THEMES IN HISTORY

WI

IDE

...CT 1300–2000

EDITED BY

BERTRAND TAITHE
& TIM THORNTON

SUTTON PUBLISHING

First published in 1998 by
Sutton Publishing Limited · Phoenix Mill
Thrupp · Stroud · Gloucestershire · GL5 2BU

British Library Cataloguing in Publication Data
A catalogue record for this book is available from the British Library

ISBN 0-7509-1683-4 (cased)
ISBN 0-7509-1684-2 (paperback)

Jacket illustration: detail from *The Battle of Issus, or The Victory of Alexander the Great*,
by Allorecht Altdorfer (Alte Pinakothek, München/Bridgeman Art Library, London).

> We dedicate this book to our teachers
> François Crouzet and C.S.L. Davies and to the memory
> of General Gulio Taithe (1925–1997).

 ALAN SUTTON™ and SUTTON™ are the
trade marks of Sutton Publishing Limited

Typeset in 10/12pt Baskerville
Typesetting and origination by
Sutton Publishing Limited.
Printed in Great Britain by
MPG, Bodmin, Cornwall.

CONTENTS

THEMES IN HISTORY

General Editors:

BERTRAND TAITHE AND TIM THORNTON
UNIVERSITY OF HUDDERSFIELD

Themes in History is a new academic series, suitable for students and the general reader. Each volume deals with a particular historical theme, including a methodological and historiographical introduction, essays dealing with the subject in different historical periods, and a concluding bibliographical essay. The essays are accessible to an undergraduate readership without assuming previous specific knowledge, while at the same time offering innovative research and approaches to appeal to all scholars. The time span covered is itself an innovation and enables unprecedented scope for contrasts and parallels. Gender, ethnicity, political and social history are continuous themes throughout the series.

EDITORS AND SERIES EDITORS

Bertrand Taithe read history at Montpellier, the Sorbonne and Manchester University where he completed a thesis on the Contagious Diseases Acts and Victorian Society. He has published *The Essential Mayhew: Representing and Communicating the Poor* (1996). He has written a number of articles on the Franco-Prussian war and has recently completed the manuscript of a monograph on medicine and war in 1870. He is a member of the French Commission Nationale d'Histoire Militaire, a fellow of the Royal Historical Society and is currently a senior lecturer in Modern French and British history at the University of Huddersfield.

Tim Thornton read history at New College, Oxford and completed a thesis on political society in early Tudor Cheshire. He has recently completed the manuscript of a monograph entitled *Political Society in Early Tudor Cheshire, 1480 to 1560* and has published a number of articles on aspects of community and identity in the late medieval and early modern period. He is currently a lecturer in late medieval and early modern history at the University of Huddersfield.

LIST OF CONTRIBUTORS

Niall J.A. Barr lectures in war studies at the Royal Military Academy of Sandhurst. He is currently working on a book with his colleague, J.P. Harris, *Amiens to the Armistice: The BEF and the Campaign of the Hundred Days, August–November 1918*. He is a member of the British Commission of Military History.

Rosalind Davies is completing a thesis on the prose writings of Sir Walter Ralegh in the School of English and Drama, Queen Mary and Westfield College, London.

Iain Donald read history and international relations and is a doctoral candidate at the University of Aberdeen. His thesis examines British perceptions of the Spanish-American War and American Imperialism at the turn of the century.

Brian Griffin lectures in history and Irish studies at Bath Spa University College. His main research interest is nineteenth-century Irish social history, particularly policing and crime. His study of the Belfast police, *The Bulkies: Police and Crime in Belfast, 1800–1865* (Dublin, Irish Academic Press), is currently in press.

Claire E.J. Herrick read history of medicine at the University of Manchester (Wellcome Unit) where she completed a doctoral thesis on the treatment of wounds and the wounded on the Western Front during the First World War. She is the 1997–8 Caird Senior Fellow at the National Maritime Museum, Greenwich, working on the history of the naval medical services, 1914–18. She has a paper on the medical events of the Russo-Japanese War, 1904–5, forthcoming in R. Cooker & M. Harrison (eds), *Medicine and the Management of Modern Warfare*.

Roisín Higgins lectures in economic and social history at the University of Edinburgh. She read history at St Andrews University where she completed a doctoral thesis on the Radical Nonconformist Press, 1886–1923. She has since carried on her work on the role of newspapers as conduits of political and religious thought.

Kirstin Howard read French and German at the University of Otago (New Zealand) where she completed her doctoral thesis. She is now a post-doctoral research fellow at the University of Cambridge.

Steve Murdoch has read history and is a doctoral candidate at the University of Aberdeen. His thesis dwells on Scottish relations with Denmark–Norway 1603–1660. He is the editor of the first Scots language historical journal, *Cairn*, and has published extensively in Gaelic, Scots and English on various aspects of Scottish history and culture.

Matthew Seligmann is a lecturer in modern world history at Nene College, Northampton. He has written a number of articles on the diplomacy and imperialism of Wilhelmine Germany for *Imago Mundi* and *German History*. A book, *Rivalry in Southern Africa: The transformation of German colonial policy*, is due out shortly from Macmillan.

David Taylor read modern history at Wadham College, Oxford. He is a principal lecturer at the University of Huddersfield and lectures in Modern British and German history. His recent writings have been concerned with crime and policing and include the recent books: *The New Police in Nineteenth-Century England* (Manchester University Press, 1997) and *Crime, Policing and Punishment in Britain from c. 1750–1914* (London, Macmillan, 1998).

Gordon Urquhart is a doctoral candidate at the University of Aberdeen. He has spoken on several aspects of Scottish cultural history and is pursuing research on the First World War and the Highlands of Scotland. His research has fuelled a play *Smoothing Creases* which received a Scottish Arts Council development award and has been presented at the Traverse Theatre in Edinburgh and the Little Theatre, Mull.

Kate Watson read history at the Universities of Glamorgan and York and at the Open University. She received her doctorate in 1996 for a thesis on popular loyalism in England, 1790–1815. Since then she has worked for Oxford Tutorial College as a tutor and academic coordinator and has taught short courses for Oxford University's Department of Continuing Education.

Philip Woodfine read history at Cambridge and is now a principal lecturer in eighteenth-century and American history at the University of Huddersfield. He is the editor, with Professor Jeremy Black, of *The British Navy and the Use of Naval Power in the Eighteenth Century* (Leicester University Press, 1988) and has written a number of articles on British political, diplomatic and military history. He has recently completed *Britannia's Glories: The Walpole Ministry and the 1739 War with Spain* (Royal Historical Society, 1998) and is currently working on a biographical study of Sir Robert Walpole.

ACKNOWLEDGEMENTS

Editing a collective work like this one is not an easy task and we have to thank the contributors first of all for putting up with our tight deadlines, our suggestions and amendments. We also have to thank the History Department of the University of Huddersfield which encouraged us and helped finance the workshop preliminary to this volume. We have to be grateful to the various good libraries our central location has enabled us to use. We have to thank Roger Thorp for his continuing support for the series and the book. Special thanks are due to Jane Smale for helping in a crucial moment of the history of this book.

1

IDENTIFYING WAR: CONFLICT AND SELF-DEFINITION IN WESTERN EUROPE

B. Taithe and T. Thornton

This chapter attempts to define and examine critically the problematic historiographies of peace, war, and identity. It moves on from controversial definitions to an assessment of the historiography of 'what war does *for* you', and that of 'what war does *to* you': from the argument that war is fundamentally creative of structures and collective identities, to the counter-case of the manner in which it affects individual identities and small communities. War fundamentally undermines often essentialist notions of ethnicity, nation, gender, state and self. Freud's answer to Albert Einstein's query on the nature of war, published in 1933, tied together a political analysis, biological determinism and a psycho-analytical framework to attempt a complex definition of both peace and war.[1]

> Paradoxical as it sounds, we must admit that warfare well might serve to pave the way to that unbroken peace we so desire, for it is war that brings vast empires into being, within whose frontiers warfare is proscribed by a strong central power. In practice, however, this end is not attained, for as a rule the fruits of victory are but short-lived, the new created units fall asunder once again, generally because there can be no true cohesion between the parts that violence has welded.
>
> You are amazed that it is so easy to infect men with the war fever, and you surmise that man has in him an active instinct for hatred and destruction, amenable to such stimulations. I entirely agree with you. . . . The death instinct becomes an impulse to destruction when, with the aid of certain organs, it directs its action outward against external objects. The living being, that is to say, defends its own existence by destroying foreign bodies.[2]

The political element to the analysis underlined the paradox of peace-seeking wars. Peace enforcement, in itself an act of war, means that any social order based on the peace–war dualism remains necessarily unstable, but also perhaps dynamic. The Clauswitzian concept of peace as war by other means links with the Latin motto, *si vis pacem para bellum* (he who desires peace, let him prepare for war), illustrating the centrality of war in the whole tradition of the western state. Put in a *longue durée* of alternating phases of warfare and peace, or of important and less important wars, this book does not intend to analyse the causes of war.[3] In fact in some contexts the causes of war can only be explored through a reification of what peace would be. In Western Europe, peace has long been either an alien concept, at most, or at least a religious one which sat uneasily with political realities. Asked to comment on the relevance of medieval practices to 'our modern, contemporary concern about world peace', Maurice Keen gently ironized on the unsuitability of medieval examples for this worthy purpose, and instead argued for a peace made of channelled violence towards crusading.[4] If one had eternity to 'rest in peace', rulers could even resent peace as a political and ideological vacuum. In 'modernity', peace is often perceived as a more concrete experience, yet even the postwar peaceful order enjoyed by European states since 1945 is in itself a relative concept. The French were almost continually at war from 1944 to 1962. Some of these 'colonial conflicts' are well known to the public, like the war in Vietnam; others like the war in Madagascar, a very bloody colonial intervention, are more obscure.[5] The British in Burma or in many other neo-colonial outposts were also at peace while at war. The fabric of the long nineteenth-century peace enjoyed by the British or the French reveals itself to be woven from a string of localized conflicts in the Indian subcontinent, New Zealand, North Africa, etc. Colonial wars are nonetheless wars and the recent emphasis on the centrality of the imperial experience in the making of European states implies a renewed emphasis on these widely reported and debated conflicts. Even though this book does not cover colonial wars and the very radical identity conflicts that they fostered or were caused by, it is worth remembering that the practice of war remained 'available' to most Europeans throughout the period of this book and until now.

The Quakers are the incarnation *par excellence* of the idea of peace as a holy political vacuum, but their peace is still clearly asocial in its opposition to the state.[6] Their Russian mission in 1854 did not stop the Crimean War; nor did their stance on war arrest the Kaiser or Edward VII.[7] From Louis XIV, allegedly advising his great-grandson to love war less than himself, to Henry V's puritanical devotion to war, historical writing barely recalls the existence of peaceful rulers.[8] A *rex pacificus* was more often a schemer who avoided wars he or she could not win, or whose peace came as a result of glorious victory, such as Louis XI and Henry IV of France, or Henry VII or Elizabeth of England.[9]

Although some of these notions are blurred, the following sections will tackle them separately and thematically from the theoretical approaches pioneered by Foucault and de Certeau to the more empirical lines of enquiry attempted by contributors to this book. The focus will shift from group identity to self-identity, from professional or ethnic identities to individual, gendered, or hyphenated definitions. In the penultimate section contributors examine the problems of the communicability of the war experience and the way this communication shapes both militarism and the role of veterans in society. Following this point the conclusion questions the role of historians as mediators of both wars and identities.

Michel Foucault's lecture programme at the Collège de France in 1975–6[10] aimed at reconstructing the double genealogy of warfare and western 'governmentability'. Foucault saw discourses on war shift from a philosophico-legal discourse to a politico-historical discourse. This shift implies that the subject who spoke in the discourse had to take sides, and that war became a part of him or her. Notions of right and wrong became irremediably biased by a sense of identity with what is right.[11] In *Discipline and Punish* Foucault was more in line with the historical writing which dates the origins of the state to larger-scale organized violence.[12] The disciplining gaze of military formations stands even now as a powerful, if teleological, metaphor for our contemporary society. This enterprise undermined the destructive liminality of the war experience which a number of historians had started to explore using the intellectual tools provided by Mary Douglas[13] and Victor Turner's anthropological work.[14] The work of Eric J. Leed which used these paradigms and borrowed from Hayden White attributed a liminality to the war experience which is at odds with the practice of a 'rite of passage' but also underestimated the centrality of war discourses in all historical narratives or understanding of society.[15] More recently the work of Daniel Pick, which combines a general Foucaultian framework with this literary tradition, and adds for good measure some of Freud's biological and psychoanalytical speculations, makes for a sinister story, in which world wars of attrition and extermination end western war-civilization.[16] In some respects this view is not new and many commentators from the 1920s viewed western civilization as a unifying cultural entity which any war shattered.[17] This view of the Second World War actually became a political motto in Britain where the war was fought for the defence of Christian civilization.[18] In a more traditional Whiggish historiography, war can kickstart an economy of exchange, political and economic, and it can also determine the shape of the state itself and the extent of its reach. The historiography of military revolution, in the revived form it assumed from the 1950s, was focused on explaining the creation of state structures as a consequence of technological and organizational developments in military affairs in the medieval and early modern period.[19] Historians of the French Revolution since Michelet have attributed the same creative power to mass volunteering,[20] but extended it to the idea of nation.[21] So deep is this image of war in western historiographies that the 'goodness' of war has been extended to a multiplicity of areas not usually associated with it, such as progress in education, medicine,[22] women's rights, agriculture, heavy industry[23] and even babies.[24] In spite of any superficial abhorrence of war, evidence in much writing since the Enlightenment perpetuates the myth and adds a new generation of scientific discoveries to this catalogue of human achievements brought from war as 'peace dividends'.

Civil wars seemingly bring few returns on violent investments, and the term 'peace dividend' is hardly ever invoked. In a war which functions internally gains are always at the expense of oneself. The term 'civil' illustrates this paradox. One of the earliest adjectival uses of the word 'civil' is recorded by the *Oxford English Dictionary* in the late fourteeenth century in the phrase 'civil war'.[25] 'Fratricidal' and 'brotherly' are other adjectives which conveniently gloss these conflicts. Benedict Anderson illustrates this point in his *Imagined Communities*, discussing the American Civil War and Renan's views on the Saint Barthélémy massacre.[26] The difference between war and civil war is somewhat spurious, for even if a civil war does not directly address the pre-eminence of a state, it deals with the structure of society within itself. Historians obsessed with the state have only recently broadened their horizons to include the diversity of societal constructs. As Tim Thornton shows, smaller-scale communities can also be shaped or even made through the organized and purposeful violence we call war.

A community of warfare is also a community of internal peace and regulated tensions, and war is only possible through the constant violent interaction of larger units, at relative peace with themselves. Rules of war and codes of war, from chivalric fictions to theoretical international conventions fix imaginary boundaries to the practice of war and give a purpose to the level of acceptable and deadly violence.[27] The ritual elements of this codification do not inevitably engage the acts of the warriors but they structure myriad self-justifying narratives of war. As Rosalind Davies shows for chivalric and humanistic codes, the violation of rules and dirty tricks are always the prerogative of the enemy and can help structure a meaningful identity for a specific community of soldiers.[28] Similar examples can be found for all legislative and theoretical restraints on war.[29] If one can perceive these legislative or rhetorical devices as an attempt to civilize war, one could also read into these often futile exercises a way of condoning the inevitability of war.[30] This is the paradox George Mosse explored in his study of the barbarization of warfare in the age of international conventions on weapons, prisoners and human rights.[31] For the soldiers themselves these fictional rules of war serve a purpose and often anchor violent groups to a common rule of law. Within these communities, the bond between 'living beings' is made of analogous stories, common fate and shared identity. What makes an identity is in itself highly complex and multi-layered. If we understand identities as being constituted of several layers or geological strata, we imply a pyramidal hierarchy which may not be there. In response to the anthropologist Richard Handler's criticism of 'identity' as a useful analytical category this book demonstrates that historians do not use it without a pinch a salt. There is no inference that identity is a unitary category or that identity and culture necessarily share many of their vague characteristics. Identity, or rather identities, do not superimpose in a neat pile of labels which could summarize for biographical purposes the two authors of this introduction as male, 'Caucasian', French, expatriate, historian or male, 'Caucasian', Yorkshire, English, British, historian etc. There is a danger in mapping from the base of an individual, through a neighbourhood and locality, to a state superstructure, via class, gender and ethnicity. The distribution of identities is not compartmentalized any more than experience or learning are. Even an individual and largely fictional 'self' can be thus divided and torn between meshed identities, and be remade or destroyed in the process. Rossel, a Protestant French career officer, who joined the Paris commune in 1871, thus rejected his social background, his political instincts and his family connections for the sake of carrying on war.[32] The irony is of course that Rossel wanted to fight off the Prussians and ended up serving a revolution in a civil war. The same point could be made about the Catholics of Elizabethan England.[33] In fact the self only exists at a given time and place through this weaving of identities which peace recomposes in similar ways to war. The major difference might lie in the intensity and the speed of change. The historiography of the First World War has been particularly aware of this, more so than the historiography of low-intensity conflicts where boundaries between armed peace and intermittent warfare are blurred beyond recognition.

Group identities may be coarser and function through a brutal process of exclusion or a possessive process of inclusion. Michel de Certeau's work on heterologies makes the point that identities build on definitions of otherness which can be very familiar and close.[34] To define the 'other' is a kind of science, and a reflexive meditation on what makes the observer or traveller different. Montesquieu,[35] Voltaire[36] and the Jesuits studied by Certeau used the literary trick of a foreigner's observation on the host culture to bring home messages about French society and politics. Historians do the same with the past. Epic narratives of war use the same rhetorical device most effectively. From the Sagas, Agincourt,[37] Duby's battle of Bouvines,[38] the historiography of the Great Armada,[39] Dunkirk, and Valmy,[40] war narratives have shaped communities composed of Nordic tribes, medieval 'races', packs of seadogs, and the revolutionary nation-in-arms. The romantic narrative of Valmy, for example, opposed the sans-culottes' armies, defending their people, to the hordes of mercenaries.[41] Spurs, and St Quentin, for Tudor Englishmen, served the same purpose.[42]

If communities can be built from without, through the constant interaction with the 'other' and otherness, they can also draw strength from within. Benedict Anderson's emphasis on the way that belief can hold together disparate elements and forces, even in an institutional vacuum, goes far beyond the choice of exotic examples he deploys.[43] The focus for such inclusive systems of belief might spring from kinship, whether real or metaphorical. Kinship can take on an ethnic connotation when it enlarges to include clannic structures. Far from being an archaic and primitive organizational system, kinship or its equivalent provides a constant recourse in response to conflict. The Anglo-Scottish borders of the fourteenth century, exposed to large-scale violence for the first time in a century, witnessed the development of a system of names and clans.[44] Gordon Urquhart's paper in this collection shows how powerful the ideal of Highland clan warfare could be, even in the most alienating context of the First World War. Beyond kinship, the focus on an individual leader of the group, especially in the form of kingship, allows the coherence and articulation of more complex groupings. Steve Murdoch's article shows how multi-layered the relationships of kingship were in Stuart Scotland between the monarch and professional soldiery.[45] At the very heart of kingship in western society lay the idea of military leadership. It is not for nothing that each German army retained a specific link with the small courts of the German empire even in 1914. Monarchs went to war until the twentieth century, when the concept of monarchy itself has been transformed and contested. Napoleon III surrendered his sword to Wilhelm I in probably the last and most incongruous example of this. The sword of the individual stood for the military might of the army in Sedan but not any longer for the nation.

Ethnicity was another unifying force that might be galvanized by war if not created outright by war practices and foundation warring myths. A.L. Epstein, for instance, describes 'military ethos' as being a constituent of an ethnic cultural identity of the African Bomba culture.[46] On the other hand the meta-identities created by wars can transcend the limitations of ethnic definitions. If, on the one hand, late-medieval German identity was a largely warring construct in the absence of a solid state or social unifying definition, French soldiers from a diversity of cultural and ethnic backgrounds could later merge, at least temporarily, into one over-arching French national identity which could then later take on some of the attributes of an ethnic national identity as defined by Anthony D. Smith.[47] Indeed some sociologists of specific cultural and ethnic groups resisting centralization in powerful states insist that war can prevent the full development of local political causes.[48] Through a war effort the state may attempt to blur ethnic divisions or use them to its benefit by sponsoring discreetly conflicting claims.[49] Conversely, competing groups might invest the act of volunteering with a real political purpose serving their interests, as Brian Griffin shows about Ireland and the Crimea.[50] Roisín Higgins' paper also shows that taking sides in a conflict can be disinterested when the conflict is deemed to reach for moral and ethical absolutes.[51] The Spanish Civil War was thus a conflict of ideology which served to strengthen the confessional divides of post-partition Ireland. Also dealing with 'morally justified' wars, Iain Donald shows the hopes of social and ethnic harmony vested in the American war against Spain. Through this successful and popular war, the American meta-identity served a clear purpose in overcoming regional, ethnic and political forms of identities. Religious identity, which can be so closely attached to the notion of ethnicity to the point of becoming indistinguishable in some historical settings, has the same dynamic relationship with war. The historiography of 'wars of religion' long glossed over the other, less divinely inspired motivations for violence to favour the more idealistic identity uniting often disparate groups under one banner.[52] War has this singular ability to sum up and simplify the more complex issues. Following our rough sketch of a Whig interpretation of war one could sum up this pattern of identity reinforcement as the effect of what war does *for* you. The group, be it ethnic, religious, or clannic, is deemed to pre-exist the conflict, at least in a latent form, and to survive the war unchanged. This sometimes simplistic historiography ignores the transient nature of all human societies and the power of war for disruption or even annihilation.

If one becomes shy of meta-narratives and pays more attention to individual involvement in warfare, the key question, naggingly unresolved and troubling, is that of volunteering.[53] That individuals might join armed forces for the money, the status or the anonymity of war can easily be understood, especially when push-and-pull factors are included. Poverty, hunger, or a shadowy past of crime or anti-social behaviour,[54] a dysfunctional family perhaps could lead men like Martin Guerre to seek an escape in armed service and war.[55] Gilbert Godbehere, a Cheshire Don Juan, had to hide among the Calais garrison from the threatening attentions of angry husbands.[56] Less clear, however, are the motivations of the volunteers who joined the disorganized bands of the French Revolution, Kitchener's Pals' Regiments, the German *Freikorps* or the many lost causes which have taken such a heavy toll of young lives.[57] The secondary literature on volunteering is thus torn between the imagery and rhetoric produced before the volunteer joins the forces, and the literature produced during and after the decision is taken. The first appears as crude and garish propaganda, while the second usually narrates war and often skips over the moment of decision. In fact the act of volunteering is frequently unproblematized in these retroactive accounts which seek to structure a life at war. Historians have on the whole emphasized the social pressures bearing on volunteers, the ideological background, the old push-and-pull mechanisms which would function for them as they did for mercenaries. There is, however, a fundamental difference between volunteers, whatever their motivation, and conscripts.[58] The real problem at this stage is that of an act of will, difficult to decipher even for the individual who exercised his/her *voluntas*, this choice. Choosing, acting on a choice, implies a clear knowledge of outcomes and options and it is the nature of war not to present the imagined predictability of peace. In the unravelling of war the individual who made the original choice ceases to exist, metaphorically or literally.

What war does *to* you can affect the existence of a stable recognizable self from the pre-war times. The elements of the self, as David Taylor points out, can be 'peeled off' the soldier's persona. The body may change at war. Physical exercise, marching, and training affect the ways in which the body can interact with the world and shape the 'perceptions' of others. War wounds, scarred tissues, disfigurement and amputations also mean that there is often not a pre-war body on which to project images of a peaceful self and that the war cannot be neatly kept between convenient but ultimately futile historiographical brackets like pre-, post-, or interwar.

Impersonations and gender crossing occur more frequently in war. This might take the form of women assuming male warring identities, from Joan of Arc to the chevalier(e) d'Éon, or the more humble Félicité Duquet, so-called *va de bon coeur*.[59] This cross-dressing is reversible, with the assumption of female attire being used in some circumstances to allow male soldiery to break the conventions of war and peace. This remains a fairly superficial level of gender identity. Beyond cross-dressers, serving in the military may affect the very definitions of gender. Masculinity and war are inextricably linked.[60] The masculine body is tested to the full in the violent games of war[61] which operates around notions of courage and gallantry,[62] while fantasies of masculinity tend to have a militaristic or warfare backdrop.[63]

As Eugen Weber noted for rural France, the ability to serve in a military capacity played an important part in the definition of masculinity and in many ways conscripted military service became a modern rite of passage. Malingerers, deserters and those who rebelled against calls to serve would have their masculinity questioned and often discursively undermined. War heroes might not fare any better. As bodily integrity and gender integrity are often merged in masculinity, returning from war maimed or disfigured could produce crises of male identity and undermine suitability for wedlock. War could become an exclusive playing-field of masculinities and even nurses might be excluded.[64] Women who care, mothers and nurses, tillers of the fields, could be patient witnesses intervening on the margins of warfare.[65] Florence Nightingale, who exemplified a 'Lady's rôle' on the battlefield, made her discipline serve the boundaries of war and peace on the front line.[66] Female legions in 1870 and legions of Amazons incurred more ridicule than admiration. Paradoxically, the *pétroleuse* of the Commune civil war, real fighters like Louise Michel or imaginary incendiaries, crossed, through their violent action, all gender boundaries to form a new and terrifying entity: a socialist woman at war.[67] Women and children as victims add pathos to war and in some instances justify the war itself. They best represent the barbarization of warfare. The civilization process described by Norbert Elias argues that civility and modes of government are inextricably linked: barbarization through warfare seems to reverse the process and yet it can be, as we have seen, the best expression of the omnipotent state.[68] War here becomes the reverse of peace. However, this barbarization process belongs to the realms of the discursive: war is and remains a socialized activity.

The barbarian at war is always the other. This is the crudest form of heterology that can be presented. If war renegotiates the self, it can also affect the group, as social priorities are reformulated with new urgency, or even as old latent debates come to the fore. Professional groups which normally see and present themselves as structuring society can be questioned and threatened. Claire Herrick's paper on the medical profession in Britain during the First World War illustrates how brittle professional identity based on knowledge production could be when challenged with heterodox yet effective answers to specific war problems. In this context the crisis can demonstrate the social and empirical basis of any professional status and undermine monopolistic claims to knowledge. War is good for 'cranks'. Many professions find their founding moment in such crises, as in the old adage that an assembly of quacks can become a profession if it finds a stable institutional and social backing. In 1914 the British medical profession survived the challenge, but was lastingly affected by this experience. In another context, as in 1792–3, medicine could be so seriously threatened as to appear, even if temporarily, defunct.[69] To face war priorities, the Revolutionary forces of France did without medical qualifications and antiquated rituals of learning. In another field, the nascent science of military architecture received a major setback in sixteenth-century England when the imperatives of defensive fortification left them wanting in Henry VIII's eyes.[70] It is therefore paradoxical that war is given such a paradigmatic importance in the development of professions or knowledge.

Group identities such as these might well be relatively simple. Although in many cases complex sub-identities might blend into a larger group sense, often the degree of overlap might be limited to one or more important elements. This can produce what we term a 'hyphen' in their identity. A hyphen implies the idea of partial integration, or even an unproblematized inclusion into a group which gradually becomes problematic or is rejected.[71] This hyphen is of course in the eye of the beholder, at least as much as it is perceived by those to whom it is applied. This is evidently the case with the Jews in Germany during the First World War. Matthew Seligmann shows how observers perceived this gradual definition of German-Jews as Jew-Germans or even Jews in Germany.[72] The hyphen was pivotal in this reversal of fortune which led to the breakdown of the German Jewry, yet this hyphen remained for many the core of their existential self-definition.[73] The articulation of identity is a discursive act which often takes place after the war or distances the author from the war. A war narrative is fundamentally a narrative of identity, which seeks a rationale to the war itself and mostly finds it in identity: an interpretative vicious circle. The paradox here is the uncommunicability of war itself, and its survival as a myth. As David Taylor points out, war rhetoric and imageries may still have currency with those soldiering even if they appear dated and contradictory in relation to the new aesthetics of war discussed by Samuel Hynes and Modris Eksteins.[74] Bertrand

Taithe's paper shows how historical identities and identifications can misfire when they appear too removed from the identity lived and practised. Historical identities employed as victory narratives meant to carry the day can fail dramatically and bring into question the whole historical process at play. The ambiguous nature of a war narrative is its one-sidedness; defeat stories make for sour reading, often only redeemed by wasteful heroism. The tropes of this rhetoric are dwelling on the sacrificial, the religious, the disincarnated. To go against these rules of representation can be dangerous. Patrick Macgill's 'realism' almost proved disastrous for him; the alternative aesthetics of war described by Hynes *et al* remained a minority interest compared with the larger and more popular production of what Rosa Maria Bracco named the 'merchants of hope' or middlebrow writers, the same conservative forces that the French regional writer Pagnol denounced as 'merchants of glory'.[75] French war painters after 1870 also seemed too keen on grime and blood and incurred the disapproval of critics.[76]

On the other hand, Kirstin Howard's paper emphasizes the effects of the incommunicability of the war experience. Harig the elder, like many documented survivors, could not articulate or even find the most basic words needed for his narrative. In his quest to express the incommunicable, he even lost language. The war narratives on which many of these papers are built are therefore more interesting for their silences or their awkward use of inappropriate literary tropes than for their apparent intent. Their purpose is also unclear beyond reclaiming identity from the vacuum of the inexpressible. An element of mediation is possible, however, and civilian society seems to cherish war narrative better than its own. Kate Watson illustrates how British people, many in their childhood years during the Napoleonic Wars, could still participate in the conflict and in the identities it shaped. Most war narrative that survives had a commercial value or served a military purpose.[77] The civilian society which on the whole consumed these war narratives and encouraged their production could simultaneously contest some of the definitions. Philip Woodfine's paper illustrates both the permeability of the nascent public sphere to war narrative, and the built-in resistance to the transgressions which make war an alternative society. Peace and war thus conflated within the same social and geographical space, and the boundaries were easily transgressed. The officer out of place did not encounter the military solidarity to which he felt entitled, yet liberal thinkers found their freedom of expression restricted for the sake of war. A hybrid space and society were created. The meaning of 'militarism', as defined by Emilio Willems for Germany, is precisely that this discourse of glorified war and soldiers is developed and functions best in the civilian sphere.[78] Paradoxically the military as a professional body can be threatened by militarism and war. Public enthusiasm can engulf the military and drag a highly structured professional body into a more openly competitive environment in which rhetorical tropes can supersede formal training and where tactics or strategy are laid open to scrutiny, lay readings and criticism.[79] Regimental culture and the military ethos can be made much more fragile by the arrival of large numbers of novice warriors and iconoclastic volunteers.[80] In 1870 Adolphe Thiers saw a great danger in the 'drowning' of the 1,500 regular soldiers in a mass of 4,000 volunteers in each French regiment; others judged this 'civilianization' a good thing for democracy.[81] The civilian/military interface is then highly charged with political and social tensions. There is an obvious difference of register between the more hot-headed militarists and the military, which can lead to misreading or open suspicion. Generals who fail can be judged literally or metaphorically by public opinion. For the likes of the careless Admiral John Byng in eighteenth-century Britain or the traitorous French Marshal Bazaine in 1872, the outcome of this conflict of interpretation of a defeat could be a death sentence.[82] It is perhaps misleading to talk about militarization in this context when the process can be shown to move from the civilian to the military up to the point when the military dilutes and includes the whole of society. In this space of militarism, the readings of war narratives can be totally unsynchronized or even delayed in time.

In a similarly hybrid position, the veteran plays a paradoxical role in western society. Reminders of war, they are often too old to fight. They may be out of tune with the society and identities they themselves helped to forge. Napoleonic veterans, a large cohort in Restoration France, aged with the legend they helped to build. The image of the Napoleonic soldier turned primary school teacher was fostered by the Second Empire which then used them to create a continuum of Bonapartist identity over the intervening years. After the First World War, veteran associations across Europe claimed a stake in the democratic societies of which they often were not part. Their democracy was a democracy of rank and file brotherhood, which nevertheless fostered a strong sense of hierarchy. Veteranship could thus become an alternative form of citizenship in most continental European countries. The problematic issue of veteran identity is illustrated by Niall Barr, who shows how issues of class riddled the smaller but unified British veterans' organization of the British Legion, while the politically oriented organizations of France and Germany grew massively.

As time passes, and the narrative of the war experience leaves behind the survivors, so their experience becomes the more alienated. Oral historians now have trouble finding survivors of the First World War who do not require extensive sub-titling. Veterans of 1870 died off after the First World War. One can safely predict a rush to microphones in the years to come as new waves of veterans begin to fade away, for the most part in silence. That some of them remain silent is indeed a blessing for the historians and their readers. Veterans have memory, not necessarily the makings of history, and as they attempt to make sense of war in their lives, that memory can indeed have many areas of darkness.

War can be a very incoherent matter and many great novelists have resisted the temptation of hindsight. Leon Tolstoy in *War and Peace* shows the general kept in ignorance of the victory he has won;[83] Stendhal describes Waterloo through the confused eyes of a conscript who has lost his regiment. On the other hand the popular British television reconstruction of Bernard Cornwell's *Sharpe* at the same battle has him move from one key engagement to another with an unerring sense of their historical importance. Supremely aware of the panoramic memory of the battle, the novelist can afford improbable tricks of which the veterans can only dream. Even more perhaps than the writer of popular fiction, historians use similar tricks to reclaim the identity lost by the soldier in the chaos of battle. They forensically dissect outcomes and intentions, meaning and historical priorities. Historical writing developed largely in order to make sense of the competing identities expressed in conflicts. The historian as narrator, authoritative yet open to challenge, cuts and pastes together fragments of imagined communities, dead individual selves and mythological identities to serve a social or epistemological order to which she or he subscribes.[84] On the other hand, this involvement with the past is not without its effects on the authors' identities, and, while many historical writings are linked to an intellectual autobiography, some historians like Richard Cobb recognized the ways in which their own sense of belonging is shaped by their writings and research.[85] When a similar empathy is turned inwards, as in Fernand Braudel's *Identity of France*, bucolic undertones can reinforce a mythology of belonging to a space or a territory.[86] Recent studies of literary production during the wars show that (a) national spatial boundaries might become so blurred that only texts can recreate this space or these imaginary borders, and (b) wars are pre-eminently times of population movements and mixing which blend peoples and do not allow for settled identities.[87] Only in the tight boundaries of historical writings might there be 'a true cohesion between the parts that violence has welded'.

Notes

1 For another instance of this syncretism see Havelock Ellis, *Essays in War-Time* (London, Constable and Co., 1916), pp. 15–42.

2 Alfred Einstein & Sigmund Freud, *Why War? 'Open Letters' between Einstein and Freud* (London, New Commonwealth, 1934), pp. 12–15.

3 There is a large literature devoted to this topic; see, for instance: Eugène Aroneanu, *La définition de l'agression* (Paris, Éditions Inter-Nationales, 1955); Michael Howard, *The Causes of Wars and Other Essays* (London, Temple Smith, 1983).

4 Maurice Keen, 'War, Peace and Chivalry', in Brian Patrick McGuire (ed.), *War and Peace in the Middle Ages* (Copenhagen, C.A. Reitzels Forlag, 1987), pp. 94–117, at p. 112. J.M. Wallace-Hadrill, 'War and Peace in the Earlier Middle Ages', *Transactions of the Royal Historical Society*, 5th series, 25 (1975), 157–74.

5 See Catherine Coquery-Vidrovitch & Charles-Robert Ageron, *Histoire de la France coloniale* (3 vols, Paris, Armand Colin, 1991), vol. 3, pp. 231–7. Robert Aldrich, *Greater France: a History of French Overseas Expansion* (London, Macmillan, 1996), pp. 234–306. The centrality of the Algerian independence war proves, if it were necessary, the crucial importance of the imperial age in the making of modern French society.

6 William K. Sessions, *They Chose the Star: Quaker War Relief Work in France, 1870–1875* (London, Friends Relief Service, 1944, rep. York, The Ebor Press, 1991).

7 Peter Brook, *Pacifism in Europe* (Princeton University Press, 1972), pp. 343–6.

8 Henry V the soldier: C.T. Allmand, 'Henry V the Soldier, and the War in France', in G.L. Harriss (ed.), *Henry V: The Practice of Kingship* (Oxford University Press, 1985), pp. 117–35; T.B. Pugh, *Henry V and the Southampton Plot* (Stroud, Alan Sutton, for Southampton Record Series, 1988); C.S.L. Davies, in J.L. Watts (ed.), *The End of the Middle Ages* (Stroud, Sutton, 1998).

9 S.B. Chrimes, *Henry VII* (London, Eyre Methuen, 1972), esp. pp. 272–97; R.B. Wernham, *Before the Armada: The Growth of English Foreign Policy, 1485–1588* (London, Cape, 1966), pp. 27–61, 234–405.

10 Michel Foucault, *Résumé des Cours* (Paris, Julliard, 1989), pp. 85–94.

11 Foucault, *Résumé*, pp. 86–8.

12 Michel Foucault, *Surveiller et punir, naissance de la prison* (Paris: Gallimard, 1975), pp. 137–71.

13 Mary Douglas, *Purity and Danger: An Analysis of Concepts of Pollution and Taboo* (London, Routledge and Kegan Paul, 1966).

14 Victor Turner, *The Forest of Symbols: Aspects of Mdembu Ritual* (Ithaca, Cornell University Press, 1967).

15 Eric J. Leed, *No Man's Land: Combat and Identity in World War I* (Cambridge University Press, 1979), pp. 12–69.

16 Daniel Pick, *War Machine: The Rationalization of Slaughter in the Modern Age* (New Haven, Yale University Press, 1993), pp. 115–35.

17 John S. Hoyland, *The Warfare of Reconciliation* (London, George Allen and Unwin, 1928), pp. 9–45.

18 Keith Robbins, *History, Religion and Identity in Modern Britain* (London, Hambledon Press, 1993), pp. 195–214.

19 The military revolution is surveyed from a medieval perspective by Andrew Ayton & J.L. Price in their introduction to *The Military Revolution*: see Philippe Contamine, *La guerre au Moyen Age* (Paris, Presses Universitaires de France, 1980), pp. 232–389. Jeremy Black has argued that the most important changes took place in the late fifteenth century and in the century after 1660: Jeremy Black, *A Military Revolution? Military Change and European Society, 1550–1800* (Basingstoke, Macmillan, 1991).

20 Châbane Harbaoui, 'Le statut rhétorique du "Peuple" et de la "Révolution" dans le discours de Michelet', in Christian Croisille & Jean Ehrard (eds), *La légende de la Révolution* (Clermont Ferrand, Université Blaise Pascal, 1988), pp. 379–92.

21 The literature on nation and nationalism is too rich to be even alluded to briefly. Some of the issues of identity are obviously at the heart of any national question but the theme of identity is both richer and more diverse. See Anthony D. Smith, *Theories of Nationalism* (London, Duckworth, 1971); Anthony D. Smith (ed.), *Nationalist Movements* (London, Macmillan, 1976); Anthony D. Smith, *State and*

Nation in the Third World (Brighton, Wheatsheaf Books, 1983); *Nation and Nationalism in a Global Era* (Cambridge, Polity Press, 1995); John Hutchinson, *Modern Nationalism* (London, Fontana Press, 1994), pp. 1–38.

22 See Roger Cooter, 'The Goodness of War', *Canadian Bulletin of Medical History*, 7 (1990), 147–59; 'War and Modern Medicine', in W.F. Bynum & R. Porter (eds), *Companion Encyclopedia of the History of Medicine* (2 vols, London, Routledge, 1993), vol. 2, pp. 1536–73. For positivist appraisals of the war see Jules Rochard, *Histoire de la chirurgie Française au XIX° siècle, étude historique et critique sur les progrès faits en chirurgie et dans les sciences qui s'y rapportent depuis la suppression de l'Académie Royale jusqu'à l'époque actuelle* (Paris, J.B. Baillière, 1875), pp. 857–76; Edmond Delorme, *Traité de Chirurgie de Guerre* (2 vols, Paris, Felix Alcan, 1888), vol. 2, p. 355; Charles A. Gordon, *The Siege of Paris: A Medical and Chirurgical Study* (London, Baillière, Tindall and Cox, 1872).

23 Arthur Marwick, *The Deluge: British Society and the First World War* (2nd edn, Basingstoke, Macmillan Education, 1991); Arthur Marwick, *Women at War, 1914–1918* (London, Fontana for the Imperial War Museum, 1977).

24 Deborah Dwork, *War is Good for Babies and Other Small Children: A History of the Infant and Child Welfare Movement in England 1898–1918* (London, Tavistock, 1987). This intelligent book undermines considerably the theory that war priorities alone shaped new welfare practices. Similar issues arise with regard to female suffrage in Britain or the coming of the National Health Service. See Keith Laybourn, *The Evolution of British Social Policy and the Welfare State* (Keele University Press, Ryburn Publishing, 1995); Pat Thane, *The Foundations of the Welfare State* (2nd edn, Harlow, Longman, 1996).

25 The *Oxford English Dictionary* shows 'civil war' to be the earliest context for the adjectival use of 'civil' in English, along with 'civil law'.

26 Benedict Anderson, *Imagined Communities* (London, Verso 2nd edn, 1991), pp. 199–202.

27 The development of concepts of just war and a corpus of laws of war which these codes continued to allow for some forms of violence which were not at the behest of the state undermines arguments that what was thereby created was the fount of all power. Frederick H. Russell, *The Just War in the Middle Ages* (Cambridge University Press, 1975); M.H. Keen, *The Laws of War in the Late Middle Ages* (London and Toronto, Routledge and Kegan Paul, 1965). War was very important to the definition of political structures, describing their authority and monopoly in the field of violence. The later definition of humanitarianism was and remains a contested concept and not a moral category. From Red Cross hagiographers like Pierre Boissier, *Histoire du Comité International de la Croix Rouge de Solférino à Tsoushima* (Geneva, Institut Henry Dunant, 1978), to detractors like A. Destexhe, *L'Humanitaire impossible ou deux siècles d'ambiguïté* (Paris, Armand Colin, 1993), or I. Vichniac, *Croix Rouge, les stratèges de la bonne conscience* (Paris, A. Moreau, 1988). Also see earlier historians: Léonce de Cazenove, *La guerre et l'humanité au XIXème siècle* (Paris, Armand de Viesse, 1869, 2nd edn. 1875). See Geoffrey Best, *Humanity in Warfare: the Modern History of the International Law of Armed Conflict* (London, Methuen, 1983).

28 On chivalric codes and the literature of honour and virtue see Malcolm Vale, *War and Chivalry: Warfare and Aristocratic Culture in England, France and Burgundy at the End of the Middle Ages* (London, Duckworth 1981), pp. 14–32.

29 Michael Howard (ed.), *Restraints on War: Studies in the Limitation of Armed Conflict* (Oxford University Press, 1979).

30 See Best, *Humanity in Warfare*, and John Hutchinson, *Champions of Charity: War and the Rise of the Red Cross* (New York, Westview Press, 1996), pp. 202–76.

31 Richard Handler, 'Is "Identity" a Useful Cross-Cultural Concept?', in John R. Gillis (ed.), *Commemorations: The Politics of National Identity* (Princeton University Press, 1994), pp. 27–40. George Mosse, *Fallen Soldiers: Reshaping the Memory of the World Wars* (Oxford University Press, 1990).

32 Jules Amigues, a notorious Bonapartist, published his papers under the title *Louis Nathaniel Rossel, papiers postumes receuillis et annotés par Jules Amigues* (Paris, Lachaud, 1875); also *Mémoires et Correspondence de Louis Rossel*, preface by Victor Margueritte with a biography by Isabella Rossel (Paris, Stock, 1908). Edith Thomas, *Rossel, 1844–1871* (Paris, Gallimard, 1967)

33 John Bossy, *The English Catholic Community, 1570–1850* (new edn, London, Darton, Longman and Todd, 1979).

34 Michel de Certeau, *Heterologies: Discourse on the Other*, Theory and History of Literature, 17 (Manchester University Press, 1986), pp. 67–79.

35 Montesquieu, *Lettres persanes* in *Oeuvres complètes* (3 vols, London, Hachette, 1866), vol. 3, pp. 1–196.

36 Voltaire, *Lettres philosophiques* (Paris, 1726 reprinted Gallimard, 1981).

37 Alfred H. Burne, *The Agincourt War: A Military History of the Latter Part of the Hundred Years War from 1369 to 1453* (London, Eyre and Spottiswoode, 1956).

38 George Duby, *Le dimanche de Bouvines, 27 juillet 1214* (Paris, Gallimard, 1973).

39 Felipe Fernández-Armesto, *The Spanish Armada: The Experience of the War in 1588* (Oxford University Press, 1988).

40 Emmanuel Hublot, *Valmy ou la défense de la nation par les armes* (Paris, Fondation pour les Études de la Défense Nationale, 1987)

41 Jean-Paul Bertaud (ed.), *Valmy, la démocracie en armes* (Paris, Archives Julliard, 1970), pp. 143–248.

42 Charles G. Cruikshank, *Army Royal: Henry VIII's Invasion of France, 1513* (Oxford, Clarendon Press, 1969).

43 Anderson, *Imagined Communities*, pp. 47–67.

44 J.A. Tuck, 'Northumbrian Society in the Fourteenth Century', *Northern History*, VI (1971), 22–39; *idem*, 'War and Society in the Medieval North', *Northern History*, XXI (1985), 33–52.

45 See also Murray G.H. Pittock, *The Invention of Scotland: The Stuart Myth and the Scottish Identity, 1638 to the Present* (London, Routledge, 1991).

46 A.L. Epstein, *Ethos and Identity: Three Studies in Ethnicity* (London, Tavistock Publications, 1978), pp. 113–38.

47 Anthony D. Smith, *National Identity* (Harmondsworth, Penguin Books, 1991), pp. 19–70. On a similar topic but obviously with more detail and more depth see Anthony D. Smith, *The Ethnic Origins of Nations* (Oxford, Basil Blackwell, 1986).

48 Patricia Elton Mayo, *The Roots of Identity: Three National Movements in Contemporary European Politics* (London, Allen Lane, 1974), pp. 1–12. Mayo dealt enthusiastically with the then flourishing movements in Wales, Brittany and the Basque Country. On the other hand a more sceptical view of 'ethnic' national entities stresses how much space defeat can give to their political expression; see for instance Maryon McDonald, '*We are not French!' Language, Culture and Identity in Brittany* (London, Routledge, 1989), pp. 122–37. See also Anthony D. Smith, *Nationalism in the Twentieth Century* (Oxford, Martin Robertson, 1979), pp. 150–65. There are obviously many more studies for Wales, Scotland,

Corsica etc. See for instance Tony Curtis (ed.), *Wales: The Imagined Nation*, Studies in Cultural and National Identity (Bridgend, Poetry Wales Press, 1986).

49 Cynthia H. Enloe, *Ethnic Soldiers: State Security in Divided Societies* (Harmondsworth, Penguin Books, 1980), pp. 210–34.

50 It is interesting to compare the experience of Irish Catholics and Scottish Highlanders with the theories of Michael Hechter; their autonomous identity allowed the state to exploit their resources for its ends in war: Michael Hechter, *Internal Colonialism: The Celtic Fringe in British National Development, 1536–1966* (London, Routledge and Kegan Paul, 1975).

51 Mediated experience of war applied for its lessons elsewhere – Joseph M. Hernon, jr, *Celts, Catholics and Copperheads: Ireland Views the American Civil War* (Columbus, Ohio State University Press, 1968), which notes the importance of Irish politicians and others in supporting the Confederate secession in the American Civil War.

52 For revisionist accounts see for instance works on France by historians such as Denis Crouzet, *Les guerriers de Dieu, la violence au temps des troubles de religion 1525–1610* (2 vols, Seyssel, Champ Vallon, 1990); for a recent but more conventional military history, see James B. Wood, *The King's Army: Warfare, Soldiers and Society during the Wars of Religion in France, 1562–76* (Cambridge University Press, 1996), pp. 6–25.

53 Large forces of volunteers form an integral part of the nineteenth-century military revolution and the drive towards infantry-based mass armies. See Geoffrey Best, *War and Society in Revolutionary Europe, 1770–1870* (London, Fontana, 1982), pp. 29–62.

54 Contamine, *La guerre*, pp. 391–5.

55 Nathalie Zemon Davis, *The Return of Martin Guerre* (Cambridge, Mass., Harvard University Press, 1983), pp. 21–6.

56 E.W. Ives (ed.), *Letters and Accounts of William Brereton* (Record Society of Lancashire and Cheshire, CXVI, 1976), pp. 86–8.

57 For an overview, see Mosse, *Fallen Soldiers*, pp. 2–33.

58 Volunteers of 1791 resented conscripts: Bertaud, *Valmy*, pp. 216–17.

59 Bertaud, *Valmy*, pp. 201–2.

60 Parodies of warfare like duels as shown in Philip Woodfine's paper also illustrate this point; see Robert A. Nye, *Masculinity and Male Codes of Honor in Modern France* (New York, Oxford University Press, 1993); Victor G. Kiernan, *The Duel in European History: Honour and the Reign of Aristocracy* (Oxford University Press, 1988).

61 Adrian Caesar, *Taking it like a Man: Suffering, Sexuality and the War Poets, Brooke, Sassoon, Owen, Graves* (Manchester University Press, 1993), pp. 3–13. Caesar reads the war poets as expressing through a lively cult of athleticism and suffering both their masculinity and their sexual orientation.

62 Masculinity and warfare are not well covered by medieval historians, but see the 'history of courage' in Contamine, *War in the Middle Ages*, chapter 9.

63 See for the best instance of a study of the Freikorps, Klaus Theweleit, *Male Fantasies* (2 vols, Cambridge University Press, 1987–9).

64 Anne Summers, *Angels and Citizens: British Women as Military Nurses 1854–1914* (London, Routledge and Kegan Paul, 1988).

65 Sharon Ouditt, *Fighting Forces, Writing Women: Identities and Ideology in the First World War* (London, Routledge, 1994), pp. 7–46.

66 Sue M. Goldie, *'I have done my duty': Florence Nightingale in the Crimean War 1854–6* (Manchester University Press, 1987); Charles Rosenberg, *Explaining Epidemics and Other Studies in the History of Medicine* (Cambridge University Press, 1992), pp. 90–108.

67 Gay L. Gullickson, *Unruly Women of Paris: Images of the Commune* (Ithaca, Cornell University Press, 1996), pp. 159–80.

68 Omer Bartow, 'The Conduct of War: Soldiers and the Barbarization of Warfare', Supplement to *Journal of Modern History*, 64 (December 1992), 32–45.

69 David M. Vess, *Medical Revolution in France, 1789–1796* (Gainesville, University of Florida Press, 1975), pp. 54–116.

70 David Ellis, *The Military Revolution in Sixteenth-Century Europe* (London, Tauris Academic Studies, 1995), p. 120.

71 In different settings the term minority has been used to describe groups which might want to define themselves as such for a diversity of reasons, to increase their access to political rights or specific recognition. See Raphael Samuel (ed.), *Patriotism: The Making and Unmaking of British National Identity* (3 vols, London, Routledge, 1989), vol. 2: *Minorities and Outsiders*. In some instances the existence of a community can be perceived as really unproblematic. Keith Sword, *Identity in Flux: The Polish Community in Britain* (London, School of Slavonic and East European Studies, 1996), pp. 22–9.

72 W.E. Mosse, *The German-Jewish Economic Élite 1820–1935* (Oxford, Clarendon Press, 1989), pp. 37–92; 164–85.

73 John Borneman and Jeffrey M. Peck (eds), *Sojourners: The Return of German Jews and the Question of Identity* (Lincoln, University of Nebraska Press, 1995), pp. 103–18.

74 Samuel Hynes, *A War Imagined: The First World War and British Culture* (New York, Atheneum, 1991); Modris Eksteins, *Rites of Spring: The Great War and the Birth of the Modern Age* (Boston, Houghton Mifflin, 1989).

75 Marcel Pagnol & Paul Nivoix, *Les Marchands de Gloire* (Produced at the Theatre of La Madeleine in 1925; Paris, L'illustration, 1926); Rosa Maria Bracco, *Merchants of Hope: British Middlebrow Writers and the First World War, 1919–1939* (Oxford, Berg, 1993).

76 See Eugène Montrorien, *Les peintres militaires* (Paris, A. Laurette, 1881). Within ten years a whole artistic genre had grown in France. *Le Siège de Paris, exposition de peinture des épisodes civils et militaires de la défense* (Rueil, Galerie Durand, February 1871). A.P. Martial, *Les femmes de Paris pendant le siège* (Paris, Codart, 1871). Denis Thomas (ed.), *Battle Art: Images of War* (Oxford, Phaidon, 1977).

77 Stéphane Audoin-Rouzeau, *Men at War 1914–1918: National Sentiment and Trench Journalism in France during the First World War* (Oxford, Berg, 1992).

78 Emilio Willems, *A Way of Life and Death: Three Centuries of Prussian Militarism, an Anthropological Approach* (Nashville, Vanderbilt University Press, 1986), pp. 5–18.

79 The military of countries where there was a lively political culture of volunteering were very wary of this and tended to cultivate a specific culture and an allegiance to the state rather than to the government of the day. Jean-Paul Charnay, *Société militaire et suffrage politique en France depuis 1789* (Paris, S.E.V.P.E.N., 1964).

80 John Keegan, 'Regimental Ideology', in Geoffrey Best & Andrew Wheatcroft (eds), *War, Economy and the Military Mind* (London, Croom Helm, Rowman and Littlefield, 1976), pp. 3–18.

81 M. Calmon (ed.), *Discours parlementaires de M. Thiers* (16 vols, Paris, Calmann Lévy, 1882), vol. 12, p. 631.

82 John Byng was shot for allowing Minorca to fall. Voltaire denounced this execution in his *Candide* and his famous 'pour encourager les autres' phrase. *Le procès du maréchal Bazaine, les causes célèbres de tous les peuples, viii–ix* (Paris, H. Lebrun, 1874).

83 See Bruno Latour, *The Pasteurization of France* (Cambridge (Mass), Harvard University Press, 1988).

84 Pierre Nora, *Realms of Memory: Rethinking the French Past* (New York, Columbia University 1996), p. 11.

85 Richard Cobb, *A Second Identity: Essays on France and French History* (Oxford University Press, 1969).

86 Fernand Braudel, *The Identity of France* (2 vols, London, Collins, 1990).

87 Frederick J. Harris, *Encounters with Darkness: French and German Writers on World War II* (Oxford University Press, 1983), pp. ix–40.

Part One

NATION MAKING WARFARE?

Following our general chronological pattern for the *Themes in History* series, the first part of this book deals with the earlier forms of identity encountered in relation to war. The making of nation-states has often been theorized by keeping closely associated the two elements 'nation' and 'state'. In such a historiography war as the attribute of the state was seen to produce identity and the evidence of national sentiment.

Rosalind Davies makes this same point for Britain but perhaps less in relation to a national identity which seeks its specificity than in relation to codes of behaviour and civility. The narratives of the raid on Cadiz, she shows, could serve both the narrators themselves and the whole nation of the English at war against barbaric Spaniards. The process of identification proceeded through opposition to 'the other'. Steve Murdoch's paper adds another layer to these early modern understandings of war and identity by showing that the house of Stuart possessed its own internal identity which enabled it to rule over many disparate territories and to be claimed by various groups as their legitimate royal house. Murdoch also shows how fragile this plural identity was and how this identification between the royal house and the people could be challenged by the subjects themselves. He shows how national identities might begin to separate from kingship. Tim Thornton demonstrates how military activity and memory could articulate communities other than the national. He suggests war against an 'external' enemy might generate separate sub-national identities, even to the point of facilitating separate regional political cultures which might serve in civil war.

This whole section demonstrates that the old orthodoxy equating nation, state and military activity can no longer stand. There was no unilinear path across the field of battle towards the western 'nation-state'.

2

NEWS FROM THE FLEET: CHARACTERIZING THE ELIZABETHAN ARMY IN THE NARRATIVES OF THE ACTION AT CADIZ, 1596

R. Davies

The English victory against the Spanish at Cadiz in June 1596 was the most resounding success of the war between England and Spain at the end of the sixteenth century.[1] It was in fear of alleged Spanish preparations of another armada that Queen Elizabeth agreed to launch a full-scale naval and military operation against the wealthy and strategic port of Cadiz. Invasion by the Spanish always threatened in the mid-1590s. There had been several localized raids along the Cornish coasts before 1596, and after the return of the Cadiz fleet in September, intelligence was received that a number of Spanish officers had landed in Ireland where the Earl of Tyrone was once more on the verge of rebellion. The Privy Council had been especially alert to the danger from late 1595 onwards. Orders were given that lieutenants of the counties should calculate the strength of their horse- and footmen, and expert captains were to be employed under every lieutenant to train soldiers. 'Nothing', decreed the Council, 'appears to [the queen] more necessary than to have her people trained in the discipline of war.'[2] A year later, after the Cadiz victory, fears of a Spanish reprisal were such that a Council of War was convened, which pooled its advice about issues such as when the armada would strike, where and with what methods.

The expedition to Cadiz went under the joint command of Robert Devereux, Earl of Essex, and the Lord Admiral, Lord Charles Howard. In addition to this, two more squadrons came under the authority of Lord Thomas Howard, as vice-admiral of the fleet, and Sir Walter Ralegh, as rear-admiral of the fleet. In charge of the land army of 6,000 men was Sir Francis Vere. As the English fleet approached Cadiz after seventeen days sailing, the plan of attack was to land as many men as possible and capture the town before the fleet itself entered the port and fought with the galleons and treasure ships in the harbour. The town was sacked by English soldiers for two weeks, and treasure was searched out relentlessly. Though a celebrated victory, the action at Cadiz was eventually coloured by criticism. The major disappointment to the English government was that the outgoing West Indies treasure fleet, which had been virtually helpless in

Cadiz harbour, had been allowed time to destroy itself when it could have been
seized. Public rejoicing at home gave way to financial investigations instigated by
Elizabeth, brought about by reports of the plunder that the land forces had
collected, as well as her concern at the small return on the seventeen ships which
she had contributed to the venture.

The division of responsibility in the leadership of the expedition has made the
Cadiz voyage invaluable to historians of Elizabethan personalities and politics.
The structure of command has been assumed to give rise to some spectacular
rivalries and aggrandizement tactics, and has fed into the more general emphasis
of Tudor historiography on competitive individualism. The naval historian J.S.
Corbett believed that the top-heavy leadership shared between six men
accounted for the failures of which the campaign was later accused. Corbett uses
this analysis to confirm the identification of heroic Elizabethan individuals, a
literary and political history of 'adventure' which was largely cast in stone in the
nineteenth century. Corbett writes,

> The cause of the failure was an old sin of Elizabethan policy. It could never be
> cured of the fallacy that the power and energy of several commanders can be
> combined into a homogenous whole, no matter how different the character of
> their genius for war. Over and over again it had been made clear that to
> exhibit the full force which the great English captains were developing, each
> must be given a free hand to act. . . . Spirits so masterful were not to be
> harnessed in teams.[3]

More recently, historians have begun to value the Cadiz expedition for the
propaganda efforts attached to the campaign; the combat at sea had a serious
counterpart in the paper war at home. Paul Hammer has concentrated on
recovering a sense of the manuscript culture of these public relations exercises as
a competitive arena of 'claims and counter-claims' which aimed to make the
events at Cadiz what Hammer refers to as 'a highly charged issue within late
Elizabethan politics'. The concern to manufacture the right kind of publicity for
the individual generals and commanders at Cadiz, evident in the mass of letters
and reports which have been traced, has rightly contributed to an understanding
of the mechanics of career fashioning in the period, and not least of all, to the
greed of the English public for accounts of the military exploits of their
countrymen on foreign soil. This then is an approach which stresses the
production of competing textual identities, generated by the true, anonymous or
falsely ascribed identity of the author. Against the older tradition of interest in
Elizabethan personalities, and the newer work which has defined individual
rivalry in terms of textual strategy, the argument followed here will present the
identity of the participants at Cadiz, and the battle itself, as a collective
stylization based on codes of military chivalry.

Before the fleet had even departed Plymouth, Vere and Ralegh were squabbling over the pecking order. Essex decided the dispute by giving Ralegh seniority at sea and Vere seniority on land. Factionalism was rife among the commanders and their men. Of Lord Thomas Howard, Sir Francis Vere and Sir Walter Ralegh, Anthony Standen wrote, 'I must saye that in no bykeringe where I haue byn I euer sawe men more fuewarde and valiant, in the matter of the combat betweene our shipps, their shipps and their galleys'.[4] Frequently quoted is Ralegh's own record of an incident in the power struggle. As well as fighting the enemy in the sea battle, the commanders were also, at times, fighting one another. In his 'Cadiz Relation' Ralegh says:

> While I was thus speaking with the Earl, the Marshal [Francis Vere], who thought it some touch to his great esteemed valour to ride behind me so many hours, got up ahead my Ship; which my Lord Thomas perceiving, headed him again, my self being but a quarter of an hour absent. At my return, finding my self, from being the first, to be but the third, I presently let slip Anchor, and thrust in between my Lord Thomas and the Marshal, and went up further ahead than all them before, and thrust my self athwart the Channel, so as I was sure none should outstart me again for that day. . . . The Marshal, while we had no leisure to look behind us, secretly fastened a Rope on my Ships side towards him, to draw himself up equally with me: But some of my Company advertising me thereof, I caused it to be cut off, and so he fell back into his place.[5]

No official despatch was written after the capture of the Cadiz, but instead certain officers were sent home at various stages of the campaign to do credit to the officers and generals of the expedition by word of mouth. These 'bearers' departed for London laden with 'private' letters, which were also probably intended for the public eye or ear. It is likely that their addressees were merely hypothetical, allowing the author to convey matters he wanted to be public under the guise of an apparently private and intimate form. The first letter-bearer to be sent home from the fleet was Sir Anthony Ashley, the queen's Secretary at War, who departed Cadiz on 9 July and reached London at the end of the month. Ashley was beaten in his journey to London by a letter about the Cadiz action which was directed to John Stanhope.[6] The anonymous author of the letter weighted his account heavily in Ralegh's favour and promoted Ralegh's interests by signalling what Essex's supporters saw as the divide between the 'sea faction' and the 'land faction' at Cadiz.[7] The sea forces, under Ralegh's command, had the opportunity to dissociate themselves from the plundering of the city on the grounds that they were still at sea when the land men disembarked. This would, of course, go a long way with the queen. Indeed it seems that the sea faction generally had more influence at the court. The queen's friends were said to be busy putting Essex and the land forces at a disadvantage, attributing most success and honour to the seamen.[8] The content of the letter to Stanhope and its particular sentiments make it very likely that it was engineered by Ralegh, or someone close to him. It is clear that copies of this letter circulated around the court in the manner that its author(s) probably intended. Essex's secretary, Edward Reynolds, sent his master a copy of the letter which he described as so immoderately in Ralegh's favour that 'a blinde man may see whereat he aimeth'.[9] According to Reynolds, all of Ralegh's friends at court were publishing his praise by letter and speech. The public intentions behind 'private' letters were thus secured and advanced by the participation of others in copying and circulating the original text.

Yet, the Cadiz participants and their supporters were denied the luxury of print. Shortly after Ashley's arrival at court, Elizabeth forbade London printers to publish any narrative that had not been scrutinized and passed by the Archbishop of Canterbury. It was an order which, according to Thomas Nashe, left all the London printers 'gaping' for copy of the voyage.[10] All the Cadiz correspondents who had intentions of publishing their narratives had to find other ways of making their versions known, seemingly by copying the text and circulating it by hand.[11] This meant that none of the competing Cadiz narratives were published, and all were withheld in favour of an official account which Cecil prepared for the press, but which appears not to have been published either.[12] A group of letters passed between the supporters of the Earl of Essex demonstrates the desire for print as a means to solidify one strain of public knowledge about the victory at Cadiz and demolish other competing versions. Essex's purpose was that 'a discourse of our great Action at Calez' 'should wth the soonest be sett in print, both to stopp all vagrant rumurs, and to enforce those that are well affected of the truth of the whole.'[13]

In contrast to the enduring interpretation of the Cadiz expedition as an event which can be wholly characterized through its personality and career fashioning of individuals, it is also possible to approach this military venture as productive of stylizations of battle and its protagonists which were collectively generated by some of its leading participants. The letters and reports written during or shortly after the event contain a subtext about the way in which the leaders of the expedition, particularly Essex and Ralegh, acted nobly, even going so far as to say that they held the command and glory equitably. This kind of sentiment in part contradicts the mileage that many historians such as Corbett have got out of the Cadiz voyage as a tinder-box of huge Elizabethan egos. Writing from Cadiz, Sir Walter Ralegh told Robert Cecil that 'ther hath bynn good agrement between the generalls', and in praise of Essex he reported that the Earl 'hath behaved hymesealfe I protest unto yow by the living god both valiently & advisedly'.[14] When he wrote to his father-in-law, the Lord Admiral Charles Howard assured him that 'there is not a brauer man in the worke then the Erle and I protest in my poore judgement a great souldier for what he doth is in great and good discipline performed.'[15] One of George Carew's letters written on 30 June is even more resounding and casts a glance beyond Cadiz to the Earl's future employments.

I do conclude him in my opinion to be as worthie a subiect as hathe bene borne in England in my adge, and yf employments be contynewed unto him I thinke he wyll prove as gallant a commander as any in Europe. . . . Many wordes in syr W R: commendation would nott do well from me, wherefore I do leave him to the vullgar savinge in a few wordes I do assure your honneur his service was inferiour to no mans, and so muche prayse worthie as those wch formerlye were his enemies do now hold him in great estimation, for that wch he did in the sea service could nott be bettred.[16]

It is important to note here that Carew was one of Ralegh's many West Country kinsmen, and his awareness of the way in which this bias would be perceived prompts him to write that praise of Ralegh 'would nott do well from me'. Instead, his praise of Essex, as Ralegh's traditional rival at court, is especially significant, as is the hint that Ralegh's enemies have been won over. The same kind of thing – clamour for Ralegh's success – is found in a letter written by Anthony Standen, not a diehard Ralegh supporter but a member of the 'Essex faction'. Standen writes, 'Sr *Water Raleghe* dyd in my iudgement no man better and hys artyllery most effect[ive,] I never knewe the gent: until this tyme, and I am sorry for yt: for there are in hym excellent things besydes his valour, and the observation he hathe in this voyage used wth my L. of *Essex* hathe made me love hym.'[17] It is my argument that these efforts to establish the successes of Ralegh and Essex, and the unity and empathy between them, were calculated to impress upon Elizabeth and the Privy Council the leadership ability of the two men. This is not to deny that ultimately they were still in personal competition, but more importantly, is an interpretation of these reiterated views as part of an attempt to shape the character of Elizabeth's military forces in the period 1596–7. The portrayal of the ideal commander was an important contribution to this aim, especially as at this time Essex in particular sought to promote strategies for a new type of land-based force, and the events at Cadiz, along with the achievements of the military leaders, became material with which to fuel his argument.

One of the chief ways in which the Cadiz writers presented the character of the English land and naval forces at Cadiz was by describing their orderliness and adherence to martial law. In these terms both the common soldier and the commanders and generals were implicated: the soldier became a chivalrous, respectful ambassador for his country, and men such as Ralegh and Essex became ideal leaders, commanding with integrity and authority. The clearest examples of this discourse in the Cadiz narratives appear with reference to the

English soldier's treatment of Spanish women.[18] Charles Howard reported that, 'The mercye and clemencie wch hath been shewed here wilbe spoken of through out the worlde. no could blud touched no woemen defiled, but haue . . . wth great care beene imbarqued and sent to St Marie Port, all the Ladies wch were manie wth all the nunes and other woemen and children and haue suffered them selues to carry also there apparell wth manie other thinges wch they caried about them and were not searched for.'[19] The principle of not killing in cold blood is testified to in Essex's account, 'The winning of Cales by the Earl of Essex', which describes the mercy shown to the Spanish prisoners by the Englishmen: 'The nexte morninge both Castle and forte surrendered themselves wthout any condition, but yeildinge to mercye. The poorer and base sorte of people were dismissed, wth all kinds of weomen, of what estate and qualytye soever . . . upon cold bloode no man was killed.'[20] Anthony Standen praised Essex for his courteous actions at Cadiz when he reported from Spain on the local reaction to the English victory. He wrote,

> Yor giving yor hande to kysse; yor remayninge in conversation wth 8 or 9 spanyerds alone and unarmed, yor protection given to al religions yor clement moderate and modest behaviour towardes nunnes virgines and dames of honor . . . have procured yow such fame love renowne & honoure in al these p*art*es that wth no treasure no myllions no Judge it is to be exchanged.[21]

The official draft compiled for the Privy Council also contains a similar description of the mercy shown at Cadiz. 'On the Monday', it read, 'all both men and women had their lyves geven them and the ladies suffred to depart uniniured any waye.' Ralegh's 'Cadiz letter' is not without its own demonstration of this code of chivalric honour. In the closing lines of the letter he writes, 'All mercy was used 4000 ladies gen*tle*wome*n* & merchants wyues sent out in all ther glorious Aparell w*i*th ther Jewells about them, w*i*thout anie tuche w*i*th the greatest honor & respecte that ever was used, by anie nation or in anie warre, to shewe that we all serued the greatest Lady of the earthe of most powere & greatest pytty.'[22]

Ralegh's letter has received little critical attention, and it appears to have gone unnoticed that a link can be made between these descriptions of English soldiers on foreign soil and the account Ralegh gives of the government of his men in Guiana. While the 'Cadiz letter' has been ignored however, Ralegh's *Discoverie of Guiana* has not, and the recent work of Louis Montrose has argued for the centrality of this discourse of chivalry to Ralegh's descriptions of Guiana and his service to Elizabeth. Readers of Ralegh's *Discoverie of Guiana*, which was published four months before the departure for Cadiz in March 1596, will recognize the letter's formulation of the mercy and justice of Queen Elizabeth as a context for her servant's clemency. The lines in the *Discoverie of Guiana* which most closely rehearse this relationship are these: 'I suffred not anie man . . . to offer to touch any of their wiues or daughters: which course, so contrarie to the Spaniards (who tyrannize ouer them in all things) drew them to admire hir Maiestie, whose commandment I told them it was, and also woonderfully to honour our nation.'[23] Dove-tailing with this line of discourse is the well-quoted line in the *Discoverie*, '*Guiana* is a Countrey that hath yet her Maydenhead'.[24] Ralegh asserts that Guiana was 'neuer sackt, turned, nor wrought', and therefore was worthy of acceptance into the empire ruled by Elizabeth. Readings of this sexualized rhetoric of discovery have formed the infrastructure of New Historicist approaches to the text. Louis Montrose's essay, 'The Work of Gender in the Discourse of Discovery', translates the domestic politics of Ralegh's career at the court of Elizabeth into the relationship between the discoverer and the new land of Guiana in the *Discoverie of Guiana*.[25] By figuring Guiana as female, Montrose contends, Ralegh indicates that it is his own masculinity that has explored and conquered her. It is clear that there is potential to revise the extent to which Ralegh's presentation of his relationship to the land of Guiana has been integrated into the poetics of the mistress-lover relationship between Elizabeth and her courtiers. It is possible to suggest instead that the Cadiz narratives define an alternative context in which Ralegh's version of an Englishman's relationship to America belongs to a shared and formulaic expression used in support of offensive or exploratory enterprises. In place of Montrose's argument about the reflexive nature of Ralegh's descriptions of discovery, and its foundation in the making of 'gendered subjective identities', another way of understanding Ralegh's descriptions of his chaste treatment of Guiana and her inhabitants is suggested by the similarities between the presentation of the exploratory venture and the offensive expedition.

In other texts written either in preparation for a voyage or in propaganda texts like the *Discoverie* the nature of the conduct of the English towards the native is carefully defined. Anonymous 'Notes for the Guidance of Raleigh and Cavendish', set out in 1584 or 1585 with a view to the settlement of Virginia, describe the manner of government to be used in Virginia. The first three orders given are these: 'First that no Souldier do violat any woman, 2 That no Souldier do take any mans goodes forcibly from him. 3 That no Indian be forced to labor vnwillyngly.'[26] Some years later when the colony in Virginia was established, William Strachey's *Laws Diuine, Morall and Martiall* for the colony instructed the private soldier that 'chastitie is a vertue much commended in a souldier'.[27] In order that the settlement's Marshall might best enforce his charges, Strachey wrote that 'ransacking, ransoming or violently outraging, and dispoiling the Country people' was forbidden. Martial law which was published regularly among armies thus had a considerable degree of influence in the context of exploration and settlement.

The cousins, the elder and younger Richard Hakluyt, propagandists for trade and empire, did much to cultivate English attitudes towards America and her

natives, and the political and economic burdens of their writings suggest the
governing rationales behind the way in which English ventures overseas were
promoted. In his *Discourse of Western Planting* written in support of Ralegh's 1584
Virginia voyage, Richard Hakluyt the younger made an all-important distinction
between popular belief about the conduct of the Spaniards in the New World,
and the conduct of the English:

> The Spaniards governe in the Indies wᵗʰ all pride and tyranie; and like as
> when people of contrarie nature at the sea enter into Gallies, where men are
> tied as slaves, all yell and crye wᵗʰ one voice *liberta, liberta*, as desirous of libertie
> and freedome, so no doubte whensoever the Queen of England, a prince of
> such clemencie, shall seate upon that firme of America, and shalbe reported
> throughoute all that tracte to use the naturall people there wᵗʰ all humanitie,
> curtesie and freedome, they will yelde themselves to her government and
> revolte cleane from the Spaniarde.[28]

In a *Pamphlet for the Virginia Enterprise* (1585) by Hakluyt senior, Christian conduct
is the behaviour which was, most literally, calculated to facilitate the easy
establishment of the economic relationship between England and America: 'for a
gentle course without crueltie and tyrannie best answereth the profession of a
Christian, best planteth Christian religion; maketh our seating most void of
blood, most profitable in trade of merchandise, most firme and stable, and least
subiecte to remoove by practise of enemies.'[29] *The Discoverie of Guiana* reproduces
the portrayal of the Spaniard's relationship to America which the Hakluyts
promoted. Describing the fears of his Arwacan navigator, that Ralegh and his
men would put him to some cruel death, Ralegh says that this was a fear inspired
by Spanish treatment of native Americans. However, when the men and women
of the Arwacan tribe became accustomed to the English presence,

> they began to conceiue the deceit and purpose of the *Spaniards*, who indeed (as
> they confessed) tooke from them both their wiues, and daughters daily, and
> vsed them for the satisfying of their owne lusts. . . . But I protest before the
> maiestie of the liuing God, that I neither know nor beleeue, that any of our
> companie one or other, by violence or otherwise, euer knew any of their
> women, and yet we saw many hundreds, and had many in our power, and of
> those very yoong, and excellently fauored which came among vs, without
> deceit, starke naked.[30]

'Nothing got vs more loue among them then this vsage,' declared Ralegh. The
sexual strategies of this discourse built between Ralegh and Elizabeth, as
proposed by Montrose, must be impacted by the broader context outlined in this
chapter, according to which the ethics of the conduct of military men originates

in propaganda issued in support of English adventure and enterprise. Ralegh himself expands the chivalric conduct of English soldiers towards American women into a more general comment on the discipline and order of his men. 'I suffred not anie man to take from anie of the nations so much as a *Pina*, or a *Potato* roote', he says.[31] Shakespeare did much the same thing in incorporating the chronicle writers' stories of how Henry V made Bardolph an example to other light-fingered conscripts who thought they could steal from the French as they journeyed towards Agincourt. Shakespeare's Henry says,

> We would have all such offenders so cut off, and we give express charge that in our marches through the country there be nothing compelled from the villages, nothing taken but paid for, none of the French upbraided or abused in disdainful language. For when lenity and cruelty play for a kingdom, the gentler gamester is the soonest winner.[32]

A regular army was not founded in England until 1645. Until this time troops had to be levied and trained for each expedition. Trained bands, which operated on the principle of selection, were introduced in 1573, and, compared to the numbers of the militia, trained military men were few at the end of the sixteenth century.[33] The unprofessional citizen forces of the militia feature prominently in Shakespeare's history plays, for example, in the recruiting scenes of *Henry IV* and among the tavern conscripts of *Henry V*. The difficulties of recruiting men of sound health and character were well known; the odds of returning home were about even and pay was poor and irregular. Preparations for war were derided by Barnabe Rich in *A Pathwaie to Military Practise*: 'In *England* when seruice happeneth we disburthen the prisons of Theeues, wee robbe the Tauernes and Alehouses of Tospottes, and Ruffines, wee scoure both Towne and Cuntrie of Rogges and vagabons'.[34] This kind of common knowledge about the quality of the English forces must also have informed the project of the Cadiz writers in their representation of discipline and leadership on Spanish ground. Indeed, instructions and ordinances issued in preparation for English campaigns in the 1590s in large part were responding to the 'grosse and manifest fraudes and deceipts' that had long been practised in armies, and they aimed to enforce tighter control and better systems of registration in the ranks.[35] The remit of the next major official venture after Cadiz, the 'Islands voyage' of 1597, was outlined in an eight-page document, part of which prescribed the 'humane' arts of war which the earlier Cadiz writers had been at pains to repeat. The instructions printed 'for the defence of the realm' in 1597 included the following directions: 'You shall also order all serving in our navy and army in no sort to spoil or destroy any church or place appointed for Divine service, nor any hospital for sick or poor persons, upon pain of death. . . . You shall also forbid all persons to kill or wilfully hurt women, children, or aged or sick persons; all these directions you shall publish for military disciplines of the forces.'[36] Thus, in some degree, the Cadiz writers were also responding to the current drive for a better organized, more accountable military force: it was an attempt to alleviate official and popular scepticism about the quality of the forces at this time, and to capitalize on the reciprocity between national identity and the 'identity' of a war.

There is yet another body of texts through which this argument runs, and which influences both the offensive and exploratory arms of England's relationship with Europe and America at the end of the sixteenth century. It is evident that the military ethics on which the Cadiz writers were drawing were those of the ideal soldier as described in Greek and Roman military discourses. In fact, one discourse of the action at Cadiz written by one 'Dr Marbecke' places the events of the expedition specifically within the programme of military discipline which was presented by the classical authors and translated into English in number from the 1540s onwards.[37] Consequently, Marbecke says that the troops at Cadiz observed holy services each day and executed offenders – one for mutiny, one for running away from his colours and another for killing one of his companions. Punishment was handed out to soldiers who had been caught stealing, and a lieutenant was cashiered for bribery and corruption.[38] All this is a close rehearsal of the orders of martial discipline laid down by the ancients.

Between the end of the fifteenth century and the mid-seventeenth century, there was widespread discussion of the art of war, out of which war emerged as a science, an object of study. As John Hale notes, interest gathered in debates about the respective merits of native and mercenary troops, the rights and wrongs of war, the nature of military virtues, the relationship between war and learning, and military and civilian life.[39] The techniques and practicalities of war were, for the English humanists who translated military texts or wrote their own, prepared for not only in physical training, but also in the careful study of ancient and modern examples of leaders, expertise and practice. Matthew Sutcliffe declared, 'What king going to make warre with a forreine prince, sitteth not downe first, and taketh counsell . . . ?'[40] The beginning of all success in war was, for Sutcliffe and other writers like him, the gathering of advice and direction. For English writers and translators in the reign of Elizabeth, the first exhortation was to make profitable use of the peaceful cautiousness which the queen favoured. Thomas Styward's *The Pathwaie to Martiall Discipline*, which went through three editions in five years, declared that peacetime (perhaps the peace of one's armchair or study) was the time to prepare for war; it was advisable to 'prosecute the ancient order of the Romanes, the which in peace were not sluggards'.[41]

Onosander's *De optimo imperatore*, translated into English by Peter Whitehorn in 1563, had a considerable influence among English proponents of military art and science. Onosander described the duties and characteristics of all the military offices – general, captain, private soldier, marshall, provost, colonel, treasurer, master of ordnance and more. An elected captain, Onosander decreed, should be temperate, continent, sober, abstinent, not excessive in eating and drinking. As an aggressor, he should conduct himself, 'using benignity and gentelnes towardes those Cities. . . . And surely that manne, which so soone as he hath obtained a City, sheweth himself sharp and cruell, putting it to sacke, tearing and cuttyng to peces al thinges, geueth occasion to other Cities, to alienate their good willes, and to take upon them selues the warre.'[42] The classical writers, generals and commanders who formed the foundations of Elizabethan military science were most often Alexander, Cicero, Emperor Justinian, Scipio and Julius Caesar. Forquevaux's *Instructions sur le faict de la guerre* (1548), translated into English by Paul Ive in 1589, set the tone for much of the later writing in English. Describing the general in the same way that Onosander had done, Fourquevaux advised the imitation of 'Scipio the chaste' and 'Caesar the iust' as the way to success. They were commanders who, 'obtained with more ease the dominions (the one of *Spaine*, & the other of *Fraunce*, through two examples which they did shew of their vertue) than by any great force that they did use. For *Scipio* although that he was yoong, & a gallant man, yet he restored a Gentlewoman of most excellent beautie, unto hir father & husband, without raunsome: and as he quitted hir freely so he restored her unto her freendes as intirely in hir honour, as shee was at the time of hir taking: which act did profit him more then all his force.'[43]

This doctrine of chaste conquest, by which better and more conquests were made, was also found in the anti-Spanish propaganda which the two Richard Hakluyts used in justification of English intervention in the West Indies where, it was said, the Spanish ruled with tyranny. Like Scipio, who profited more through clemency than force, these classical precepts were contiguous with economic projects for exploration and settlement and with characterizations of the English soldier in the 1580s and 1590s. George Whetstone's *The Honourable Reputation of a Souldier* makes the link for us:

> When God deliuereth any Citie or towne into their hands they (especially the *Spaniard* and the *Italian*) take small compassion of the Inhabitantes afflictions: but to iniurie them in the hyest extreamitie, as the sweetest part of their spoile, they most impiously, and barbarously abuse honest matrones and deflower their daughters. . . .
> The Continencie of ALEXANDER, SCIPIO, and many other most illustrious Captains, ar worthy presidents, to brydle the intemperate affections of the multitude of Souldiers.[44]

Fourquevaux's discourse on war includes a list of 'chiefest lawes', a format for summarizing martial law which by 1599 had been repeated in many various forms in books on military science. This group of texts ranges from Leonard Digges' *Stratioticos* (1579), and other manuals like it, to publications of rules laid down for specific English campaigns, such as *Lawes and Ordinances set downe by*

Robert Earle of Leycester (1586) and *Lawes and Orders of Warre established for the good conduct of the seruice in Ireland* (1599). Some of the most repeated tenets of military discipline were those which outlawed treason, correspondence with the enemy, changing camp, breaking truce with the enemy, mutiny, falling asleep on the watch and registering in two musters.[45] To maintain order among the troops, it was stated that killing another soldier in a private quarrel was in breach of martial law, as was attacking any victualler, dicing, carding, stealing and blasphemy. The orders that were published before Essex led his army into Ireland stated among other laws that 'No man shall rauish or force any woman, vpon paine of death. And adulteries or fornications shalbe punished by imprisonment, banishment from the Army, or such other penaltie'.[46] The Earl of Leicester notified his army that pregnant women, women lying in childbed, old people, widows, young virgins and babies, were to be exempt from 'violent handes'.[47]

In April 1596, as the time for the Cadiz voyage approached, Essex produced a manuscript pamphlet entitled 'Instructions and Articles sett downe by us Robert Erle of Essex and Charles L. Howard . . . generalls of her Ma[ties] forces imployed in this action bothe by sea and land'.[48] This document ordered every captain and chief officer of the navy to observe and enforce during their employment many of the rules of conduct which are rehearsed in the other texts which have been described. It has been argued here that, in repeating the endorsements of the ideal soldier and ideal commander, the Cadiz writers collaborated to publicize England's military machine as much as an ambassadorial vehicle as an aggressor. On the strength of the narratives and reports of the action written by Ralegh and others, which characterized the leadership as respectful and cooperative and the troops as chaste and temperate, Essex was able in his version of the action at Cadiz, the 'Relation of the winning of Cales', to propose new military strategies.

In September and October 1596, controversy about the Cadiz expedition was still raging. Elizabeth had instigated financial investigations into the reports of pillaging which had gone on after the victory, and accusations were flying as to who was to blame for allowing the treasure fleet to escape unharmed from Cadiz harbour. A thirty-two page manuscript in Essex's hand, written between September and October 1596, contains Essex's arguments for the reform of the Elizabethan army, specifically for a complementary relationship between naval and land forces.[49] With command of the sea, it says, Spain's Indian traffic can be interrupted, and the squeeze on Iberian resources can be increased. Yet in order to capitalize on the successes of English sea power, it was necessary to transform what Essex called 'the idle wanderings upon the sea' of privateers and semi-official fleets, through the authorization of a land force which could secure bases at strategic locations, giving English ships somewhere to water and the army somewhere to 'conquer and dwell'.

The Hulton manuscript describes the current state of the Elizabethan land force as a 'monstruous unweldy' body of men, which could not be kept in order.

'Ther numbers do for the most part consist of artificers and clownes who know nothing of the warres and litle of the use of the armes they carry . . . ther leaders men of quality dwelling neere, butt as insufficient commonly as the soldiers; ther furniture only fitt to hang over the skreene in a halle.'[50] Essex proposed that quality was more important than quantity. Whereas a mainly volunteer land force of approximately 6,000 men had served at Cadiz, Essex stated radically that an army of 3,000 was sufficient for any action if it was composed of 'disciplined men'. Essex's point, that it was the character of the land force which was crucial – what L.W. Henry calls the key to the difference between the old and new ideas – had not been expressed by any other English military leader of the time. These projects for reform, along with a less specific impulse towards the increase in England's offensive operations, were the potential beneficiaries of the military identities generated and reinforced at Cadiz.

The narratives of the expedition illustrate the competitive rivalry and individualism which have so often been caricatured in the Elizabethan period. However, they also endorse a challenge to this dominant ideology through the collective endeavour to shape the identity and quality of soldiers and their leaders. The attempt to trace the diverse impulses behind this discourse of military identity has recovered the extent of the interleaving of late Elizabethan anti-Spanishness, of propaganda for trade and settlement in America, of the humanistic display of the reading of classical precepts and military science, of the legitimation of war, and of Essex's proposals for a small, skilled land and sea force. The writers of the Cadiz narratives were participating in a drive for offensive warfare which was intended to have repercussions beyond what eventually devolved into tawdry investigations and inventories. The usefulness of the military exploit in the career of Elizabeth's courtiers is undeniable. The Earl of Essex in particular dined out on the victory at Cadiz for some time, and until his death in 1601 he sported a spade-shaped beard which he had grown on the voyage. His new and fixed facial image remained as an ever-present reminder of his glory at Cadiz, and the style was immortalized in a painting by Marcus Gheeraerts.[51] Yet the personal profit to be secured from the victory against the Spanish had a counterpart which has remained more discreet over the centuries, in the collective fashioning of military men as civilized ambassadors for England.

Notes

1 Analysis of the Cadiz action can be found in Julian S. Corbett, *The Successors of Drake* (London, Longmans, Green & Co., 1919); Alan Haynes 'The Cadiz Expedition, 1596', *History Today*, 23 (March 1973) 161–9; Stephen & Elizabeth Usherwood, *The Counter-Armada, 1596. The Journall of the Mary Rose* (London, The Bodley Head, 1983). Paul Hammer has traced the manuscripts and authors involved in the propaganda war which followed the battle in his unpublished paper, 'Myth-making: Politics, Propaganda and the Capture of Cadiz in 1596'. I am grateful to Dr Hammer for a copy of this paper.

2 The Council to the Lord Lieutenant of Lincolnshire, *Calendar of State Papers, Domestic, Elizabeth 1595–7* (London, Longmans, Green, Reader and Dyer, 1869) (07/09/1597).

3 Corbett, *Successors of Drake*, p. 134.

4 Anthony Standen to Lord Burghley, from Cadiz, 5 July 1596. British Library [BL], Harleian MS 6845, ff. 101–2.

5 Sir Walter Ralegh, 'A Relation of the Action at Cadiz' in Phillip Ralegh (ed.), *An Abridgement of Sir Walter Raleigh's History of the World* (London, privately printed, 1700), p. 23. Besides the 'Relation', Ralegh wrote a 'letter' (hypothetically) addressed to his cousin Arthur Gorges, which will be referred to as his 'Cadiz letter'. The letter is Huntington Library [HL], San Marino, HM 102, ff. 10ᵛ–12, and is printed by Pierre Lefranc in 'Ralegh in 1596 and 1603: Three Unprinted Letters in the Huntington Library', *Huntington Library Quarterly*, 29 (1965–6), 337–45.

6 Lambeth Palace Library [LPL], MS 658, f. 116. Stanhope was master of the posts and a friend and relative of Robert Cecil.

7 Edward Reynolds to Essex, LPL, MS 658, ff. 259–60ᵛ.

8 Edward Reynolds to Essex, LPL, MS 658, ff. 259–60ᵛ.

9 Edward Reynolds to Essex, LPL, MS 658, ff. 259–60ᵛ.

10 BL, Cotton MS Julius C. III, f. 280.

11 This was certainly the tactic of Essex and his secretariat. Reynolds advised Essex that 'by sending abrode copies wᶜʰ ye rest of your freinds to whom they are communicated will allsoe do so and they will passe very shortly into all partes & speake all languages.' Responsibility for introducing the script into various parts of Europe was divided among Essex's supporters: Anthony Bacon circulated it in Scotland, Thomas Bodley in the Low Countries and Monsieur La Fontaine in France. (Reynolds to Essex, LPL, MS 658, ff. 259–60ᵛ).

12 Cecil's official version is Public Record Office [PRO], SP 12/259 no. 114. In 1599 references to the Earl of Essex and his victory at Cadiz had to be removed from unsold copies of Richard Hakluyt's *Voyages* (1598). This has been cited as an example of the extent of the censorship of Cadiz documents, but in fact it must have had more to do with Elizabeth's fears at Essex's growing popularity after his return from Ireland in 1599. See Charles E. Armstrong, 'The "Voyage to Cadiz" in the Second Edition of Hakluyt's "Voyages"', *The Papers of the Bibliographical Society of America*, 49 (1955), 254–62.

13 Henry Cuffe to Edward Reynolds. LPL, MS 658, f. 88. The account which Essex and his secretaries produced is 'The winninge of Cales by the Earle of Essex'. BL, Stowe MS 1303, ff. 3–6ᵛ.

14 Walter Ralegh to Robert Cecil, 7 July. BL, Cotton MS Vespasian C.XIII, f. 290.

15 LPL, MS 658, ff. 55–6.

16 George Carew to Robert Cecil, 30 June. BL, Cecil Papers vol. 41, no. 99.

17 BL, Harleian MS 6845, ff. 101–2.

18 It would appear that the claims of these authors about the military chivalry of the English invaders did have some correspondence with reality. A canon of the Church of Cadiz, Francisco de Quesada, who observed the actions of the English at the time of the victory, recorded the cordiality with which the locals were on the whole treated. He wrote, 'ninguna mujer ha sido forzado ni llevada à Inglaterra; a nadre han tormento por haber dineros sino fueron dos otres; ninguna persona murió à sangre fria; casi ninguna insolencia se ha hecho.' [No women were raped or abducted to England; a woman was tormented for money; no people were killed in cold blood; no insolence has been done.]

Archivo general de Simancas, MS Estado 177, cited in Edward Edwards (ed.), *The Life of Sir Walter Ralegh* (2 vols, London, Macmillan, 1868), vol. 2, p. 134.

19 LPL, MS 658, ff. 55–6.

20 BL, Sloane MS 1303, ff. 3–6ᵛ.

21 BL, Cecil Papers vol. 138, no. 59.

22 HL, HM 102, f. 12.

23 Sir Walter Ralegh, *The Discoverie of Guiana*, ed. V.T. Harlow (London, The Argonaut Press, 1928), p. 44.

24 Ralegh, *Discoverie*, p. 73.

25 Louis Montrose, 'The Work of Gender in the Discourse of Discovery', in Stephen Greenblatt (ed.), *New World Encounters* (Berkeley & London, University of California Press, 1993), pp. 177–217, 218–40. See also Montrose, 'The Elizabethan Subject and the Spenserian text', in Patricia Parker & David Quint (eds), *Literary Theory/Renaissance Texts* (Baltimore, The John Hopkins University Press, 1986), pp. 303–40.

26 'Anonymous Notes for the Guidance of Raleigh and Cavendish', printed in D.B. Quinn (ed.), *The Roanoke Voyages* (2 vols, London, Hakluyt Society, second series, 1955), vol. 1, pp. 130–9.

27 William Strachey, *For the Colony in Virginia Britannia. Lawes Diuine, Morall and Martiall* (London, n.p., 1612), pp. 81, 43.

28 Richard Hakluyt, *Discourse of Western Planting* (1584), in E.G.R. Taylor (ed.), *The Original Writings and Correspondence of the Two Richard Hakluyts* (2 vols, London, Hakluyt Society, second series, 1935), vol. 2, p. 318.

29 Richard Hakluyt senior, *Pamphlet for the Virginia Enterprise*, in Taylor (ed.), *Original Writings*, vol. 2, p. 334.

30 Ralegh, *Discoverie*, pp. 43–4.

31 Ralegh, *Discoverie*, p. 44.

32 William Shakespeare, *Henry V*, ed. Gary Taylor (Oxford University Press, 1984), III, vi, 108–14.

33 On this subject see Lindsay Boynton, *The Elizabethan Militia 1558–1638* (London, Routledge & Kegan Paul, 1967); John R. Hale, *The Art of War and Renaissance England* (Washington, Folger Shakespeare Library, 1961).

34 Barnabe Rich, *A Pathwaie to Military Practise* (London, J. Charlewood for R. Walley, 1587), sig. G3.

35 See for example the Ordinances and Instructions for Musters issued for captains and soldiers in the pay of the Crown in the Low Countries in 1590. PRO, SP 12/234, no. 76.

36 *Calendar of State Papers, Domestic, Elizabeth 1595–7* (15/06/1597), p. 99.

37 For a survey of English military writing and translation see Maurice J.D. Cockle, *A Bibliography of English Military Books up to 1642* (London, Simpkin, Marshall, Hamilton, Kent & Co., 1900).

38 BL, Stowe MS 159, ff. 353–69ᵛ.

39 Hale, *The Art of War*, p. 1.

40 Matthew Sutcliffe, *The Practice, Proceedings and Lawes of Armes* (London, C. Barker, 1593). Sutcliffe quotes from the gospel of Luke 14:31.

41 Thomas Styward, *The Pathwaie to Martiall Discipline* (London, T. East for Myles Jenyngs, 1581), Preface to the Reader.

42 *Onosandri Platonici de Optimo Imperatore*, translated from Greek into Italian by Fabio Cotta, and from Italian into English by Peter Whitehorn (London, William Seres, 1563), p. 113. Between 1539 and 1572 three other ancient books on the art of war were translated: Frontinus, tr. Richard Morison, *The Strategemes, Sleyghtes and Policies of Warre* (London, T. Berthelet, 1539); Julius Caesar, tr. Arthur Golding, *The Eyght Bookes of Caius Julius Caesar Conteyning his Martiall Exploytes in Gallia* (London, William Seres, 1565); Vegetius, tr. J. Sadler, *The Foure Bookes of Martiall Policye* (London, Thomas Marshe, 1572).

43 Paul Ive tr., *Instruction for the Warres* (London, T. Man and T. Cooke, 1589) pp. 260–1. Fourquevaux's treatise is usually (and wrongly) attributed to Guillaume du Bellay.

44 George Whetstone, *The Honourable Reputation of a Souldier* (Leyden, n.p., 1586), p. 48.

45 The texts which I take these martial laws from are, besides Forquevaux's, Leonard Digges, *An Arithmeticall Militarie Treatise named Stratioticos* (London, Henry Bynneman, 1579); Thomas Styward, *The Pathwaie to Martiall Discipline* (London, T. East for Myles Jenyngs, 1581); *Lawes and Ordinances set downe by Robert Earle of Leycester* (London, C. Barker, 1586); Gyles Clayton, *The Approued Order of Martiall Discipline* (London, John Charlewood for Abraham Kitsonne, 1591); Matthew Sutcliffe, *The Practice, Proceedings and Lawes of Armes* (London, C. Barker, 1593); Robert Barret, *The Theorike and Practike of Modern Warres* (London, R. Field for W. Ponsonby, 1598); *Lawes and Orders of Warre established for the good conduct of the seruice in Ireland* (London, n.p., 1599).

46 *Lawes and Orders of Warre*, sig. A2ᵛ. The authors of these rules were the Earl of Essex, the Earl Marshall of England, Viscounts Hereford and Bourgcher, and Lord Ferrers of Chartley.

47 *Lawes and Ordinances*, sig. A3.

48 Several copies exist. See PRO, SP 12/257, nos 45, 46 and 47. Also LPL, MS 250, ff. 339–41ᵛ.

49 Study of this manuscript in the Hulton Papers at the British Library has revealed that an extract from the longer work has had a better known existence as *The Omissions of the Cales Voyage*. L.W. Henry's work on the entire manuscript has concluded that the *Omissions* was extracted from the rest of the work in order to act as a justification of Essex's actions at Cadiz. Internal evidence suggests that the original transcription (now lost) was made by Edward Reynolds at Essex's direction. See L.W. Henry, 'The Earl of Essex as Strategist and Military Organiser (1596–1597)', *English Historical Review*, 68 (1953), 363–93.

50 Henry, 'The Earl of Essex', p. 370.

51 Reproductions of this portrait can be found in Roy Strong, *The Cult of Elizabeth: Elizabethan Portraiture and Pageantry* (London, Thames and Hudson, 1977); and *Tudor and Jacobean Portraits* (2 vols, London, HMSO, 1969).

3

THE HOUSE OF STUART AND THE SCOTTISH PROFESSIONAL SOLDIER 1618–1640: A CONFLICT OF NATIONALITY AND IDENTITIES

S. Murdoch

In 1639 Charles I undertook a military operation against his native kingdom of Scotland in an attempt to force through his centralizing policies, especially in ecclesiastical reform. This action was strongly resisted by the Scots, who took up arms against their king and engaged in what has become known as the 'Bishops' Wars'. These 'wars' were the result of the conflicts caused by the perceived identities of the protagonists, and this paper is divided into three sections which try to make sense of these conflicting identities. The first section follows the evolving identity of the House of Stuart from a Scottish Royal House to a multi-national institution. Having established a successful dynasty in Scotland, the Stuarts added England, Ireland and France to their titles in 1603, though the status of the French claim as anything other than a traditional title of the English realm is debatable, especially given James Stuart's desire to avoid conflict with his neighbours.

The second section investigates the motivations of the Scottish professional soldier from 1618 to 1640. During this period, the Scots sent some 40,000 men to fight on the continent; first in the army of the Palatinate and Bohemia, then Denmark–Norway, and latterly in the armies of Sweden, France and Russia. Contemporary sources reveal that the defence of the honour of the House of Stuart was a prime motive for their participation in the European conflict. The war that began in Bohemia became one for the Palatinate itself and gave the Scots an opportunity to demonstrate their particular degree of loyalty to the House of Stuart through their endeavours in the defence of Princess Elizabeth. The war also ensured that Europe was replete with experienced and disciplined Scottish soldiers more zealous than their fellow Stuart subjects from England and Ireland in pursuing the anti-Habsburg cause. The number of these men was instrumental in ensuring that the evolution of the Scottish identity that took place in the seventeenth century would continue to have a strong martial component, as it had done in previous centuries

The third section addresses an apparent paradox which resulted from the conflict between the House of Stuart and the Covenanters at the end of the 1630s. The Covenanting army was led by General Alexander Leslie, who, like the majority of his officers and NCOs, had served in the Swedish army. The Swedes could ill afford to release so many men from their army as they were engaged in a war with the Holy Roman Empire. This led to a remarkable debate in the Swedish state council at which Scottish delegates were invited to explain their reasons for opposing their king and preparing to resort to arms against him. In this unusual forum, the Scots were forced to define their motivations and their national identity in a way that home-based subjects did not have to do. This debate should form an important component of any evaluation of Scottish identity in the seventeenth century and here it has been combined with additional evidence to highlight the importance of multiple kingdoms historiography when studying that period.

This paper seeks to explain the transformation of the Scottish professional soldiers from 'loyal Stuart subjects' to 'radical Scottish rebels'. In doing so it challenges many long-established beliefs relating to the identity of the House of Stuart and the military participation of the Scots on the continent. An illustration of this historiography is the Folio Society's edition of Clarendon's *History of the Great Rebellion*. This edition begins in 1642, missing out the first five books of Clarendon's work and therefore the Bishops' Wars between Charles I and the Scottish Covenanters, which are important in understanding the development of English military resistance to the king. After 1642, 'cuts have also been made in order to produce a fast moving, narrative account of the civil war as Clarendon saw it.'[1] The text left to the reader is not the one that Clarendon saw at all. By including the Bishops' Wars and ongoing events in Scotland and Ireland in his text, Clarendon clearly viewed them as intrinsic to events in England. The editor's decision to remove large sections because they did not take place in England is both parochial and absurd. It is hoped that in combination the following three sections, with their emphasis on a 'multiple kingdoms' approach to their subject, will partially redress such historiography.

THE HOUSE OF STUART: A SCOTO-BRITISH INSTITUTION?

The House of Stuart as an institution has been the focus of a considerable body of investigation. An uninformed observer could easily conclude that soon after James Stuart took the English throne, the House of Stuart cast off its Scottish attachments and became thoroughly English. Mention of his Scottish heritage becomes incidental in most works about James VI (though often raised to explain some fault in his character or policy). In the case of Charles I, the Scottish element is usually lost altogether. As a result many historians fail to appreciate the motivations behind the actions of both monarchs which a different perspective can clarify. To gain such a perspective we must address some of the neglected features of the individual monarchs themselves and reinterpret much of the extant information relating to the Stuart kings.

There are startling differences of opinion over James' abilities and his contrasting personae in Scotland and England. Regardless of any belief concerning ability, the important point is often reiterated that after 1603 'a foreign king sat on the English throne, an absentee on the Scottish'.[2] The current historical consensus concludes that to English and Scottish subjects alike James was firmly Scottish and in England often resented for being so. When James moved to England he gave prominent positions to the many Scottish nobles he brought with him. His English critics dreaded the 'Scotticization' of their institutions.[3] The king, however, had many reasons to maintain his Scottish entourage. His Scottish servants had aided the successful government of Scotland since the 1580s and had served him well abroad. James knew them and trusted them and did not see the need to build up duplicate relationships. The myth that 'British' foreign affairs were conducted from London in England's interests is crucially flawed.[4] Foreign relations were not conducted in England's interests, but in the interests of the House of Stuart, and frequently by pre-1603 Scottish agents such as Robert Anstruther, James Spence and Francis Gordon.[5]

An example which shows how the Scots dominated in other areas comes from the experiment to integrate some Englishmen into James' Bedchamber. That trial lasted there less than a year and the Bedchamber remained an exclusive Scottish enclave until 1615, when George Villiers was admitted. Such a strong Scottish presence prompted Sir John Holes in 1610 to write that the Scots stood 'like mountains between the beams of his grace and us' and indeed some 158 Scots found places in his government and household during James' English reign.[6]

Conrad Russell has recently commented on another significant Scottish influence in James' post-1603 government noting that 'James's proverbial "stroke of the pen" only worked because the Scottish Privy Council and the Scottish members of the Bedchamber had carefully prepared the piece of paper on which the stroke of the pen was to be placed'.[7] Jenny Wormald claims that James ensured that Scotland essentially remained Scottish, but 'England – or, more specifically, the English Capital and the English Court as well as, to an extent, the English government – had been made Anglo-Scottish.'[8] Scottish influences on James' administration remained strong after 1603, not just for Scotland, but also in his political relationship with England.

If James brought a distinctly Scottish element to the English government and court life, his wife Anna, sister of the Danish king Christian IV, not only added a continental European element but also compounded the Scottish. When Anna arrived in Scotland she quickly became Scotticized and learned the court language, Scots.[9] Her presence facilitated much cross-fertilization of cultural and political ideas with the continental mainland. Anna brought her Scottish and Danish companions with her to England in 1604. Anna Kroas remained the queen's personal attendant between 1589 and 1619, and other Danish attendants, such as her doctor, her chaplain and the official Danish resident, remained in her household.[10] Her Scots attendants included Lady Jean Drummond, Anna's First Lady between 1603 and 1617, and the Countess of Nottingham, Margaret Stuart, daughter of the 2nd Earl of Moray and lady of the Drawing Chamber.[11] Anna never gave up her Scottish attendants or lost her love for Scotland, telling the Venetian ambassador, Antonio Foscarini, that Scotland 'seemed to her like her native land'.[12]

The Scottish dimension to the House of Stuart in England after 1603 did not stop at the king and queen. The connection was also maintained by the royal children. Historians have proffered many contrasting views of the personal identity of Charles I. Charles is most often regarded as an Englishman, Kevin Sharpe advancing the claim that he was 'the first adult Englishman to succeed to the throne since Henry VIII'.[13] John Morrill suggests that to the Scots Charles was 'an authoritarian, unfeeling, foreign king'.[14] The Scottish view usually concludes that Charles was either 'thoroughly anglicised'[15] or 'wholly English'.[16] Keith Brown is one of the few to challenge that view and call Charles I a Scot.[17] Perhaps a more interesting evaluation is given by Sir Charles Petrie who argued that Charles was 'half Englishman and half Scot, [and] it was an irony of fate that made the king an Englishman at Holyrood, and a Scot at Westminster'.[18] Gerald Howat adds another hybrid dimension during his discussion of the marriage of the Elector Frederick of the Palatinate to Elizabeth Stuart, Charles' sister. He footnotes her description as an 'English addition to European Calvinism' with the incidental comment that 'in fact, Elizabeth was half-Scottish and half-Danish'.[19] The consistent conclusion here would be to transfer the same description to her brother Charles. Charles is, however, referred to in the same book as an Englishman and English king where 'king of England' would have been more accurate and appropriate. On the whole the assessments of Charles' identity are made in spite of either his country of birth or his parentage and upbringing.

In England, Charles was educated by several Scottish tutors, including William Alexander, 1st Earl of Stirling, and Thomas Murray. In his Bedchamber Charles employed seven Scots grooms to one English one.[20] Being surrounded by these Scots may have prompted the request from Charles to James Stuart in 1617 'to let me see the country where I was born and the customs of it'.[21] James refused and Charles was left with a limited insight into the workings of Scottish government and the traditional relationship between the Scottish monarch and his subjects.[22] Despite this, Charles continued to foster his Scottish friendships and developed close associations with Lennox and Hamilton which must have affected the way he perceived Scotland and his own relationship to that kingdom. In 1618 a foreign source wrote that 'having been born in Scotland and his attendants being mostly Scots, he is naturally more inclined to that nation, a matter which is very distasteful to the English'.[23]

The Scottish element of Charles' character filtered through in his letters, proclamations and actions. Charles' Scottish identity was expressed in his use of the Scots language and in his repeated identification with the Scottish nation.[24] It is also worth reiterating that it was during the reign of Charles I that the highest number of Scots held places on the English Council and not during the reign of the more overtly Scottish James.[25]

There were, however, strong non-Scottish influences during Charles' formative years. From the age of four until the age of eleven, Charles was placed into the care of Sir Robert and Lady Carey and must have absorbed from them an English perspective on life. Queen Anna spent time with Charles during his formative years in a way that she had not been permitted to do with Prince Henry. Arguably Danish influences on the future king were stronger than they might have been had he been heir to the throne from birth. Anna taught her children a sense of pride in their ancestry and in doing so must have made them very aware of their Scoto-Danish heritage.[26] In addition, Charles met both his Danish uncles, Duke Ulrik and King Christian IV, on several occasions.[27] As well as European influences from Denmark, Charles also had ties in Germany through his cousin Christian of Brunswick and because of his sister Elizabeth's marriage to Frederick, the Elector Palatine. These ties would grow stronger during Charles' involvement with the later conflict over Bohemia in his capacity both as prince and king. Charles also spent time in Spain and married the French princess, Henrietta-Maria. Keith Brown argues that many of the perceived 'anglicisations' of James' and Charles' reigns were in fact continental European influences filtering through to Scotland via the Stuart court.[28]

Understanding all the formative elements in the personal identity of Charles Stuart is vital to the interpretation of his later actions. Barry Coward, for example, points out that early seventeenth-century England was as remote from the Stuart court as Scotland and 'witnessed the development of a Court culture under the patronage of Charles I, which most articulate English people found alien and abhorrent'.[29] Allan Macinnes, however, highlights James' error in denying the prince's request to visit Scotland when he tells us that Charles 'had no appreciation of the ready familiarity between Scottish monarchs and their leading subjects prior to 1603. Charles's concern that order, seemliness and decency should prevail undoubtedly served to make his Court a model of decorum. But such concerns entailed the deliberate distancing of the king from his subjects and, simultaneously, compounded his remoteness from Scotland.'[30] Historians from Scotland and England seem to agree then that Charles was not in touch with most of his subjects. If both nations found Charles to be an 'alien' king it might be because, for most of his life, that is what he was. He was, however, not alien for being 'an Englishman at Holyrood and a Scot at Westminster', but for trying to be something else in both.

James VI and I is believed to have been determined to use his personal dynastic union of the kingdoms to push for a more complete political union. Such schemes had been advocated in the sixteenth century by several Scots, including the historian John Major and the Highland cleric, John Elder.[31] Yet it was James Stuart who introduced the concept, for the first time with any serious prospect, of a 'Great Britain'. In April 1604 the English House of Commons received a proposal from James that England and Scotland should henceforth be known as Great Britain and he proclaimed himself 'James by the grace of God King of Great Britain, France and Ireland'.[32] James claimed to have chosen the name Britain since it was ancient, already appeared in maps and charts, and was used by previous kings of England although they had 'not had so just and great cause as we have'.[33] The English Parliament rejected the new title, but the Scottish Parliament accepted and adopted the name of Great Britain in its proceedings with the king.

The various debates over seventeenth-century 'Britain' and 'Britishness' are lengthy and as yet unresolved.[34] Yet the fact remains that Charles Stuart was born neither English nor British and, unless he is to be considered a Scot for the duration of his life, his identity must, after crossing the Tweed in 1604, have evolved into something else. To refer to Charles as a Scottish, Anglo-Scottish or a Scoto-Danish king would be as inaccurate as to call him an English king. It could be argued that given his upbringing Charles was in fact the first 'British' king of Scotland and England.

There is another possibility to consider, however, and that is that James and Charles were keen to promote not 'Great Britain' but the House of Stuart. The succession of the House of Stuart was difficult to swallow for the majority of Englishmen. Jenny Wormald argues that James pressed the idea of 'Great Britain' as a device to deflect the attention of his English subjects away from that fact. Many Englishmen simply chose to ignore the origins of the Stuarts. Conrad Russell for one argues that as far as the English were concerned, if James 'chose to be king of Scots in his spare time, that was nothing to do with them'.[35] The alternative way of looking at this of course is that the Scots could go along with the concept of Great Britain so long as that actually meant that the Scottish Royal House gained in prestige. If this meant that they had to call their Scottish king 'British', then so be it.[36]

Russell seems to have missed the point. During his reign, James took on possessions in the Americas, claimed Greenland and Spitzbergen from his brother-in-law, the king of Denmark, and even considered the annexation of northern Russia for a time.[37] When James VI left Scotland for England, it was not to assimilate Scotland into England under the guise of Britain, it was to assimilate England into his personal portfolio. As Scotland had been for centuries, England, Wales and Ireland were to be institutionally and constitutionally 'Stuartized'.[38] The policies which the Stuarts pressed in England after 1603 were an extension of those formulated and tested in Scotland before that date. The raising of the nobility of service had been tested out in Scotland since 1600, and reform of the church in England resulted from ideas of church government James had formulated in Scotland.[39] In this it was an extremely successful institution. The parochial nature of English and Scottish historians has, however, often led to a failure to see it as such.

If James could not actually gain control of a region he sought to influence it. In doing so he often employed forceful solutions to curb destabilizing elements within his sphere of influence – hence the Lewis and Ulster plantations. Radical measures, including the use of policing troops, became a trade mark of James' international policy. He used them in 1609 when he moved 4,000 troops from the Netherlands to the Dukedoms of Julich and Cleves to stave off increased Imperial influence.[40] In the remaining years of his reign he would employ the tactic on several other occasions, including sending several thousand troops to Poland in 1621 and 1623. These troops had officially been recruited to fight the Turks. Yet this was an unusual time for James to be sending troops to a Catholic king since James was the acknowledged leader and defender of the Protestant faith. Poland was also at war with Protestant Sweden. The sending of Stuart troops to the war zone was a move probably calculated to make Gustav Adolf reconsider his attack on another Christian country as much as it was to protect Sigismund III from the Turk.[41]

James also sent troops to the Palatinate in 1620 to help his son-in-law, the Elector Palatine, in his dispute with the Holy Roman Empire. Howatt tells us that the troops had strict orders that they were to protect the Elector and his family but were not to fight for Bohemia.[42] The Scottish troops in the field, however, took a very active part in the war.[43] If these troops were intended by James to be part of a European policing operation, that is certainly not how they behaved.[44]

THE LOYALTY AND IDENTITY OF THE SCOTTISH SOLDIER 1618–40

Sir Andrew Gray, Elizabeth Stuart's quartermaster since 1613, arrived in London in February 1620 having been sent by the new king of Bohemia to levy 2,000 foot in Britain.[45] By the end of May he set sail for Hamburg with 1,500 Scottish volunteers. They were soon followed by 1,000 recruits who left from London. These troops were to join another 1,000 Scots already in Bohemian service with Colonel Seton.[46] Under Gray and Seton, there were probably more Scots fighting to defend Bohemia at the time of the White Mountain than Spaniards trying to capture it.[47] The outcome of that battle is well recorded (the

Imperialists won), but Seton's regiment fought on in Bohemia until February 1622, long after the Elector had fled.[48] Indeed by the end of 1622 the Scots had contributed at least 5,000 of the 8,000 soldiers who had left the British Isles for the war to defend Elizabeth Stuart.[49]

On James' death, responsibility for any contribution from the British Isles to the continental conflict fell to Charles I. The degree of support given by Charles to the European campaigns is usually severely underestimated. E. Beller erroneously declared that Sir Charles Morgan's unsuccessful expedition to Germany in 1627–9 was 'the only military assistance given to Christian by his nephew Charles I [and] the King of Denmark's military situation demanded more than the army of under 5,000 men which Morgan commanded'.[50] Such a view ignores the contribution of some 13,400 Scots soldiers who entered the Danish army at the same period.[51] Nonetheless it remains a common belief among many historians of Charles I that he sanctioned only minimal support for the conflict. Kevin Sharpe, for example, states that in 1630 Charles I allowed the levy of only 6,000 troops for Swedish service and 'contributed no more to the Swedish campaigns'.[52] The Sharpe figure falls well below that cited by Scottish and Scandinavian historians of the period, who usually conclude that the number of Scots in the Swedish army exceeded 20,000.[53] The sheer number of Scots who took part in the conflict, some 40,000 compared to perhaps 15–20,000 Englishmen, suggests that there were motivating factors which did not apply to England.

The Scottish professional soldiers who took part in the continental wars are often regarded or referred to as mercenaries. The word 'mercenary' is usually applied to a soldier who remains unattached to any particular state or government, who sells his services to the highest bidder and has little or no interest in the cause for which he is fighting. A well-quoted line on the nature of Scottish military motivation, originating in the memoirs of Sir James Turner, seems to confirm that the Scots soldiers fulfil this definition of mercenaries. Turner wrote that he 'had swallowed without chewing, in Germanie, a very dangerous maxime, which militarie men there too much follow; which was, that so we serve one master honestlie, it is no matter what master we serve'.[54] The problem with this source is that it is seldom placed into any kind of perspective. Sir James wrote his memoirs well into the Restoration period, at a time when Covenanters were being severely persecuted in Scotland by the Stuarts. Turner had served the Covenanting army and, in writing this defence of his actions in that service, he was trying to place as much distance between himself and the Covenanters as possible. In truth, the mercenary behaviour Turner emphasizes was the least of the reasons for the majority of Scottish enlistments.[55]

Another well-recited belief is that the bulk of the soldiers were pressed into service. Scrutiny of the Scottish Privy Council records shows that missives were sent out to various Scottish burghs regarding the enlistment of beggars and masterless vagabonds that might have been 'in danger of punishment of death'. They all had a chance to enlist with Gray and similar orders were sent out to all 'incorrigible Border outlaws'.[56] Regardless of this, a contemporary observer, the Venetian ambassador, concluded that Gray's regiment 'included a larger number of Scots than English and of better quality, owing to the efforts of that Colonel to show more honour to those of his own nation'.[57] That the men were of better quality indicates that the numbers of beggars and bandits must have been low, and at most several hundred out of tens of thousands of men.

Although the Thirty Years' War was conducted largely by religious division, the motivation of the opposing forces cannot always be explained through ecclesiastical affiliation. Examples of leading Catholics, such as Sir John Hepburn and Sir Andrew Gray are found in the 'Protestant' army while Presbyterians, like General Walter Leslie and Colonel John Gordon, were to play important roles within the ranks of the Empire. The number of Presbyterian Scots that served the Empire is small and it is probable that there were more Catholic Scots on the 'Protestant' side than *vice versa*.[58]

The Stuarts were in the remarkable position of being the monarchs of three kingdoms in which a different confession of faith was dominant: Anglicanism in England, Calvinism in Scotland and Roman Catholicism in Ireland. The fact that the king was of a different faith had little bearing on the loyalty of his subjects in Scotland or Ireland who did not share his Anglican faith. As far as the Scots Calvinists were concerned, the king's personal confession of faith was his own business so long as he left the Kirk in Scotland to its own devices. To the Irish learned class the fact that the king was, in their eyes, a heretic was of little consequence. The theological teachings of the Jesuits, Bellarmine and Suarez meant that 'as temporal and spiritual authority were to be clearly distinguished it was possible for a Catholic people to give allegiance at least *in temporalibus* to a "heretical" Prince'.[59] This doctrine was accepted at the clerical synods of Drogheda and Kilkenny in 1614, Armagh in 1618 and Cashel in 1624. It is very likely that Scottish Catholics would have been aware of these teachings and they may have had a bearing on their loyalty to the king.

An attack by the Empire on Bohemia was more than simply an attack on Protestantism, however; it was also a direct attack on the House of Stuart. Since the queen of Bohemia was a Scottish princess and the House of Stuart was perceived as a Scottish institution, Colonels Gray and Hepburn, and indeed other loyal Roman Catholics, had two valid reasons to return to Bohemia, regardless of religious affiliations: defence of Queen Elizabeth and her family in particular, and defence of the honour of the House of Stuart in general.[60]

While the official role of the Scots may have been to protect the Bohemian king, there is little doubt that their true loyalty lay with the Stuart queen. Mackay notes that even among the non-commissioned officers and privates there were high numbers of gentlemen's sons.[61] Monro spoke of fighting a good cause against the enemy of the daughter of his king, the queen of Bohemia, and ascribed similar motives to Mackay.[62] Mackay himself related to a friend that he was no true soldier of fortune but served abroad because of his loyalty and affection for Charles I, and even Count Mansfeld's commission to Captain David Learmonth related to those prepared to bring Scots into the service of the king and queen of Bohemia.[63] In both primary and secondary sources the cause of Elizabeth Stuart is the reason cited above all others for which the majority of Scottish officers appear to have volunteered.

The loyalty of the Scottish soldier to the Stuarts could cause friction in the armies of their allies. In one incident in the Danish army, a hitch arose with the regimental colours of Mackay's regiment which 'ranked the breast' of the Danish king. The incident was recorded by Monro:

> His majesty of Denmark would have the officers to carry the Dane's crosse, which the officers refusing, they were summoned to compeare before his majestie at Raynesberge to know the reasons of their refusals; at the meeting none would adventure, fearing his majestie's indignation, to gainestand openly his majestie's will, being then his majestie's sworne servands; and for the eschewing of greater inconvenience the officers desired so much time of his majesty as to send Captain Robert Ennis into England to know his majestie of Great Britaine's will, whether or no they might carrie without reproach the Dane's crosse in Scottish colours: Answere was returned they should obey their will under whose pay they were, in a matter so indifferent.[64]

As a result of this answer from King Charles, the Danish flag was carried as one of the regimental colours, while the Saltire was carried as the other. This incident illustrates that loyalty to their country and king was strong on the part of the Scottish soldiers. They were not willing to fight under anyone's banner without thought for or consultation with their own monarch.

The loyalty of the Scots was complex and steadfast. It was directed first towards the House of Stuart, and secondly to those European leaders prepared to fight against the Habsburgs in defence of the Protestant cause – a way of attempting to restore the Palatinate in the eyes of the Scots. As if to underscore this point, the Scots formed the royal bodyguard in the Bohemian, Danish and Swedish armies respectively and prosecuted the war on behalf of the House of Stuart with a determined resolve quite out of proportion to the size of their population within the three kingdoms. The Swedish national council noted that recruiting in England was difficult and the troops they got from England were not good enough for their campaigns, a view that had been shared earlier by the king of Denmark. The Swedes added that the Scottish troops readily enlisted, were of better quality than the English and that Sweden did well from their recruitment.[65] One Swedish historian of Scottish descent, Archibald Douglas, concluded that the Scots also took a totally different stance from the Germans in relation to their service in the Swedish army. Scottish national interests notwithstanding, Douglas believed that the Scots showed a fidelity in Swedish service which almost surpassed that of the Swedes themselves. He also noted that the Scots did not desert on any occasion, unlike troops of other nationalities, the implication being directed here again towards the Germans.[66] The Germans had shown their fickle nature while in Danish service. Of the whole of the Duke of Weismar's army, only Mackay's regiment did not surrender to the Imperialists in 1628. The Germans changed sides without firing a shot after the retreat from Oldenburg, and in fact the Scots had to skirmish their way through them to avoid capture.[67] A similar episode occurred in 1635 when Robert Douglas fought his way back to the Swedish lines after the Germans he was with made their peace with the Empire.[68]

The Scots might not have deserted from the Swedes, but there is a recorded incident of their desertion from an army, which actually strengthens rather than weakens the argument of loyalty to the House of Stuart. A most bizarre incident occurred in 1622 when King James allowed the recruiting of 800 Scottish troops by the Spanish, when Scots and Spaniards were killing each other elsewhere on the continent. Their recruitment was part of James Stuart's complex European diplomacy and an attempt to gain Spanish favour for a marriage alliance. Many of the Scots thought they had been recruited to fight against the Habsburgs, not for them, and promptly deserted to the Dutch when they arrived in Flanders.[69] This incident should have highlighted to the Stuarts that when challenged to compromise some aspect of his conscience, the Scottish professional soldier was quite capable of actions independent of, or even against the wishes of his monarch.

Not only did the Scots demonstrate that they were capable of developing a personal professionalism in the armed forces of Europe, but also they can easily be shown to have had a significant impact on the professionalization of European armies as a whole. Whether or not one believes James Grant's claim that 'Military discipline was introduced into Sweden by the Scots',[70] the Swedes were certainly influenced by the Scots by virtue of the fact that their army contained so many Scottish officers and military innovators, such as General Sir Robert Scott, inventor of the 'Swedish' leather cannon, and Colonel Alexander Hamilton, the perfector of it. Accompanying the new artillery piece came the evolution of new tactics and improved discipline to enhance its use.

In Denmark–Norway, there is also evidence of the professionalization of the army and navy by Scottish influence. Gunner Lind argues that the period between 1614 and 1660 can be described as the era in which the Danish army completed its transformation to a professional army.[71] An important part of this development took place during the Danish period of the Thirty Years' War, Kejserkrigen, and it is probably not coincidental that during this period the Scots formed over a third of the Danish officer corps.[72] The professionalization process was effected in the navy by Admiral John Cunningham, a Scot, who in 1632 successfully argued for the introduction of taxes in Norway to pay for a regular navy rather than further deplete the manpower of the region.[73]

The professionalization of military forces was not confined to Scandinavia. In 1630 Alexander Leslie of Auchintoul was sent with about sixty Scottish officers to Russia by Gustav Adolf of Sweden in order to 'modernize' the army of Tsar Mikhail Romanov. This was done in the hope that the Russians would attack the Poles and prevent a Polish strike at the flank of the Swedish forces entering Germany. The removal of Leslie to Russia did not therefore constitute the simple migration of a mercenary from one army to another. As Professor Dukes has shown, Leslie was 'the most significant' modernizer in the Russian army and part of a larger anti-Habsburg scheme which ended with the recruitment of 66,000 foreign soldiers into Russian service in 1631 and the opening of the war on the eastern front by the anti-Habsburg alliance.[74] In recognition of his success, Leslie became the first soldier in the Russian army to hold the title of 'General'.

During the 1630s the Scots played a significant part in the evolution of several major European armies. This was a process which, whether they started it or not, the Scots certainly developed and employed to their advantage throughout the decade.

Whether in personal discipline or in structuring the military environment in which they found themselves, the Scots can be seen to be far from simply a rabble of mercenaries. In whichever army they served, or opposed, they gained respect and left their mark of military professionalism from Musselburgh to Moscow.

THE PARADOX

The previous sections have demonstrated that the first half of the seventeenth century witnessed the strengthening of the Scottish institution of the House of Stuart. The Scots had shown that they were more willing to volunteer in its defence than were their co-subjects in England and Ireland. How then can we explain the return of those soldiers to fight the very institution so many of them left to defend? The extent of the about-face by the Scottish soldiers becomes evident when we note the commander of the first Covenanting regiment in the field in 1639: the same Colonel Monro who had written so clearly that the defence of the House of Stuart was his primary motivation for going to the German wars in 1626. Lord Reay, his former Colonel-in-Chief, soon followed him into the field, and thousands of veteran officers rallied in defiance of the orders of their king.

The background to the National Covenant and the Bishops' Wars in Scotland has been well documented.[75] Charles I's Act of Revocation of 1625 threatened to deprive the nobility of their rights to vast areas of former church land. Furthermore, the nobility found that the bishops were being given a leading role in civil government at the expense of the nobility. The king never summoned the assembly and treated the Scottish Parliament with contempt. Even the rights of subjects to petition for redress were infringed. Lord Balmerino was condemned to death for his part in drafting such a petition after the king's visit to Scotland in 1633. The main cause of resentment in Scotland, however, remained the attempt by the king to bring the Scottish and English Churches together within one common system of order and discipline. A Book of Canons was imposed on the Church of Scotland by royal prerogative without negotiation and a new prayer book was to be introduced to Scotland in July 1637. James Hamilton went to Scotland as king's commissioner to pacify the Scots by promising a temporary suspension of the prayer book if they would repudiate the Covenant. As a result of the failure of the two parties to reach an agreement, Charles I resolved on war with his native kingdom.

While this general background to the Covenanting conflict is well known, the motivation of the professional soldiers in the conflict is not. These men were not detached from Scottish politics; they were very much a part of it. Often Scottish officers would act as Stuart diplomats and negotiators overseas. Perhaps because of this Charles Stuart expected their services when his authority was challenged in Scotland. Charles, like the leaders of the Scottish Kirk, issued circular letters to the soldiers on the continent ordering them to return and support his cause. The response of the Scots to Charles' request is epitomized by the answer he received from Sir John Seton, a colonel in the Swedish army who replied that he could not bring himself to serve the king against his native kingdom.[76] In contrast, the call for men to defend their country was well supported.

The Swedish army was still engaged in the war against the Habsburg Empire when the request came for the officers to return home. Obviously the Scots had to justify their withdrawal to the Swedish government. In June 1638 Alexander Leslie wrote to the Swedish national council regarding the nature of the Scottish Covenant. His letters stated that there were two driving factors behind the movement: the defence of religion and of national liberty.[77] Leslie desired to be allowed to leave Swedish service quickly before Charles, whom the Swedes described as the king in, not the king of, England, surrounded Scotland and attacked with his ships.[78] The council decided that he could not really be refused since he had so long and loyally served the Swedish Crown and because it was *solus amor patriae* – patriotic love alone – which drove the field marshal. The council also agreed to provide discreetly some artillery and muskets.[79] Back in Scotland, Alexander Leslie maintained a correspondence with the Swedish chancellor, telling Oxenstierna that 'le Roy nous attaque encore avec ses armees tant par terre que par mere. Cela fait que tout coeur loyal soit froisse de voir un Roy bouder contre son ancien et native royaume par les boutfeues de Rome'.[80]

In 1640 another Scottish veteran soldier, John Cochrane, went further and complained that the king planned something akin to the Spanish Inquisition should he defeat the Scots.[81] Most important from the point of view of identity, however, was when Cochrane concluded that the polity of Scotland itself was being changed by the king; Scottish laws and liberty were being dismantled and the kingdom of Scotland reduced to a province by the Stuart monarch.[82] The Covenanters had taken to arms to show they were prepared to defend what they held dear for God and for their 'fatherland'.[83]

By 1638 the concept of national identity for the majority of Scots had evolved into a quite distinct and separate entity from their identity as Stuart subjects. When confronted by the need to rank these two allegiances, national loyalty won over regal affiliations. It could be argued that the loyalty to Scotland's religious integrity which the Covenanters displayed was part of a national identity forged in defiance of a king. That would be too simplistic. A strong sense of national identity had existed in Scotland prior to the Covenanting period. It would be more accurate to state that the actions of the Covenanters were a confirmation of an identity that already existed, but which Charles Stuart had obviously underestimated and misunderstood. His uncompromising stance on ecclesiastical reform forced an issue which his father had wisely dropped before the situation got out of control. Charles' overconfidence in the strength of his position ultimately led to armed confrontation which eventually cost him his kingdoms and his head.

Charles I held a variety of identities for the subjects of his kingdoms. To the Scots, Charles was a native of Scotland, and head of their royal house. To the English he was the descendant of the house of Tudor and their true king. Modern academics usually label Charles restrictively, attaching him too closely to one nation or another. When that is blatantly inappropriate the erroneous label of 'British' is exhumed as a concessionary identity. But Charles was more than British. He was also king of Ireland – the Irish reinvented the Stuarts as descendants of their 'high kings'. The Stuarts also claimed the throne of France in their title and had a strong continental European dynastic heritage. The dynastic significance of this is clear from the motto of Christian of Brunswick, Elizabeth Stuart's cousin and Christian IV's nephew, who entered the war for the Palatinate not for Frederick V but 'für Got and für Sie' – for God and for Her. Bearing this in mind, Charles' attempts to deploy Danish cavalry to fight the Scots in 1640 can be seen in a more charitable light than that portrayed by Mark Fissel. He claims that Danish troops were to be employed because they could ride roughshod over native soldiers.[84] Charles simply asked his uncle, Christian IV, for support in his time of troubles. Christian for his part was prepared to help Charles in principle since he was a member of the Danish royal family.

A fundamental problem for the three kingdoms lay with Charles' failure to recognize his multiple identities and responsibilities. Instead, Charles Stuart sought to remain aloof from the issues of the nationality and identity of his subjects. As head of the House of Stuart he acted without discrimination toward them; they should obey his commands, regardless of their self-perceived identities. He attempted to restructure the institutions his father had put in place. In this he was aided by the Anglo-Scottish élite who had joined the Stuart institution. During the conflict with the Covenanters and the English Parliament, these Scoto-Stuarts remained Charles' most loyal supporters.[85]

The majority of Scots chose another course which is exemplified by the action of the Scottish professional soldier. They had remained loyal to the House of Stuart during difficult times. In contrast, their monarch demonstrated by his actions that their loyalty to him was misplaced.[86] When Charles tried to interfere with the integrity of their country, they quickly re-evaluated their personal loyalty to him. This resulted in a shift away from allegiance to the king and a strengthening of Scottish national identity. The problem for the Stuart king lay in the fact that the Scots, unlike the monarchy, were now in possession of a professional military organization to support their position. The professional soldiers returned to officer, impart experience and give strength to their countrymen in their preparation to defend the integrity and polity of the nation.

If the Covenanters challenged the king's perception of himself as a universal monarch, then Charles I tested the unity of the nation when he acceded to their demands. By taking the Covenant himself, Charles caused a split within the ranks of the movement which fragmented the nation into, in his words, four major groupings.[87] Ironically their challenge to his absolutist identity encouraged others to question their perception of, and loyalty to, the king. The resulting wars in the three kingdoms led to the eventual conquest of Scotland by Cromwell.

The Bishops' Wars can be attributed to a classic clash of identities. Charles Stuart failed to recognize the integrity of Scotland and the traditional relationship of a Scottish king with his people. The Scots for their part failed to appreciate the distance that had developed between themselves and their Royal House after the Stuarts succeeded to the English throne. The failure to define an adequate identity for the House of Stuart – even simply to concede that 'Stuart' is a sufficient description in its own right – has surely prejudiced our understanding of the conflict. Had the Scots recognized that once at the head of multiple kingdoms the king's identity would lie more with his family's dynastic position than with any geographic location, they may have been able to impose safeguards for their nation before James Stuart ever left for England. Where the seventeenth-century Scots and English failed, the modern historian must surely now succeed in understanding the complex identity of the House of Stuart. Once that is done, the Stuart motivation for war – in all three kingdoms – can be reinterpreted and more accurately understood.[88]

Notes

1 Edward Hyde, Earl of Clarendon, *The History of the Great Rebellion*, Folio Society reprint, (ed.) Roger Lockyer (London, Oxford University Press, 1967), p. 24.

2 J. Wormald, 'James VI and I: Two Kings or One?', *History*, 68 (1983), 189. Cf. J. Wormald, 'The High Road from Scotland: One King, Two Kingdoms', in A. Grant & K.J. Stringer (eds), *Uniting the Kingdom? The Making of British History* (London, Routledge, 1995).

3 K.M. Brown, 'Courtiers and Cavaliers: Service, Anglicisation and Loyalty among the Royalist Nobility', in J. Morrill (ed.), *The National Covenant in its British Context 1638–1651* (Edinburgh University Press, 1990).

4 D. Stevenson, *The Covenanters: The National Covenant and Scotland* (Edinburgh, Saltire Society, 1988), pp. 11–16.

5 S. Murdoch, 'Robert Anstruther: A Stuart Diplomat in Norlan Europe', *Cairn*, 1 (1997), 46–55.

6 J. Wormald, 'James VI, James I and the Identity of Britain', in B. Bradshaw & J. Morrill (eds), *The British Problem, c. 1534–1707: State Formation in the Atlantic Archipelago* (London, Macmillan, 1996), pp. 158, 164.

7 C. Russell, 'Composite Monarchies in Early Modern Europe: The British and Irish Example', in Grant and Stringer (eds), *Uniting the Kingdom?*, pp. 138–40.

8 Wormald, 'James VI, James I and the Identity of Britain', pp. 150–65.

9 Rigsarkivet Denmark (hereafter DK. RA.) TKUA Skotland A II 4 (25/05/1595). Johannes Seringius to the Rigsraad; *nunc tam scotici loquitur, quam aliqua princeps faemina in hoc regno nata*.

10 *DNB*, vol. I, Anne of Denmark, p. 440. Wilhelm Below was the official Danish agent at the Stuart court between 1606 and 1626. See T. Riis, *Should Auld Acquaintance be forgot. . . . Scottish Danish relations c. 1450–1707* (Odense University Press, 1988).

11 Scots at Anna's court also included her chief maid, Barbara Abercrombie, her chief gentleman usher, John Stewart, and her 'master cook', John Ferris; one of her favourites was Malcolm Groat, her 'musician for Scotch music': *Calendar of State Papers Domestic* (hereafter *CSPD*), vol. cvii, *1619–23*, p. 30; cf. L. Barroll, 'The Court of the First Stuart Queen', in L.L. Peck (ed.), *The Mental World of the Jacobean Court* (Cambridge University Press, 1991), p. 199. *Calendar of State Papers Venetian* (hereafter *CSPV*), vol. 15, *1613–1616*, pp. 5–6. M. Lee Jnr, 'James VI's Government of Scotland after 1603', *Scottish Historical Review*, LVI (1976), 47.

12 Antonio Foscarini to the Doge and Senate, 2 September 1613, *CSPV*, vol. 13, *1613–1616*, pp. 36–7.

13 K. Sharpe, *The Personal Rule of Charles I* (New Haven & London, Yale University Press, 1992), p. 196.

14 J. Morrill, 'The Covenant in its British Context', in J. Morrill (ed.), *The National Covenant*, p. 22.

15 A.I. Macinnes, *Charles I and the Making of the Covenanting Movement 1625–1641* (Edinburgh, John Donald, 1991), p. 1.

16 Wormald, 'James VI and I: Two Kings or One?', p. 209.

17 K.M. Brown, *Kingdom or Province? Scotland and the Regal Union 1603–1715* (London, Macmillan, 1992), p. 99.

18 C. Petrie, *The Letters, Speeches and Proclamations of King Charles I* (London, Cassel, 1935), p. ix.

19 G.M.D. Howat, *Stuart and Cromwellian Foreign Policy* (London, Adam and Charles Black, 1974), p. 18. Th.A. Fischer, *The Scots in Sweden* (Edinburgh, Otto Schuler, 1907), p. 88.

20 C. Carlton, *Charles I: The Personal Monarch* (London, Routledge, 1983), pp. 26, 37. See also G.E. Aylmer, *The King's Servants: The Civil Service of Charles I, 1625–1642* (London, Routledge, 1974), p. 317.

21 Carlton, *Charles I*, p. 17.

22 See D. Stevenson, 'The English Devil of Keeping State: Élite Manners and the Downfall of Charles I in Scotland', in R. Mason & N. Macdougall (eds), *People and Power in Scotland: Essays in Honour of T.C. Smout* (Edinburgh, John Donald, 1992).

23 *CSPV*, vol. 15, *1617–1619*, p. 393. Antonio Foscarini's 'Relation of England', 19 December 1618.

24 Examples of Charles' Scots writings can be found in several places, especially the *Records of the Privy Council of Scotland*, second series, passim. Non-governmental examples can be found in *The Miscellany of The Spalding Club*, vol. 1 (Aberdeen, Spalding Club, 1841) p. 233 (Charles I to The Lords of Session, 16 May 1634), and vol. 2 (Aberdeen, Spalding Club, 1842) p. 11 (Charles I to Robert Gordon of Straloch, 8 October 1641). For an example of Charles' identification with the Scottish nation from a hostile source see J. F. Larkin (ed.), *Stuart Royal Proclamations Volume II: Royal Proclamations of King Charles I 1625–1646* (Oxford, Clarendon, 1983), No. 280 (Charles I from Whitehall, 27 February 1639), pp. 662–7.

25 Wormald, 'James VI, James I and the Identity of Britain', p. 159.

26 E.C. Williams, *Anne of Denmark, Wife of James VI of Scotland, James I of England* (London, Longman, 1970), p. 104.

27 Anna's children were aware of their Danish heritage. Cf. Miss Benger, *Memoirs of Elizabeth Stuart* (2 vols, London, Longman, 1825), vol. 2, p. 224. See also *DNB*, section on Anna of Denmark, pp. 437–9. P. Gregg, *King Charles I* (London, J.M. Dent and Sons, 1981), pp. 21, 24, 41.

28 Brown, 'Courtiers and Cavaliers', p. 156.

29 B. Coward, *The Stuart Age: A History of England, 1603–1714* (London, Longman, 1980), p. 2.

30 Macinnes, *Charles I*, p. 2.

31 J. Major, *Historia Majoris Britanniae tam Angliae quam Scotiae* (Paris, 1521); John Elder, 'A proposal for Uniting Scotland with England, addressed to Henry VIII', in *Bannatyne Miscellany*, vol. I (Edinburgh, Bannatyne Club, 1827).

32 J.R. Tanner, *Constitutional Documents of the Reign of James I* (Cambridge, University Press, 1930), p. 34. (Proclamation of Union, 20 October 1604). It should be observed that Ireland and Britain were seen as separate entities by James. See also G.P.V. Akrigg (ed.), *Letters of King James VI and I* (London, Berkeley, University of California Press, 1984), p. 224.

33 Tanner, *Constitutional Documents*, p. 34.

34 C. Russell, 'The British Problem and the English Civil War', *History*, 72 (1987), 395–415. Morrill (ed.), *The National Covenant*; R.G. Asch (ed.), *Three Nations – A Common History? England, Scotland, Ireland and British History, c. 1600–1920* (Bochum University Press, 1993); Grant & Stringer (eds), *Uniting the Kingdom?*; Bradshaw & Morrill (eds), *The British Problem*; C. Russell, *The Fall of the British Monarchies 1637–1642* (Oxford University Press, 1991).

35 Russell, 'Composite Monarchies in Early-Modern Europe: The British and Irish Example', p. 146.

36 Cf. Morrill, 'The British Problem', in *The British Problem*, pp. 3–17.

37 For James' claims to Greenland and Spitzbergen from his brother in law see DK. RA. TKUA England A I, 2: Breve fra kong Jacob I til kong Christian den fjerde. The proposal for the annexation

of Russia: Inna Lubimenko, 'A project for the acquisition of Russia by James I', *English Historical Review*, xxix (1914), 246–56.

38 The Irish perceived the House of Stuart as an institution derived from their own Irish kingdom: B.Ò. Buachalla, 'Na Stíubhartaigh agus an t-aos léinn: cing Séamas', *Proceedings of the Royal Irish Academy*, 83, c (1983) 127–9, and B.Ò. Buachalla, 'James Our True King: The Ideology of Irish Royalism in the Seventeenth Century', in D.G. Boyce *et al*, *Political Thought in Ireland Since the Seventeenth Century* (London, Routledge, 1993). Another Irish perspective is presented in N. Canny, 'The Attempted Anglicisation of Ireland in the Seventeenth Century: An Examplar of British History', in Asch (ed.), *Three Nations – A Common History?*

39 K. Brown, 'British History: A Sceptical Comment', in Asch (ed.), *Three Nations – A Common History?*, p. 123.

40 *CSPV*, vol. 13, *1613–1615*, pp. 171–2 (Antonio Foscarini to Doge and Senate (8/08/1614)).

41 DK. RA. TKUA England A I, 2: Breve fra kong Jacob I; and Meldrum, *The Letters of King James*, p. 219 (Christian IV to James VI, 31 August 1621) and p. 221 (James VI to Christian IV, 6 October 1621); *CSPD, 1619–23*, p. 237. Alvise Valaretio, 15 September 1623, *CSPV*, vol. 18, pp. 111–12.

42 Howat, *Stuart and Cromwellian Foreign Policy*, p. 28. S.H. Steinberg, *The Thirty Years' War* (London, Edward Arnold Ltd., 1966); T.K. Rabb, *The Thirty Years' War: Problems of Motive, Extent and Effort* (Boston, D.C. Heath and Co., 1967); J.V. Polisensky, *The Thirty Years' War* (London, B.T. Batsford Ltd, 1971); G. Parker, *Europe in Crisis 1598–1648* (New York, Correll, 1980); G. Parker *et al*, *The Thirty Years' War* (London, Routledge and Kegan Paul, 1984); S.J. Lee, *The Thirty Years' War* (London, Routledge, 1991).

43 *RPCS*, vol. 12, *1619–22*, pp. 255–61, 412, 431, 453; Polisensky, *The Thirty Years' War*, pp. 125–6, 159.

44 DK. RA. TKUA England A I, 2: Breve fra kong Jacob I., and Meldrum, *The Letters of King James*, p. 206 (James VI to Christian IV, 3 June, 1620). Also *CPSV*, vol. 16, *1619–1620*, pp. 276–7 (Girolamo Lando to Doge and Senate (11/07/1620)).

45 26 February 1620, *CSPD*, vol. cxii, *1619–23*, p. 125.

46 *CSPV* vol. 16, *1619–1621*, pp. 204–7 (Girolamo Lando to Doge and Senate, 19 March 1612). Also in letters no. 266, 288, 295, 373, 411 and 427; *RPCS*, vol. 12, *1619–1622*, pp. lxxvii–lxxviii, pp. 255 and 257–61.

47 The numbers are derived from Polisensky's figures in combination with those of the Records of the Privy Council of Scotland. We also know that Gray left Leith with 1,500 Scots. Colonel Seton is listed as having 1,000 men in his Scottish regiment. *RPCS*, vol. 12, *1619–1622*, pp. 255–61; Polisensky, *The Thirty Years' War*, pp. 125–6; Polisensky gives the number for Spaniards at White Mountain as not much over 2,000.

48 Polisensky, *The Thirty Years' War*, p. 159.

49 *CSPV*, vol. 16, *1619–1621*, pp. 326–7 (Girolamo Lando to Doge and Senate (9/07/1620)). See pp. 617–20 (Girolamo Lando to Doge and Senate (26/03/1621)).

50 E. Beller, 'Recent Studies on the Thirty Years' War', *Journal of Modern History*, 3 (1931), 74.

51 J. Fallon, 'Scottish Soldiers in the Service of Denmark and Sweden, 1626–1632' (unpublished Ph.D. thesis, University of Glasgow, 1972). Grant, *Memoirs of Sir John Hepburn*, p. 3.

52 Sharpe, *The Personal Rule*, p. 79. Sharpe ignores royal warrants allowing for the levying of 41,400 for continental service. See *RPCS* second series, passim., and E. Furgol, *A Regimental History of the Covenanting Armies* (Edinburgh, John Donald, 1990), p. 2; Macinnes believes that the number in the Protestant army alone exceeds 40,000: *Charles I*, p. 31.

53 W.S. Brockington, Jnr., 'Scottish Mercenaries in the Thirty Years' War', in *Proceedings of the South Carolina Historical Association* (South Carolina, 1986), p. 41, suggests that *c.* 12,000 troops, one sixth of the Swedish army, were Scottish in 1630 alone.

54 Sir James Turner, *Memoirs of his Own Life and Times* (Edinburgh, n.p., 1829), pp. 3–14.

55 Turner quotation is used without qualification in Parker, *The Thirty Years' War*, p. 195.

56 *RPCS*, vol. 12, *1619–1622*, pp. lxxvii–lxxviii, 255, 257–61; Parker, *The Thirty Years' War*, p. 194. J. Mackay, *An Old Scots Brigade* (Edinburgh, William Blackwood and Sons, 1851), p. 5, footnote.

57 *CSPV*, vol. 16, *1619–1621*, pp. 326–7 (Girolamo Lando to Doge and Senate (9/07/1620)).

58 Some who had been in Imperial service left. Sir Henry Bruce, Imperial governor of Mikulor, left Imperial service to raise a Scottish regiment for Elizabeth Stuart whom, he declared, 'he no longer wished to fight'. J.V. Polisensky, *Tragic Triangle* (Prague, Universum Karlova, 1991), p. 181.

59 See B.Ò. Buachalla, *Aisling Ghear; Na Stíubhartaigh agus an t-aos léinn* (Dublin, An Clochomhar, 1996), p. 47. Ò. Buachalla, 'James Our True King', p. 11.

60 This is best shown by the words of Colonel John Seton, who refused in 1622 to surrender to the Imperialists. He answered them with the words, 'Since I have promised my king my loyalty unto death, my only course if I do not wish to deserve the name of a liar is to declare that I wager my life on the struggle.' Polisensky, *Tragic Triangle*, p. 245.

61 Monro, *His Expedition with the Worthy Scots Regiment called Mackay's* (2 vols, London, n.p., 1637), vol. i, p. 21. Grant, *Memoirs of Sir John Hepburn*, p. 12. J.H. Burton, *The Scot Abroad* (Edinburgh, n.p., 1864), p. 315; Thomas Fischer, *The Scots in Germany* (Edinburgh, O. Schulze & Co., 1902), pp. 73–5.

62 Monro, *His Expedition*, vol. i, p. 21.

63 R. Mackay, *The House and Clan of Mackay* (Edinburgh, n.p., 1829), p. 272. Scottish Record Office (SRO), Reay papers GD 84/2/148. Fallon, 'Scottish Soldiers', pp.191–2.

64 Monro, *His Expedition*; Mackay, *Old Scots Brigade*, p. 17; Fischer, *Scots in Germany*, p. 75.

65 *Svenska Riksrådets Protokoll*, vol. v (Stockholm, P.A. Norstedt & Söner, 1888), p. 15. Antonio Foscarini in his 'Relation of England'. See *CSPV*, vol. 15, *1617–1619*, p. 397.

66 A. Douglas, *Robert Douglas – en krigaregestalt från vår storhetstid* (Stockholm, Bonniers, 1957), p. 48.

67 Monro, *His Expedition*; Mackay, *Old Scots Brigade* , pp. 38–44.

68 Douglas, *Robert Douglas*, p. 48.

69 See *RPCS*, vol. 12, *1619–1622*, pp.730–1, 755–6, 780, 781; *CSPV*, vol. 17, *1621–1623*. Letter nos 317, 327, 552, pp. 230–86.

70 Grant, *Memoirs of Sir John Hepburn*, p. 29.

71 G. Lind, *Haeren og Magten I Danmark* (Odense University Press, 1994).

72 G. Lind, *Danish Data Archive 1573* (Officers in the army of Denmark–Norway 1614–1662); S. Murdoch & A. Grosjean, *Scotland, Scandinavia and Northern Europe 1580–1707* database.

73 Riis, *Should Auld Acquaintance be Forgot*, vol. 2, p. 58.

74 J. Barnhill & P. Dukes, 'North-East Scots in Muscovy in the Seventeenth Century', *Northern Studies*, 1 (1972), 52–3; P. Dukes, *The Making of Russian Absolutism 1613–1801* (London, Longman,

1990), p. 19; D. Fedosov, *The Caledonian Connection* (Centre for Scottish Studies, University of Aberdeen, 1996), p. 68.

75 D. Stevenson, *Scottish Covenanters and Irish Confederates* (Belfast, Ulster Historical Foundation, 1981); M. Lee jnr, *The Road to Revolution: Scotland under Charles I 1625–37* (Urbana, University of Illinois Press, 1985); Stevenson, *The Covenanters*; Morrill (ed.), *The National Covenant*; Macinnes, 'Covenanting, Revolution and Municipal Enterprise', in J. Wormald (ed.), *Scotland Revisited* (London, Collins, 1991); Macinnes, *Charles I*.

76 D. Lang (ed.), *The Letters and Journals of Robert Baillie, A M., Principle of the University of Glasgow MDCXXXVII–MDCLXII* (Edinburgh, Robert Ogle, 1841), p. 72; Burton, *The Scot Abroad*, p. 226.

77 *Rikskansleren Axel Oxenstiernas Skrifter och Brefvexling, senare afdelningen*, vol. IX (Stockholm, 1898), pp. 480–1: 'confederati causam religionis et patriae libertatis', *Svenska Riksrådets Protokoll*, vol. vii, *1637–39* (Stockholm, P.A. Norstedt & Söner, 1895), p. 252, 28 June 1638.

78 *Svenska Riksrådets Protokoll*, vol. vii, p. 272 (28/07/1638).

79 *Svenska Riksrådets Protokoll*, vol vii, pp. 274–9 (2, 9, 10/08/1638).

80 Riksarkivet Sweden (hereafter SV. RA.), Brev till Axel Oxenstierna, Leslie to Oxenstierna (18/11/1639); *Rikskansleren Axel Oxenstiernas Skrifter*, vol. IX, pp. 483–5.

81 DK. RA. TKUA. Skotland A II no. 79a.

82 Russell, 'The British Problem', p. 400.

83 *Svenska Riksrådets Protokoll*, vol viii (Stockholm, P.A. Norstedt & Söner, 1898) pp. 97–9, 118. July 1640.

84 M.C. Fissel, *The Bishops' Wars: Charles I's Campaigns against Scotland 1638–1640* (Cambridge University Press, 1994).

85 Brown, 'Courtiers and Cavaliers', p. 158.

86 I. Grimble, 'The Royal Payment of Mackay's Regiment', in J. MacDonald (ed.), *Scottish Gaelic Studies*, vol. 8–9 (Aberdeen University Celtic Department, 1955-62), p. 24

87 Petrie, *Letters of King Charles I*, p. 182. Charles to Henrietta Maria (17/06/1646).

88 I would like to thank Alexia Grosjean, from the Scottish–Scandinavian Project at the University of Aberdeen, for her comments on this paper.

4

'The Enemy or Stranger, that shall invade their Countrey': Identity and Community in the English North

T. Thornton

The aftermath of the battle of Flodden Field in 1513 was one of glorious triumph for most of those involved on the English side. Twelve Scottish earls, the archbishop of St Andrews, two bishops, two abbots, and King James IV himself were dead. Thomas Howard, Earl of Surrey, the English commander, was able to send to Queen Catherine of Aragon the bloodied coat of a dead monarch, and the event was recorded for ever in an augmentation to the Howard arms. Howard was restored to the Duchy of Norfolk forfeited by his father after Bosworth Field. More generally, ransoms and booty abounded.[1] Yet the victory was not so complete that no room was left for recriminations. Three different viewpoints illustrate the way failure on the battlefield was perceived. The first, from the poem 'Scottish Field' in the Bishop Percy Folio Manuscript, is almost certainly by a Cheshire gentleman active in the military campaigns of 1513–14, although probably in France rather than Scotland.

> Than bespake Sir Raphe Egerton, the knight,
> And lowlye kneeled vpon his knee,
> And said, 'My soueraigne lord King Henry,
> Yf it like your Grace to pardon me,
>
> If Lancashire and Cheshire been fled and gone,
> Of these tydings wee may be vnfaine;
> But I dare lay my life and lande
> It was for want of their captaine.
>
> For if the Erle of Derby our captaine had beene,
> And vs to lead in our arraye,
> Then noe Lancashire man nor Cheshire
> That euer wold haue fled awaye.[2]

The second is a state paper, reporting the result of the battle to Henry's council and probably by someone close to the English commander on the day, the Earl of Surrey. This report is known as the 'Articles of the bataill bitwix the Kinge of Scottes and thErle of Surrey'.[3]

> Edmond Howard had with hym 1000 Cheshire men, and 500 Lancanshire men, and many gentilmen of York shire on the right wyng of the Lord Haward; and the Lord Chamberlain of Scotland with many Lordes dyd sette on hym, and the Chesshire and Lancasshire men never abode stroke, and fewe of the gentilmen of Yorkshire abode, but fled.

The third comes from the chronicle of Raphael Holinshed, published in 1577, over sixty years after the event.[4]

From each of these perspectives, squabbles about the failings of the English were conducted in terms of the role played by different county contingents in the conflict. Command was ignored, both at the overall strategic level and at the individual level of the divisions of the army on the battlefield. Within the English host the crucial determinants were the county contingents and their characteristics. This might be linked to the leadership provided by a particular noble family. In the case of Lancashire and Cheshire, the sixteenth century saw a long drawn out struggle by the Stanleys to achieve and retain a position of military and political leadership in the face of challenges from other noblemen, such as the Talbot family, Earls of Shrewsbury.[5] To an extent the presentation of the behaviour of county contingents in terms of the presence or absence of their leadership (most noticeable in 'Scottish Field') is special pleading related to this dispute. The main point therefore stands – that the behaviour of the English forces at Flodden was conceived in terms of county forces, or even of personified counties, since it is explicitly 'Lancashire' and 'Cheshire', not the *men* of Lancashire and the *men* of Cheshire, that are held to blame.

For a long time now, since the military revolution discussed first by Michael Roberts and extended to the earlier part of the sixteenth century by Geoffrey Parker,[6] a school of military historians has argued that dramatic changes in military technology and organization occurred in the early modern period and that these were vital in transforming government and society. Military technology and organization were employed by many of the exponents of state-building in early modern Europe as a major factor in the emergence of the early modern European state, which is also allotted a prominent role in the Marxist analyses of scholars like Perry Anderson. In the words of Charles Tilly, 'war made the state, and the state made war.'[7] War is correctly seen as driving virtually all the most dynamic elements of the royal state.[8] The raising of taxation to pay for war strengthened the sinews of power in the king's hands.[9] The mustering and training of troops put in place organizational mechanisms responsive to the central government rather than to the traditional medieval local self-government at the king's command. In England, lieutenants and deputy lieutenants began to force through unpopular measures for the defence of the realm, more or less closely defined.[10] And the experience of war behind the king's banner provided for many men of early modern Europe the horrific personal baptism into subjecthood of the early modern state.

Viewed in the longer perspective, some of the early enthusiasts for sixteenth-century state-building in its more exciting concrete manifestations now seem foolishly rash. In the case of England, the administrative revolution proposed by Geoffrey Elton has been diluted by historians who have found precursors for the developments he proclaimed, or discovered that their lasting impact was dubious, and who would now argue that change took place across the whole of the sixteenth century and beyond.[11] The same fate has befallen the perhaps even more ambitious statements about French absolutism.[12] Now the arguments about state-building have shifted towards the idea of cultural revolution. Rather than the erection of new bureaucracies, the destruction of old élites and the imposition of new mechanisms of control, we have a changing ethos throughout society which allows the king's subjects to see the state as the proper mechanism for the regulation of economy and society.[13] Given this trend, we cannot employ military revolutions in quite the same crude manner to explain revolutions in state-building. Military activity is, however, still important for those who argue for a cultural revolution of state-building, although no longer given the priority it previously received in such writing. To the idea that disputes should best be resolved through the state, that marriage and the other key events of the lifecycle should be recorded by the state, and that the state might become the arbiter of the codes of honour, is added the idea that service in war should be expressed through the armies of the state. Ultimately, this is the most powerful expression of the new power of the state – no longer do people die for their own personal honour, or for a community that might be personal, of knighthood, for example, or religious, or geographical; now they sacrifice their lives for an idea of the state.

There are of course problems with the military revolution thesis, even when applied in support of a more subtle concept of social and political change. As was pointed out soon after its first exposition, it employed a partial and even dubious view of medieval warfare – especially in terms of organization and the ethos of those who fought. Michael Howard's view of the glorious chaotic individualism of the medieval man-at-arms, expressed in his 1977 publication, *War in European History*, was highly questionable. One of the most important innovations of the military revolution, the introduction and development of gunpowder weapons, occurred in the fourteenth and fifteenth centuries.[14] There has, in consequence, been a tremendous amount of writing which suggests that the cultural revolution represented by national political motivation in war should be considerably predated. In the English case there has been the vigorous emphasis on the Hundred Years' War as a formative experience for the English. Direct expressions of English sentiment might be largely about xenophobia rather than an immediate emphasis on the unity of the English – witness the poet Thomas Hoccleve's 'I am an Englyssh-man and am þi foe / ffor þou a foo art vnto my lygeànce'[15] – or might find an identity to coalesce around in the figure of the monarch – most notably Henry V, most disastrously Henry VI. Yet the simple act of organizing and supporting such a major effort as the war in France has been seen as uniting the English in a way never seen before. Alison McHardy's work on the diocese of Lincoln shows that special prayers were requested there over fifty times during the Hundred Years' War, and that on two-thirds of these occasions the intention was linked directly or indirectly to war or peace. One of the main ways that the outside world impinged on the villagers of Leicestershire, Oxfordshire, or Lincolnshire during the fourteenth and fifteenth centuries was therefore with reference to wars being conducted by their king against France and Scotland.[16] It might even be argued that the cultural confrontation detected by John Gillingham between the English and barbarous Irish in the late twelfth and thirteenth centuries was a crucial moment in defining Englishness against a cultural opposite.[17] In fact, war is such a potent force in catalysing identities that the search might be projected back as far as evidence survives. The real question is the nature of the identity defined.

War may have produced changes to social and political organization, it may have required the gathering of resources through taxation and purveyance,[18] it may even have thrown men together in camp or on the battlefield, but in doing so it did not necessarily mean that a sense of national identity was created, or even that any other sense of communal identity was enhanced. Two reasonably well-known examples make the point. The Scrope–Grosvenor dispute 1385–91 over the use of heraldry showed that although groups of soldiers from Yorkshire and Cheshire had served in close proximity they had very distinct memories of who had worn which arms – Grosvenor relied on over 200 Cheshiremen and Lancastrians, Scrope mainly on Yorkshiremen and members of the Lancastrian affinity.[19] This was a distinction apparent in the minds of those who served, but it should also be remembered that those who organized the military resources of the king could conceive of them in terms of geographical origins. In the 1430s and 1440s fears of treachery led those who administered the troops serving the Lancastrian dynasty in France to list them by name and by nationality. Muster lists therefore describe soldiers as Norman, Gascon, Irish, Welsh and so on.[20]

In fact, we have to be very specific about what we mean by the effects of war on identity when we try to recruit it to the cause of the rise of the nation-state. A couple of points immediately suggest themselves about the way that war was developing in the fifteenth and sixteenth centuries. The first was an increasing use of mercenaries. This recruitment of paid troops from elsewhere is a core element of the military revolution thesis: because war was getting more technologically advanced, specialists were needed to fight it. These might be permanent standing armies, but as often as not, especially in England, they were mercenaries. Such mercenaries were often not of the home nation; in English armies these specialists were often men from the Low Countries, Germany and Switzerland.[21] Secondly, the shift towards more 'national' service that undoubtedly took place during this period in England was a transition from contract armies, raised through agreements with individual captains who tended to draw on the resources of the 'bastard feudal' affinity, to levies, and these levies were inevitably conducted on a county level.[22] The implication, as the historians of the county community have never been slow to point out, was that county priorities could be placed above national priorities – as when in 1625 the people of Huntingdonshire refused to have anything to do with the people of Essex during an invasion scare.[23] This emphasis has of course been heavily challenged in recent years and it is absurd to suggest that the England of gentry republics proposed by Conrad Russell, John Morrill and their precursors like Alan Everitt extended to gentry republican armies defending their shires.[24] If Staffordshire managed as a result of a meeting three weeks after the battle of Edgehill to levy an army of 800 foot and 200 horse to defend the shire against the forces of either king or Parliament, then this effort did not survive long as the intervention of troops from Shropshire and an uprising in the Staffordshire Moorlands broke the county's neutrality.[25]

Even so, it is vital to remember that we cannot abandon all forms of local identification simply because the county community school has been shown to be flawed in its analysis. The county, the region, the sub-kingdom, the autonomous territory – all of these remained extremely significant foci for military identification. Discussing the phrase, 'then stood Cambridgeshire firm', from the *Anglo-Saxon Chronicle*'s relation of a battle in 1010 against the Danes, James Campbell recently observed that 'one of the principal keys to the long success of the English state [was] the development of loyalties to local units which had been created for the purposes of central authority, loyalties which generally did not so much contradict as reinforce that authority'.[26]

Even at the most basic level of the formation of identity, of xenophobia cultivated through military activity, it is apparent that the counties of the north of England had a different experience from those further south and west. This is very clear until the end of the sixteenth century in England because of the immediacy of the Scots to the north and the French to the south. War with the Scots had been a common feature of the fourteenth, fifteenth and sixteenth centuries.[27] Edward I's massive efforts to subdue the Scots in the 1290s had resulted only in a long drawn out struggle with Robert the Bruce and his successors, producing a disastrous defeat at Bannockburn in 1314, and drawn to a close by treaty in 1328.[28] This proved short-lived, since Edward III resumed the war in the 1330s, achieving victory at Halidon Hill in 1333 and forcing a settlement which deprived the Scots of a large section of their lowland shires. Edward's attention was distracted after 1340 by his attempt to make conquests in France, but Scottish involvement in the Hundred Years' War led to another great Scottish defeat at Neville's Cross, and the capture of the Scottish king.[29] Fighting continued on and off through the remainder of the century; the Lancastrian dynasty's first actions included a campaign against the Scots and, although James I was captured at sea in 1406, tension and war on the Scottish border was a regular feature of the 1450s and 1460s. The presence of Margaret of Anjou and supporters of Henry VI in Scotland during the latter decade ensured that it would be an important theatre of war. The loss of Berwick was only reversed in 1482. Henry VII's pursuit of a peaceful foreign policy produced, after the abortive expedition of 1497, a truce and subsequently peace of Ayton, which saw the marriage of Margaret Tudor to the Scottish King James IV in 1502.[30] In spite of this, the resumption of the Hundred Years' War in France by Henry VIII meant war against the Scots, resulting in Flodden Field in 1513. Intermittent hostilities were a feature of the 1520s, and in the 1540s the death of James V left the Scottish throne in the hands of his infant heir, Mary. Henry's determination to win her for his son Edward VI then resulted in large-scale conflict in the 1540s, culminating in Protector Somerset's attempts to control Scotland through garrisons.[31] Tensions again erupted at the start of Elizabeth's reign, and it was only late in the sixteenth century that the queen's determination to be succeeded by her Scottish cousin, James VI, meant the beginning of a long alliance between the countries.

Scottish wars impinged upon the lives of men and women in the north of England in a far from abstract way. The memory and fear of destruction and raiding south of the border affected communities as far south as the Aire and Wharfe. In 1318 and 1319 particularly devastating raids were mounted into northern England, the latter seeing a battle at Myton-on-Swale; Silsden and Riddlesden on the Aire were among the vills exempted from the lay subsidy of 1319 as a result of Scottish destruction. In 1322 Edward II himself only narrowly avoided capture when the Scots came upon English forces at Byland in North Yorkshire.[32] The memory of these raids lived on well into the early modern period,[33] and they were a major cause of the chronic impoverishment of the region.[34] For those living close to the border, of course, continuous raiding meant changes to social organization, with the establishment of the clannic system of 'names' on both sides of the border.[35]

It was therefore only a certain area of England which suffered destruction at Scottish hands. Conversely, it was troops from a similarly limited area of the realm which inflicted devastation in turn on the Scots. There was a continuing localization of recruitment against different enemies. From at least the early fourteenth century, once Edward III's main attentions switched to France, the troops levied to deal with the Scots tended to come for immediate crises from Northumberland and, in more prolonged troubles, from the shires of Cheshire, Nottinghamshire, Yorkshire and further north.

If we seek a crystallization of the elements of community in the counties of Tudor and Stuart England, we find it most clearly in volumes of county history. The vast majority of these studies are structured around an account of the manors and great houses of the shires, but they also express the shire's identity through other material, not least the record of the ancestors of the county gentry in war. The works of Smith and Webb on Cheshire indicate vividly the importance of the Scots as the county's enemy.[36] The people of Cheshire were, according to William Smith, 'of stomack, bold, and hardy; of stature, tall and mighty; withall impatient of wrong, and ready to resist the Enemy or Stranger, that shall invade their Countrey: The very name whereof they cannot abide, and namely, of a Scot.'[37]

Success against the Scots was also the key theme of the poetry of the northwest and of the Borders. In Lancashire and Cheshire, a medieval tradition of alliterative poetry remained vigorously alive, much of it devoted to celebrating defeats of the Scots.[38] Flodden was a favourite subject, being described by the poem 'Scottish Field' and its variants, with which we started. The men of Lancashire and Cheshire are proudly recalled in the ballad 'Musleboorrowe ffeild', about the battle of Pinkie:

> The Lord Huntley, we had him there,
> with him hee brought 10000: men
> yett, god be thanked, wee made them such a banquett
> that none of them returned againe[39]

By contrast, in spite of their considerable presence on the field of Agincourt and the massive riches won by the likes of Sir Hugh Calveley and Hugh Browe, little was made in this poetic tradition of war against the French.[40] On the Borders, the ballads which celebrated the exploits of Percy and Douglas at Otterburne remained a part of the local culture throughout the early modern period.[41] The importance of the Scottish threat was also clear in the cartographical portrayal of the north of England. Attempts to use the maps of the late sixteenth and seventeenth centuries to support an argument for the effective social and political independence of counties will not stand up – counties remained building blocks of the newly visualized realm of England.[42] Yet the portrayal of the battle of Neville's Cross on Saxton's map of Durham illustrates the importance of the war with the Scots to the county's image.[43]

There is an even greater chance of penetrating the mentality of the whole population of these counties when we look not for overt references to war, but seek instead the use of national stereotypes as metaphors for fearsome enemies in literary works. At the most elementary level, the need to conjure up the horrors of Biblical villains such as Herod's men often led the writers of the northern mystery cycles to refer to more contemporary threats.[44]

Such an identity with a specific focus on the Scottish threat might have aided those in power at the centre in ensuring strong local defence. Campbell's formulation is, however, too optimistic – opposition was very possible when the Crown needed a more general mobilization against one enemy. This kind of division of response was clearest when it produced regional revolts, such as that of the Cornish against Henry VII in 1497: they were determined that their money was not to be spent on a campaign against the Scots. In the 1410s a more passive but nonetheless effective resistance to service in France was shown by the gentry of Yorkshire. A summons to serve in France was not well received: of a total of ninety-six summons sent out, only five were returned with a promise of unequivocal support in return for wages. Two other gentlemen said they were already engaged in military service, five promised a substitute each and five more promised to associate to support one substitute. More than seventy made excuses, however, mainly citing financial reasons.[45]

When considering the impact of conflict on identities, therefore, we have to ask for what military forces were used, with specific questions about the way they were organized as a group and the manner in which they identified their purposes. If we look at the purposes of the army in the early seventeenth century there is a singular lack of identification with a foreign policy that few understood and which resulted in such catastrophic disaster as the Île de Ré expedition in 1627.[46] There was also a lack of identification through a uniform code of dress. The adoption of a single colour, red, for the English troops did not occur until 1645. Before that, English troops might wear a common identifying mark, as with the cross of St George in Normandy in the early fifteenth century. Far more striking, however, were the badges and liveries that denoted individual commanders and their followers. The first 'uniform' to make any kind of impact in France in the fourteenth century was the green and white of the men of Cheshire and North Wales.[47]

In order for a clear unified identity to form, it is likely that the clarification of a single national enemy needs to occur. If we have a complex of enemies these must be enemies against which all elements within the national entity feel equally committed, and this was highly unlikely to occur for geographical and cultural reasons. One of the factors that served to make the French threat such a powerful force for unity from the end of the seventeenth century, as described by Linda Colley, was its uniqueness: the subjects of the English Crown now had, as never before, a clearly identifiable source of hatred and fear against which to unite.[48]

It is particularly important that we ask, with Jean-Philippe Genet, which state rises? The state which fought wars in the early modern period was the royal state – and that permitted a variety of expressions of identity because of the complexity of the state which the king ruled and which he and his kin represented.[49]

It might also be possible to suggest that there was a remarkable persistence of this complexity of identity in the military activity of what might be loosely called the British state. It is in Britain of course that we still have regiments which in many cases bear county names or the titles of great regional noble families; a colonial effort that was in large part conducted by an army operated by a colonial company, the East India Company; and a contemporary volunteer force, the Yorkshire Territorial Army, whose motto is 'For Queen and County'. In concluding, however, it is worth suggesting a more immediate consequence of this argument for the early modern British historian. This relates to choices of allegiance in the period immediately before and during the English Civil War. Attempts to explain the way the gentry and their inferiors chose sides have tended to centre on their perceived social and economic interests, or their religious outlook. Both interpretations have come up against problems in explaining the clearly regional response to the conflict. The gentry of the north of England tended to be royalist in their sympathies, and this has often been explained ultimately by a blanket theory of northern conservatism. Yet the question as to why so many in the North refused to follow what might have been their natural social or religious interests requires more than this near circular argument – conservatism results in allegiance to the Crown, something which itself indicates conservatism.[50] A far clearer explanation for the choices made by gentry in northern England is the importance of the Scottish threat, not simply in direct material terms but to the way their identity as members of their local communities was defined.[51] It made little difference that the majority of the devastation and the most serious threat of social breakdown in the northern counties came from English troops.[52] While a radical Protestant well out of harm's way in Shropshire, Brilliana Harley, might hint that the Scots' cause was the Lord's 'caus',[53] the autobiographies of men like Sir Hugh Cholmley, initially of parliamentary sympathies, and the letters of a northern family like the Lowthers in the period of the Bishops' Wars show their real fears centred on the Scottish threat. It was at the start of the First Bishops' War that Sir Henry Slingsby of Scriven wrote in his diary, '[t]hese are times for historians to write who seek to avoid all calm narratives as a dead water, to fill their volumes with cruell wars and seditions. I desire not employment at these times.'[54] Even for the Protestant Adam Martindale, the arrival of the Scots in England was a key event: 'The Scots had invaded England, and entered Newcastle, and though a pacification followed, that seemed onelie to remove the seate of warre into our owne quarters; great animosities were set on foot concerning monopolies and ship money.'[55]

The alliance of the Scots and the group in the English parliament led by John Pym meant that the Parliamentarian cause was identified with 'the Enemy or Stranger, that shall invade their Countrey': the Scots.

Notes

1 J.J. Scarisbrick, *Henry VIII* (London, Eyre and Spottiswoode, 1968), pp. 37–8; R.B. Wernham, *Before the Armada: The Growth of English Foreign Policy, 1485–1588* (London, Cape, 1966), p. 86.

2 J.W. Hales & F.J. Furnivall (eds), *Bishop Percy's Folio Manuscript: Ballads and Romances* (3 vols, London, N. Trübner & Co., 1867–8); David A. Lawton, 'Scottish Field: Alliterative Verse and Stanley Encomium in the Percy Folio', *Leeds Studies in English*, new series, X (1978), 42–57.

3 *State Papers Published under the Authority of His Majesty's Commission* (11 vols, London, Record Commission, 1830–52), vol. 4, *King Henry the Eighth, Part IV*, pp. 2–3.

4 Raphael Holinshed, *Holinshed's Chronicles of England, Scotland and Ireland* (6 vols, London, J. Johnson *et al*, 1807), vol. 3, pp. 592, 596, 598. On Holinshed, see *DNB* (1891 edition), vol. 27, pp. 130–2; M. McKisack, *Medieval History in the Tudor Age* (Oxford, Clarendon Press, 1971), pp. 116–20.

5 G.W. Bernard, *The Power of the Early Tudor Nobility: A Study of the Fourth and Fifth Earls of Shrewsbury* (Brighton, Harvester, 1985); Barry Coward, *The Stanleys, Lords Stanley and Earls of Derby, 1385–1672* (Manchester University Press for Chetham Society, 1983); *Historical Manuscripts Commission: Report on the Manuscripts of the late Reginald Rawdon Hastings, esq. of the Manor House, Ashby de la Zouch* (4 vols, London, HMSO, 1930), vol. 2, p. 4.

6 Michael Roberts, *The Military Revolution, 1560–1660* (Belfast, Queen's University Press, 1956); Geoffrey Parker, 'The Military Revolution, 1550–1660 – a Myth?', *Journal of Modern History*, 48 (1976), 195–214; Geoffrey Parker, *The Military Revolution: Military Innovation and the Rise of the West, 1500–1800* (Cambridge University Press, 1988).

7 Charles Tilly (ed.), *The Formation of Nation States in Western Europe* (Princeton and London, Princeton University Press, 1975), p. 42.

8 Michael Mann, *The Sources of Social Power* (2 vols, Cambridge University Press, 1986, 1993), vol. 1, *A History of Power from the Beginning to A.D. 1760*, pp. 453–8, 475–83; R. Bean, 'War and the Birth of the Nation State', *Journal of Economic History*, 33 (1973), 203–21; B.M. Downing, *The Military Revolution and Political Change: Origins of Democracy and Autocracy in Early Modern Europe* (Princeton University Press, 1992).

9 The classic accounts of major periods of innovation linked to war include G.L. Harriss, *King, Parliament and Public Finance to 1369* (Oxford, Clarendon Press, 1975); cf., however, the assertion that the high levels of expenditure of the late thirteenth and fourteenth centuries were a reversion to earlier high levels of expenditure in M. Prestwich, 'War and Taxation in England in the Thirteenth and Fourteenth Centuries', in Jean-Philippe Genet & Michel Le Mené (eds), *Genèse de l'état moderne: prelevement et redistribution* (Paris, Éditions du C.N.R.S., 1987), pp. 181–92.

10 Gladys Scott Thomson, *Lords Lieutenant in the Sixteenth Century: A Study in Tudor Local Administration* (London, Longmans and Co., 1923); Penry Williams, *The Tudor Regime* (Oxford, Clarendon Press; New York, Oxford University Press, 1979; reprinted 1986), pp. 416–17; J. Goring & J. Wake, *Northamptonshire Lieutenancy Papers, 1580–1614* (Northamptonshire Record Society, XXVII, 1975);

A. Hassell Smith, *County and Court: Government and Politics in Norfolk, 1558–1603* (Oxford, Clarendon Press, 1974), chapters 11–13.

11 Geoffrey Elton, *The Tudor Revolution in Government* (Cambridge University Press, 1953). Criticism includes: G.L. Harriss & Penry Williams, 'A Revolution in Tudor History?', *Past and Present*, 25 (July 1963), 3–58; Christopher Coleman & David Starkey (eds), *Revolution Reassessed: Revisions in the History of Tudor Government and Administration* (Oxford, Clarendon Press, 1986); David Starkey *et al* (eds), *The English Court from the Wars of the Roses to the Civil War* (London and New York, Longman, 1987).

12 Nicholas Henshall, *The Myth of Absolutism: Change and Continuity in Early European Monarchy* (London, Longman, 1992).

13 Michael Braddick, 'State Formation and Social Change in Early Modern England: A Problem Stated and Approaches Suggested', *Social History*, 16 (1991), 1–17.

14 Michael Howard, *War in European History* (Oxford University Press, 1976), p. 56; Philippe Contamine, *War in the Middle Ages*, translated by Michael Jones (first published in French as *La Guerre au moyen Âge* (Paris, Presses Universitaires de France, 1980; Oxford, Blackwell, 1984), pp. 137–50, 193–207; R. Smith, 'Artillery and the Hundred Years War: Myth and Interpretation', in Anne Curry and M. Hughes (eds), *Arms, Armies and Fortifications in the Hundred Years War* (Woodbridge, Boydell, 1994), pp. 151–60; C.J. Rogers, 'The Military Revolutions of the Hundred Years War', *The Journal of Military History*, 57 (1993), 258–75.

15 Thomas Hoccleve, *Works*, ed. F.J. Furnivall (EETS, London, Kegan Paul, Trench, Trübner, 1892–1925), vol. 3, *The Regement of Princes*, p. 191 (ll. 5307–8).

16 A.K. McHardy, 'Liturgy and Propaganda in the Diocese of Lincoln during the Hundred Years War', in *Religion and National Identity*, ed. S. Mews (Studies in Church History, 18, Oxford, Blackwell, 1982), pp. 215–27.

17 J. Gillingham, 'The English Invasion of Ireland', in B. Bradshaw *et al* (eds), *Representing Ireland: Literature and the Origins of Conflict, 1534–1660* (Cambridge, 1993), pp. 24–42. For the claims of the period 1272–1327, Barnaby C. Keeny, 'Military Service and the Development of Nationalism in England, 1272–1327', *Speculum*, 22 (1947), 534–49.

18 M.J. Braddick, *Parliamentary Taxation in Seventeenth-Century England: Local Administration and Responses* (Royal Historical Society, Studies in History, 70, 1994); Michael J. Braddick, *The Nerves of State: Taxation and the Financing of the English State, 1558–1714* (Manchester University Press, 1996); John Brewer, *The Sinews of Power: War, Money and the English State, 1688–1783* (Alfred A. Knopf, New York, 1989).

19 R. Stewart-Brown, 'The Scrope and Grosvenor Controversy, 1385–91', *Transactions of the Lancashire and Cheshire Historical Society*, 89 (1938 for 1937), 1–22; Simon Walker, *The Lancastrian Affinity, 1361–1399* (Oxford, Clarendon Press, 1990), p. 56.

20 Anne Curry, 'The Nationality of Men-at-Arms serving in English Armies in Normandy and the *pays de conquête*, 1415–1450: A Preliminary Survey', *Nottingham Medieval Studies*, XVIII (1992), 135–63. The administrative imperative demanded greater precision in the naming of those from continental Europe, with the result that the Welsh, as Curry notes, are underrepresented: p. 151.

21 John Gilbert Millar, *Tudor Mercenaries and Auxiliaries, 1485–1547* (Charlottesville, University Press of Virginia, 1980); Michael Mallett, *Mercenaries and their Masters: Warfare in Renaissance Italy* (London, Bodley Head, 1974).

22 J.J. Goring, 'The Military Obligations of the English People, 1511–1558' (Unpublished Ph.D. thesis, University of London, 1955); *idem*, 'Social Change and Military Decline in Mid-Tudor England', *History*, 60 (1975).

23 Conrad Russell, *Parliaments and English Politics 1621–1629* (Oxford, Clarendon Press, 1979), p. 8.

24 Important early examples of the county community school include Alan Everitt, *The Community of Kent and the Great Rebellion, 1640–1660* (Leicester University Press, 1966) (based on his thesis written 1952–57); Thomas G. Barnes, *Somerset, 1625–1640: A County's Government during the 'Personal Rule'* (Cambridge, Mass., Harvard University Press, 1961); Hassell Smith, *County and Court.* Criticism: Clive Holmes, 'The County Community in Stuart Historiography', *Journal of British Studies*, XIX (1980), 54–73; Ann L. Hughes, 'Warwickshire on the Eve of the Civil War: A "County Community"?', *Midland History*, VII (1982), 42–72; Christine Carpenter, 'Gentry and Community in Medieval England', *Journal of British Studies*, 33(4) (October 1995), 340–80.

25 John Morrill, *The Revolt of the Provinces: Conservatives and Radicals in the English Civil War* (London, Allen and Unwin, New York, Barnes and Noble, 1976), p. 37.

26 James Campbell, 'The United Kingdom of England: The Anglo-Saxon Achievement', in Alexander Grant & Keith J. Stringer (eds), *Uniting the Kingdom? The Making of British History* (London and New York, Routledge, 1995), pp. 31–47, at p. 35.

27 For a brief summary of the main phases of the war as they affected the north of England, Richard Lomas, *North-East England in the Middle Ages* (Edinburgh, John Donald, 1992), pp. 41–52. The Scots also hated the English: 'there is nothing the Scots like better to hear than abuse of the English': Pius II in 1435, cited in *Early Travellers in Scotland* (1891; facsimile edition, Edinburgh, James Thin, The Mercat Press, 1973), p. 27.

28 For a graphic account of the effects on the English population, see J.R. Maddicott, *The English Peasantry and the Demands of the Crown, 1294–1341* (Oxford, *Past and Present* Supplement, 1975).

29 Ranald Nicholson, *Edward III and the Scots* (London, Oxford University Press, 1965).

30 Wernham, *Before the Armada*, chapters 12–15; D.M. Head, 'Henry VIII's Scottish Policy: A Reassessment', *Scottish Historical Review*, 61 (1982), 1–24.

31 M.L. Bush, *The Government Policy of Protector Somerset* (London, Edward Arnold, 1975), chapter 2.

32 Colm McNamee, *The Wars of the Bruces: Scotland, England and Ireland, 1306–1328* (Tuckwell Press, East Linton, East Lothian, 1997), chapter 3; J.F. Willard, 'The Scotch Raids and the Fourteenth Century Taxation of Northern England', *University of Colorado Studies*, V(4) (1908), 240–2; Ian Kershaw, 'The Scots in the West Riding, 1318-19', *Northern History*, XVII (1981), 231–9.

33 e.g. for Durham, R. Surtees, *History and Antiquities of the County Palatine of Durham* (London, 1816), I (I), 2–3 – on damage to Dalton, Morton, and Hesilden.

34 Edward Miller, *War in the North* (University of Hull Publications, 1960), pp. 8–12.

35 J.A. Tuck, 'Northumbrian Society in the Fourteenth Century', *Northern History*, VI (1971), 22–39; *idem*, 'War and Society in the Medieval North', *Northern History*, XXI (1985), 33–52.

36 Both their works are entitled 'The Vale-Royall of England', and were printed in *The Vale-Royall of England, or the County Palatine of Chester Illustrated* (London, Daniel King, 1656).

37 William Smith, 'Vale-Royall of England', p. 19; cf. Philip Morgan, *War and Society in Medieval Cheshire, 1277–1403* (Manchester, Chetham Society, 3rd series, XXXIV, 1987), pp. 3–4 (where the creation of the tradition is dated to 1540–1620). Cf. the emphasis on the Scots in William

Hutchinson, *The History of the County of Cumberland* (2 vols, F. Jollie, Carlisle, 1794–7; republished East Ardsley, Wakefield, E.P. Publishing Ltd. with Cumberland County Library, 1974), vol. 1, pp. 18–32.

38 M.J. Bennett, 'Sir Gawain and the Green Knight and the Literary Achievement of the North West Midlands: The Historical Background', *Journal of Medieval History*, 5 (1979), 63–88; M.J. Bennett, *Community, Class, and Careerism: Cheshire and Lancashire Society in the Age of Sir Gawain and the Green Knight* (Cambridge University Press, 1983), pp. 231–5; Lawton, 'Scottish Field: Alliterative Verse and Stanley Encomium', pp. 42–3; C.A. Luttrell, 'Three North-West Midlands MSS', *Neophilologus*, 42 (1958), 38–50 (Thomas Ireland of Hale and the Booths of Barton).

39 *Bishop Percy's Folio Manuscript*, vol. 1, pp. 123–6 (at ll. 25–8).

40 J.C. Bridge, 'Two Cheshire Soldiers of Fortune: Sir Hugh Calveley and Sir Robert Knolles', *Journal of the Architectural, Archaeological and Historical Society for the County and City of Chester, and North Wales*, 14 (1908), 112–231. It is intriguing that the glorification of the French wars found in some gentry families, in historical writing and the forgery of monumental sculpture in the late sixteenth and early seventeenth centuries in Cheshire (Morgan, *War and Society*, pp. 3–5) did not get translated into the poetic tradition.

41 James Reed, 'The Ballad and the Source: Some Literary Reflections on The Battle of Otterburn', in Anthony Goodman & Anthony Tuck (eds), *War and Border Societies in the Middle Ages* (London and New York, Routledge, 1992), pp. 94–123; Anthony Goodman, 'Introduction', in ibid., pp. 7–8.

42 Victor Morgan, 'The Cartographic Image of "The Country" in Early Modern England', *Transactions of the Royal Historical Society*, 5th series, 29 (1979), 129–54.

43 These maps may be found in E. Lynam (ed.), *An Atlas of England and Wales: The Maps of Christopher Saxton, England 1574–1579* (London, 1936, revised edn 1939).

44 *The Chester Mystery Cycle, volume 1, Text, and volume 2, Commentary and Glossary*, ed. R.M. Lumiansky & David Mills (EETS, s.s., 3 and 9, 1974 and 1986).

45 A.E. Goodman, 'Responses to Requests in Yorkshire for Military Service under Henry V', *Northern History*, XVII (1981), 240–52.

46 Conrad Russell, *The Crisis of Parliaments: English History 1509–1660* (Oxford University Press, 1971, reprinted with corrections, 1974), pp. 304.

47 Contamine, *War in the Middle Ages*, pp. 188–92; H.J. Hewitt, *The Black Prince's Expedition, 1355–1357* (Manchester University Press, 1958), p. 16. On the provision of uniforms, E.M. Carus-Wilson, 'Evidences of Industrial Growth on some Fifteenth-Century Manors', *Economic History Review*, 2nd series, XII (1959–60), 190–205, esp. pp. 197–8.

48 Linda Colley, *Britons: Forging the Nation, 1707–1837* (New Haven, Yale University Press, 1992), esp. chapter 7. The possible previous example is the Spanish, for which see William S. Maltby, *The Black Legend in England: The Development of Anti-Spanish Sentiment, 1558–1660* (Durham, North Carolina, Duke University Press, 1971).

49 Jean-Philippe Genet, 'Which State Rises?', *Historical Research*, LXV (1992), 119–33.

50 e.g. Frank Musgrave, *The North of England: A History from Roman Times to the Present* (Oxford, Basil Blackwell, 1990), pp. 228–37: the northern gentry as essentially conservative and royalist.

51 John Morrill provides a useful assessment of the historiography of Northern gentry loyalties in 'The Northern Gentry and the Great Rebellion', *Northern History*, 15 (1979), 66–87. It should be

noted that the importance of the Scottish threat is recognized by Conrad Russell, but it is interpreted by him entirely in terms of its religious connotations: Conrad Russell, *The Fall of the British Monarchies, 1637–1642* (Clarendon Press, Oxford, paperback edn,1995), pp. 83–5, 86, 139–40, 142.

52 The impact of the Scottish rebellion on Yorkshire and the northern counties is described by J.T. Cliffe, *The Yorkshire Gentry from the Reformation to the Civil War* (London, Athlone Press, 1969), chapter 14.

53 *Letters of Lady Brilliana Harley*, ed. T.T. Lewis (Camden Society, 51, 1853), p. 30; discussed in Russell, *Fall of the British Monarchies*, p. 85. Sir William Brereton, a Cheshire gentleman, while noting the 'sluttishness and nastiness' of some of the Scots, was more impressed by their religion, commenting extensively on the absence of bells and King Charles' need to bring Englishmen to Scotland to teach the craft of bellringing, for example. 'The Journal of Sir William Brereton, 1635', in John Crawford Hodgson (ed.), *North Country Diaries* (Second Series) (Surtees Society, 124, 1915 for 1914), pp. 1–50, esp. pp. 32, 36.

54. *The Memoirs of Sir Hugh Cholmley* (London, n.p., 1787); Cumbria Archives, Carlisle, D/LONS/L1/1/4; *The Diary of Sir Henry Slingsby of Scriven*, ed. Daniel Parsons (London, Longman, Rees, Orme, Brown, Green and Longman, 1836), p. 14.

55 Richard Parkinson (ed.), *The Life of Adam Martindale, Written by Himself* (Chetham Society, IV, 1844), p. 28.

Part Two

VOLUNTEERING: INDIVIDUAL, SELF AND COMMUNITY

The great turning point in military terms is probably not linked to tactical innovations of one sort or another but to the rise of militarism and volunteering at the turn of the eighteenth and nineteenth century, at a time when peace and war had become reified and more theoretically defined. Philip Woodfine's paper shows the tensions between the military and the civilian in an era when Britain was deeply involved in continental wars against the French Revolution. Using a precise type of source which gives us an insight into the civilian resolution of cultural clashes between various professional and cultural groups, Woodfine demonstrates a double evolution of British society towards contained militarism and restricted civil freedoms. Kate Watson follows this analysis by showing how perceptions of the war permeated even childhood memory and shaped individual and collective identities by opposition to the enemy, the French in this instance. In these first two papers the focus is on the impact of the conflict on civilian society in the age of the first mass armies.

Looking in more depth at the volunteering movement in Ireland, Brian Griffin shows how even a foreign and distant conflict like the Crimea could be interpreted along the lines of a native sectarian divide and how the act of volunteering could be deeply motivated by political reasons and home issues. The war abroad became a way of legitimating political claims at home and a way of structuring a sectarian community in relation to the (British) state and other Irish factions. Iain Donald shows a similar but slightly more complex pattern occurring in the United States at the time of a short victorious war against Spain. In this instance ethnic divisions added to the trauma of the civil war and the complex makeup of American identity to turn this conflict into a test of national and sub-national identities. Issues of loyalty and ethnic and political claims here explain both the volunteering process and the uses of the conflict to shape a modern overarching and unifying American identity. Bertrand Taithe's paper covers many of the above themes. In 1870 the issue of volunteering was reminiscent of revolutionary wars, but in practice it was more representative of the deep dissension among Frenchmen. Moreover, the disastrous defeats of 1870 could not compare with the largely mythologized war effort of the 1790s. The differences between Frenchmen then and now made observers question not only the nature of French national identity but also Frenchmen's identities and their worth.

By the end of the nineteenth century mass volunteering had lost its novelty value and in many countries had been subsumed by conscription. The subsequent conflicts often did away with the practice of mass volunteering; total war questioned more radically all forms of identity simultaneously.

5

'UNJUSTIFIABLE AND ILLIBERAL':
MILITARY PATRIOTISM AND CIVILIAN
VALUES IN THE 1790S

P. Woodfine

T his chapter sets out to examine some of the complexities of social relations and political views in England which lay beneath the broader descriptive labels of loyalist and radical during the French wars of the 1790s. It results from an attempt to sample some underused manuscript sources, the records of the court of King's Bench, for this purpose.[1] Those records might help to illuminate conflicts of values and belief which, as recent scholarship has made clear, were both highly polarized and also far from straightforward. There were ambiguities in the ways in which people responded to the strains of war and the demands of the state, financial and military. In contemporary France the Directory and Napoleon put great efforts into shaping a loyalism which embraced military values and success.[2] Even so, the research of Alan Forrest has shown that, despite the astonishing degree of militarization caused by the successive *levées en masse* and, from 1794, by conscription, the short-term effect was to reinforce 'village archaisms' and threaten the success of the new civic order being introduced from above.[3] The state never fully succeeded in persuading its citizens that voluntary service either in militia or in the regular forces was a basic civic duty. Indeed, the very ideals of revolution and *patrie* which were used to call citizens to arms were often used to resist conscription. It was easy to point to exemptions and privileges for officials, or for particular regions or towns, which were in conflict with revolutionary ideals and therefore justified resistance.[4] 'Despite all the innovation of the revolutionary years', he concludes, 'large parts of France remained traditional and largely autarchic, impervious to the propagandist appeal of the nation-state.'[5] In the same way, the loyalism so actively promoted by the Pitt ministry could not eradicate a strongly entrenched civilianism, buttressed by a long tradition – in political terms, almost invariably an adversarial one – of opposition to the existence of a large standing army.[6]

The very occurrence of war was a seeming paradox for those who followed David Hume and Adam Smith in praising the progressive, modernizing commercial society with a well-established civic culture. That kind of progress was, in the event, often accompanied by international conflict and the evolution of a state geared to maintain and enhance its military capability.[7] In the case of

Britain, and many of its European neighbours, this militarism was symbolized in society by the rise of the fashion for uniform dress. By 1789 the normal dress of George III, and most of those in high society who were in even the loosest sense attached to his service, was the 'Windsor Uniform' which had been created during the American War.[8] Patriotic citizens did not, despite these trends, necessarily embrace narrowly militaristic values. Furthermore, love of country was always, for the individual, bound up with a complex of other values and beliefs, not least a narrower provincialism and suspicion of the outsider – the person from another valley or county as well, though not to the same degree, as the foreigner. The values which went along with loyalty to country could include a belief in law and conciliation rather than the soldierly resort to personal resentment and challenge. Such complex outlooks were not simply reshaped by the patriotic response of loyalism into a simple endorsement of the military codes which flourished in wartime. The abrasiveness of military values and the pressures on local communities of mass enlistment are likely to have aggravated and complicated rather than simplified political choices. Yet if we look at, for instance, Home Office papers, or local newspapers, or the writings of radicals on the one hand and loyalists on the other, we inevitably see the opposed ends of the spectrum far more often than the shadings towards the middle.

This is the rationale for an attempt to sample the voluminous records of King's Bench. Though it was the highest court of common law, it had also over the centuries acquired the right to remove from inferior courts into its own jurisdiction a variety of complex or vexed cases, many of them trivial in themselves.[9] Poor law disputes, especially cases of removal and settlement, were a frequent aspect of the work of the court as parishes were misguidedly tempted to spend, sometimes heavily, on lawyers to avoid supporting their neighbours' poor.[10] Only a small minority of King's Bench cases actually went to trial, and the main business of the judges was to weigh the merits of cases and issue rules or writs to parties in dispute.[11] For example, writs of *mandamus* could be used in disputed cases to install people in offices, so the records contain details of many contests over clerical and even churchwardens' appointments.[12] Formal instructions, 'rules', were issued to parties in all manner of civil disputes, which made up a great deal of King's Bench business, and usually the judges seem to have given their views and recommended a peaceful settlement. The advantage for historians of these civil disputes is that the initial way of bringing a case into court was through affidavits sworn by the parties: these were depositions, not made out to any strict formula, but simply the sworn statements of witnesses or parties to disputes. At times they are extremely full and revealing. These records of King's Bench do seem to offer evidence of areas in which, under the strain of war, clusters of values came into collision.

Only in the caricatured world of the graphic satirists of the day was there a simple and outright choice, for the mass of the people, between plebeian patriotism and radical dissidence, even though these polarized extremes are indeed part of the story.[13] On the one hand were affirmations of Britishness and an upsurge of loyalty to the constitution and the monarchy. Linda Colley's 'apotheosis of George III' was depressingly evident to one radical in 1792: 'No nation ever seemed more stupidly rooted in admiration of the glare and parade of royalty than the English.'[14] Church and King mobs had a more or less coherent set of prejudices which typically informed their actions. They hated dissenters and reformers (and there was a significant overlap), rich people and foreigners. Popular attitudes might sometimes be articulated in a reactive and basic way, but Malcolm Thomis and Peter Holt have argued that the nearest we come to finding a popular political consciousness is this 'sub-political' response to the threat of revolutionary France and its ideas.[15] Linda Colley and Kathleen Wilson are not alone in discerning a 'plebeian patriotism', a crude but real national and imperial sentiment among the masses.[16] On the other hand historians, inspired by the seminal work of E.P. Thompson, have seen an emerging proletarian outlook, the rudiments of a class consciousness which was to be fully articulated in the generation after the Napoleonic wars, and was perhaps even strong enough to have had a potential for revolution.[17] This radicalism was augmented by the poverty, hardship and dislocation of a period of rapid change.

One bitter and highly informed satire on the characters of some fifty leading politicians characterized the reign of George III:

A reign, where every abuse of true government has been committed, – where the system of favouritism, corruption, and of war, has been carried to the utmost extent – where the reputed domestic virtues of the sovereign . . . are the sole compensation for all the above evils – for the fruits of an inordinate selfish avarice extracted from the very entrails of the people, and for a load of taxes, that must eventually either rouse or destroy them.[18]

The expense of monarchy was highlighted by the proposal in 1795 that Parliament should pay off the staggering debts accumulated by the Prince of Wales. The money, notoriously, was principally expended in womanizing, gambling and art collecting, and the character of the prince's associates was an easy target for anti-monarchists. One radical publication denounced them in 1792: 'They are the very *lees* of society: creatures, with whom a person of morality, or even common decency could not associate.'[19] The prince had contracted debts, by 1795, of around £800,000, and the issue generated a great deal of debate both inside and outside parliament.[20] It was hard to resist the simple protest arising from the contrast in such difficult times between the hard living of the poor and the improvident luxury of the prince and his followers: 'At a moment when the accumulation of taxes and the calamities of an unsuccessful war have raised the necessaries of life to so high a price as to occasion universal discontent, and even to excite, in some places, dangerous tumults, a bill has passed the Commons for burdening the people with near a million of debt contracted by the Prince of Wales.'[21] The most successful defence of the prince, which went through three editions in that year, dismissed 'the juvenile specks that dim, for a moment, the lustre of his Royal Highness the Prince of Wales'.[22] The main weapon of this pamphlet was a vicious attack on the reformer, Charles Grey, whose arguments were dismissed as 'spleen, presumption, and triteness, aided by a pert and verbose confusion'. On the lustre of Prince George, by contrast, the author was eloquent: 'Every unprejudiced man of sense acknowledges, that there is not a more accomplished gentleman than his Royal Highness the Prince of Wales; whether we consider the talents, the virtues, or the graces, that he possesses.'[23] However, the appeal to common judgement was belied by the fact that this was a production of a government agent, financed by secret service funds. Stuart, the author, wrote to his paymaster: 'I flatter myself the Letter will meet with the approbation of you and your friends, as it is the strongest and most pointed that I have ever yet written.'[24]

In this highly partisan climate, the choices facing citizens were unusually stark, and allegiances could be sharply placed on one side or the other of a divide. Beneath this straightforward polarity, though, were other levels of conviction and outlook. People might hold clusters of values which (potentially) could embrace apparent opposites. For instance, love of the king and his domestic virtues could easily accommodate, even encourage, contempt for the Prince of Wales and a fear of the potential for monarchical corruption. Indeed, the very force of a patriotism centred upon the Christian family values of George III and his embodiment of the national spirit could prompt attacks upon those members of the royal family who were not themselves sufficiently patriotic to live up to those high standards. This little-explored aspect of the outlook of 'Britons' has been recently shown at work by Philip Harling in the Duke of York affair of 1809.[25] Sexual and financial scandal, vigorously pursued in the Commons as well as in the press, prints, and radical broadsheets, forced the second-in-line to the British throne to resign as commander-in-chief of the armed forces. As Harling concludes: 'Above all else, the York affair revealed that the Crown and the government could still be the victim as well as the beneficiary of what Colley calls the "conventional, xenophobic, and complacent" brand of British patriotism, even at the height of a popular war in defence of the established order.'[26]

Censure of individual members of the royal family was not the same thing as a belief in the 'secret influence' of the Crown, spreading governmental control through places, bribery, spying and repression. For some reformers, though, this influence of the Crown was still as potent a symbol of the menace to freedom as it had been for the generation of the American wars.[27] In propounding these arguments, of course, constitutional reformers were at least implicitly, and sometimes explicitly, seeking to emulate the French. Unease over this subversive threat from reformers led the government increasingly to use the military as an adjunct of the police power. In 1792 Pitt began building barracks in mainland England, an almost unprecedented move. And he made clear the political and policing purpose of the barracks, telling the Commons in February 1793: 'The circumstances of the country, coupled with the general state of affairs, rendered it advisable to provide barracks in other parts of the kingdom. A spirit had appeared in some of the manufacturing towns which made it necessary that troops should be kept near them.'[28] Six of the new barracks were set up in industrial centres where in 1792 radical activity had been prominent, including Birmingham, Manchester and Sheffield. The barracks not only kept the soldiers on hand in case of trouble, but also confined them to military society at night, away from the temptations of inns and the seductions of radical propaganda and political discussion.

An important move against subversion came in late November 1792 when, to counter the London Corresponding Society, John Reeves set up his Association for the Preservation of Liberty and Property against Republicans and Levellers. Michael Duffy has recently shown that, though the Association movement was an independent initiative by Reeves, it was promptly manipulated by Pitt, in whose hands the 'associations were one of the major expedients . . . employed to defuse the domestic crisis of late 1792'. Part of this work consisted of persuasion. A characteristic pamphlet was printed in 1792 by the 'Hackney association for the preservation of peace, liberty and property', and sold at a penny, or nine pence the dozen, evidently with a design to lead literate plebeians away from the path of anarchy. In it, after fifteen pages of avuncular persuasion by his wise master, a reform-minded workman determines to embrace instead the hardworking path to prosperity and the vote:

> instead of going to the liberty-club I will begin my work; for, I should not like to see a Frenchman lie with my wife, or take the bread out of my children's mouths; and I now see, that, if I go on as you do, and mind my business, I may in time be as rich and as happy as you.'[29]

Essentially, though, associations were concerned not so much to persuade those attracted by reform as to check seditious publications by bringing their authors and printers before the magistrates.[30] Pitt's defusing initiative certainly reached the West Riding of Yorkshire, where loyalist meetings were held in all the major towns in December 1792. The one at Bradford was called under the auspices of the Bradford Association against Levellers and Republicans.[31] The success of this tactic of portraying reformers as levellers can be seen in the anxiety which reform groups showed to counter it: for example, the handbill distributed in Liverpool, and reprinted in the leading West Riding newspaper, which warned its readers against the way that the word 'equality' was being distorted to mean equality of property, whereas they only meant an equality of rights to the benefits and protection of society.[32] The conflict of reform and loyalism was intensified by the prosecutions mounted by the government in 1793–4 of the organizers of the Scottish conventions and then of the leaders of the London Corresponding Society. John Thelwall, the most popular and violent of the London reform speakers, was even more embittered after his acquittal, repeatedly denouncing 'the sanguinary ambition of a *Pitt*, the aristocratic enthusiasm of a *Burke*, the metaphysical frenzy of a *Wyndham*'.[33]

In this heightened atmosphere of political tension, one King's Bench case furnishes the details of an overtly political clash between reform and loyalism, complicated by a military man's intemperance. The quotation in this paper's title comes from this case, which disturbed the gentlefolk and trading élite of mercantile Wakefield in the early 1790s. A doctor who had practised there for fifteen years, William Dawson, used the phrase 'unjustifiable and illiberal' when Major John Tottenham and his friends, including the staunchly loyalist vicar, banned reform advocates Robert Bakewell and John Smith from their newspaper reading room.[34] The reform societies were active in the autumn of 1792, and the Leeds Constitutional Society was instituted on 27 November 1792 to press for parliamentary reform, despite the extent to which 'the Public Mind is agitated by the Jarrings of Faction'. The society's officers of course had to counter the charge that they favoured a levelling equality of property, a story 'palmed upon us by wicked or foolish Men, for the worst of Purposes'.[35] Cleverly quoting the arguments of Pitt and the Duke of Richmond in 1782 in favour of reform, they made a moderate appeal for the 'dissemination of political knowledge', a call which was bound to be seen by loyalists as subversive and dangerous. One Leeds merchant bought and distributed two hundred copies of the sixpenny pamphlet version of Paine's *Rights of Man*, and while journeymen cloth-dressers were reading those, a pro-government parade in the town of some three thousand people burnt an effigy of Tom Paine and sang 'God save the King'.[36] In a direct response to the corresponding societies, the government on 21 May 1792 issued a Royal Proclamation against seditious writings, designed to put pressure on printers and publishers. This pressure was soon followed up by direct action. In the papers of the Treasury Solicitors is a letter from James Hebden, attorney in Leeds, who had been invited to act for them in stamping out seditious writings but pleaded pressure of business. He wrote in December 1792 wishing them success in their plan: 'I think it will put a stop to the Circulating of Paine's Books and others of a seditious Nature; indeed it appears to me the proclamation has already had a good effect. I believe that the Booksellers here will not sell any more, and a certain sect of People have lately been more moderate in their Arguments and Conversation.'[37] These tensions, so evident in Leeds, were also felt in the nearby textile town of Wakefield.

The twin centres of social life for Wakefield gentlefolk were the Assembly Rooms, in which the sexes mixed, and the News Room, a male preserve. It was in the News Room that controversy arose in the years 1792–3. The immediate context was the reception in Wakefield of the May 1792 Royal Proclamation. John Tottenham, late major in the 90th Regiment of Foot, was active in supporting the lead given by the Crown against subversive publication. He was prominent among about thirty neighbouring gentlemen who called a meeting, chaired by an active clerical magistrate, the Revd Henry Zouch of Sandal Magna, at Wakefield's Moot Hall on Monday 11 June. They met 'to consider of some proper Mode of expressing the grateful sense they had of his Majesty's goodness in issuing his Royal Proclamation solemnly warning his Subjects to guard against every attempt which aimed at the Subversion of the Constitutional Government of this Country'.[38] A vocal minority disagreed with the object of the meeting, and distributed a handbill deploring its divisive intentions. This was produced, amid indignation, at the loyalist meeting, and was later found to have been written by Robert Bakewell, a merchant woolstapler, and Thomas Johnston, a dissenting teacher. They appealed to their fellow townspeople:

> we intreat you before you interrupt the tranquil state of the Town by Political Discussion to reflect on the nature and principle of that Proclamation and what Persons and Writings you are called upon to reprobate. The Proclamation was issued immediately after a Society had been formed in London called the Friends of the People, a Society which hath for its Object the Security and happiness of the Nation by promoting a timely and temperate Reform of the Abuses of our Constitution, a Society composed of Men the most respectable for Knowledge and Integrity this Country can boast. With the Character and Virtues of two of its Members who reside in this Town and Neighbourhood you are all well acquainted one of whom represents the City of York. Will you then assemble to sanction a Proclamation which in the Opinion of several Members of both Houses of Parliament is intended to criminate that Society and is only calculated to raise a Spirit of distrust and jealousy in the Nation at large.[39]

This moderate appeal did not match the mood of the town, or the district, at a time when the press was keenly reporting developments in the National Convention and, as the *Leeds Mercury* declared, 'the fate of Louis XVI appears to interest every British bosom'.[40] Wakefield was the earliest Yorkshire town to respond to the appeal of Reeves' loyalist association. On 10 December 1792 a meeting was called by the gentry, clergy and merchants. It attracted over 4,000 people and, in order to accommodate them, had to be adjourned from the Moot Hall to the choir of the parish church. This mass meeting unanimously adopted a number of loyal resolutions, condemning inflammatory and seditious writings, blaming them upon 'evil-disposed Persons, acting in Concert with Persons in Foreign Parts', and affirming their own loyalty to 'the goodly Fabrick of the English Constitution, reared and upheld by the successive Virtue and Wisdom of all the great and good Men who, for Centuries, have gone before us'.[41] The meeting resolved to 'use every Exertion in our Power' to discourage seditious publications, and to prosecute the authors, printers and publishers of them. The crowd then twice sang 'God save the King', accompanied by the organ, and many of them then followed the mayor and the town music to the market cross and other places to sing the anthem there also. An effigy of Tom Paine had earlier been whipped through the streets, a halter round its neck. That evening the jubilant crowds saw the effigy hanged and thrown onto a large bonfire.[42]

Perhaps the strong lead given by prominent citizens and the vociferous public assertion of loyalist values was a response to the popular alienation which Edward Thompson argued was so pervasive in the West Riding at this time. Certainly volunteers for military service did not come forward in the same degree as in other comparable areas. Colley has found that Yorkshire was the only industrializing county to have had notably low levels of volunteers in the 1803–4 militia returns: 20 per cent of the male population as opposed to 35 per cent in the ten other industrial counties.[43] Whatever the underlying sentiments in Wakefield though, on the surface the town's loyalism had been mounting in a highly demonstrative way. Meanwhile, Bakewell and Johnston, together with a merchant, John Frederick Smith, had distributed in December 1792 a handbill called *Equality*, which ended with the words 'God bless the People'.[44] The reformers were caught in the act by the vicar of Wakefield, the Revd Dr Bacon. As Edward Greene, a labourer, was distributing the *Equality* handbills he met Bacon, and offered him one of them, 'on seeing which the Doctor was very angry and asked this Deponent how he durst deliver the same, and by whose orders he did it'. He handed over to Bacon his remaining handbills and went back to Smith and Bakewell, refusing to distribute any more and telling them 'he should think himself well off, if he did not get into the House of Correction for what he had already done'. The next morning the hapless labourer went to Dr Bacon to tell him he was very sorry for having distributed the handbills and to beg he might be forgiven. Bacon told him 'that he ought to take care not to distribute any bills that came from the said John Frederick Smith, Robert Bakewell or the Presbyterian Parson . . . on political subjects'.[45] Greene was not wrong about the house of correction, which was the fate of a counterpart of his in London in the same month, William Carter. An illiterate porter, watchman and bill-sticker, Carter was arrested for posting copies of a London Corresponding Society address, and on 7 January 1793 he was sentenced to six months' imprisonment for sedition.[46]

Pressure on dissidents was a direct outcome of the December loyalist meetings. Patriotic gatherings like the one at the Wakefield Moot Hall had been held in each of the major towns, the Huddersfield one following the Wakefield pattern very closely. In both cases, the resolutions arrived at, menacing in tone and promising action against subversive writers, were published in all the leading Yorkshire newspapers, and also written out on parchment, to be passed from house to house for mass signature.[47] The intimidatory intent of this is clear: loyalists were evidently doing their best to suppress reform sentiments. The outraged patriots of Wakefield, though, despite their public resolutions, did not actually take legal action through the magistrates. Instead, on 2 January, they called a meeting of the newsroom subscribers and resolved to exclude the two incendiaries in their midst from Michaelmas next, when annual newsroom subscriptions were due to be renewed. Another of their resolutions revealingly provided that 'Officers on Recruiting Service or on Military Duty' were to be allowed free use of the room.[48] On 16 September 1793 a meeting was duly held, attended by a group of gentlemen and merchants, the Revd Michael Bacon and the Revd William Bawden, along with Major John Tottenham and his brother Lieutenant-General Loftus Tottenham. They signed a unanimous resolution banning Bakewell and Smith from the room after 29 September.

For Tottenham the soldier it was a matter of simple honour and patriotism to cut subversive men out of polite society. For Dawson the doctor it was a question of free speech and liberal society. In this tense atmosphere, in which reform proponents were depicted as agents of the French bent on introducing anarchy, Dr Dawson at least dared to express dissent. 'Conceiving the said resolution to be an unprecedented unjustifiable and illiberal act', and claiming that several others felt the same way and were about to resign from the News Room, Dawson and two others signed and put up a protest at what had been done. The affidavits on either side give entirely opposed ideas of how many supported the exclusion and how many the objection to it. This of course could be crucial to knowing just how great the divides in Wakefield society were. Bakewell claimed that the subscribers did not exceed fifty-four, apart from Bakewell and Smith themselves, and of thirty-four of them to whom he had personally applied, thirty-one of them declared their disapprobation of the Tottenham resolution. Against this, Tottenham's witnesses said that after the exclusion notice, some forty-six subscribers signed up to the News Room, as against fifty the year before, so it was clear that few gentlemen if any would refuse to subscribe on that account, while many would refuse to do so if they had to associate with Smith and Bakewell.[49] The News Room in consequence, said Tottenham, was then entirely given up.[50]

On 30 September, both men meeting in the News Room, Major Tottenham gave the doctor a piece of his mind: 'Doctor Dawson, no man in Wakefield but you would have brought in that paper which you have done, signed by three names– I tell you, you are a mere tool.' Dawson said to Tottenham, 'Take care, Sir, what you say', and Tottenham replied, 'I'll repeat the same – even at the muzzle of your pistol. If you want anything further with me, you know where I live.' Another witness recalled the words as 'Take care, Sir, what I say? What I say now I would tell you any Hour at the Muzzle of your Pistol. – If you have any thing to say to me you know where I live.'[51] At this point, the honour code seems to have aggravated the political divide. For Major Tottenham, the honourable course was clear, and he told a friend, Martha Andrews, that if Dawson took the law upon him he would post him a coward and a scoundrel.[52] Dr Dawson on the other hand responded to the challenge by bringing an action against Tottenham. The procedure was that King's Bench was asked to issue a rule to Tottenham 'to shew cause why an information should not be exhibited against him for certain misdemeanours'.[53] First the court received the affidavits on Dawson's side, then Tottenham was given the chance to respond with his affidavits, and after that he was served with a copy of the rule on Monday 18 November and summoned to attend the court. In the following term he was tried before a jury.

That the case went to trial testifies to the bad feelings involved, and the further complications that arose. It emerged from Tottenham's side that Dawson was not entirely unacquainted with duels, and that in around 1785 he had applied to Tottenham and 'as his friend placed his Honour in his Hands and requested his Advice how to act in regard to a Challenge'. Dawson claimed that he had not asked Tottenham to act as his second, but simply to offer advice, and that he and the challenger had for some years past been on civil and neighbourly terms.[54] It would be damaging to the doctor's standing, of course, to be seen as a duellist. Another problem arose from a rather misleading report of the initial King's Bench hearing in the *Leeds Intelligencer*, in November 1793.[55] Dawson set right what he saw as a prejudicial account and wrongly believed that Tottenham had inserted it. Major Tottenham, visiting York at the next Assizes, was told that Dawson had even placed his revised paragraph in the *York Chronicle* and he argued before King's Bench that Dawson, in using the newspapers, had 'a view to prejudice this Deponent either in the Opinion of the Jury . . . or his Friends and of the Public at large'. In February 1794, having received the rule absolute of King's Bench against him, Major Tottenham made a very stiff attempt at a reconciliation, but neither party could unbend enough for this to be possible, and the jury trial went ahead.[56] Tottenham was found guilty and his fine had then to be fixed by the Justices of the court of King's Bench, who at this very time were actively proceeding against seditious libels. For instance, James Ridgeway, publisher of various radical works, received harsh penalties in May 1793: for publishing *The Jockey Club* he was fined £100 and imprisoned for two years in Newgate; for publishing *A Letter Addressed to the Addressees* a further £100 fine and one year's imprisonment; for *The Rights of Man* the same penalty again (all to run consecutively) and was further required to provide two securities of £100 each for his good behaviour for five years after his release.[57] In this context, it may not be surprising that the King's justices took an indulgent view of Major Tottenham's combative loyalism and his sensitivity to slurs on the crown. He was ordered to pay costs and fined one shilling.[58]

This was a case in which the military honour code seems to have aggravated an already stark clash of political sympathies. In other and more direct ways, too, these legal records suggest a clash of military and civilian outlooks. The most obvious perhaps lies in the area of military recruitment, which was likely to touch every town in the country. Recruitment could mean an appeal to patriotism through advertising well judged to produce the right kind of applicant. One such advertisement appeared in Leeds early in 1793:

> Leeds Independent Rangers. Wanted. A few spirited Yorkshire Heroes to form an independent Company of Infantry, to be commanded by Captain Cockell of Leeds, who will freely serve their King and Country in any Quarter of the Globe, and by their services render the name of the Leeds Independent Rangers immortal; such are the brave fellows Yorkshire can produce, and such are the Volunteers wished to be commanded by Mr Cockell, who will be always happy to accompany them wherever they may be ordered.[59]

In this and similar advertisements, those who brought good recruits were encouraged by a guinea or more in addition to the bounty of five guineas received by the recruit. Unfortunately, the offer of bounties brought forth unsuitable applicants and caused legal and administrative difficulties. One of the more tangled poor law settlement cases which had to be resolved by King's Bench in these years was posed by John Barrett, an ex-soldier in his late forties who answered Captain Cockell's call and left the magistrates of Leeds and Halifax to decide on the care of his pauperized wife and children.[60] One regiment, able to promise home service only, could afford to exclude the troublesome categories: 'it is requested that no Man will offer himself when in liquor, or who is an Apprentice, or belonging to the Army, Navy, or Militia.'[61] Not all regiments could afford to be so punctilious, and most recruiting officers depended upon the systematic use of drink and chicanery.

One vivid example comes from Newcastle-under-Lyme: the affidavits sent to King's Bench provide clear evidence of the overbearing behaviour of the army's recruiters and their tactic of pouring strong drink into potential recruits, followed by the King's guinea and an oath. In this case, the tactic was foiled by the exertions of an active and determined woman, willing to face the considerable lawyers' fees necessary to get a case through King's Bench: Mary Liversage, wife of John, a shoemaker. John spent the evening of Monday 1 December 1794 drinking rum with the soldiers, and came home late, 'exceedingly sick [and] quite senseless'.[62] Next morning he said he had taken a gold guinea from 'Old Ensor', William Ensor, ironmonger, then charged with raising troops along with his stepson John Edensor. John Liversage set off before the break of day to put matters right. Between 8 and 9 that morning Mary found him at a public house next to Ensor's, with Edensor, once more very drunk.[63]

William Ensor had been particularly active in raising men and the night before had sworn in a drunken man. Mary Liversage was afraid that the same would happen to John, 'knowing the extraordinary effect which Liquor always had on her . . . Husband', and so warned Edensor not to swear John in that condition. Returning again about ten o'clock to take care of her husband, she met him coming out of Ensor's shop, and he told her '"they have sworn me"'. He was then blind drunk, 'being entirely deprived of his Strength and Understanding'. On recovering, and within twenty-four hours, her husband offered Ensor his guinea back again with a further pound to make the matter up, but though the mayor was on his side, the recruiting officers and the Justice who had sworn him were adamant that he should not be released from his oath. William Ball and Gerrard Gosling, the officers concerned, made a highly significant admission. They 'often declared that the matter of the discharge of this Deponent's husband was not of so much consequence to them of itself but that if he got off the greatest part of the Men they had raised in the neighbourhood would also be released from them.' Their regiment was called the Stamford Volunteers (*sic*). Liversage was kept in prison for some time, and when the mayor sent him home the army seized him again. William Ball, the officer in charge, said to Mary 'that if she brought the Attorney he would horsewhip him'. While in captivity, Liversage was repeatedly menaced with severe punishments if he did not drop his King's Bench proceedings. Mary testified that '. . . William Ball called her . . . Husband a damned rascal and declared that he deserved to be flogged to death'. The drunken and now no doubt much-chastened shoemaker was imprisoned in Stamford, kept in irons and fed only on bread and water until his release on a writ of habeas corpus of 26 January 1795.

The aggressive and contemptuous attitude of the officer was striking, and was evidenced in an even more extreme form by a recruiting party in the West Riding of Yorkshire. A new regiment, the Wakefield Rangers, was looking for men in 1795 in Slaithwaite, a village in the Colne Valley perhaps rather too far from the displays and effigy-burnings of Wakefield itself to have much enthusiasm for volunteering. The sadistic recruiting sergeant, Charles Elliott, went into the Shoulder of Mutton late on the evening of 5 March and shook hands with a man in drink, John Meal, slipping the king's guinea into his hand. Though Meal dropped it at once, he was dragged about the floor, beaten, robbed and finally carried in a cart along the road to Huddersfield, during which journey he was 'damned for an old Rascal', beaten repeatedly, had his testicles violently pulled and some ribs stoved in with a rifle butt. He was finally left propped up in a doorway at the entry to the town, when the serjeant commented, 'the Old Bugger is good for nothing, we'll leave him', and the recruiting party went to the George Inn for a drink.[64] Meal died of his injuries within thirty-six hours, and on 24 March 1795 Sergeant Elliot was found guilty of murder, sentenced to hang on 30 March and his body to be dissected and anatomized.[65]

These were severe and brutal encounters, but even where enlistment was voluntary and part-time, the line between military and civilian outlook could obstinately remain. The volunteer companies of the 1790s brought civilian (largely middle-class) patriotic enthusiasm into play but did not for that reason necessarily mean the triumph of military values. Volunteering was a complex civic and local phenomenon: the regiments raised under an Act of April 1794 were overwhelmingly formed from among the urban middle classes, asserting for themselves a place within the aristocratic state.[66] In Leeds, in the last week of May 1795, when the town was 'crowded with genteel and fashionable company', was staged the supreme provincial expression of this movement. The 'Military Festival of the West Riding Corps of Gentlemen Volunteers' was held from Tuesday to Friday, with extensive manoeuvres and firing on Chapeltown Moor that Wednesday. On Thursday was held a review of the corps from the five major textile towns of the West Riding, Leeds, Bradford, Wakefield, Huddersfield and Halifax. The Huddersfield Corps was led by Sir George Armytage, Baronet, who had been chairman of the patriotic meeting in Huddersfield on 20 December 1792, denouncing incendiaries and declaring loyalty 'at the present alarming Crisis of this Country' to the government and constitution.[67] At the head of the Wakefield corps was Major John Tottenham, whose brother the Lieutenant-General was prevented from inspecting the troops only by illness. The display by the 1,000 volunteer troops drew a huge crowd: 'there were present about three hundred carriages, an immense number of people on horseback, and not less than sixty thousand astonished and delighted spectators.'[68] The following summer a similar review took place at Wakefield.[69]

ˌ Despite the appeal of such spectacles and the military fervour which they could engender, the volunteer movement should also be studied as an aspect of the working of urban élites. In the growing commercial towns of eighteenth-century England, a wide range of institutions and charities were promoted with the aim of creating a culture of civic virtue and respectable bourgeois values.[70] This was not a context in which militarism could easily flourish. Some three quarters of the nation's volunteer corps were raised by the leaders of the rising towns, with their followers among the artisan classes.[71] Yet, as J.E. Cookson has pointed out, the leadership of military units did not mean that the urban middle class embraced a military outlook: there was not yet an ideology which would imbue the notion of citizenship with a belief in the duty to defend the state through military service. 'The result, without exaggeration,' he claims, 'can be described as a continuous, largely ineffective struggle by the army to "decivilianize" the volunteers.'[72] To begin with, the motives for enlistment were not always purely patriotic or military, especially for those units which demanded that a volunteer bring his own horse and which offered the attractions of a uniform and of regular meetings with friends. Sometimes the social rewards were even grander, as in Leeds in late September 1795: 'On Friday last the Gentlemen Volunteers of this

Borough (and several others) partook of an elegant entertainment given by their Colonel, Thomas Lloyd, Esq., at his hospitable mansion at Horsforth near this town. Four large marquees were pitched in the Park, where the corps dined, and where liberality and hospitality were eminently conspicuous.'[73] One young would-be volunteer was Thomas Butler, who wanted diversion from the family foundry at Kirkstall Forge, where he worked from early morning to late at night. In December 1796 he wrote, unsuccessfully, to his father asking to be allowed to join the Leeds Gentlemen Volunteer Cavalry: 'Some relaxation from business I am determined to have for I cannot much longer endure the confinement I have for a considerable time experienced – and what I now propose is the relaxation I wish to have.'[74] In the following February his father objected to his building a new house at a distance from the foundry itself, and young Thomas won the argument by saying that sooner than comply he 'would rather be a soldier'.[75]

The blurring of civilian identity involved in joining a volunteer regiment could even *sharpen* the clash between civilian and military outlooks, especially where the civil code of law met the military code of the challenge. The duel was firmly rooted in military society at this period, even though it was forbidden by both military and common law.[76] In the very long view, the code of the duel has been claimed by Lawrence Stone to have actually tamed and regulated the violence of the upper classes.[77] By the late eighteenth century, though, the survival of the duel was an anomaly in an increasingly prosperous commercial society. Donna Andrew has shown that 'In eighteenth-century England duelling was not dead, nor was it seen as a charming antique custom. To many it represented a major threat to public peace and the sanctity of religion.'[78] The code of honour which underpinned the duel was seen by many as a threat to civil society, civic virtue, and therefore the urban culture of the day: 'the debate about duelling was an important element in the formation of the middle class, and the gestation of middle-class culture.'[79] The final victory over the honour code came only in the second quarter of the nineteenth century, when there emerged 'a new vision of society based on reasonableness, Christianity and commerce, in which duelling ceased to be practised simply because it appeared incongruous and foolish'.[80] Before that final change, however, the honour code retained its power as a way of resolving and shaping antagonisms between individuals. Duelling was especially rife in Irish society at this period.[81] In England, too, the demands of the honour code could prevail over even the most powerful considerations. In 1809 a duel between the Minister of War, Viscount Castlereagh, and the Foreign Secretary, George Canning, threatened to bring down both the ministry and the war effort.[82] In this case, the demands of political and national prudence, all of which favoured the side of law and rationality, gave way to an important underlying pressure from the expectations of peers. This peer pressure was especially strong upon a military officer for whom unimpeachable honour and courage were career qualifications.

A good example of this military code of honour in action can be found in the way in which two officers attempted to settle their mutual grievances. This was the case of Sir George Thomas, Baronet, versus Major John Cotton Worthington, both late of the Sussex Fencible Cavalry.[83] The case centred on a libel upon Thomas which Worthington had posted in the regimental mess, but this was only the final act in a long play. In August 1798 Colonel Thomas had brought charges of irregularity against Major Worthington, maliciously, as Worthington believed. He was fully exonerated by the Commander-in-Chief in Scotland, Sir Ralph Abercromby, and praised for his conduct by the Duke of York. In March 1799 Worthington in turn brought charges against his Colonel for misconduct, in what Abercromby later described as 'the most enormous Abuse which had taken Root in the Sussex Light Dragoons'.[84] Those charges were upheld in part, and the king was so persuaded of Thomas' guilt that he soon after removed him from his command. As well as offering abuse and provocation, Thomas then brought fresh charges against Major Worthington in late July 1799, directed to the Commander-in-Chief, the Duke of York. The most serious accusation laid was one which Thomas must have known the Duke could not investigate with any propriety. It was that, in October 1798, when challenged by Captain Ferguson, Worthington had contrived to be stopped from fighting. This charge was the one which passionately concerned Worthington, who explained to the court that he:

> should have thought it highly improper in his situation to have adopted the Conduct imputed to him by the said Charge as in consequence thereof he this Deponent would have reduced himself to a situation which would have rendered him infamous in the eye of the world and of his Profession. And this Deponent saith that the last mentioned Charge was wholly and absolutely false . . . and being apprehensive of the effect it might have on the Military Men who were to be his judges on his approaching Trial on the other Charges against him he this Deponent suffered indescribable distress of mind upon receipt of the said Letter.[85]

Such was his distress in fact that he went immediately to the mess room in the Ringrose Inn, York, where the regiment then was, and posted Thomas – as Major Tottenham had threatened to post Dawson – pinning up a paper denouncing Colonel Thomas as 'an infamous liar and calumniator after the exhibition of his miserable Charges'. This, the offence which brought him before King's Bench, was purely to justify himself before his brother officers in regard to the charge of avoiding a challenge. In proof that he had not acted in this dishonourable way, Worthington testified that three months after the challenge from Ferguson he had brought forward an offer of unlimited foreign service, and the whole Corps had concurred in it, which they never would have done if he had really rested under any imputation of cowardice.

Volunteer officers, who did not live under the same peer pressures to justify their honour and courage, were less likely to endorse the duel as a way to resolve disputes. An example of the difference can be found in an action taken out in 1799 by William Wilcock, a Halifax attorney, against Eccles McConagal. McConagal was a lieutenant in the 52nd Regiment of Foot, sent to Halifax on the recruiting service before leaving for the Indies. In debt to the tune of £17, and refusing to pay despite every indulgence of time, McConagal found himself served with a writ by Wilcock, a part-time Grenadier officer in the Halifax Volunteer Corps. Wilcock's clerk, a fellow lodger of McConagal, heard the soldier abuse the attorney: 'It is a very shabby thing for a Brother Officer to arrest an Officer, and a Granadier too. . . . We will see whether a Light Bob . . . will not meet a Granadier.'[86] On 9 May a friend of McConagal, Lieutenant George Burrell of the 15th Foot, called to deliver a challenge:

> I am sorry to come to you upon unpleasant business, but Mr McConagal is so much hurt that you should order the Bailiff to take him into Custody when arrested, especially as you some times wear the same Cloth with himself, that he expects you will give him the satisfaction of a Gentleman by meeting him tomorrow morning and you'll bring a friend along with you.[87]

Even when taken into custody and brought before two justices of the peace, McConagal and Burrell were unrepentant in insisting on their right to challenge Wilcock. 'McConagal said he might have been called before a Court of Enquiry and broke at his Regiment if he had not called this Deponent out.'[88] For the part-time officer and full-time attorney, his duty to the law came before military solidarity, though revealingly he also felt the need to defend his stance in terms of the honour code: 'he was as Nice in point of Honor as Mr McConagal could be . . . but was bound in Justice to himself, to the Public in General and to the Gentlemen in the Profession of Law in particular, to bring the matter before this honourable Court.'[89]

The final response of the officers was a kind of sullen intimidation, firing off half a dozen pistol balls into a door.[90] A similar instance of a military man disgruntled with justice occurred in November and December 1798. The Revd Frederick Dodsworth, a justice of the peace at Thornton Watlass, in the North Riding, was repeatedly disturbed by Captain Matthew Hutton of the 106th Regiment of Foot, who prowled about his isolated house firing off guns and shouting menaces. On 18 December Hutton discharged a gun behind his garden wall at eight in the morning and called out, 'Damn you, it was I myself that fired the Gun, and if you are a Man come hither.' That same evening, Hutton and a friend fired a large gun outside the parlour window, making the room shake, and when Dodsworth went out they shook him and repeatedly called him a 'damned scoundrel'.[91]

A larger-scale study of these minor disputes brought before the court of King's Bench would no doubt reveal other instances of the aggression implicit in the officer code. Such cases have a parallel, worse in degree but similar in kind, in the ex-soldiers who were involved in the Mohock violence in London in 1712. They were, as Daniel Statt has recently argued, driven by 'a culture of violence acquired by young officers during service in the war'.[92] Despite the extent of volunteering and the considerable body of plebeian patriotism, this culture, and its honour code, were essentially alien to a population in which civilian and civic values were strong. The new prominence of the army and militia was bound to cause conflict, despite the widespread appeal of 'romantic militarism' in this period, not only to the crowds who flocked to reviews but also to Wordsworth and other more articulate admirers of the moral spectacle of the nation at war. As Nancy Rosenblum has shown, 'romantic militarists did not share the typical social attitudes of professional military men who are conservative in a variety of respects; their conservatism arises first from the need for discipline, order, and established arrangements'.[93] During the French wars, not only those who volunteered, for various reasons, in the militia or volunteer regiments, but a large part of the urban civilian population had thrust upon them a considerable number of touchy military men, confident of the need for discipline and order, and among whom the code of honour and the duel were vigorously cultivated. It must have been the case for many that a belief in the nation, and in the war, was strained by the conflicts thus created. Little wonder that, at the end of the earlier Seven Years' War, one pioneer novelist, Francis Gentleman, had excluded soldiers from his utopian paradise set on the moon: 'all Military Persons, as turbulent, dangerous Animals, incompatible with a Region of Peace, are excluded without Exception.'[94]

Notes

1 I sampled the main categories of King's Bench Crown Side materials from Michaelmas 33 Geo III (November 1792) to Trinity 40 Geo III (July 1800), reading mainly but not exclusively papers relating to Yorkshire. I am grateful to Ruth Paley of the Public Record Office for her assistance in exploring the administrative procedures of the Court.

2 James Leith, 'Deradicalization and Militarization: some Architectural Projects under the Directory', *Proceedings of the Consortium on Revolutionary Europe 1750–1850*, 15 (1985), 29–44.

3 Alan Forrest, *Conscripts and Deserters: The Army and French Society during the Revolution and Empire* (Oxford University Press, 1989), pp. 43–73, 235–7.

4 Forrest, *Conscripts and Deserters*, pp. 24–8.

5 Alan Forrest, *Soldiers of the French Revolution* (Durham (NC), Duke University Press, 1990), pp. 187–8.

6 H.T. Dickinson, *The Politics of the People in Eighteenth-Century Britain* (London, Macmillan, 1994), pp. 149–50, 199–200.

7 This seeming paradox is discussed for the modern period in Charles Townshend, 'Militarism and Modern Society', *Wilson Quarterly*, 17 (1993), 71–82.

8 Philip Mansel, 'Monarchy, Uniform and the Rise of the Frac', *Past & Present*, 96 (1982), 103–32.

9 For instance two innkeepers in York, John Ringrose and Matthew Dawson had an undue number of dragoons and their horses billetted on them by the local Justices in Autumn 1792, and protested successfully to King's Bench. King's Bench rule book, 29 November 1792, PRO, KB 21/46, p. 17. In June 1794 Thomas Foster of Heptonstall successfully appealed against his parish's highway accounts, KB 16/21/3 unfoliated; KB 21/46, Easter 34 Geo III, p. 218.

10 Unfair rates are one source of dispute: see affidavits of Thomas Garforth and others, PRO, KB 1/30, Trinity 39 Geo III, 21, 54. One particularly tangled case of cruelty by an overseer in Bowling can be traced in KB 1/28, Michaelmas 36 Geo III, 46; KB 1/29, Hilary 36 Geo III, 2; KB 21/46 pp. 445, 477.

11 Still the most complete guide to the scope and practice of King's Bench, including its awesome structure of fees, is Richard Gude, *The Practice of the Crown Side of the Court of King's Bench, and the Practice of the Sessions, The General Rules of Court, from the Reign of James I to the present Time; And the Statutes relating to the Practice. Together with a Table of Fees, and Bills of Costs. Also, an Appendix of Forms and Precedents* (2 vols, London, 1828; repr. Littleton, Colorado, Fred B. Rothman, 1991).

12 For example, the cases in King's Bench controlment rolls 1793/4, PRO, KB 29/453, *passim*.

13 Linda Colley, 'The Reach of the State, the Appeal of the Nation: Mass Arming and Political Culture in the Napoleonic Wars', in Lawrence Stone (ed.), *An Imperial State at War: Britain from 1689 to 1815* (London, Routledge, 1994), pp. 170–1.

14 [Anon], *The Jockey Club, or a Sketch of the Manners of the Age* (London, n.p., 1792), p. 13. L. Colley, 'The Apotheosis of George III: Loyalty, Royalty and the British Nation, 1760–1820', *Past & Present*, 102 (1984), 94–129.

15 M. Thomis & P. Holt, *Threats of Revolution in Britain 1789–1848* (London, Macmillan, 1977), p. 23.

16 Phrase used in Colley, 'Reach of the State', p. 165. See also Raphael Samuel (ed.), *Patriotism: the Making and Unmaking of British National Identity* (3 vols, London, Routledge, 1989); Linda Colley, *Britons: Forging the Nation, 1707–1837* (New Haven, Conn., Yale University Press, 1992); Colin Kidd, 'North Britishness and the Nature of Eighteenth-Century British Patriotisms', *Historical Journal*, 39 (1996), 361–82. Kathleen Wilson, 'Empire of Virtue. The Imperial Project and Hanoverian Culture, *c*. 1720–1785', in Lawrence Stone (ed.), *Imperial State at War*, and *The Sense of the People: Politics, Culture and Imperialism in England 1715–85* (Cambridge University Press, 1995).

17 See, for example, E.P. Thompson, *The Making of the English Working Class* (Harmondsworth, Penguin Books, 1968); R.A.E. Wells, *Insurrection: The British Experience 1795–1803* (Gloucester, Alan Sutton, 1983); M. Philp (ed.), *The French Revolution and British Popular Politics* (Cambridge University Press, 1991). Useful surveys can be found in H.T. Dickinson, *British Radicalism and the French Revolution 1789–1815* (Oxford, Basil Blackwell, 1985) and *The Politics of the People in Eighteenth-Century Britain* (London, Macmillan, 1994).

18 *Jockey Club*, p. 3.

19 Ibid.

20 Debates on the issue lasted from 1 to 25 June 1795: [William Cobbett], *The Parliamentary History of England*, XXXI (London, 1818), pp. 99–138.

21 [A Hanoverian], *A Letter to the House of Peers on the Present Bill depending in Parliament, Relative to the Prince of Wales's Debts* (London, 1795), p. 6.

22 [E. Stuart], *A Letter to Charles Grey, Esq. on his Parliamentary Conduct, respecting his Royal Highness the Prince of Wales, in which are some remarks on 'A Letter to the Prince of Wales, on a Second Application to Parliament', and likewise on the 'Observations'* (London, 1795), p. 2.

23 Ibid., p. 18.

24 Though the pamphlet is listed in the British Library catalogue as anonymous, the recently released Secret Service accounts prove it to have been written by Stuart. E. Stuart to John King, 6 June 1795, PRO, HO 387/1/3, fo. 24.

25 Philip Harling, 'The Duke of York Affair (1809) and the Complexities of War-Time Patriotism', *Historical Journal*, 39, 4 (1996), 963–84.

26 Harling, 'Duke of York affair', p. 979.

27 *Address from the London Corresponding Society to the Inhabitants of Great Britain on the Subject of a Parliamentary Reform*, 16 August 1792, in Mary Thale (ed.), *Selections from the Papers of the London Corresponding Society 1792–1799* (Cambridge University Press, 1983), p. 19.

28 C. Emsley, 'The Military and Popular Disorder in England 1790–1801', *Journal of the Society for Army Historical Research*, 61 (1983), 17. For an earlier period, T. Hayter, *The Army and the Crowd in Mid-Georgian England* (London, Macmillan, 1978).

29 *Equality, As Consistent with the British Constitution, In a Dialogue between a Master-Manufacturer and One of his Workmen* (London, 1792), pp. 14–15.

30 M. Duffy, 'William Pitt and the Origins of the Loyalist Association Movement of 1792', *Historical Journal*, 39 (1996), 943–62. See H.T. Dickinson, 'Popular Conservatism and Militant Loyalism 1789–1815', in Dickinson (ed.), *Britain and the French Revolution 1789–1815* (London, Macmillan, 1989).

31 Meeting of 20 December 1792, *Leeds Mercury* (29/12/1792).

32 *Equality* (Liverpool, 1 December 1792); the British Library catalogue dates this handbill as 1795, but it is reprinted – curiously enough, without comment – in the *Leeds Mercury* (15/12/1792).

33 John Thelwall, *Tribune*, 1795, cited in G. Claeys (ed.), *The Politics of English Jacobinism: Writings of John Thelwall* (University Park, PA, Pennsylvania State University Press, 1995), p. 114.

34 Affidavit of William Dawson (11/11/1793), PRO, KB 1/28, Michaelmas 34 Geo III, 35.

35 Printed address of the Leeds Constitutional Society, PRO, TS 24/3/30A.

36 R.I. & S. Wilberforce, *The Life of William Wilberforce* (5 vols, London, 1838), vol. 2, pp. 4–5.

37 Hebden to Chamberlayne and White, December 1792, PRO, TS 24/2/16. Hebden is listed as an attorney, of Mill-hill, in the national directory of 1790, *The Universal British Directory of Trade, Commerce and Manufacture* (3 vols, London, 1790), vol. 3, p. 536. He is not listed in the more detailed Leeds directories of 1798 and 1800.

38 Affidavit of Major John Tottenham (28/12/1793), PRO, KB 1/28, Hilary 34 Geo III, 1.

39 Ibid. The York member was Richard Slater Milnes of Fryston Hall; see R.G. Thorne (ed.), *The History of Parliament: The House of Commons 1790–1820* (5 vols, London, Secker & Warburg, 1986), vol. 4, p. 598.

40 *Leeds Mercury* (29/12/1792). Nationally, there may have been as many as 1,500 loyalist associations engaged in similar activity: R.R. Dozier, *For King, Constitution and Country: The English Loyalists and the French Revolution* (Lexington, KY, Kentucky University Press, 1983), pp. 60–3.

41 *Leeds Mercury* (15/12/1792).

42 'Extracts from the *Leeds Intelligencer*, 1791–1796', *Thoresby Society Publications*, 44 (1956), *Leeds Intelligencer* (24/12/1792), p. 36.

43 Colley, *Britons*, p. 298.

44 Affidavit of Edward Greene (20/11/1793), PRO, KB 1/28, Hilary 34 Geo III, 1.

45 Ibid.

46 Thale (ed.), *Papers of the London Corresponding Society*, p. 34. At this same time, a cloth dresser from Upperthong, near Huddersfield, who had uttered disrespectful comments on the king and constitution, had to compound with the magistrates to avoid further prosecution by inserting a large advertisement in both Leeds newspapers asking pardon of the public. *Leeds Mercury* (9/02/1793).

47 Meetings, for example, at Ripon, 12 December 1792; Leeds 17 December; Bradford and Huddersfield 20 December; Knaresborough 22 December. *Leeds Mercury* (22, 29/12/1793).

48 Affidavits of Henry Andrews, Lieutenant-General Loftus Anthony Tottenham, Thomas Charnock, John Lee, the Revd William Bawden, William Charnock, Thomas Mathewman, John Smalpage and Edward Brooke (20/11/1793), PRO, KB 1/28, Hilary 34 Geo III, 1.

49 Affidavit of Major Tottenham (28/12/1793), ibid.; and Robert Bakewell (11/11/793), ibid. Michaelmas 34 Geo III, 35.

50 Affidavit of Major Tottenham (20/11/1793), ibid. Hilary 34 Geo III, 1.

51 Affidavits of Major Tottenham and William Bawden (20/11/1793), ibid., Michaelmas 34 Geo III, 35.

52 Affidavit of William Dawson (11/11/1793), ibid.

53 PRO, KB 21/46, Michaelmas 34 Geo III, p. 259; KB 29/453, Hilary 34 Geo III, fo. 11.

54 Affidavit of William Dawson, 29 May 1794, PRO, KB 1/28, Easter 34 Geo III, 61.

55 Affidavits of Major Tottenham and Thomas Wright, printer, 17 May 1794, ibid., 62.

56 Affidavit of Colonel Marwood Turner Van Straubenzee, 18 May 1794, ibid.

57 PRO KB 21/46, Easter 33 Geo III, pp. 108–9.

58 PRO KB 21/46, Michaelmas 34 Geo III, pp. 176, 187; ibid. Easter 34 Geo III, p. 231.

59 *Leeds Mercury* (26/01 & 2, 9, 16, 23/02/1793).

60 PRO, KB 16/21/5, 36 Geo III, unfoliated.

61 Loyal Durham Fencibles, *Leeds Mercury* (13/06/1795).

62 Affidavit of Mary Liversage (12/01/1795), PRO, KB 1/28, Hilary 35 Geo III, 12.

63 Affidavit of Joseph Jordan (12/01/1795), ibid.

64 Affidavits of Private Thomas Whitaker, Samuel Haigh, Private John Wilshore, Thomas ffrance (9/03/1795), Assize Depositions, Northeastern Circuit, PRO, ASSI 45/38/3.

65 PRO, ASSI 42/10.

66 Debates on the Bill in *Parliamentary History*, XXXI, 206–35. Here I draw on a valuable recent discussion of the movement: J. E. Cookson, 'The English Volunteer Movement of the French Wars, 1793–1815: Some Contexts', *Historical Journal*, 32 (1989), 867–91.

67 *Leeds Mercury* (29/12/1792).

68 *Leeds Intelligencer* (1/06/1795); *Leeds Mercury* (30/05/1795).

69 'W. R.', 'Review of Volunteers at Wakefield in 1796', *Bradford Antiquary*, N.S. 6 (1933–9), 90.

70 Anne Borsay, '"Persons of Honour and Reputation": the Voluntary Hospital in an Age of Corruption', *Medical History*, 35 (1991), 281–94; R. J. Morris, 'Voluntary Societies and British Urban Elites, 1780–1850: an Analysis', *Historical Journal*, 26 (1983), 95–118.

71 Cookson, 'English Volunteer Movement', p. 868.

72 Cookson, 'English Volunteer Movement', p. 870.

73 *Leeds Intelligencer* (21/09/1795).

74 Thomas Butler jr to Thomas Butler sr (15/12/1796), cited in R.F. Butler, *The History of Kirkstall Forge through Seven Centuries 1200–1954 AD. The Story of England's Oldest Ironworks* (York, Ebor Press, 2nd edn 1954), p. 75.

75 Diary entry (15–17/02/1797), in A.E., B.F. & H.M. Butler (eds), *The Diary of Thomas Butler of Kirkstall Forge, Yorkshire, 1796–1799* (London, Chiswick Press, 1906), p. 116.

76 A.N. Gilbert, 'Law and Honour among Eighteenth-Century British Army Officers', *Historical Journal*, 19 (1976), 75–87.

77 Lawrence Stone, 'Interpersonal Violence in English Society, 1300–1980', *Past & Present*, 101 (1983), 29.

78 Donna T. Andrew, 'The Code of Honour and its Critics: the Opposition to Duelling in England, 1700–1850', *Social History*, 5 (1980), 409–34.

79 Andrew, 'Code of Honour', p. 434.

80 Andrew, 'Code of Honour', p. 411.

81 James Kelly, *That Damn'd Thing called Honour: Duelling in Ireland 1570–1860* (Cork University Press, 1995).

82 John Kenneth Severn, 'An Affair of Honour?', *British Heritage*, 2 (1981), 56–63.

83 The various affidavits detailing the case are in PRO, KB 1/30, Easter 40 Geo III, 40 and 41.

84 Affidavit of Major John Worthington (17/05/1800), PRO, KB 1/30, Easter 40 Geo III, 41.

85 Affidavit of Major John Worthington (12/05/1800), ibid.

86 Affidavit of Walter Edward Hodgson (16/05/1799), PRO, KB 1/30, Trinity 39 Geo III, 4.

87 Affidavit of William Wilcock (16/05/1799), PRO, KB 1/30, Trinity 39 Geo III, 4.

88 Ibid.

89 Ibid.

90 Affidavit of William Hoyland (16/05/1799), ibid.

91 Affidavit of Frederick Dodsworth (12/01/1799), ibid., 61.

92 Daniel Statt, 'The Case of the Mohocks: Rake Violence in Augustan London', *Social History*, 20 (1995), 197–8.

93 Nancy L. Rosenblum, 'Romantic Militarism', *Journal of the History of Ideas*, 43 (1982), 259.

94 [Francis Gentleman] Sir Humphrey Lunatick, Baronet, *A Trip to the Moon. Containing an Account of the Island of Noibla. Its Inhabitants, Religious and Political Customs, &c.* (York, 1764: repr. New York, Garland Publishing, 1974), p. 101.

6

BONFIRES, BELLS AND BAYONETS: BRITISH POPULAR MEMORY AND THE NAPOLEONIC WARS

K. Watson

In 1793 Britain embarked on war with France. Conflict between the two nations was of course nothing unusual. Indeed France was in many respects Britain's significant, traditional 'other', the hallmark of everything that Britons were not: 'corrupt', 'Papist' and even 'feminine'. However, two factors made this war rather different from those that preceded it and meant that its impact on individual and national identity was potentially heightened. First, war was largely a response to a French *ideological* threat rather than the usual motives of trade and conquest, the 1789 Revolution appearing to the British Establishment as a danger to their own *status quo*. And secondly, that war was to continue on and off for almost twenty-five years, touching, changing and shaping the lives of a whole generation. We might expect then that the consequences for self and national identity of fighting a war of such complex and arduous duration would be merely to strengthen that sense of British cultural and political superiority. It was Britain after all that finally emerged from the wars victorious, having defeated not only 'French Principles' at home and abroad, but also the mighty Napoleon.

Yet, while such a conclusion is justified in the sense that loyalism did apparently assert itself as the dominant mass allegiance of the period, artisans and merchants alike eagerly participating in loyalist volunteer forces and political clubs in their thousands, it is neither the whole nor the end of the story. For that loyal artisan who willingly offered up his services for the defence of the nation as a volunteer soldier frequently showed a marked reluctance to engage in conflict when the nation's enemy was defined not as the alien French forces, or even troublesome political radicals, but a food rioter from his own town or village. Similarly the bourgeois merchant classes, who played an active role in the loyalist association campaigns to hunt out and arrest French sympathizers, were also equally prominent in the numerous campaigns to end hostilities between the two nations, particularly after the rise to power of Napoleon at the turn of the century. Thus while most British people could be defined as loyalist throughout this period, and would willingly define themselves as such, it was a loyalty that was neither static nor uniform but highly adaptive to the particular concerns of the individual.

This paper seeks to address the British reaction to the French Revolution through a study of those particular concerns, as expressed in a variety of memoirs, diaries, and autobiographies of the period, by those people who lived, worked and fought through this emotive, unsettling time. It attempts to understand not only why they remained so predominantly loyal, but also the ways in which that loyalty was perceived and constructed, for we cannot begin to explain why loyalty was so dominant a force in Britain during the 1790s and beyond until we ask to what and to whom they believed their loyalty was owed.

Most of the writers to whom this paper refers can indeed be classified as coming from an explicitly or implicitly loyalist position and most retained that position throughout the period. Otherwise, differences between them are wide and varied. Some, for instance, treated the political aspects of the time merely as a backdrop to their more personal concerns; others regarded those aspects as of crucial significance in their lives. A few retained only childhood memories of the experience. There are crucial differences too in the social backgrounds of those concerned, from the peasant-turned-soldier, to the 'respectable' Evangelical. The manner in which they recorded their memories also differs substantially. Some noted occurrences contemporaneously, largely for their own private purposes; others wrote retrospective accounts, often from thirty or forty years' distance, which were destined for the public arena. Yet, whatever their perspective, what they have to say on the subject, or even not say, is both interesting and, sometimes, enlightening since these writings, while in no way comprising a fully comprehensive view of popular loyalism, do at least give rise to a number of significant questions about its practical implications. These questions are about the influence of propaganda on their loyalty, about the effect of the lived experience of war on their preconceptions of French and English culture, and questions about how and why their views might change over time. In exploring these questions one therefore gains a useful insight into both popular loyalism itself, as it was experienced and as it was remembered, and into its long-term implications, as an ideological positioning defined by its appeal to unity at a time when society as a whole was undergoing a period of significant strain.

That autobiographical writings exist for this period, from a variety of different social perspectives, is in itself revealing. In the case of the lower-class authors, for instance, even their authorial status reflects certain significant social trends, such as the growing progress of mass literacy in Britain, indicative of David Vincent's findings that 'by the third quarter of the Eighteenth Century . . . at least one labourer and servant in three could sign the marriage register'.[1] The existence of these kinds of publications also indicates the emergence of a new market after the wars, or at least of a new demand for works that gave a lower-class perspective, as was noted in the introduction to the autobiography of a tailor, Thomas Carter, in 1845, wherein the editor speculated how different the reception of such a work would have been only half a century before:

Had a *Tailor* written his Memoirs, who had nothing to record of marvellous adventure, nothing of precarious talent . . . if such a person had appeared with his 'Memoirs' half a century ago, how utter would have been his neglect! Contempt would have been too much honour for him. But the circle is widened. He has now his own *class of students* to sympathise with him, and to cherish his lessons and examples.[2]

This impression, as stressed by Carter's editor, that a new market for works by and for the lower classes had indeed opened up in the post-Napoleonic period is also indicated by the considerable demand shown after the wars for eye-witness accounts of major battles, as recorded by the ordinary soldier or sailor.[3]

Carter's memories of the wars, however, are largely those of a child; born in 1792, he was only twenty-three when hostilities ended. His recollections of the period therefore retain a degree of innocence, in that, except for the latter stages of the war, Carter offers not his own perceptions of the war's socio-political implications, but rather the received opinion of the adults around him. In this respect his memoirs bear comparison with the autobiographical recollections of a rather different figure, Harriet Martineau, who offers a similarly youthful perspective on the situation, having been born in 1802.[4] However, while both authors' accounts are relatively lacking in direct political comment, there are nevertheless substantial differences in their accounts of its perceived effects, both in their own cases and those of their families, largely it seems because of the differences in their social backgrounds: Martineau came from an altogether more 'respectable', comfortably-off background than Carter.

The social differences between the two are most marked in terms of the levels of political awareness with which the two were surrounded. Carter, for instance, noted on several occasions, that while the adults around him certainly knew the war was on, they only ever made reference to it in the vaguest terms, leaving him with little understanding about wider political issues.[5] What is more, he was not even aware of this deficiency in his education until he reached the age of around fifteen, when he first began to reflect on his relative political ignorance:

> I think it was somewhere about [that] time . . . that my thoughts were first directed to political questions. Until then I had not been in the way of hearing anything respecting them. . . . It was generally affirmed that it was a good thing to beat the French, but as to either the quality or the extent of this asserted good, I was totally uninformed.[6]

In comparison, Martineau, although similarly and understandably vague about the real implications of the war, seems, through frequent contact with her parents and teachers, to have been much more aware of the actuality of events, describing, for instance, her awareness of the death of Nelson when she was only a small child:

My first political interest was the death of Nelson. I was then four years old.
My father came in from the counting-house at an unusual hour, and told my
mother, who cried heartily. I certainly had some conception of a battle, and of
a great man being a public loss. It always rent my heart-strings (to the last day
of her life), to see and hear my mother cry; and in this case it was clearly
connected with the death of a great man.[7]

The fate of the French royal family also seemed to have attracted the young
Martineau's attentions.[8] As Martineau acknowledged, her interest in the fate of
the French royals was understandable considering the romance surrounding it,
but her 'knowledge' of the war seems to have extended to more mundane,
domestic issues:

I remember my father's bringing in the news of some of the Peninsular
victories, and what his face was like when he told my mother of the increase of
the Income tax to ten per cent, and again, of the removal of the Income-tax.[9]

This extract indicates perhaps a further aspect of the war which was every bit as
politically charged as the ideology, the terror or the glamour – that is the financial
costs of it. The tax issue was, and still is, one of great concern to the middle classes
of Britain in particular. For while they were among the most outwardly loyal
groups of all, proud to defend King and Constitution, to set up petitions and
sponsorship lists and even to knit clothes for 'our boys' overseas, they did this
through *voluntary* contributions. When governments tried to regulate their efforts
in the financial arena, and particularly when they tried to make financial
contributions to the war effort mandatory through taxation, they frequently got
their fingers burnt, as middle and upper classes alike objected vehemently to the
further intrusions of the State into 'private' concerns. Loyalism went so far but no
further, or rather the very notion of loyalism, even for the most loyal, was
frequently different from State conceptions of it – in this case perhaps because one
of the things middle-class loyalists were most concerned to defend was the notion
of the independent Englishman, free from undue State interference.[10]

Martineau's account of her father's concerns also indicates once more the
sharp differences between the political environments of the two children, for
Carter observes that he could not ever remember seeing even a newspaper in his
father's house throughout the whole of his childhood.[11] Indeed, Carter's only
recollection of a newsworthy event was limited to the peace celebrations of 1802,
the sheer spectacle of the occasion making a lasting impression on his memory:

The town was generally illuminated; the streets were filled with people; the
church bells were ringing; bonfires were blazing; and everybody seemed to be
happy. . . . But there was a subject connected indeed with these rejoicings, but

of far greater importance, especially to such as had endured privations through the recent scarcity. This was the great and numerous benefits that were to be expected to arise from the returns of general tranquillity. 'Peace and Plenty' was the motto to many a device exhibited at the illuminations. This had already become the general watchword, and everybody seemed to expect that their hopes of general and lasting prosperity would soon be realised.[12]

The war was only truly significant in Carter's world, then, when it had real, practical and personal implications. Otherwise it was just a complex, confusing and distant issue which had little bearing on his daily life.

Yet, even in Martineau's case, her most vivid and frequent memories relate not to 'news' itself, but to a general perception of a single figure, Napoleon Bonaparte. The strength of these memories indicates both the extent of the propaganda and mythology surrounding Napoleon and their consequences, creating a kind of super-human, demonic figure of the man. Indeed this image proved to be so captivating and disturbing for Martineau that on one occasion her father felt compelled to reassure her that Napoleon was, after all, only a man like any other:

I had my own notions of Bonaparte too. One day at dessert, when my father was talking anxiously to my mother about the expected invasion, for which preparations were made all along the Norfolk coast, I saw them exchange a glance, because I was standing staring, twitching my pinafore with terror. My father called me to him, and took me on his knee, and I said 'But, papa, what will you do if Boney comes?' 'What will I do?' said he, cheerfully, 'Why, I will ask him to take a glass of Port with me,' – helping himself to a glass as he spoke. That wise reply was of immense service to me. From the moment I knew that 'Boney' was a creature who could take a glass of wine, I dreaded him no more. Such was my induction into the department of foreign affairs.[13]

Neither Carter nor Martineau, however, nor any member of their respective families, had any direct contact with the war or the political action inspired by it, other than through the fear of the anticipated invasion. As such their experiences differed greatly from those of a third child of the time, Sergeant 'Thomas', who was born in the year 1790. Thomas' background was by far the most deprived of the three. He was the son of a poverty-stricken Irish Catholic family, and the severity of this experience clearly had an effect on his retrospective account of the period. However, what is most notable about Thomas' account of his childhood is the degree to which his personal experiences of suffering were interpreted as directly resulting from the wider political circumstances of the time, namely, the Irish rebellion against British control. Note, for instance, his description of Ireland in the year 1798, when Irish discontent reached breaking point:

Although not quite nine years of age when our neighbourhood rang with war's alarms, the scenes I was then compelled to witness cannot be forgotten. . . . The rebels had taken possession of the place, and had murdered a magistrate who attempted to oppose them. . . . My poor mother was in the midst of these dangers; and I well remember that she experienced great rudeness from the ruffian rabble. . . . That night we were afraid of entering into any house, lest we should attract the notice of the rebels, who were now flushed into insolence and inebriety by their recent victory: we therefore crept behind the foliage of some low trees, and passed the night in the open air.[14]

Thus while Carter and Martineau merely aimed to recall the perspective of their own childhood years, Thomas actually attempted to contextualize it according to his own distinct agenda, an agenda that placed Catholicism and 'French Principles' as mutually supporting and inseparable evils:

Hair-brained but hot-headed men became the self-elected orators of secluded nocturnal assemblies. Liberty and equality, and reason versus religion, neat as imported from the French Directory at Paris, was the order of the day . . . nothing less than the dismemberment of the British Empire, and the establishment of a republic, formed probably on the model of citizen Robespierre, would suit their purpose. . . . The sons of Irish misrule assumed several names: there were white-boys, and steel-boys, oak-boys, and right-boys. Distinctions are, however, needless, – they were all bad boys; and . . . this body consisted chiefly of persons professing the Roman Catholic religion.[15]

Thomas' account of his childhood years thus highlights the problem for the historian of relying on autobiographies as 'authentic' sources, in that his memories of the period were clearly substantially affected by his later conversion to Protestantism. This is not to suggest that other forms of self-narrative are necessarily more reliable as 'objective' accounts, since each was similarly defined by the author's own personal agenda at the time of writing. Diaries, chronicles, and other contemporaneous texts do, however, at least offer an immediacy of reaction to a given event or time that autobiographies lack. This is particularly true for this period, the historical importance of which would have been only too well known to those people publishing their writings in the mid-nineteenth century.[16]

The fact that Thomas' autobiography was so clearly defined by the reactionary nature of his adult politics, however, makes his accounts of his 'loyalism' even more compelling, in that at no point does he recall an instance where ideological considerations worked as inspiration for direct action. His account of his decision to enlist in the militia in his early teenage years, ultimately the most self-consciously 'loyal' activity he was to take part in, is especially noteworthy in this respect:

I had arrived at the fourteenth year of my age; a period, generally speaking, of no small vanity and self-complacency, and in which many men think themselves qualified, by the dignity of their teens, to shake off the trammels of parental guidance. . . . Among the youths with whom I contracted some acquaintance, was a dissolute lad about my own age; by whose enticement, when only just fifteen, I enlisted in the Queen's County militia. . . . Evil communications corrupt good manners; and perhaps the apparent freedom, the frankness and gaiety of an open-hearted soldier's holiday life, had an influence which, though not acknowledged, was really felt.[17]

Peer pressure, rather than politics, then, inspired Thomas' one practical expression of loyalty. Similarly pragmatic motives seem to have guided the decision of other young men of Thomas' age and social class to enlist in one branch or another of Britain's military forces.[18] Joseph Mayett, for instance, recalled in his autobiography how, as a young agricultural worker, he had initially tried to enrol in the militia in 1802 because of an attack on his bravery by his employer's teenage son:

When I was Coming with the Cows my masters son met me he was about 13 years of age and a strange boy to sweare and he began to sweare at me and said he thought I had been gone for a soldier but I was not that fool then he swore I was afraid of a red Coat signifying that I had not Spirit enough to be a soldier this stung my pride and iritated me afresh and off I set to Buckingham but when I arrived there the recruiting party was gone out of town and it being peaceable times they would not enlist me in the militia.[19]

The soldier Thomas Morris recalled that his own decision to enlist had been inspired not by any ideological considerations, but derived from a childhood spent reading heroic tales of British victories:

I was particularly fond of reading the heart-stirring accounts of sieges and battles; and the glorious achievements of the British troops in Spain . . . created in me an irrepressible desire for military service . . . and, oh! how proud did I feel when having gone through my course of drill, I was permitted to join the ranks. Even now I often think of the delightful sensation I experienced . . . where our evolutions and martial exercises excited the admiration and wonder of crowds of nursery-maids and children, who invariably attended on such occasions. Then, how delightful on our return home, to parade the streets in our splendid uniform, exhibiting ourselves as the brave defenders of our country, should the Corsican attempt to carry into effect his threatened invasion of England.[20]

The ceremony and pageantry that surrounded loyalist activity, from the Volunteer review to the martial band, could therefore be as influential in bringing in recruits as any ideological considerations, and perhaps even more so in the case of the lower-class recruits, who otherwise lived lives where occasions for ceremony, and indeed glory, were noticeably absent.[21] War offered them that chance at glory and an exciting and rare opportunity to break free from their often harsh and drab lives and in this context it is hardly surprising that political questions arising from the war and its conduct were rarely discussed, or even identified. Indeed, in a rare anecdote relating to the ideological aspects of the conflict, Mayett recalled how he received, within a few days of each other, both a radical and a loyalist pamphlet, each setting out from very different perspectives and in very simple language why the conflict against France had occurred. Convinced by each in turn, and yet vaguely aware of their mutually contradictory nature, Mayett resolved the resulting sense of confusion by simply refusing to contemplate the matter further.[22]

Such an attitude, so far divorced from ideological motives, raises interesting questions about the nature, audience and effectiveness of loyalist propaganda – had the lower classes, for instance, been led to this uncontemplative level of patriotism through the culture created by propaganda, even though, with the single exception of Mayett's reference to his sense of confusion, it appears in these instances to have been little read by them? Or did that propaganda merely reinforce and reflect an already existing mass reactionary climate? In this sense, can they even be said to be 'loyalist' at all, or merely responding, in an apolitical way, to the demands of a culture in which radicalism of any kind already appeared dangerously alien, innovative and therefore threatening? One might argue that the loyalty of those closest to the war – the soldiers, sailors, and militiamen – was both understandable and necessary, whatever their initial reasons for enlistment, since the real and ever-present dangers of their situation almost demanded from the individual a degree of blind faith in the relative ideological and moral 'rightness' of their cause. For civilian loyalists the position was rather different, in that their experience of war remained a highly personalized one, its demands and effects necessarily having to be accommodated into the trappings of daily life rather than defining, and even justifying, their patriotism. What made these people loyalist, then, and the ways in which they expressed it, was necessarily more complex since the 'enemy' was always rather more distanced, both at home and abroad; who could really be sure where Jacobinism might lurk? Yet civilian loyalist accounts of this period, and particularly those kept in diary form without the benefit of an autobiographer's hindsight, suggest that for many of these people too, in various ranks and social positions, the wars and the paraphernalia which surrounded them were something to be dealt with rather than contemplated. This applied even if they were directly involved in it in some way, as was the prosperous tenant farmer, John Carrington.[23]

As a prominent and well-respected member of his community, Carrington held several official posts in wartime, including that of Chief Constable. In this latter role he was assigned supervisory duties relating to Volunteer organization and Militia balloting, and in his diary for the years 1798–1810 we have many accounts of these occasions. Yet, while these records are of interest in that they provide details of the sheer time and organization such activities demanded, the reader is rarely offered anything beyond a strictly factual account. Although we may learn how frequently ballots were called and what allocation was demanded from each village under his control, Carrington fails, on all but a few occasions, to place Volunteering and Militia activity within a wider social and political context and to comment on local feeling on balloting, or even on the war in general. This is partly due to the nature of his diary, clearly kept as a simple personal and businesslike account of his duties and usually restricted to one or two lines an entry. Even when Carrington does go into more detail, as in his account of the year 1803, it quickly dwindles into a statement of official duties:

This month we are Threatened to be Invaded by one Boneparte, by the French, and England is to be Divided amongst the French And Every man to be killed, and the Women to be saved, so we are Raiseing of Men from 17 to 55 one class, and 15 to 60 the other class, so Nothing but Soldiering three times a week. To St. Albans to Draw and Swear Inn Burges the Constable of Bramfield and my self, fine work.[24]

A similarly unenlightening coverage of the politics behind the war is found higher up the social scale in the chronicles of Joseph and John Saville, members of a very successful cloth-making family, who again adopt a brief one-line approach to events, be they personal or political, as in the following entry for the year 1793:

Jany: Louis the 16th King of France, beheaded.
Mch 23: Jno. Turner, my mother's coachman died. . . .
Octor 16: The Queen of France beheaded.[25]

Indeed the Saville brothers' coverage of the wider political situation is so limited, that the invasion scare year of 1803 does not merit even a single entry.

The adoption of this perspective demonstrates that the childhood interest in war expressed by Martineau, Thomas and Carter was far from exceptional. There were adult diarists and autobiographers of this period who saw the wars as of central importance in their lives, and, as with Carter, and to a lesser extent Martineau, one of the reasons for this heightened sense of involvement may be the geographical area within which they lived. The farmer, Charles Hicks, for instance, came, like Thomas Carter, from the Colchester area and in his diaries he recalled how in 1803 invasion fears were particularly acute there:

When Buonaparte had his flat-bottomed boats made and threatened to invade England, it was thought probable he might attempt a landing on the Essex coast. It created considerable alarm in this neighbourhood. Orders were received in the parishes along the coast to appoint persons to take charge of the live stock and have it removed, if necessary, to the upper part of the county on the borders of Cambridgeshire. . . . The Revd. Shaw King, residing at Commarques at Thorp, had all his plate and valuables packed ready for starting. It was said several families in Colchester made similar preparations.[26]

The immediate and real sense of danger which surrounded coastal and garrison towns seems to have inspired their inhabitants into various kinds of social and political activism, which those from other 'safer' areas frequently appeared to lack. Within the town of Colchester, for instance, public concerns had become, in a very real way, personal ones, and this is particularly apparent in the memoirs and correspondence of a brother and sister of that town, Jane and Isaac Taylor, who found themselves as children evacuated to a place of safety in Suffolk in 1803. As the eldest child, Jane assumed control of her younger sibling's welfare. She kept in touch with her mother by letter, primarily to reassure her parents that the children were coping successfully with their enforced separation. Their correspondence also reveals how the Taylors' strong sense of involvement in the war remained with them throughout this time:

We have safely received your parcels and letters which were very acceptable to us. I am now quite comfortably settled in my new house. . . . Thank you for the carpet: it is quite a luxury to us. Although we brought every thing absolutely necessary we have few conveniences; and though, if we were all huddled together in a barn, expecting the French to overtake us every instant we might be very well contended with–
'An open broken elbow chair;
A caudle cup without an ear; etc.'
Yet, living quietly, like our neighbours, we rather miss the conveniences we have been used to.[27]

Her sense of stoic acceptance of the situation became more fragile as the separation continued. Within months she appeared desperate for the exile to end, and wrote to her mother:

Could you see us just now; I cannot tell whether you would most laugh at, or pity us. I am sitting in the middle of the room, surrounded with beds, chairs, tables, boxes, etc. And every room is the same: but our brains are in still greater confusion – not knowing what to do. Have you heard this new alarm? It is said the French are actually embarking. Mr —— strongly advises us not to move till we hear something more: so we are quite perplexed.[28]

Particular events, then, such as the anticipated invasion of 1803, and particular circumstances, such as living in a garrison and/or coastal area, could combine to personalize the war for those otherwise likely to be little affected by it. The dividing line between public and private issues accordingly became blurred, and war-related events became more likely to occupy the thoughts and writings of diarists and autobiographers.

Again, even in these circumstances, the loyalty expressed by writers tended to be a deeply personalized one, and at times could prove somewhat problematic. Jane Taylor, for instance, though clearly loyalist at heart, found that at times her patriotism could not easily be reconciled with her other great passion, that of Evangelical Christianity, as she explained in a letter to a friend in 1805. She outlined why Nelson's recent victory at Trafalgar was an occasion to which she responded with mixed emotions:

> Now for your grave and appropriate question, namely – 'What do you think of this famous victory?'. . . [F]irst, I thought that it was a very 'famous victory'; did not you? – and besides this, and much more I thought a great many things that the newspapers had very obligingly thought ready for me . . . to speak in a graver strain . . . read on. . . . Every man who performs his part with zeal and success claims respect:– and who can deny that Nelson has nobly performed his? But tell me is the character of the warrior in itself to be admired? . . . From what motives does a man at first devote himself to war? Do you not think it is more often from a desire of glory, than from patriotism? . . . If so many brave men must be sacrificed, I heartily rejoice that the dear bought victory was ours. But how is it possible, while we regard them not merely as the machines of war, but as immortal beings, to rejoice without sorrow and dismay in the result of the rencontre?[29]

Taylor's aversion to the idea of 'the hero' was clearly religiously inspired. It is also indicative of one of the most notable issues of the wars – the rise of the heroic figure – when leaders such as Nelson, Napoleon, and Wellington, among others, came to represent a kind of idealized symbol of the nation for the mass of the population. Their various exploits, victories, and defeats were avidly followed and celebrated. Heroes had existed before in the public imagination of course, performing a similar function, in that they were at once both personal and public figures, transcending the gap between the notion of personal sacrifice for the public good and its lived reality. In the 1790s, however, the cult of heroism reached significant heights, as identified, for instance, in the massive commercial and cultural potential of the trade in Nelson memorabilia, from the production of commemorative items, such as medals, bowls and snuff boxes, to the founding of numerous friendly societies in his name. In this respect Nelson proved a deeply unsettling figure to the establishment, even while he boosted popular support for

ministerial war policy, since his cult proved once again how the basis of
patriotism, even in this period of external and internal threat, remained a
populist one, despite the best efforts of the élite to reconstruct it in a new royalist
dimension.[30] This is not to suggest that royalism and populism could not be
mutually supportive, but it is worth noting in this respect that while Nelson's
private affairs, and most notably his relationship with Lady Hamilton, arguably
did him little harm and may even have added further to his image as a man of
the people, the public's attitude to the Prince of Wales' infidelities was far less
tolerant, contributing to the image of him as one who was both sexually and
politically corrupt.

In this context it is hardly surprising that the notion of 'the hero', or even 'the
anti-hero' in the case of Napoleon, figured so frequently in various self-narratives
of the period, in both contemporaneous and retrospective form. He (and it was
invariably 'he') acted as a bridge between public and private suffering, and
between the ideological assumptions about the war and its perceived realities,
creating for many authors a space in which they could feel personally involved in
a public issue. This may have been particularly true for female authors, who were
otherwise excluded from so many of the active demonstrations of loyalty and
patriotism. It might also be one explanation for the interest shown in the affairs
of the war by Sarah Spencer, Lady Lyttleton, in her letters to her brother Bob,
himself cast in a heroic role as an officer in the navy:

> I can't wonder at people's desire to meet and talk now tho', when we have all
> this battle of Corruna to talk about. . . .
>   And don't it appear as if every man belonging to us, as soon as he begins to
> rise above all others, is taken off? Nelson, Abercrombie, so many, many more,
> and now the best land officer we had left. How dreadful is the state we are
> now in, without any returns; the anxiety for their arrival is painful to see! All
> those circumstances and every other about this dear-bought victory, make out
> the whole of conversation, as you may suppose.[31]

The patriotism and loyalty of the British people, therefore, as reflected in these
self-narratives, while rarely appearing to be seriously undermined or even
substantially critical, was never either a uniform stance or an uncomplicated one.
Furthermore, its inspirations appear not to have been direct propaganda at all
but rather the personal concerns and fears of the individual, since, as previously
noted, reference to such propaganda material was rarely made. This is not to say
that those concerns did not arise in part from the general tide of loyalism that
swept Britain at that time, fed and encouraged by the 'official' loyalist discourse,
as heard in court, at church, in caricatures or the newspapers. Nor is it to say that
that loyalism was not real, in the sense that many people, and certainly most of
those discussed here, did genuinely express a fear of and hostility to France and

'French Principles'. However, what they feared was not the ideological consequences as such of the French experience, but rather its daily, practical implications for themselves, their families and their neighbours. Images of the French as wicked *sans-culottes*, or as slaves to the tyrannical Napoleon were certainly effective in creating an atmosphere of fear about the French, and effective too in creating an atmosphere of mistrust and even hatred towards those in Britain who appeared to support them. Such imagery, however, was only effective when experienced at a distance. Once soldiers, like Morris or Thomas for instance, actually confronted that enemy and saw that they were not demons but men, much like them, or, worse still, realized that in some ways life for the French soldier was actually better than for them, then the power of the loyalist discourse was substantially undermined. Such discourse relied heavily on that element of contrast between life for the Frenchmen, tyrannized, impoverished and depraved, and that of the Englishman, free, nourished and pure in his 'free-born' status.

For those in civilian life, exempt from the actual experience of meeting the enemy, that distance between imagery and reality, in terms of the French, could not so easily be drawn. Yet even in this case the sheer toll of the war, in terms of its financial, moral or human costs, made the ideological reasoning behind the conflict increasingly difficult to bear, particularly as the Revolutionary state was replaced by the Napoleonic one. Thus what kept these people loyal as the wars proceeded was not the discourse of loyalism itself, as constructed by the ministry or those loyalist members of the élite, but rather a sense of loyalty to what they themselves held dear – family, home, religion and country – in the belief that what British society represented at its best was a constitutional recognition of those individual attachments. While government could appeal to the threat to each of these in various ways and at various stages in the conflict, it could not define what each of those concepts meant for each of its people, and hence it could not define how they would be protected. Loyalists were loyal, then, because they wished to be so, but ultimately it was a loyalty deeply rooted in the personal and buttressed by a cultural perception of the unassailable benefits of the British constitution.

This notion of the peculiar strengths of the British tradition was so ingrained in popular culture that it not only fuelled the popular reaction against 'French Principles', as was well recognized by those orchestrating loyalist initiatives, but also served as something of a counter-balance to the many hardships and disappointments of the war years for many people. It explains too why for so many loyalism truly was an instinctive reaction rather than an ideological 'choice'. However, for others, loyalty was tested to its limits when the British state or even people appeared to be undermining what it was supposedly defending – that tradition of the liberty of the individual – simply to achieve short-term gains in the wars. Something of this sense of concern, bewilderment and even dismay can be seen in the fears of Taylor, for instance, that popular glorification of the hero figure was blinding people to their moral responsibilities. It was most aptly and absolutely expressed in the diaries of Francis Horner, the son of an Edinburgh merchant, who became an MP.[32]

Horner spent the early years of the wars separated from his family in England, where he had been sent by his father in order that 'he should be freed from the disadvantages of a provincial dialect'.[33] While there he began the study of law, which was eventually to become his career, and started to keep the diaries and letters which made up his memoirs. Initially a loyalist in an uncomplicated sense, although always with Whig leanings, in 1797, at the age of nineteen, he wrote a letter to his father confirming his support for Pitt's handling of the war. Two years later, however, this support was looking less certain, as Horner confided to his diary:

> I daily find it more necessary to be anxious about the formation and expression of my political opinions. . . . On the one hand the majority of the country runs strongly and implicitly in favour of a minister who has made the greatest inroads on the constitution; on the other, there is a set of people who, undoubtedly, some from wicked and ambitious reasons, others from honest views, pout after a new and republican order of things. Between these two fires, there is some courage in pleading the cause of our neglected constitution.[34]

This change in Horner's perspective is instructive for a number of reasons. First, it indicates the effect changing social and political circumstances could have on an individual's ideological allegiances, since Horner's response was clearly influenced by a series of disruptive incidents, such as the sailors' mutinies of spring 1797 and the Irish rebellion of 1798; both of these events may have provoked fears in him not only of the political volatility of the masses, but also of the government's harsh response. Secondly, it offers further confirmation of the difference between the diarist's account of a period and that of an autobiographer, in that Horner's account is that of a man responding to circumstances on a day-to-day level, rather than of one who was reflecting from a distance of ten years or more on the general feeling of the times. Thirdly, and perhaps most significantly, it also suggests how for Horner, and perhaps others like him, neither the loyalist response to the ideological repercussions of the French Revolution nor the radical one was ultimately satisfying, since Horner feared that both stances failed to offer adequate protection for the British constitution.

Horner remained what might loosely be called 'loyalist', then, since he genuinely feared for the safety of the country in relation to the literal and ideological French threat, even joining a Volunteer corps during the invasion scare of 1803, and offering to contribute to a friend's loyalist propaganda campaign. Yet his discontent with Britain's own ideological position continued to haunt him, and in a letter to his friend, Francis Jeffries, in 1807, he argued that the current destruction of traditional liberties was of far greater significance than the external French threat. By 1816 his dismay at that process of destruction was so great that even British victory offered Horner little comfort, as he confided to Jeffries:

> There are changes in the whole frame of European politics, and in our domestic scheme of liberties, which are going on much faster than politics ever before seemed to me to move. . . . In the most formidable periods of the French military power, my dread never was of its prevailing against us in this island by conquest, but of the inroads that our system of defence was making upon the constitutional forms of our parliamentary government, and upon the constitutional habits of the English commons. We are nearly declared to be a military power. If this design is not checked, of which I have slender hopes, or does not break down by favour of accidents, we shall have a transient glory, for some little while . . . but it is a glory in which our freedom will be lost, and which cannot maintain itself when the vigour, born of that freedom is spent. Do not tell any body of these gloomy visions of mine; they will appear absurd and insincere. . . . I have in my heart infinitely more apprehension, about the future of English liberty, than I ever permit myself to express in public.[35]

Loyalism could mean many things, then, for many people, according to personal circumstances and conditions. It could, and did, act both as a vehicle for individual empowerment and as a nationally unifying force, whereby the French example was ultimately found wanting in contrast to the British constitutional tradition. For some, like Carter or Martineau, that experience was truly a politicizing one, leading them on to new radical political expression. Others, like Morris, found that their experience of loyal activism left them with a sense of self-worth and self-belief that was valuable enough in itself, needing no translation into a demand for greater political rights. The experience of the war years for people like Horner was by contrast a deeply disheartening one; their belief in the superiority of the British constitutional system, indeed their 'loyalty' itself, was profoundly undermined not because of what France represented, or even achieved, but because of what Britain appeared to lose – popular and state acknowledgement of the necessity of the British tradition of liberty. When that acknowledgement was perceived to be lacking, as Horner believed absolutely, and as many of the other authors expressed on individual occasions, they reacted with varying degrees of isolation and dismay, caught in a space between loyalty and radicalism which no contemporary political grouping adequately addressed, in a society already beset by social and cultural change and by the disruptive effects of war itself.

Thus while the experience of the Revolutionary and Napoleonic Wars did arguably leave its mark both in terms of the development of class-consciousness that E.P. Thompson has described and in terms of the boost it gave to popular nationalism, the evidence of these texts suggests that its most profound consequence for British society as a whole, was to thrust the deeply rooted belief in the exceptional character of the British tradition of liberty, shared by radicals and loyalists alike, into the spotlight. Loyalists everywhere came to realize what being loyal meant practically for them, and what was the object of their loyalty – the survival of one's home, family, culture or religion; hence, in some cases such realization led to an examination of the ways in which those various allegiances were given true constitutional recognition. When the long period of war ended and people had to decide what kind of peace they wanted, it was those issues that loyalism had made pertinent which formed the centre of political debate – issues about what and whom parliament should represent, what kinds of responsibility the individual should be expected to have and what role the state itself should be expected to play in determining these issues. After the conflict British society struggled to deal with the gaps between constitutional ideals and practical realities which loyalism had unwittingly exposed.

Notes

1 David Vincent, *Literacy and Popular Culture, England 1750–1914* (Cambridge University Press, 1989), pp. 11–12.

2 Thomas Carter, *Knights Weekly Volume: Memoirs of a Working Man* (London, Knights, 1845), pp. vi–vii.

3 Clive Emsley, 'The Social Impact of the French Wars', in H.T. Dickinson (ed.), *Britain and the French Revolution 1789–1815* (Basingstoke, Macmillan, 1989), p. 226.

4 Harriet Martineau, *Autobiography: Volume One* (London, Virago, 1983 [1855]).

5 Carter, *Memoirs*, p. 35.

6 Carter, *Memoirs*, pp. 83–4.

7 Martineau, *Autobiography*, p. 23.

8 Martineau, *Autobiography*, pp. 78–80.

9 Martineau, *Autobiography*, pp. 78–80.

10 See Kate Watson, 'Liberty, Loyalty, Locality: The Discourses of Loyalism in England, 1790–1815' (unpublished Ph.D. thesis, Open University, 1995), chapter 1 for a wider discussion on the nature of the middle class and volunteering.

11 Carter, *Memoirs*, p. 84.

12 Carter, *Memoirs*, pp. 43–4.

13 Martineau, *Autobiography*, p. 23.

14 Sergeant Thomas, *Memoirs of A Sergeant, Late in the 43rd Light Infantry Regiment* (London, 1835) p. 5.

15 Thomas, *Memoirs*, pp. 3–5.

16 Thomas' autobiography was published in 1835, six years after the Catholic Emancipation Act had finally been passed, and perhaps worked for him in this respect as some kind of cathartic exercise, enabling him to express publicly his resentment about this extension of official religious tolerance. The fact that Thomas was able to find a publisher for his book, however (and presumably a market), also suggests that he was not alone in his prejudice – and that Linda Colley may perhaps be overstating the case with her assertions that by 1829 'the mass of poorer Britons no longer felt so aggressively on the subject of Catholicism as they had done in the past', and that anti-Catholic sentiment was largely confined to 'the poorer, more marginal and less literate folk who were . . . more dependant on that traditional, largely oral culture in which Protestant intolerance was so deeply imbedded'; Colley, *Britons: Forging the Nation, 1707–1837* (New Haven, Yale University Press, 1992), pp. 332–3.

17 Thomas, *Memoirs*, p. 12.

18 Both John Nicol and John Green also seem to have initially enrolled in their country's service less from a sense of patriotism than from a desire to satisfy their particular need to travel, Nicol noting that he had always wished to go to sea since 'The first wish I ever formed was to wander, and many a search I gave my parents in gratifying my youthful passion'; *The Life and Adventures of John Nicol, Mariner* (London, n.p., 1822), p. 2. Green described how he had joined the army after various attempts at civilian life had failed since he had 'in vain tried to settle, having a disposition to wander, which left me no rest until it was gratified'; John Green, *The Vicissitudes of a Soldier's Life, Late of the 68th Durham Light Infantry* (Louth, n.p., 1827), p. 1.

19 Ann Kussmaul (ed.), *Autobiography of Joseph Mayett of Quainton, (1783–1839)* (Aylesbury, Buckinghamshire Record Society, No. 23, 1986), p. 22.

20 John Selby (ed.), *Thomas Morris: The Napoleonic Wars* (London, Longmans, 1967), p. 2.

21 'Britons who were poor, more so perhaps even than the prosperous, were drawn into military service not just by apprehension but by the excitement of it all, by a pleasurable sense of risk and imminent drama, by the lure of a free, brightly coloured uniform and by the powerful seduction exerted by martial music': Colley, *Britons*, pp. 306–7. Note too Clive Emsley's comment that 'Such attractions, together with the pull of patriotism which was especially strong in the early stages of the Napoleonic War, should not be underestimated as encouragements to recruitment': Emsley, 'Social Impact of the French Wars', pp. 218–19.

22 Kussmaul, *Autobiography*, p. 70.

23 W. Branch Johnson (ed.), *Memorandums for . . . the Diary between 1798 and 1810 of John Carrington* (Chichester, Phillimore, 1973).

24 Branch Johnson (ed.), *Memorandums*, p. 89.

25 A.F.J. Brown (ed.), *Essex People, 1750–1900* (Chelmsford, Essex Record Office Publications, 59, 1972), pp. 46–7.

26 Brown, *Essex People*, pp. 70–9.

27 Isaac Taylor, *Memoirs and Poetical Remarks of the late Jane Taylor* (London, n.p., 1825) (18/10/1803), pp. 74–5.

28 Taylor, *Memoirs*, p. 76.

29 Taylor, *Memoirs*, pp. 142–5.

30 G. Jordan & N. Rogers, 'Admirals as Heroes: Patriotism and Liberty in Hanoverian England', *Journal of British Studies*, 28 (1989), 211–24. Jordan and Rogers compared for instance the popular attention paid to Nelson's tour of the Midlands and the West Country in 1802 with the far less warm response which the king received on his visit to Weymouth in 1805 and argued that 'There was . . . a crucial element of spontaneous, rapturous acclaim that characterized Nelson's tour . . . one that contrasted with the studied promotion of royal spectacle', p. 222.

31 Hon. Mrs. Wyndham, *Correspondence of Sarah Spencer, Lady Lyttleton, 1787–1870* (London, n.p., 1912), letter dated (24/01/1809), p. 59.

32 Francis Horner, *Memoirs and Correspondence of Francis Horner, MP* (2 vols, London, n.p., 1843).

33 Horner, *Memoirs*, p. 6.

34 Horner, *Memoirs* (11/02/1799), p. 70.

35 Horner, *Memoirs* (27/02/1816), pp. 314–15.

7

IRISH IDENTITY AND THE CRIMEAN WAR

B. Griffin

In November 1854 the *Londonderry Journal*, in keeping with its policy of promoting public enthusiasm for Irish participation in, and support for, the Crimean War, published a stirring ballad entitled 'The Islemen of the West'. The ballad painted a picture of the constituent parts of the United Kingdom rallying together to make common cause against the Russian Empire. The stanza devoted to Ireland's role in this common cause stressed, in particular, the message of a nationwide support for the war effort. This message was conveyed both by referring to men from specific regions of Ireland – a Tipperary mountaineer, Connaught Rangers and 'he who kiss'd his sweetheart last by Shannon's silver rills' – and by more generalized references to 'the daring sons of Eire' or the 'septs of our old Celtic land'.[1] The unity depicted in the ballad was, then, twofold: a unity between Great Britain and Ireland, and a unity between Irishmen.

It is with this notion of a national Irish support for the war in the Crimea that this essay deals; it demonstrates that there was indeed broad support from the Irish public for Irish participation in the Crimean War. This, at first sight, is surprising, given that the Great Famine was still a recent and painfully vivid memory and is believed, by many historians, to have left a legacy which irrevocably soured Ireland's attitudes towards Britain.[2] This antipathy did not, however, become immediately apparent in Ireland; apart from some typically vitriolic attacks by John Mitchel and other Irish Americans, openly expressed hatred of Britain was relatively uncommon in the early to mid-1850s. As we shall see, most Irish people in those years were willing to work within the Union rather than heed the call of Mitchel and other republican separatists for a rebellion to overthrow British rule in Ireland. This does not mean, however, that the *Londonderry Journal* was entirely accurate in depicting an Ireland unambiguously united behind Britain in its war effort. This essay shows that, underneath this apparent unity towards participation in the war, Ireland was riven by deep divisions. A close examination of Ireland's response to the Crimean War reveals much about the tensions and divisions in Irish society and the ambiguities and complexities of Irish identity in the mid-1850s.

That Irish soldiers played a substantial role in the Crimean conflict should not be doubted, even if one cannot give a precise figure for the numbers of Irishmen serving in the British army in the 1850s.[3] We are on surer ground when

discussing Irish enlistment in the British army before the 1850s. During the
Napoleonic Wars and the decades thereafter Ireland proved a fruitful recruiting
ground for the British army. Indeed, in 1830, when Ireland's proportion of the
United Kingdom population was some 32.3 per cent, 42.2 per cent of the British
army was Irish. Irishmen, in fact, outnumbered Englishmen in the British army
in that year.[4] Unfortunately, there are no statistics available for Irish
representation in the British army from 1840 (when 37.2 per cent of the army
was Irish) down to 1861 (when 28.4 per cent of the army was Irish).[5] Despite this
hiatus in the statistical evidence, one still gets a general picture of a very large
Irish contingent in the British Crimean army from a variety of sources.

   First, one can point to the active role played in the war by those infantry
regiments that traditionally recruited almost exclusively in Ireland. These
consisted of the 18th Royal Irish Regiment, the 88th Connaught Rangers and the
89th Regiment.[6] It appears from the memoirs of a veteran of the 7th Royal
Fusiliers that the 18th Regiment was an Irish-speaking regiment, judging from
the fact that the regiment was addressed in Irish by its commanding officer just
before it went into battle on 18 June 1855.[7] Among the cavalry, the Irish
regiments which fought in the Crimea included the 4th Royal Irish Dragoon
Guards, the 5th Princess Charlotte of Wales Dragoon Guards and the 6th
Inniskilling Dragoons, comprising three of the Heavy Brigade's five regiments.[8]
The Light Brigade also included one Irish regiment, the 8th Royal Irish Hussars.[9]
While these infantry and cavalry regiments constituted an important part of the
Irish contingent serving in the Crimean War, nevertheless most Irish soldiers who
fought in the Crimea served in regiments which are not usually identified as
Irish. In fact many nominally Welsh, Scots or English regiments in the Crimea
contained either an Irish majority or a substantial Irish minority in their ranks.
Those with an Irish majority included the 14th Buckinghamshire, 3rd Buffs (East
Kents), 19th Princess Alexandra of Wales' Own Yorkshire, 23rd Welch Fusiliers,
33rd Duke of Wellington's Own, 41st Welch, 47th Loyal North Lancashire, 49th
Royal Berkshire, 55th Westmoreland, 62nd Wiltshire, 63rd West Suffolk and the
97th Regiment.[10] Crimean regiments that were divided almost equally between
British and Irish soldiers included the 1st Royals, 17th Leicestershire Foot, 20th
Lancashire Fusiliers, 21st Royal North British Fusiliers, 34th Cumberland and
77th East Middlesex regiments.[11] The 30th Cambridgeshire and 61st South
Gloucestershire regiments and the 90th Perthshire Volunteers also had
substantial Irish contingents, as did the 11th Hussars and 17th Lancers.[12]

   There is also plenty of anecdotal or impressionistic evidence, such as claims
that 'nearly one-half' of the British troops in the Crimea sported sprigs of green
in their caps on St Patrick's Day in 1855, to support further the picture of a very
substantial Irish presence in the British Crimean forces.[13] Catholic chaplains and
the fifteen Irish Sisters of Mercy serving in British military hospitals in Scutari
and the Crimea added their opinions that half, or even the majority, of the

British army's casualties in the conflict were Catholics,[14] and most of these, of course, would have been Irish. Irish newspapers added claims that most of the British army in the Crimea was Irish, sometimes basing their assertions on analyses of the surnames of the dead and wounded in official casualty lists.[15] These efforts of Irish newspapers notwithstanding, it is not possible to give a definite figure for the number of Irish troops serving in the Crimea. Sister Evelyn Bolster, in her study of the Irish Sisters of Mercy in the Crimean War, estimates that one third of the British soldiers were Catholics from Ireland.[16] If her estimate is accurate, then it does not seem implausible that around 40 per cent of the total was Irish, when one includes Irish Protestant troops; this estimate certainly accords well with estimates of the peacetime Irish presence in the British army.[17] Whatever the exact number of Irish troops serving in the Crimea may have been, there seems no reason to doubt either the disproportionate Irish representation in the British Crimean army or the support which Irish civilians gave to the war.

As noted above, this obviously raises important questions concerning historians' assertions about Irish attitudes towards the link with Britain and Ireland's role in the empire in the decade after the Great Famine.[18] The supposed lasting resentment of the Irish people towards Britain, as a result of the British government's mishandling of the famine crisis, did not prevent massive Irish volunteering for the British army and, to a lesser (but still unknown) extent, the Royal Navy; nor did it prevent most Irish people from supporting Irish participation in the war. This support requires some explanation from the historian. The support is evidenced not merely in the form of Irishmen flocking to the British colours, but also, and perhaps more tellingly, in the form of Irish civilians' contributions to the Patriotic Fund (a fund throughout the United Kingdom, under the patronage of Queen Victoria, to relieve the widows and orphans of servicemen killed in the conflict).[19] Other indications of Irish support for the war are manifested in the form of popular ballads such as 'Kate on the Crimea' and 'The Gallant Escape of Pat McCarthy from the Russians', as well as the 'best-selling' collection entitled *Lays of the War*, written by a Corkonian[20] and also by amusements with anti-Russian themes at the annual Donnybrook Fair.[21] The enthusiasm with which many returning veterans were greeted further suggests that the war met with popular approval.[22] The reception given to Captain William H. Newenham, 'one of the heroes of Inkerman' as he is described by a contemporary newspaper, is a good example of the type of welcome given to returning veterans by local people. An eye-witness records that when Captain Newenham visited his brother, the Revd Edward Newenham of Coolmore, in May 1855 he received an enthusiastic welcome from the local community: 'On his approach to that beautiful residence he was met by several hundreds of the peasantry, who gave him a most enthusiastic reception, took the horses from his carriage, and drew him to the house, passing under several

triumphal arches which were tastefully erected by them to greet his arrival'.[23]
The avid interest of the Irish public in news from the theatre of war is attested to
by contemporaries.[24] This intense interest was not lost on the editors of Irish
newspapers, who fed the public a stream of accounts of Irish bravery and printed
hundreds of letters written from the Crimea and the other areas of conflict by
Irish soldiers and sailors.[25] These letters ranged from rather formulaic accounts,
in which Irish soldiers bragged of their deeds or those of their regiment and
made light of the hardships which they endured,[26] to quite graphic descriptions
of the privations which were the daily lot of the Irish and other allied troops.[27]

How does one explain the keen interest in and the general support of the war
which Irish people displayed? The large-scale involvement of Irish servicemen
would, of course, be sufficient to explain this interest for a large part of the
population, as relatives and friends of Irish soldiers and sailors were unlikely to
have been indifferent to their fate. For others, their interest was no doubt kindled
and sustained by the fact that a large cross-section of the Irish landed classes
fought in the Crimea and their deeds were recounted in the Irish national and
provincial press. It stands to reason that people whose members of parliament,
landlords, or landlords' relatives were active in the Crimean conflict should have
maintained more than a passing interest in the war. Several Irish members of
parliament fought in the war. Two of these were killed at the battle of Inkerman:
Lieutenant Colonel E.W. Pakenham of the Grenadier Guards, MP for Antrim,
and Lieutenant Colonel Thomas Vesey Dawson of the Coldstream Guards, MP
for Louth from 1841 to 1847 and MP for Monaghan from 1847 to 1852.[28]
Another Irish soldier-politician, Major J.P. Maxwell, MP for Cavan, was
wounded while serving in the Crimea.[29] Other members of prominent Irish
landed families who were killed or who died of disease in the war included Lord
Fitzgibbon of the 8th Hussars, Captain Cavendish Brown of the 7th Fusiliers (son
of Lord Kilmaine), Major Charles Daly of the 89th Regiment (brother of Lord
Dunsandle), Captain William Hely Hutchinson of the 13th Light Dragoons
(brother of the Earl of Donaghmore), Captain William Monck of the 7th Fusiliers
(brother of Viscount Monck) and Major Charles Luke Hare, also of the 7th
Fusiliers (son of Viscount Ennismore).[30] One could also point to economic
motivation behind Irish interest in, and support for, the war. Irish agriculture was
undergoing a boom period from the early 1850s onward, and many farmers,
especially in Ulster and Munster, prospered from supplying the British and
French forces during the war. Irish provision merchants and other Irish
businesses also benefited from the war.[31] It would, however, be too reductionist or
simplistic to cite economic motives, or ties of friendship or family, or natural
interest in the military activity of prominent local men, as the main factors at
work, although these cannot be totally discounted. There were other, more
important factors which contributed to the generally positive attitude towards the
war which most Irish people *in Ireland* displayed.[32] This is not to say that Ireland

should be considered, by virtue of this support, a contented part of the United Kingdom, slavishly loyal to Britain. There is little evidence of spontaneous, disinterested or unconditional Irish support for the war, even among Irish Protestants – with the exception of those gentry families with a tradition of serving in the British army. There is plenty of evidence that these families genuinely welcomed the outbreak of the war as an opportunity to maintain their martial tradition.[33] Most Irish people who supported the war effort, however, did so mainly from purely domestic, Irish considerations rather than because of intense loyalty to Britain or her empire. The Irish supporters of the war can, broadly speaking, be divided along religious lines into two mutually hostile camps, with Catholics and Protestants vying with each other in promoting participation in the war effort and advertising the contributions of their combatant and non-combatant co-religionists to the war effort. The main reason for this behaviour is not that they were convinced of the justice of Britain's cause, but because they were involved in point-scoring against the rival community. Each community wanted to prove to British public opinion that it was worthy of more favourable consideration when it came to resolving the interminable sectarian disputes of mid-century Ireland. A parallel can be drawn here with developments in Ireland during the First World War, when the leaders of the anti-Home Rule Ulster Volunteer Force urged their followers to fight for Britain in the hope that the British government would resolve the Home Rule issue in their favour, and the leaders of the pro-Home Rule Irish Volunteers urged their followers to fight for Britain in the hope that the British government would reward them by granting Home Rule.

 During the Crimean War, Catholic clergy and civic leaders presented the war as a golden opportunity to win kudos where it mattered – in Britain. This should be placed in the context of the profound changes which had occurred, and were still ongoing, in post-Famine Irish society. The Catholic community of the mid-1850s had, relatively speaking, never been so well off;[34] although increasing in general prosperity it still had numerous grievances ranging from the land question to real and perceived sectarian discrimination.[35] In this era of rising expectations frustration at real and perceived restrictions on further social advancement was felt all the more keenly by the leaders of the Catholic Church and community. These leaders, in contrast to Irish republicans, wanted to work within the United Kingdom political system to further the interests of Irish Catholics.[36] This explains why most of the Catholic hierarchy and most nationalist newspapers urged young Catholic Irishmen to serve in the British armed forces and urged Catholic civilians to support the war effort in a variety of ways, including contributing to the Patriotic Fund, supplying Catholic troops with devotional literature and supporting the work of Catholic chaplains and the Irish Sisters of Mercy.[37] Supporting the war was represented as a religious duty, one which would not only benefit oppressed Catholics at home but also oppressed Catholics abroad, such as the Poles.[38] The tsar of Russia was, significantly, portrayed as an enemy of the Catholic Church, particularly in Poland. One ballad refers to the Russians as 'nun-floggers', and portrays the war as a contest between Russia and 'Catholic Europe' (meaning Ireland and France), a contest whose result shall be that 'our convents must still be free'.[39] It is important to remember here that Irish Catholics saw themselves as members of a universal church, that they took vicarious pride in notable achievements by non-Irish Catholics and that they also viewed with alarm threats to the Catholic Church abroad.[40] During the Crimean War the achievements and sacrifices not only of Irish Catholic soldiers and sailors, but also those of their French Catholic allies, were trumpeted in the Catholic press and used as polemical debating points against Irish Protestant opponents of further Catholic advancement and their allies in Britain. This is perhaps best exemplified by the rhetoric surrounding the ill-judged attempt by some British MPs to abolish the parliamentary grant to the largest Irish Catholic seminary, Maynooth College, in 1855. The response of the *Freeman's Journal*, the leading nationalist newspaper, to the proposal to abolish the grant sums up how Irish Catholic civilians pointed to the sacrifices of their co-religionists in the Crimea in order to defend their own interests. In a leading article on the Maynooth proposal the newspaper stated that 'The only argument with which we would resist such a declaration [against the Maynooth grant] would be, "Sebastopol"'.[41]

In a mirror image of these developments within the Catholic community, there were regular calls from Protestant newspapers and pulpits for Irish Protestants to join the British army and Royal Navy or otherwise to support the war effort. The war was frequently portrayed as a religious struggle, one in which Irish Protestants could defend their interests at home while promoting the cause of Protestantism abroad.[42] The Revd S.J. Moore, in a sermon in Wellington Street Presbyterian Church in Ballymena in December 1854, gave one of the best expositions of this view of the war. Moore presented a number of reasons why Irish Protestants should support the war against Russia; probably the most telling for his audience was that to allow the tsar to establish a protectorate over Turkey's Christians would be analogous to admitting that 'all the papists of this empire should be accountable only to Pio Nono', and that the pope could 'take military possession of Ireland' as a result.[43] When Catholic Piedmont joined the war on Britain's side early in 1855, the Protestant *Belfast Newsletter* comforted its readers with the assurance that Piedmont was actively anti-clerical and proto-Protestant and that it was only a matter of time before it produced another 'Harry the Eighth' who would suppress Piedmont's convents and monasteries.[44] Irish Protestants, then, were encouraged to view the war as a struggle against the pretensions of Rome, whether in Ireland or abroad. Tsarist Russia was, of course, easily portrayed as a crypto-Papist state, hostile to Protestantism in both Russia and Britain.[45]

This survey of the Irish *supporters* of the war effort shows that the picture of a country united behind Britain was a false one. As we have seen, although the lay and clerical leaders of the Protestant and Catholic communities supported the British war effort, they did so for contradictory reasons. Public discourse on the war – at least as it is reflected in the form of newspaper editorials and coverage – reveals a strong and antagonistic confessional trend in how the war was presented to the Irish public. Certainly Catholics and Protestants were encouraged to perceive the conflict in the terms constructed by clerics, journalists and newspaper editors in their respective communities, but would it be accurate to claim that the large-scale Irish participation in the Crimean War was a result of appeals from pulpits and newspapers? Probably all that can be stated with certainty is that these emotive appeals provided a boost to Irish enlistment in the British armed forces in the mid-1850s, but the evidence of the mainly plebeian origins of Irish recruits in this period suggests that, for most volunteers, social and economic motives were probably the most important factors.[46] E.M. Spiers' description of the motives for Irish enlistment in the British (and other) armies in the nineteenth century gives a good idea of the many reasons for Irishmen's volunteering for service in the Crimean War:

> Their military participation, like their emigration overseas, reflected elements of 'push' and 'pull': the 'push' coming from attempts to escape the poverty, the lack of prospects and the restricted confines of life in Ireland; the 'pull' deriving from the attractions of regular army pay and provisions, the sense of community and comradeship in regimental life, and the appeal of action and adventure, often in distant locations.[47]

These 'push' and 'pull' factors are not unlike the factors which Alan Ramsay Skelley has identified as the motives prompting British men to enlist in the British army from the late 1850s onwards.[48] W.J. O'Neill Daunt gave a rather jaundiced account of how successful these factors were for British army recruiters in Cork in 1854. He noted that 'starvation is a good recruiting sergeant, and many poor fellows enlist to escape from the hunger to which misgovernment consigns them in their own fertile land'.[49] No doubt poor employment prospects also account for the fact that a Tipperary labourer named Hallinan had ten sons serving in the British army during the Crimean War.[50] Although few were compelled to join the British army against their will, apart from those who were convicted of crimes and offered the choice of enlistment as an alternative to imprisonment,[51] it is simplistic to suggest that all those Irishmen who volunteered in the British army during the Crimean War did so from motives of loyalty to the Crown. While many, including Catholics, did join from loyalist motives,[52] there was such a wide variety of motives for joining the British army that it seems unreasonable to reach the conclusion that Irishmen were making a political statement of loyalty merely by enlisting in that army, either during the Crimean War or at any other period.[53]

As the preceding discussion shows, beneath the apparent unanimity of support for the war there were many rifts in Irish public opinion and diverse motives for supporting the war. This picture of a fragmented society is made even more apparent when one examines Irish opposition to the war. Those who opposed Irish participation in the conflict, though a minority of the population, should not be omitted from an examination of the Crimean War and Irish public opinion. There were two main groups of opponents to the war: the Irish Quakers and Irish republicans. The Quakers, although only a tiny fragment of Ireland's population, were nevertheless vocal in their opposition to the Crimean conflict and were, indeed, the only Christian denomination to oppose the war on pacifist principles.[54] Republican opponents of the war were much more numerous than the Quaker opponents, but their hopes that England's difficulty in the Crimea would prove to be Ireland's opportunity to overthrow British rule were shattered as a result of the indifferent or hostile reception to anti-war sentiment in Ireland. Indeed, the *Belfast Newsletter*, an inveterate opponent of Irish nationalism and especially Irish republicanism, even went so far as to publish the text of the appeal of the New York-based John Mitchel for a rebellion in Ireland while Britain was distracted by the war with Russia, so sure was it that Mitchel's appeal would fall on deaf ears. The *Newsletter*'s editorial on Mitchel's appeal stated that

> the vast mass of the people . . . is essentially loyal, whether Roman Catholic or Protestant, Conservative or Liberal. The ghastly phantoms which Mitchel summons forth from the famine years no longer appeal to the hearts of the people. The country, so long in a transition state, is beginning to shine out in a clear and distinct perspective of prosperity; and the prophet of mischief, who only recalls the melancholy past, has no honour among the people.[55]

The *Newsletter* exaggerated the extent of the antipathy towards Mitchel's viewpoint. There was some public display of republican hostility toward Ireland's fighting on Britain's side, as evidenced by the posting of anti-recruiting placards and posters in some parts of the country, a few seditious public meetings in Cork city and the short-lived *Tribune* newspaper edited by the future Fenian leader, Thomas Clarke Luby, in which Luby expressed the hope that the Crimean War would lead to the fatal weakening of Britain's grip on Ireland.[56] Nevertheless, republican opponents of Irish participation in the war were unrepresentative of Irish public opinion; hence the despairing verdict in the memoirs of the future Fenian leader, Jeremiah O'Donovan Rossa, when he recalled the period of the Crimean War: 'The Irish National Cause was dead or asleep those times.'[57] Despite the fact that republican opponents of the war were in the minority, their stance against Irish participation in the conflict on Britain's side shows that not all of Catholic Ireland (most republicans were Catholics) went along with the pro-war stand of the Catholic Church and of most nationalist newspapers. In conclusion, it is fair to say the Irish public's response to the Crimean War was much more complex than that suggested by the author of 'The Islemen of the West'. This varied response throws important light on the deep divisions within Irish society and on the complexities of Irish identity in the mid-1850s.

Notes

1 *Londonderry Journal* (15/11/1854).

2 For some examples see Cecil Woodham-Smith, *The Great Hunger: Ireland 1845–9* (London, Four Square, 1962), p. 410; Donal McCartney, *The Dawning of Democracy: Ireland 1800–1870* (Dublin, Helicon, 1987), pp. 173–4; John Newsinger, *Fenianism in Mid-Victorian Britain* (London, Pluto, 1994), p. 21.

3 H.J. Hanham, 'Religion and Nationality in the Mid-Victorian Army', in M.R.D. Foot (ed.), *War and Society: Essays in Honour and Memory of J.R.Western 1928–1971* (London, Paul Elek, 1973), pp. 161, 176.

4 Hanham, 'Religion and Nationality', p. 162; E.M. Spiers, 'Army Organisation and Society in the Nineteenth Society' in Thomas Bartlett & Keith Jeffery (eds), *A Military History of Ireland* (Cambridge University Press, 1996), pp. 336–7.

5 Hanham, 'Religion and Nationality', p. 162.

6 There are accounts of these regiments' Crimean campaigns in Lieutenant Colonel Nataniel Steevens, *The Crimean Campaign and the Connaught Rangers, 1854–55–56* (London, Griffith and Farran, 1878); Captain Rowland Brinckman, *Historical Record of the Eighty-Ninth Princess Charlotte's Regiment* (Chatham, Gale and Polden, 1888), pp. 110–11; G. le M. Grettan, *The Campaigns and History of the Royal Irish Regiment from 1684 to 1902* (Edinburgh and London, William Blackwood, 1911), pp. 182–3; Henry Harris, *The Royal Irish Fusiliers (The 87th and 89th Regiments of Foot)* (London, Leo Cooper, 1972), p. 62; Marcus Cunliffe, *The Royal Irish Fusiliers 1793–1950* (London, Oxford University Press, 1952), pp. 209–16.

7 T. Gowing, *A Soldier's Experience or a Voice from the Ranks: Showing the Cost of War in Blood and Treasure* (Nottingham, Thomas Forman, 1899), p. 126.

8 E.S. Jackson, *The Inniskilling Dragoons: The Records of an Old Heavy Cavalry Regiment* (London, Arthur L. Humphreys, 1909), pp. 157–8, 178; J.J.W. Murphy, 'Three Irish Cavalry Regiments at Balaklava', *Irish Sword*, iv (1959–60), 182–90.

9 The Revd Robert H. Murphy, *The History of the VIII King's Royal Irish Hussars* (2 vols, Cambridge, W. Heffer, 1928), vol. 2, pp. 423–4, 433.

10 Public Record Office of Northern Ireland, D.2133, box 3; undated *Newry Examiner* extract in *Cork Examiner* (10/10/1855).

11 Undated *Newry Examiner* extract in *Cork Examiner* (10/10/1855).

12 *Galway Express* (13/05/1854); *The Times* (London) (14/11/1854); *Londonderry Standard* (31/01/1855); Sister Evelyn Bolster, *The Sisters of Mercy in the Crimean War* (Cork, Mercier Press, 1964), p. 211.

13 Undated extract from *Morning Herald* in *Freeman's Journal* (Dublin) (4/04/1855).

14 *Cork Examiner* (1/01/1855); *Freeman's Journal* (Dublin) (7/08/1855). For a recent account of the Irish Sisters of Mercy in the Crimea see Mary Ellen Doona, 'Isabella Croke: A Nurse for the Catholic Cause during the Crimean War', in Margaret Kelleher & James H. Murphy (eds), *Gender Perspectives in Nineteenth-Century Ireland: Public and Private Spheres* (Dublin, Irish Academic Press, 1997), pp. 148–56.

15 See, for instance, *Cork Examiner* (10/10/1855).

16 Bolster, *Sisters of Mercy*, p. 35.

17 Peter Karsten, 'Irish Soldiers in the British Army, 1792–1922: Suborned or Subordinate?', *Journal of Social History*, 36 (Autumn 1983), 31–64, p. 36; K. Theodore Hoppen, *Elections, Politics and Society in Ireland, 1832–85* (Oxford, Clarendon Press, 1984), p. 413.

18 The topic of Ireland's role in and attitude toward the British Empire is one of the great neglected areas of Irish historiography. A recent volume of essays edited by Keith Jeffery, *'An Irish Empire'? Aspects of Ireland and the British Empire* (Manchester University Press, 1996), goes a considerable way toward redressing this neglect.

19 For some examples of Irish support for the Patriotic Fund see *Londonderry Journal* (1, 8/11/1854); *Freeman's Journal* (Dublin) (1, 4, 17/11/1854).

20 Michael Joseph Barry, *Lays of the War* (London, Longman, 1855); *Belfast Newsletter* (15/01/1855); W.E. Vaughan (ed.), *A New History of Ireland. V: Ireland under the Union, I: 1801–70* (Oxford, Clarendon Press, 1989), plate 20.

21 *Galway Express* (26/08/1854 & 9/09/1854).

22 *Cork Examiner* (7/01/1856); *Freeman's Journal* (Dublin) (25/01/1856); *Belfast Newsletter* (27/05/1856); *National Banquet Given to the Victorious Soldiers Returned from the Crimean War and Stationed in Irish Garrisons, by the People of Ireland, in the City of Dublin, October 22, 1856* (Dublin, Alexander Thom, 1858).

23 *Cork Examiner* (25/05/1855).

24 For an account of the 'painful excitement' which gripped Dublin on the arrival of news of the battle of Balaklava, see *The Times* (London) (14/11/1854).

25 The first Irish serviceman to be fêted during the Crimean War was Captain James Armar Butler of Kilkenny, who died on 20 June 1854 while marshalling the Turkish defence of Silistria. Butler had the dubious distinction of being the first British soldier in the Crimean War to die as a result of Russian action. Other notable Irish 'firsts' in the Crimean War included the first soldier and sailor, respectively, to win the Victoria Cross. An Armagh man, Lieutenant Charles Dawson Lucas of HMS *Hecla*, was the first British serviceman to win the Victoria Cross. He was awarded the medal for throwing a live Russian shell overboard during the naval bombardment of the Bomarsund battery. The first soldier to win the Victoria Cross was Sergeant Luke O'Connor of the 23rd Foot. O'Connor, a native of Roscommon, won the medal for his actions at the Alma and Redan, in September 1854 and September 1855 respectively. See George Ryan, *Our Heroes of the Crimea: being Historical Sketches of Our Military Officers, from the General Commanding-in-Chief to the Subaltern* (London, George Routledge, 1855), pp. 141–3; Anon., *The Victoria Cross* (London, O'Byrne Brothers, 1865), pp. 46, 83–4.

26 See, for example, the letter of Sergeant Michael Flattery of Clare, serving in the 88th Regiment, to his father, in *Daily Express* (Dublin) (12/01/1855) and the letters of Corporal Michael O'Connor of Cork, serving in the 47th Regiment, to his father, in *Freeman's Journal* (Dublin) (9/02/1855) and *Galway Express* (24/02/1855).

27 See, for example, the letter of R.A. Johnson of the 8th Hussars to his mother in *Cork Examiner* (17/01/1855) and the letter of Privates Philip and William Flynn of Mallow, serving in the 77th Regiment, to their mother in *Cork Examiner* (7/02/1855)

28 *Freeman's Journal* (Dublin) (24/11/1854); *Belfast Newsletter* (30/05/1856)

29 *Freeman's Journal* (Dublin) (13/01/1855).

30 *Illustrated London News* (11/11/1854); *Cork Examiner* (24/01/1855); *Dundalk Democrat* (14/04/1855); *Freeman's Journal* (Dublin) (29/05 & 27/06/1855).

31 *Daily Express* (Dublin) (10/07/1854); *Belfast Newsletter* (15/01/1855); *Freeman's Journal* (Dublin) (7/06/1855); James S. Donnelly jr, *The Land and the People of Nineteenth-Century Cork – the Rural Economy and the Land Question* (London and New York, Routledge and Kegan Paul, 1987 edn), p. 81; Jonathan Bardon, *A History of Ulster* (Belfast, Blackstaff Press, 1992), p. 318.

32 It should be stressed here that there was much more hostility among the emigrant Irish, particularly in the United States of America, toward Irish participation in the Crimean War than there was among those Irish who did not emigrate.

33 Ryan, *Heroes of the Crimea*, pp. 86–8; E.H. Nolan, *The Illustrated History of the War against Russia* (2 vols, London, James S. Virtue, 1857), vol. 1, p. 226.

34 R.V. Comerford, 'Ireland 1850–70: Post-Famine and Mid-Victorian' in Vaughan (ed.), *New History of Ireland*, p. 381.

35 Strictly speaking, the land question should not be seen as a religious question. Nevertheless, in his pastoral message of February 1855 Bishop John Cantwell of Meath listed the lack of Tenant Right as one of the Catholic grievances which would be remedied as a result of the sacrifices of Catholic Ireland and France in the war. See *Cork Examiner* (16/02/1855).

36 For a discussion of the increasing confessional rivalry between Irish Catholics and Protestants in the 1850s, and of Catholics' desire for redress of their grievances within the Union, see Comerford, 'Ireland 1850–70', pp. 385–8 and D. George Boyce, *Nineteenth-Century Ireland: The Search for Stability* (Dublin, Gill and Macmillan, 1990), pp. 124–32.

37 *Cork Examiner* (1/01 & 4 /06/ & 17/10/1855); *Freeman's Journal* (Dublin) (1, 4, 17/11/1854 & 25/01/1855).

38 *Cork Examiner* (19/02/1855); Bishop Patrick Francis Moran (ed.), *The Pastoral Letters and Other Writings of Cardinal Cullen, Archbishop of Dublin* (3 vols, Dublin, Browne and Nolan, 1882), vol. 1, pp. 300–1; John Devoy, *Recollections of an Irish Rebel* (New York, Charles P. Young, 1929; repr. Shannon, Irish University Press, 1969), p. 347.

39 The text of the ballad, 'A New Song on the Russian War!!', is in Vaughan (ed.), *New History of Ireland*, plate 20.

40 For further discussion of the distinctive Irish Catholic political-religious view of the world in the late nineteenth century and in the 1930s see Mary Kenny, *Goodbye to Catholic Ireland* (London, Sinclair-Stevenson, 1997), pp. xiv–xv and also Roisín Higgins' contribution to this volume.

41 *Freeman's Journal* (3/05/1855).

42 *Belfast Newsletter* (10/01/1855); The Revd S.J. Moore, *A Contribution to the Patriotic Fund; or, the Necessity of the Present War with Russia, and Our Duties with Regard to it* (Belfast, Shepherd and Atchison, 1855).

43 Moore, *Patriotic Fund, passim*.

44 *Belfast Newsletter* (19/01/1855). The description of the inhabitants of the convents and monasteries was that of '40,000 bachelors and virgins . . . black locusts, male and female, before whose ceaseless circuit every green thing on the face of nature, and every fresh germ in the heart of man, vanish as though under the scorching breath of a sultry summer's blight'.

45 Moore, *Patriotic Fund*, *passim*. On 15 October 1856 the Protestant *Belfast Newsletter* announced that an Irish Protestant soldier, Sergeant Philip O'Flaherty, was to return to Turkey as a Free Church missionary. O'Flaherty's decision is a telling testimony to the religious slant which the *Newsletter*, and other Protestant sources, placed on the issues at stake in the Crimean War.

46 David Fitzpatrick makes the telling observation that soldiering was 'often the occupation of last resort for Irish townsmen without regular employment.' See David Fitzpatrick, '"A Peculiar Tramping People": The Irish in Britain, 1801–70', in Vaughan (ed.), *New History of Ireland*, p. 641.

47 Spiers, 'Army Organization', pp. 356–7.

48 Alan Ramsay Skelley, *The Victorian Army at Home: The Recruitment and Terms and Conditions of the British Regular, 1859–1899* (London, Croom Helm, 1977), pp. 247–9.

49 National Library of Ireland, MS 3041, journal of W.J. O'Neill Daunt (24/02/ & 14/04/1854).

50 Undated extract from *Tipperary Free Press* in *Londonderry Journal* (17/10/1855). For more on the economic motivation for Irish enlistment in the British army in the late nineteenth and early twentieth centuries, see Keith Jeffery, 'The Irish Military Tradition and the British Empire', in Jeffery (ed.), *An Irish Empire?*, pp. 97, 103, 118.

51 For some examples of these reluctant 'volunteers' see *Daily Express* (Dublin) (5/01/1855) and *Cork Examiner* (12/02 & 27/07/1855).

52 Karsten, 'Irish Soldiers in British Army', *passim*.

53 For a different point of view, see D.H. Akenson, *The Irish Diaspora: A Primer* (Toronto, P.D. Meaney, and Belfast, Institute of Irish Studies, 1993), pp. 143–5. David Taylor's examination in this volume of the experiences of one Catholic Irishman in the British army, Patrick Macgill, shows how difficult it is to generalize about Catholics' motivations for enlistment.

54 *Belfast Newsletter* (4/04/1855); *Freeman's Journal* (4/05 & 8/08/1855); Samuel Haughton, *Memoir of James Haughton* (Dublin, E. Ponsonby, 1877), pp. 122–4.

55 *Belfast Newsletter* (14/04/1854).

56 *Belfast Newsletter* (17/01/1855); *Cork Examiner* (27, 30/04 & 4/05/1855); *Tribune* (Dublin) (3, 10, 24/11/1855).

57 Jeremiah O'Donovan Rossa, *Rossa's Recollections, 1838 to 1898* (Mariner's Harbor, New York, privately published by the author, 1898), p. 210.

8

THE SPANISH-AMERICAN WAR AND
AMERICAN NATIONAL IDENTITY

I. Donald

The Spanish-American War of 1898 was fought ostensibly to free Cuba from the colonial rule of Spain. The causes of the war have been ascribed to a variety of factors including territorial aggrandizement, commercial expansionism, naval strategy and manifest destiny.[1] Widespread popular support for Cuban independence throughout the United States critically motivated the American intervention. American public opinion, encouraged by the liberal reporting of Spanish atrocities on the island by the sensational press, was further enraged by the De Lomé letter affair and the mysterious sinking of the United States battleship *Maine* while on a courtesy call to Havana. After this latter incident President McKinley could ill afford to oppose popular feeling against the Spanish.

During the course of the war the United States annexed Hawaii and at the resultant peace treaty gained the Philippines, Puerto Rico and Guam from Spain. Cuba became an American protectorate until it found a stable government. The war affected America in several different ways, raising questions of how Americans perceived their founding principles, what it meant for national identity and how their role in world politics should now be directed.

A problem that inevitably arises when discussing 'national identity' is devising a definition that is broad enough to ensure a cohesive discussion of the topic, while, at the same time, providing parameters so as to limit its scope.[2] American national identity is difficult to define because it cannot be based, as in the case of older and more homogeneous nations, on the obvious criteria of common language, race, ethnicity, religion, or cultural uniformity.[3] The development of a sense of national identity was both helped and hindered by various factors. The fact that the United States was founded and fostered by immigration created not only a sense of a new beginning away from the Old World but also problems of assimilation. Was it possible for immigrants to overcome rivalries and antagonisms from the Old World, in order to forge a new nation? Later immigrants were faced with either assimilating to an existing identity that was still derived from the colonial relationship with Great Britain or addressing the problems of dual cultural loyalties. These hyphenated identities often constrained the feeling of a new national identity further restricted by the geographic scale of the country – how could the New England mixed farming states relate to the Southern plantation mentality, and how could either relate to the people who flooded westwards? In part the Americans' sense of identity remained regional or local. It manifested itself in the strong feelings of state loyalty which were often more resolute than any feeling of national loyalty. Such divisions led to the war between the North and South from 1861 to 1865. The effects of the Civil War and reconstruction left the nation united in theory but still deeply divided in practice. As the nation expanded in both population and territory, the problems were compounded. The idea of an American national identity had to be superimposed rather than forged. Thus American identity related to the political sphere and principles of liberty, equality, democracy and human rights. These principles were embodied in the Declaration of Independence, the Constitution and Bill of Rights, Washington's Farewell Address, Lincoln's Gettysburg Address and other speeches, addresses and documents. America was portrayed as one sovereign people, a homogenized nation bound together in love of liberty and equality. The unity of the people was symbolized by the flag or 'Old Glory', with its design of stars and stripes representing the founding colonies and each new State. The Constitution and Bill of Rights were applicable to all. The adoption of the motto *E pluribus unum* on the Great Seal of the United States after the Revolution, served to represent not only the political union of the thirteen former colonies but also the acceptance of the diverse ethnic makeup and emergence of common nationality in America.

In the 1890s, the existing ethnic mix and changing patterns of immigration meant the concept of national identity was hard for many Americans to perceive. The factors that seemed to be bringing the nation closer together could also be regarded as divisive. The winning of the west, the closure of the frontier[4] and the growth of transcontinental railroads and communications bound the nation together physically, but also seemed to bring to an end the perceived opportunities that the frontier had held and emphasized the regional differences that existed. Increased industrialization, agrarian production, bureaucratization and urban growth produced common experiences in the long term but any benefits were masked in the short term by the 1893 depression.[5] Richard Hofstader has referred to this as 'the psychic crisis of the 1890s'.[6] The bitter labour struggles such as the Homestead and Pullmann strikes, the widespread support for the populist movement and the expansion of the trusts all seemed to threaten the fragile makeup of the nation.

The concept of national identity remained open to contest. Some people attempted to apply the criteria of language, race, ethnicity, religion and cultural uniformity to the United States. In 1891 John W. Burgess argued that 'national unity was the determining force in the development of the modern constitutional states. The prime policy, therefore, of each of these states should be to attain proper physical boundaries and to render its population ethnically homogenous.'[7] Such views gained considerable prominence and the image of America as a White, Anglo-Saxon, English-speaking and Protestant nation was encouraged. As the pattern of immigration changed in the 1890s, some Americans sought to exaggerate the Anglo-Saxon ties to northern Europe, while at the same time encouraging the exclusion of races perceived as less desirable. Other contemporary commentators preferred to dismiss the idea of common blood ties. Frederick Jackson Turner, who published his famous frontier thesis in 1893, stressed the importance of environment over heritage.[8] Yet others preferred to emphasize the idea of America as the great melting pot. Lyman Abbott, editor of *The Outlook*, speaking in March 1898 asked, 'What is America? Anglo-Saxon? Hardly. It is German, it is French, it is Italian, it is Hungarian, it is Polish, in some localities it is preeminently Irish; it is every nation on the face of the globe.'[9]

As American identity was woven from the principles of liberty, equality, support for self-determination and self-government, the nation naturally sympathized with the cause of the Cuban insurrectionists. The United States was overwhelmingly motivated by humanitarian concern, but in support of a republican cause. Americans were genuinely horrified by the Spanish policies on the island, especially the reconcentration policy which General Weyler initiated in 1896. This policy required the populace to move to locations under Spanish military jurisdiction and aimed to deny aid that the populace could provide to the insurgents. Reconcentration was misconceived and badly administered, and the Spanish were faced with feeding thousands of civilians who otherwise would have been tending the fields themselves. The problem increased as the insurgents burned the crops of those fields still being farmed. The result was starvation for those in the camps. As the policy struck directly at civilians and only indirectly at the insurgents the outcry in the United States was particularly vehement.[10]

The humanitarian outrage was fostered by the press and ensured popular sympathy for the Cuban cause and support for American intervention. The only other war to come close to being as popular as the Spanish-American War in American history was the Second World War. America was fighting for a 'just cause', the horrors of the Civil War were to the majority a distant memory and it was not until the First World War that Americans would be 'baptised in blood' to such a degree that it would scar the nation again. As Frank Freidel has stated, the 'Spanish-American War, lasting only a hundred days, was too brief and too successful to become unpopular'.[11]

The reasons given at the time for American intervention in Cuba were very specific. At the start of 1898 the *Literary Digest*, which surveyed American and world press comment, stated 'as a rule the Cuban policy of the United States is looked upon abroad as inspired by jingoism, unjustifiable desire for aggrandisement, and a want of knowledge of the condition of the island. Occasionally, however, we run across an article in which our attitude is explained satisfactorily.' The *Digest* continues, 'The *Boersen Zeitung*, Berlin, explains that we could not, from a strictly business point of view, preserve strict neutrality. Our industry, our trade, our shipping are too closely bound up with the Pearl of the Antilles.'[12] This cynical view was atypical and quickly ignored in favour of more noble reasons a month or two later. In a similar vein arguments in favour of a war to avenge the *Maine* or for territorial aggrandizement were played down in favour of intervention on the grand principles of liberty, humanity, democracy and Christian duty.

The demand for intervention on the grounds of liberty and humanity was combined with the belief that Cuba would become the newest addition to democracy and republicanism. A typical report from the Atlanta *Constitution*, after the destruction of the *Maine*, asserted 'Humanity demands, not that the United States shall declare war as the result of an incident which can not by any possibility be traced officially to Spain, but that the great republic shall put an end to Spanish butchery in Cuba and aid in setting that island on its feet as an independent republic.'[13] In Congress, Republican Senator Redfield Proctor of Vermont reported to the Senate on 17 March 1898 the conditions he had witnessed in a recent trip to Cuba. The speech is widely believed to have turned the opinion of the more cautious members of Congress towards intervention. Proctor concluded,

> I have endeavoured to state in not intemperate mood what I saw and heard and to make no argument thereon, but leave every one to draw his own conclusions. To me the strongest appeal is not the barbarity practised by Weyler nor the loss of the *Maine*, if our worst fears should prove true, terrible as are both these incidents, but the spectacle of 1,500,000 people, the entire native population of Cuba, struggling for freedom and deliverance from the worst misgovernment of which I ever had knowledge.[14]

This support was shown by many diverse groups, including, for example, the United Mine Workers, one of the largest trade unions of the time, which hoped that

> the lengthy arms of Uncle Sam, will be stretched across the Florida straits, extending aid, LIBERTY and INDEPENDENCE, to the starving, struggling, fighting, freedom loving Cubans, so that the flag of 'CUBAN LIBRE' will become a permanent fixture in the bright constellation of Republics in the western hemisphere.[15]

American sympathy for the Cuban cause and aversion to Spanish policies, so effectively encouraged by the Cuban lobby in New York and the popular press,[16] was further outlined by President McKinley. A diplomatic exchange between the representatives of Great Britain, France, Germany, Russia, Austria-Hungary and Italy and the President at the Executive Mansion was presented to the American public in the terms, 'We hope for humanity's sake you will not go to war.' McKinley was reported to have replied, 'We hope, if we do, you will understand it is for humanity's sake.'[17] This was repeated in his special message to Congress on 11 April 1898 which summarized the need for American intervention in Cuba. Intervention was necessary for 'the cause of humanity and to put an end to the barbarities, bloodshed, starvation, and horrible miseries now existing there'.[18]

Members of the clergy were quick to help the President define and justify intervention. Understandably they emphasized the Christian duty of the nation in pursuing such a course of action, as well as liberty and humanity. The minister and author, Henry Van Dyke, portrayed the conflict as Good against Evil: 'The forces that have led to this conflict are far deeper than politics or commerce. They are in fact the primal forces of society; the elements that contend forever in the mighty strife between light and darkness . . . the love of liberty against the pride of power; the passion of humanity against the interests of ancient oppression.'[19] The Unitarian minister, Samuel Burns Weston, who was also the editor and publisher of the *International Journal of Ethics*, stated, 'with Spanish inhumanity at our very door and in our constant sight, we are irresistibly compelled to concern ourselves. It was our special duty to put an end to it, as it was the special duty of the Christian nations of Europe to interfere and put an end to the Armenian atrocities, but which, to their everlasting disgrace, they neglected.'[20] Weston was not alone in comparing the Cuban situation to the Armenian atrocities committed by the Turks a few years earlier. The fear that inaction would result in similar bloodshed in Cuba and that the responsibility would fall to the United States encouraged intervention. It is ironic that Americans regarded Spanish colonial rule as barbaric and cruel and as a remaining evil of the Old World but they often failed to see the similarities with their own internal problems, especially in their attitudes towards Black Americans and Native Americans.

Spanish tyranny was consistently viewed in the same way as the colonies viewed Great Britain in 1776. Weston commented that

the conflict which has been going on in that island between those aspiring for freedom and those determined upon despotism and oppression is by its very nature an irrepressible one. . . . I cannot see how any one that believes in the Revolution of 1775 and in the principles of the Declaration of Independence, can fail to sympathise with the Cuban cause.[21]

William R. Huntington, a member of the clergy in New York, argued that 'the Cubans have stronger reasons for their revolt against Spain than our colonies had for revolting against England'.[22] Historical analogies were employed to appeal to patriotism and to remind the nation of its own struggle for freedom. The majority of Americans believed they were fighting a just war, as they had in 1776, 1812, and in 1861. It was essential for the war to be seen as a just cause, because association with 'ignoble motives' were far more suited, so Americans thought, to the power politics of the Old World.[23]

The war was deliberately portrayed in the terms of a conflict for traditional American ideals in order to foster a greater sense of loyalty and unity. Congressmen were quick to emphasize the loyalty of their own States and especially where loyalty may have been questioned because of ethnicity, language or religion. Harvey Butler

Fergusson, the delegate representing New Mexico Territory, reminded Congress that he represented 'a people largely Spanish in descent', but challenged any other State in the Union 'to furnish, in proportion to population, more or braver or more loyal soldiers than . . . New Mexico'. At the end of his speech Fergusson duly concluded that 'This is a composite nation, composed of people of German descent, of English, Scotch, Irish, Italian, and Spanish descent, and, in my judgement, no portion of our patriotic population of whatever descent, can surpass the people that I represent in devotion to the flag of this great nation.'[24] Similarly, John F. Fitzgerald of Massachusetts spoke up for American Catholics. In response to press articles and editorials which reported that as Spain was a Catholic country then a large proportion of the Catholic people in the United States would refuse to take up arms against the Spanish government or be otherwise disloyal, Fitzgerald stated,

> I know I voice the sentiments of the members of that grand old faith when I say that if war does come, no more valiant, brave, and heroic defenders of the national honor . . . will be found than the members of the Catholic Church. . . . The identity of the Catholic and Protestant, Jew and Gentile, is swallowed up in the single term America.[25]

Congressmen representing areas with very different ethnic compositions used strikingly similar language. There was the need to vouch loyalty and then to dissolve any doubts by reflecting on the meaning of America. President McKinley was presented with assurances from various immigrant groups. Charles G. Dawes noted in his journal that on 6 July, he 'went with the committee of German-Americans to the White House and introduced them to the President, where they tendered a regiment of German-Americans to him as an evidence of the loyalty of these citizens'.[26]

The strongest demonstrations of loyalty and unity of the nation were given by the South. The Spanish-American War allowed the defeat of the Confederacy to be forgotten. The generation of men who fought in 1898 could hardly remember the horrors of the Civil War; they were more familiar with the literature which glamorized war. Nevertheless, not all psychological scars from the Civil War had healed. Bitter memories still remained, especially of General Sherman's 'March to the Sea'; however, the Spanish-American War came to represent a reconciled Union.[27] The South was eager to pledge its loyalty to the Stars and Stripes and the press in the major Southern cities was quick to pick up on this. On 9 March the Atlanta *Constitution* asserted,

> There still lingers in the country on both sides of the old line some slight touch of sectionalism, but when the order to march against Spain is given, the last vestige of sectionalism will disappear from the land and mutual brotherhood will once again assert itself under the folds of the star spangled banner.[28]

The Richmond *Times* remarked that,

> It will be a case of 'the country, whether right or wrong, the country'. And the
> nation may turn its eyes with perfect confidence to the south. Upon any
> battlefield of the war the confederate veterans and their sons will be seen
> upholding the national honor and guarding the country's safety with all the
> steadiness and resolution that characterized them in the early sixties.[29]

The surge of enthusiasm and patriotism led to many offers in the South from
Confederate veterans to enlist in a war against Spain, ignoring the fact that many
were past the suitable age requirements.[30] The South was also keen to prove that
it was equal in every way to the North. The New Orleans *Times-Picayune* stated,
'it is an assured fact that the men of this southland will be equal to every demand
upon their devotion to the union and the honour of the nation.'[31]

In Congress, Southern Senators and Representatives, the majority of whom
were Democrats, voted down the line with McKinley's Republican administration.
During the debate regarding the Defence Appropriation Bill, requesting the
appropriation of $50 million for national defence and presented before Congress
on 8 March 1898, there were strong assurances of the South's loyalty to the
Union. Representative John T. Allen of Mississippi reminded Congress that,

> The people of the South probably know more what actual war means than
> any other section of this country. . . . But they stand ready to honour any draft
> upon their resources either in money, men, sacrifice, and patriotism to uphold
> the glory of the American flag and to make our country what it should be in
> the eyes of the world.[32]

Thomas C. McCrae of Arkansas regarded the occasion as the most important in
the nation's history since the Civil War: 'It is an occasion when patriotism should
and I daresay will, obscure sectionalism and partisanship. It is an occasion when
Americanism should assert itself in behalf of the defence of American honor.'[33]
Albert S. Berry of Kentucky asked Congress to rejoice, 'should war come it will
not be brother against brother, but a united country against a foreign foe.'[34]
Western and Northern Congressmen also recognized the spirit of reconciliation
and unity. John C. Bell of Colorado joined other Congressman in stating that,
'we have no North, no South, no East, no West, but an indivisible nation'.[35] The
reassurances of national unity were tied to the cause America was fighting.
Representative James T. Mann of Maine remarked that, 'the noblest and most
inspiring example of history is President McKinley holding aloft the Stars and
Stripes over an undivided North and South . . . for the sake of humanity'.[36]
Charles G. Dawes forwarded resolutions for presentation to the Republican State
Convention of Illinois which included the words, 'We believe that the present war

with Spain is in a righteous and just cause. We rejoice that the American people are a unit in sustaining the Government and that the Spirit of patriotism has swept away the last vestige of sectional feeling.'[37]

Several individuals symbolized the reunification of North and South. Ex-Confederate Fitzhugh Lee, who was the American Consul in Havana in the period leading up to the outbreak of war, returned to a hero's welcome. On 26 March 1898, The Milwaukee *Journal* even had a headline calling for Lee to run for President.[38] On his conduct *Leslie's Weekly* stated, 'He had simply done his duty as a brave, loyal and patriotic American Citizen. He had shown his profound love for his country, its institutions, and above all, its flag.'[39] It then went on to comment that the South was the home of the best American patriotism. The Richmond *Dispatch* accurately remarked that 'Lee is just now not only the idol of the South but of the whole country'.[40] The New Orleans *Times-Picayune* stated, 'The splendid course of General Lee at Havana will forever remove the prejudice which has heretofore existed against the employment of Confederate soldiers in the public service.'[41] The feeling of unity was further enhanced when President McKinley, for political reasons, commissioned Lee and another ex-Confederate, Senator Joseph Wheeler of Alabama, as Major Generals of the volunteer units.

A more powerful symbol of the reunification of North and South was the war's first official death on 11 May 1898. The victim was a young Ensign from North Carolina, Worth Bagley. Despite the fact that four other sailors died with Bagley when their torpedo boat *Winslow* was hit by fire from the Spanish shore batteries in Cuba, it was Bagley who became a martyr.[42] *Leslie's Weekly* commented that Bagley 'has once more made "Old Glory" the flag of us all'.[43] Southern heroes fighting for the stars and stripes demonstrated the new feeling of sectional reconciliation to the American people. Less than a month later the American navy attempted to block the Spanish fleet in the harbour of Santiago de Cuba by sinking the collier *Merrimac*. The operation failed, but the officer in charge, Lieutenant Richmond P. Hobson of Alabama, became the next great hero of the war. One New York journal enviously remarked, 'The South is having its share of the heroes in the present war.'[44]

The old rivalries were not completely forgotten. The Richmond *Dispatch* reported on 8 March, the same day that Congress experienced the overwhelming support of Southern Congressmen for the Defence Appropriation Bill, that the former Confederate General Bradley T. Johnson had declared he 'did not wish to see the South enter into any such war. It was no fight of ours.'[45] Some Northerners argued that as Southerners were more used to the climate they were more fit to make up the bulk of the volunteer regiments.[46] Some Southerners responded that they should remain on their shores, as it was the Southern States that would most likely come under bombardment from Spanish fleets. In March the Chattanooga *Times* praised the cautious attitude of the government and the South:

More especially would the south be slow about crying 'war', when the brunt of any attack must fall on her, as it would if we fought with Spain, over Cuba. The southern coast, illy defended as it is, would be attacked by Spanish ships. Some of our cities would suffer great losses of property and some loss of life. Society would be distracted, diverted from the usual avocations. Material affairs would languish. Failures in business would be a necessary consequence. If Spain found an ally in France – and it's not very unlikely she would – we might have to repel invasion, which would be directed at the shores of the south. Our warm-blooded young men would be sacrificed in thousands, and what, pray, would be the compensation for all these losses, supposing we won the fight in a half year? 'Free Cuba', you answer?[47]

When war came, however, Southern towns welcomed with open arms the same regiments that had invaded the South during the Civil War.[48] Together with the renewed feeling of unity, there was also a feeling of national greatness. James Marcus King, a clergyman from Pennsylvania, summarized the feeling when he commented on 15 May 1898, 'Nationality is asserting itself. . . . Sectionalism is being blotted out. . . . [W]e have served notice upon the family of Nations, that, looking this way, they must face an undivided nation.'[49]

The feeling of unity was not forgotten after the cessation of hostilities. On a visit to Atlanta, for the Peace Jubilee in December 1898, President McKinley, who had fought for the Union during the Civil War, addressed the Georgia legislature and delivered what was described at the time as an 'epoch-making' speech. In it McKinley said, 'Sectional lines no longer mar the map of the United States. Sectional feeling no longer holds back the love we bear each other. Fraternity is the national anthem.'[50] The common themes for most of the speakers at the Jubilee were peace, unity and fraternity.

The reconciliation of North and South and the general feeling of unity in America were remarkably different for Black Americans, the majority of whom argued against intervention in Cuba.[51] Most felt that the grand principles for which America was allegedly fighting ought first to be applied across the United States. As the *American Citizen*, a Black American paper published in Kansas City, commented, 'Let Uncle Sam keep hands off of other countries till he has learned to govern his own. Human life at home is at a low ebb now and should be protected before reaching out to protect others.'[52] A month later the same paper repeated, 'Let this government see that all laws are obeyed by our fire-eating southerners before going to war with Spain or any other country.'[53] The Washington *Bee* on 5 March 1898 stated that 'A government that claims to be unable to protect its own citizens against mob law and political violence will certainly not ask the negroes to take up arms against a foreign government. . . . He is as much in need for independence as Cuba is.'[54] Most of the other members of the Black press were in agreement that for Black Americans civil rights had to come first. Yet, while warning against war or annexation, most of the papers compromised their position, pledging loyalty if the government was forced to change its policy. This illustrates the dilemma of the Black American community during the Spanish-American War: they were expected to prove their loyalty to the United States by defending her interests, yet the United States could or would not protect Black Americans by ensuring them the civil rights guaranteed to other Americans.

Nevertheless, many Black Americans vowed to pledge their support should it be necessary. On 30 April, the Richmond *Planet* simply stated, 'The wisdom of [the war] is questioned. However all loyal citizens must do their duty.'[55] In May 1898 the Washington *Bee* argued that 'The Spanish American War will mark a new era for the Negro in our national history. . . . This is a fight for humanity and for liberty and as Americans let there be no division among us.'[56] The *Iowa State Bystander* stated

> The love of our country, its flag and its laws should enthuse and stimulate each of us to that higher degree of patriotism. . . . True, we may not enjoy the full blessing of our rights and there are many injustices done to the race. . . . Now in regard to us having no country to fight for, it is folly to think and absurd to speak it because this is our country by adoption and by importation as well the whites. . . . Let us be men and show loyalty and we shall be rewarded.[57]

The hypocrisy of United States policy was not lost on Black Americans. The *Afro-American Sentinel* asked, 'Does it not appear ludicrous for the United States government to be waging a war in the interest of humanity and to bring home the cessation of Spanish outrages in Cuba, when it has such a record at home?'[58]

Despite the fact that at home they faced lynchings, disenfranchisement and other examples of racial prejudice, Black Americans still organized to fight for the United States. The war was regarded as an opportunity for Black Americans to advance their rights by proving their worth as citizens of the United States. The Black press vigorously campaigned for the right to fight, and the right to be led by their own officers. The cry, 'No Officers! No Fight!',[59] coined by the Richmond *Planet*, was used throughout the war in an attempt to get Black officers above the rank of lieutenant for the four Black regular regiments and the four Black volunteer regiments. In the end only six states (North Carolina, Virginia, Ohio, Kansas, Illinois and Massachusetts) permitted Black officers above the rank of lieutenant. The issue of Black officers for Black troops led to accusations of treason from White papers but was a direct response to the question of civil rights. At the same time the Black press expressed a fear that Black troops commanded by White officers would either be used as cannon fodder or for menial duties. In the end only the four Black regular units saw action and they performed very well, much better than contemporaries expected. The Black troops were in agreement with the Black press. On 1 May, Theophilus G. Steward, Chaplain of the 25th

Infantry, a coloured unit, recorded, 'I believe this war will very greatly help the colored man of the South, and result in the further clearing of the national atmosphere.'[60] If the hope of the Black soldier was echoed in that letter, another provided a different perspective. George W. Piroleau, Chaplain of the 9th Cavalry, another Black unit, remarked upon the reception of the Black regiments in the South on their way to Cuba and commented,

> You talk about freedom, liberty etc. Why sir, the Negro of this country is freeman and yet a slave. Talk about fighting and freeing poor Cuba and of Spain's brutality; of Cuba's murdered thousands and starving reconcentradoes. Is America any better than Spain? . . . The four Negro regiments are going to help free Cuba, and they will return to their homes, some then mustered out and begin again to fight the battle of American prejudice.[61]

In spite of these hopes, the war did little in the long run to enhance the Black American's position within the United States and the initial gratitude shown to Black soldiers was tarred by accusations of cowardice, mainly as the result of comments by Theodore Roosevelt, which he only retracted in part after considerable pressure was applied and long after the damage had been done. All the same, Black Americans had rallied round the flag and, while more discerning of the true motives behind the war, they were willing to present a united front in support of the war in order to enhance their own rights after the war.

If the Spanish-American War was considered a just and righteous one and this helped to invoke a sense of unity, the war also seemed to demonstrate to Americans and the world that the nation had come of age. The success of the Spanish-American War reaffirmed the belief in national greatness. Two prominent works espousing extreme forms of nationalism had been published in 1885 – *Our Country: Its Possible Future and Its Present Crisis*, by Josiah Strong, and an essay entitled 'Manifest Destiny', by John T. Fiske. Strong, a Protestant clergyman, advocated that it was the destiny of the Anglo-Saxon to carry the ideals of civil liberty and spiritual Christianity to the remote peoples of the world. Although Strong talked about Anglo-Saxonism it was clear to him that the United States was the natural successor to Great Britain in leading the way.[62] The popular historian, John T. Fiske, argued in similar terms that 'The work which the English Race began when it colonized North America is destined to go on until every land on the earth's surface that is not already the seat of an old civilization shall become English in its language, in its religion, in its political habits and traditions, and to a prominent extent in the blood of its people.'[63] The overwhelming success of the Spanish-American War seemed to justify this rationale.

The arguments in favour of expansion on the basis of race and destiny were not new or radical but gained prominence because a number of key policy-makers adopted them. These included the naval strategist Alfred T. Mahan,

Senators Henry Cabot Lodge, Albert T. Beveridge, and the archetypal imperialist, Theodore Roosevelt. Mahan's *The Influence of Sea Power upon History, 1670–1783*, published in 1890, argued international influence and prestige rested upon naval strength. Thus the power of great nations hinged upon their ability to wage war and control the sea. Mahan argued that America required a strong navy and a more aggressive foreign policy that would expand trade and acquire colonies.[64] It was an attractive thesis for many Americans. After all, the nation had a history of expansion and with the closure of the frontier it seemed only natural to look elsewhere, but that necessitated a change in direction for the United States. Reflecting upon American foreign policy and its guiding principles during the nineteenth century in 1895, Henry Cabot Lodge argued:

> Washington withdrew us from the affairs of Europe, but at the same time he pointed out our true line of advance was to the West. He never for an instant thought that we were to remain stationary and cease to move forward. . . . We have a record of conquest, colonization, and territorial expansion unequalled by any people of the nineteenth century. . . . Small States are of the past and have no future. The modern government is all toward the concentration of people and territory into great nations and large dominions. The great nations are rapidly absorbing for their future expansion and their present defence all the waste places of the earth. It is a movement which makes for civilization and the advancement of race. As one of the great nations of the world, the United States must not fall out of the line of march.[65]

At no point did these writers assume that the United States was not already a great power. Instead it was the fear that America was not utilizing its potential and was going to lose out in the long run to the European powers that prompted them to call for a more aggressive foreign policy. Without exploring the influence that the expansionists had on bringing about the Spanish-American War, it is important to recognize the widespread support that such ideas found in 1898. Americans believed that they were a great nation, an idea best expressed by the fictional Irish-American saloon-keeper and philosopher, Mr Dooley, created by Finley Peter Dunne. In discussing the war preparations of the United States, Mr Dooley's friend, Mr Hennessy, proudly boasts, 'We're a gr-eat people'; Mr Dooley agrees and then replies, 'We ar-re that. An' th' best iv it is, we know we ar-re.'[66] Certainly in the 1890s the United States liked to consider itself as a more democratic and upright nation than those of Europe, because it was generally assumed that the nation was not party to the power politics that dictated European foreign policy.

Ironically it was the moral necessity of intervention in Cuba that was, on the one hand, to reassure American self-belief in national greatness but, on the other, to bring about the most serious debate about the nation's principles and vocation. The self-belief that Americans held in their nation was vindicated by the overwhelming defeat of Spain. It did not matter that the armed forces had been seriously under-equipped and ill-managed, because the nation had still succeeded in annihilating the Spanish fleets, capturing Santiago in Cuba and Manila in the Philippines, and forcing Spain to seek terms of peace. The downfall of Spain was regarded as a defeat of the evils of the Old World. The American ideals of liberty, equality, democracy and Christian duty had overcome the tyrannical, unjust, monarchical, militaristic, colonial and medieval Catholicism of Spain. It was thus argued that the war was itself part of American destiny. The conquest of Cuba, the Philippines, Puerto Rico and Guam were not a part of a deliberate expansionist policy; rather they were necessary military and naval manoeuvres for the United States to destroy Spain. In turn the ease of victory seemed to point to destiny and the fact that Americans were God's chosen people. Admiral George Dewey's one-sided victory at Manila Bay, where the United States fleet lost one sailor as a result of heat stroke, effectively ended Spanish rule in the Philippines and made America the master of the islands. In April 1899 Theodore Roosevelt, in a speech to the Hamilton Club, reflected on the acquisition of the Philippines as a necessary test for the nation, saying that it was only through this test that the nation 'shall ultimately win the goal of true national greatness'.[67] Similarly Albert Beveridge argued that God's hand was at work:

That [the American] flag has never paused in its onward march. Who dares halt it now – now, when history's largest events are carrying it forward; now, when we are at last one people, strong enough for any task, great enough for any glory destiny can bestow? How comes it that our first century closes with the process of consolidating the American people into a unit, just accomplished and quick upon the stroke of that great hour presses upon us our world opportunity, world duty, and world glory, which none but a people welded into an indivisible nation can achieve or perform?[68]

Beveridge was responding in part to the mass movement against imperialism, under the auspices of the Anti-Imperialist League, founded in June 1898, which gained prominence between 1898 and 1902. The League was organized initially to prevent the annexation of the Philippines, which it reasoned was against American principles. Not only did annexation run against the republican principle of consent of the governed, it was argued that this would indirectly affect liberty and equality in America. The movement attracted support from many diverse groups, in many cases from people who had supported the Spanish-American War, but ultimately it was to fail to obtain its aims, partly because of the diversity of the motives of groups that supported the movement.

The Spanish-American War was fought for the perceived traditional American values. As it was a war for just and righteous reasons it provided an opportunity for the nation to come together and overcome geographical, religious and racial divisions. Finally, the success of the war elevated American feelings of national greatness to unprecedented heights. The war seemed to prove that America could overcome its diversity when it felt threatened, but the consequences of the war re-divided the nation and actually questioned the very reasons and ideals for which America had fought and the basis of what it meant to be American.

I would like to thank Dr E. Ranson of the University of Aberdeen for his suggestions and comments on this paper.

Notes

1 For a comprehensive examination of the literature available on the Spanish-American War see Anne Cipriano Venzon, *The Spanish-American War: An Annotated Bibliography* (New York, Garland Publishing, 1990). See also Joseph Smith, *The Spanish-American War: Conflict in the Caribbean and the Pacific, 1895–1902* (London, Longman, 1994), which provides a good introduction to the study of the war and includes a useful guide to further reading. The best overviews are David F. Trask, *The War with Spain in 1898* (New York, Macmillan, 1981); Ernest R. May, *Imperial Democracy: The Emergence of America as a Great Power* (New York, Harcourt, Brace and World, 1961), Julius W. Pratt, *Expansionists of 1898: The Acquisition of Hawaii and the Spanish Islands* (Baltimore, John Hopkins University Press, 1936). Also see Walter Millis, *The Martial Spirit: A Study of Our War with Spain* (Boston, Houghton Mifflin Company, 1931).

2 See Walker Connor, 'A Nation is a Nation, is a State, is an Ethnic Group is a . . .', *Ethnic and Racial Studies*, 1 (1978); Benedict Anderson, *Imagined Communities: Reflections on the Origin and Spread of Nationalism* (London, Verso, 1983); Anthony D. Smith, 'War and Ethnicity: The Role of Warfare in the Formation, Self-Images and Cohesion of Ethnic Communities', *Ethnic and Racial Studies*, 4 (1981), 375–97.

3 Arthur Mann, *The One and the Many: Reflections on the American Identity* (University of Chicago Press, 1979).

4 Frederick Jackson Turner, *The Frontier in American History* (New York, Holt, 1920), pp. 1–38.

5 The modernization and bureaucratization of American society is examined by Robert H. Wiebe, *The Search for Order 1877–1920* (New York, Hill and Wang, 1967); and Alan Trachtenberg, *The Incorporation of America: Culture and Society in the Gilded Age* (New York, Hill and Wang, 1984). H. Wayne Morgan, *Unity and Culture: The United States 1877–1900* (Harmondsworth, Penguin, 1971), gives a more general account of how the changes affected American culture and society.

6 Richard Hofstader, 'Cuba, the Philippines and Manifest Destiny', in idem, *The Paranoid Style in American Politics* (London, Cape, 1966), pp. 145–87.

7 John H. Burgess, *Political Science and Comparative Constitutional Law*, I (Boston, Ginn & Co., 1891), vol. I, pp. 30–48, cited in Perry E. Giankos & Albert Karson, *American Diplomacy and the Sense of Destiny* (4 vols, Belmont, California, Wadsworth Publishing Co., 1966), vol. 1, p. 26.

8 Turner, *The Frontier in American History*, pp. 110, 243–68.

9 Lyman Abbott, 'Is it Peace or War?' *The Plymouth Morning Pulpit*, I, 5 (15/03/1898) (New York, R.G. Brown, 1898), p. 10.

10 Geoffrey Best, *Humanity in Warfare: The Modern History of the International Law of Armed Conflicts* (London, Methuen & Co., 1983), p. 191.

11 Frank Freidel, 'Dissent in the Spanish-American War and the Philippine Insurrection', in Samuel Eliot Morison, Frederick Mark & Frank Freidel *Dissent in Three American Wars* (Cambridge, Mass., Harvard University Press, 1970), p. 67.

12 *The Literary Digest*, XVI (15/01/1898), p. 82.

13 *The Literary Digest*, XVI (12/03/1898), p. 303.

14 *The Literary Digest*, XVI (26/03/1898), p. 363.

15 *United Mine Workers Journal* (31/03/1898), in Philip S. Foner & Richard C. Winchester (eds), *The Anti-Imperialist Reader: A Documentary History of Anti-Imperialism in the United States* (2 vols, New York, Holmes & Meier Publishers, Inc., 1984-5), vol. 1, p. 189.

16 See Marcus Wilkerson, *Public Opinion and the Spanish-American War: A Study in War Propaganda* (Baton Rouge, Louisiana University Press, 1932), and Joseph Wisan, *The Cuban Crisis as Reflected in the New York Press* (New York, Columbia University Press, 1934).

17 Margaret Leech, *In the Days of McKinley* (New York, Harper and Row, 1959), pp. 185–6. See also New York *World* (8/04/1898).

18 James D. Richardson, *A Compilation of the Messages and Papers of the Presidents* (14 vols, Washington, DC, Bureau of National Literature, 1911), vol. 8, p. 6289.

19 Henry Van Dyke, *The Cross of War: A Sermon* (New York, n.p., 1898), p. 5; Charles G. Ames, *In War Time: A Sermon Preached in the Church of the Disciples, 24 April 1898* (Boston, Geo. H. Ellis, 1898), p. 5.

20 Samuel Burns Weston, *The Ethics of Our War with Spain: A Lecture Given before the Society for Ethical Culture of Philadelphia, 8 May 1898* (Philadelphia, S. Burns Weston, 1898), p. 16.

21 Weston, *The Ethics of Our War*, pp. 10–11.

22 William R. Huntington, *Duties of War Time: A Sermon* (New York, Thomas Whittaker, 1898), p. 6.

23 In his first annual message, of 6 December 1897, President McKinley had stated that American intervention for the purpose of annexation surmounted to 'criminal aggression'. Likewise, it was a fear of 'ignoble motives' that led the Senate to adopt the Teller amendment on 19 April 1898, which disclaimed 'any disposition or intention [of the United States] to exercise sovereignty, jurisdiction, or control' over Cuba, except in a pacification role. It also promised that the United States would 'leave the government and control of the island to its people'. See Richardson, *Messages and Papers of the President*, vol. 8, p. 6258; and *US Congressional Record*, XXXI, pp. 3791, 3954.

24 *US Congressional Record*, XXXI, p. 2613.

25 *US Congressional Record*, XXXI, p. 2606.

26 Charles G. Dawes, *A Journal of the McKinley Years*, ed. Bascom N. Timmons (Chicago, The Lakeside Press, 1950), p. 164.

27 Richard E. Wood, 'The South and Reunion', *Historian*, 31 (May 1969), 415–30.

28 Atlanta *Constitution* (9/03/1898), p. 4.

29 Richmond *Times* (17/03/1898), in *Public Opinion*, p. 326.

30 Richmond *Dispatch* (8/03/1898), p. 6.

31 New Orleans *Times-Picayune* (17/03/1898), in *Public Opinion*, p. 327.

32 *US Congressional Record*, XXXI, p. 2604.

33 *US Congressional Record*, XXXI, p. 2604.

34 *US Congressional Record*, XXXI, p. 2610.

35 *US Congressional Record*, XXXI, p. 2604.

36 James R. Mann, *The War to Free Cuba: Remarks of Hon. James R. Mann, of Illinois, in the House of Representatives, 8 March and 28 April 1898* (Washington, n.p., 1898), pp. 6–7.

37 Dawes, *Journal of the McKinley Years*, p. 161.

38 *The Literary Digest* (26/03/1898), p. 367.

39 *Leslie's Weekly* (28/04/1898), p. 258.

40 Richmond *Dispatch* (8/03/1898), p. 2.

41 New Orleans *Times-Picayune* (8/03/1898), p. 4.

42 Willard B. Gatewood, Jr, *Black Americans and the White Man's Burden, 1898–1903* (Urbana, University of Illinois Press, 1975), notes that Eligah B. Tunnell, a cook aboard the *Winslow*, became known as a 'second Attucks'. On the whole it was Bagley who grabbed the nation's attention.

43 *Leslie's Weekly* (2/06/1898), p. 360.

44 *Leslie's Weekly* (23/06/1898), p. 402.

45 Richmond *Dispatch* (8/03/1898), p. 2. See also *New York Times* (9/03/1898), p. 6.

46 Richmond *Dispatch* (21, 24/04/1898), p. 4.

47 Chattanooga *Times* (17/03/1898), in *Public Opinion*, p. 325.

48 Charles Johnson Post, *The Little War of Private Post* (New York, Signet Books, 1961), pp. 34–5.

49 Revd James Marcus King, *The Situation and Justification of the Nation at War with Spain: An Address before the Empire State Society Sons of the American Revolution* (New York, n.p., 1898), p. 12

50 Atlanta *Constitution* (15/12/1898), p. 1.

51 Perry E. Giankos, 'The Spanish-American War and the Double Paradox of the Negro American', *Phylon*, 26 (Spring 1965), 34–49.

52 *American Citizen* (Kansas City, Kansas) (14/01/1898), in George P. Marks III, *The Black Press Views American Imperialism, 1898–1900* (New York, Arno Press, 1971), p. 8.

53 *American Citizen* (Kansas City, Kansas) (24/02/1898), in Marks, *Black Press*, p. 10.

54 Washington *Bee* (5/03/1898), in Marks, *Black Press*, p. 13.

55 Richmond *Planet* (30/04/1898), in Marks, *Black Press*, p. 32.

56 Washington *Bee* (7/05/1898), in Marks, *Black Press*, p. 56.

57 *Iowa State Bystander* (20/05/1898), in Marks, *Black Press*, p. 59.

58 *Afro-American Sentinel* (9/07/1898), in Marks, *Black Press*, p. 70.

59 Marks, *Black Press*, p. 33.

60 Willard B. Gatewood, *'Smoked Yankees' and the Struggle for Empire* (Urbana, University of Illinois Press, 1971), p. 26.

61 Gatewood, *'Smoked Yankees'*, pp. 28–9.

62 Josiah Strong, *Our Country: Its Possible Future and Its Present Crisis* (New York, The Baker & Taylor Co., 1885), p. 170.

63 John T. Fiske, 'Manifest Destiny', *Harper's New Monthly Magazine*, 70 (March 1885), 588.

64 Alfred T. Mahan, *The Influence of Sea Power upon History, 1670–1783* (Boston, Little, Brown and Co., 1890).

65 Henry Cabot Lodge, 'Our Blundering Foreign Policy', *Forum*, 19 (March 1895), 16–17.

66 Finley Peter Dunne, *Mr Dooley: In Peace and in War* (Boston, Small, Maynard & Company, 1899), p. 9.

67 Theodore Roosevelt, *The Strenuous Life: Essays and Addresses* (New York, The Century Co., 1901), p. 21.

68 Albert C. Beveridge, speech in the Senate (9/01/1900): *US Congressional Record*, 56th Congress, 1st Session, pp. 704–12, in Giankos and Karson, *American Diplomacy*, vol. 1, p. 64.

9
RELIVING THE REVOLUTION: WAR
AND POLITICAL IDENTITY DURING
THE FRANCO-PRUSSIAN WAR

B. Taithe

'The war of 1870 has been the primary cause of a great ideological upheaval, the most powerful, perhaps, to have taken place since the French Revolution.'[1]

Like many historians since, Commandant Palat, who began his study of the 1870 war bibliography with this line, certainly had a vested commercial interest in selling *his* war as paradigmatic to the late nineteenth century. Most historians of the period would agree as far as ideas are concerned[2] and, with the added proviso of a greater emphasis on the Commune of Paris (18 March 1871–May 1871), they too, like Daniel Pick[3] or Robert Tombs,[4] would emphasize the importance of the Franco-Prussian war.[5] The link with the French Revolution (1789–99) is also a recurrent theme in the historiography produced at the time and since. In his thought-provoking study, François Furet ended the French Revolution in the immediate aftermath of the 1870 war.[6] Arguably the posthumous victory of the French republic only became apparent in 1877 when the Third Republic eventually found a constitutional stability which enabled it to last another sixty-three years.[7]

The 1870 war thus works three ways: it serves as a turning point in French institutions, as a starting point for armed socialist insurrections,[8] 'modern' revolutions,[9] and as a reference, an almost nostalgic echo of the 'Great Revolution' and, indeed, the revolutions of 1830 and 1848.[10] In this chapter I wish to focus on this umbilical link with French historiography and on the historical identity of the men who went to war in 1870, who carried on the struggle after the fall of the Second Empire and lived the days of the Commune and the civil war of 1871.

The Franco-German war, summed up in a few lines, started in July 1870, was lost militarily by September and continued only through a spirited call to arms by French republicans until January–February 1871. The Commune, in itself a complicated political animal, then started a civil war across France in March 1871 only to end in the massacres of May.[11] In 1870 the Second Empire, partly a parody of Napoleon I's empire, collapsed in severe military defeats, a republic was proclaimed which claimed simultaneously the inheritance of the democratic social harmony of

February 1848 and the revolutionary enthusiasm and vigour of the volunteers of
1792. Within Paris and several other cities, radicals went further in reclaiming the
revolutionary ideals and resumed the political debates of the Jacobins, Robespierre,
Baboeuf and the various terrorist groups of 1793 onwards. Their identities were
structured around the past through specific readings of history which became
politically relevant in the context of 1870. Their identification reflected a desire to
re-enact the past to achieve a similar outcome by the same means. The French
experience of 1870 is perhaps primarily that history does not repeat itself and that a
historical identity cannot be applied literally without paying a severe and traumatic
toll to the past.[12] In the rest of this chapter I wish to look more closely at this
dimension of French political discourses, examining how historical myths and
traditions shaped afresh a new call for volunteers to defend the 'nation' and
discussing the ways in which the defeat affected the individuals who answered these
calls. This means that the topic of this paper is perhaps less a study of battered or
contested identities than a study of assumed identities and of the process of historical
identification with the past. To use the theoretical framework sketched in the
introduction, identification functioned through the discovery of another, historical
self coming to the fore in case of emergency. At the grass-root level, identification
with a historical *alter ego* may have been determinant in the act of will of
volunteering; at the governmental level this discursive historical identity legitimated
the war effort and made it possible. As this study will show, historicizing identities
sometimes conflicted with one another and with deeper, entrenched regional,
parochial and class identities. The focus will shift from the wider French 'imagined
community' to a study of the individual fragility of an interiorized national identity.

1870–1871: L'ANNÉE TERRIBLE

On 1 October 1870 *La guerre illustrée*, a popular Parisian periodical providing a
twice-weekly diet of illustrations and 'cut-and-paste' articles from a diversity of
newspapers to the besieged Parisians, printed on the first page:

Aux Armes Citoyens!
Here are the words used by the Commissars of the Convention, delegated to
the Northern armies addressed the people to urge them to take arms in
September 1792.
    'Citizens, city and country folks! Listen to the voice of the people's deputies
who delegated us; listen to those who are sent to you to express the deep
concern of the National Assembly and who employ all their efforts and means
for your salvation and that of the fatherland (*patrie*).
    Citizens, enemies, or rather frenetic criminals, have invaded the French
territory; they bring everywhere desolation and death; they pillage your homes,
they steal your rich harvest, fruits of your labour and sufferings; they take life

away from your dearest ones, and their criminal sword threatens you too. They violate too without pity all the rights of humanity and propriety which even the fiercest ancient warriors honoured. Nothing is Sacred to them, their exploits are as many crimes of which you are the victims. . . . Citizens! Be worthy of the name Frenchman, and show them what, in their legitimate anger, a people of free men attacked without reason and so cruelly robbed can do.

Arm yourselves, unite at the first sign, march against these criminals with the legitimate and pitiless anger which must move you. Bring among them fear and anguish, and swear as you leave your homes to exterminate them to the last. . . .'

These lines written seventy-two years ago [*sic*] are still valid. As in 1792, barbaric and devastating enemies have invaded our land. As our fathers rose, let us all rise, and we will do what they have done because what they wanted we want. But no discord. Unity of all our hearts and wills, salvation is at that cost.[13]

A month earlier this newspaper still had Napoleon III's coat of arms crushing the coat of arms of the king of Prussia as a logo. The first issue of the journal presented a relatively flattering portrait of the monarch simply captioned, 'His Majesty the Emperor'. After the military disaster of Sedan and the surrender of Napoleon III, the armorial and references to the imperial dynasty had been swiftly removed, and the journal progressed in time to use 1792 rhetoric and calls to arms to compensate for the failure of the Bonapartist myth. This quotation is remarkably banal in besieged Paris and only serves to illustrate how even 'middle-of-the-road' liberal publications became suddenly animated with revolutionary fevers. The commentary, however, is an interesting rewriting of history. The choice of 1792 as a founding date of volunteer armies reflects the idealized vision projected by Michelet, Lamartine or even Adolphe Thiers of the early days of the Revolution and the Revolutionary Wars. In 1792 the Terror had not yet happened, the Church was not yet banned, the counter-revolutionary insurrection had not yet started. The call to volunteers extracted from its historical context builds on an a-historical view of French citizenship constructed entirely in opposition to the barbaric hordes. The rhetoric suddenly seemed to acquire a new freshness and relevance. Quoting from Michelet may help us understand this faith in volunteers:

No, the anarchy of Paris did not fool anyone on the meaning of this moment. This death was a life. . . . Defensive does not suit France. France is not a shield. France is a living sword. She went by herself to the enemy's throat. Every day, eighteen-hundred volunteers left Paris, and up to twenty thousand. There would have been far more if they had not been stopped. . . .[14]

In spite of such a lively mythology of the volunteers of 1792, the commentary is intriguing and shows clearly that even enthusiastic journalists knew that revolutionary rhetorical tropes could become as many red flags to their prosperous readers. Many readers would make the comparison between 1793, the year of the *levée en masse*, with 1870 mass mobilization,[15] and this sort of comparison could prove more divisive than inspirational.

To use revolutionary language in 1870 was to challenge a substantial fraction of the political landscape. Legitimist royalists, high-brow aristocrats celebrating Louis XVI's martyrdom, Orléanist royalists evicted in 1848, Bonapartists angry at the 4 September 1870 coup would all object to revolutionary myths. Across many of these political divisions, all Catholics would fear a radical and anticlerical republic, in spite of the Archbishop of Paris, Mgr Darboy, who noisily supported the new republic.[16] The journalists, like the government, had to widen the revolutionary discourse and to broaden their definition of French citizens at war to include even those who did not consider themselves citizens but subjects. The revolutionary identity of the French citizen at war thus became a broad label in which coexisted the revolutionary forces of various *montagnard* Parisian forces which referred directly to Robespierre or Hébert and the heady days of the Terror, and *zouaves pontificaux* who left the service of the Pope to defend France.[17] The *zouaves pontificaux* especially went to war behind the Sacred Heart of Jesus flag and under the leadership of famous *Chouan* names like Cathelineau and Charette. Catholic Breton soldiers who did not speak French were also reminiscent of counter-revolutionary forces.[18] On the other side of the political world, their old enemies, the Garibaldian red shirts had followed their old leader to help the French Republic and defend the Rhone valley from German invaders.[19]

At the margins of the revival of volunteering this diametrically opposing identification with the enemies of the Vendée civil war meant that, in the event of a victory, peace would probably not last long. There were other signs that the volunteering of 1792 and that of 1870 were not identical. *Francs-tireurs* units or other registered bands of irregulars were also a sort of volunteer fostered by a republic which could ill afford to discourage even the most uncontrollable manifestations of public enthusiasm.[20] This almost instinctive answer to calls for volunteers fitted with an already long history of guerrilla warfare which had proved its effectiveness in Spain against Napoleon and, more recently, in Mexico against the French.[21] German forces responded with exceptional harshness to *francs-tireurs'* and volunteers' ambuscades, treating local populations as war enemies.[22] Prussian troops always refused military status to guerrillas and armed civilians.[23] Occupying armies denied them neutrality and considered them as the equals of spies, and executed hostages and partisans' families.[24] The whole concept of neutrality originated from a strict understanding of the unwritten right of the people, *droit des gens*, including the right to property and life.[25] When Prussian, Bavarian or Saxon troops (whom the French only gradually considered as one German collective entity) shot down villagers after short-lived resistance, on the sole grounds of their having broken the rules (or so-called laws) of war, they were applying a strict understanding of illegitimate enemies.[26] This view compared modern warfare to the Prussian *Nationalverein* when German volunteers resisted French occupation in 1813. During this episode the French occupiers had been pitiless and had hanged a number of them. Forgetful of this, French historians of the generations following 1870 echoed the French press of the war and argued that such violence after the Geneva Convention demonstrated the hypocrisy of the Prussian government.[27]

The French government could not exclude such volunteers and had at its disposal a medley of forces that could be used for war. The remnants of the imperial army, including the chief of the government, General Trochu, had participated in the imperial adventures of Napoleon III. The active French reserve or *garde mobile*, based on the model of the German *Landwehr*, was made up mostly of provincial soldiers, many of whom acquired a specifically military ethos and discipline from contact with professional soldiers.[28] Last but not least the government had re-created, with its full revolutionary rights, the *garde nationale*, the urban revolutionary militia dating from the Revolution which had been involved in the 1830 and 1848 revolutions.[29] To broaden its social basis the *garde nationale* had been opened to all, irrespective of wealth or status. Both *garde mobile* and *garde nationale* enjoyed the right to elect their officers.[30] The 1870 volunteer therefore had some of the characteristics of his 1792 counterpart, as recent historians have shown us. As in 1792, the 1870 volunteers were in fact merged with the professional armies of the previous regime.[31] Gambetta's efforts produced prodigious results and the call to volunteers of 1870 was in many ways superior to that of 1792: 600,000 men were gathered and equipped, virtually conjured from nowhere.[32] After the defeat many commentators poured scorn on Gambetta's rhetoric and minimized the scale of the mobilization to such an extent that the German historiography had to be translated to defend Gambetta's reputation.[33] In 1870, however, the common historical perception was that the 1792 volunteers constituted a homogenous whole which painfully contrasted with the uneven fighting capability of the 1870 armies. In spite of several attempts to reorganize *gardes nationales* into operational fighting units, the identity of 1870 volunteers remained contested.

The *garde nationale*, numerically the largest military group, even if the least 'military' of all, was structured around a notion of citizen-soldier which was deeply defiant of the military traditions which had enabled Napoleon III to rule for eighteen years.[34] The concept of citizen-soldier was not new and obviously used the old paradigms established during the Revolution; it also implied a use of mass armies which seemed somewhat redundant considering the technological challenges of long-distance rifles and modern armament.[35] To summarize, the military concepts attached to citizen-soldiery were deeply entrenched in the past in military terms but contained a number of innovative elements. Among the most important aspects of this citizen-soldiery were its universal nature, replacing decades of selective and highly class-biased military service, and its integrative influence on French identity. This latter point has been much emphasized in Eugen Weber's book which considers that universal conscription did much to unify the

French under a single French identity. The experience of 1870 seems to prove his point. If revolutionary rhetoric argued for a defence of a common Frenchness, the practice proved how fragile this identity was. Units of the *garde nationale* and *mobile* defined themselves in parochial terms. Landlords billeted with *mobiles* in Paris insisted on receiving soldiers from the same region to avoid the many, and potentially dangerous, quarrels between *pays* over the dinner table where they had to meet. Parisian volunteers also objected to merging with units from different streets or neighbourhoods. Soldiers resented having to serve with people 'from streets absolutely foreign' to their own.[36] Within Paris too, class difference and political orientation meant that the mass of volunteers could be reasonably clearly divided into bourgeois and workers' units, into revolutionary and partisans of order units. These divisions meant that even the Commune could not rely on a unified set of volunteers.[37] The defence of Paris in May 1871 was piecemeal, and each neighbourhood fought for itself without a general overview of the urban battle or even the clear demonstration of a Parisian identity above that of the *arrondissement*.[38]

Universal mobilization also conspired to turn this nation-in-arms into a dangerous servant of the state. Elected officers had little control over their elector soldiers and the *garde nationale* of Paris could easily turn into a permanent armed referendum. The attempted coups against the Paris government in October 1870 and January 1871 confirmed a danger which eventually materialized in March 1871 in the proclamation of the Commune. Within the Commune itself the democratic war institutions of the *garde nationale* coexisted uneasily with elected civilian institutions and often competed in the violence of their proclamations.[39] The volunteer of 1792 had outlived his useful purpose.

At the governmental level flirting with a strong historical model and well-defined historical identities was tempting, especially in a strongly deterministic vision of the past in which the same causes could obtain the same effects. The Parisian government thus ruled through bombastic calls to arms and re-enactment ceremonies such as the one that took place opposite the Panthéon to organize the volunteer armies.[40] Outside Paris, Gambetta assumed the difficult role of a republican dictator ruling by decrees and sending numerous telegrams, using both the language and the historical references of the Revolution.[41]

> Let us rise *en masse*, and let us die rather than suffer the shame of a dismemberment. Through all these disasters, in spite of ill fate, we still have the sentiment of French unity, the indivisibility of Republic. Paris besieged asserts even better its immortal motto [*fluctuat nec mergitur*, afloat it cannot sink] which will dictate that of the whole of France. *Vive la nation! Vive la république une et indivisible.*[42]

This parody had a real purpose: the revolution of 4 September did not have the democratic credentials of the late Liberal empire, being the result of a riot rather than a vote, and it thus ruled as a compromise of forces and found its legitimacy in history. The identity of France, to use Braudel's phrase, was also a difficult issue.[43] The sentiment of national unity might not be enough to guarantee the borders. Since September the German invaders had made it clear that Alsace and German-speaking Lorraine, containing most major eastern fortresses, would have to be surrendered in any peace settlement. What made the historical borders of France an intangible reality which justified the continuation of the war against all odds was the Revolutionary constitution which declared the republic to be one and indivisible. Within France the separatist tendencies of the Ligue du Midi [44] and the Lyons commune,[45] and, in March 1870, the federalist tendencies of the Commune ideology expressed simultaneously in Paris, Lyons, Marseilles, Narbonne, St Étienne, Le Creusot and Toulouse, could only be crushed by recourse to centralist, Jacobin political traditions and Revolutionary discourse.[46]

The dangers of addressing issues of 1870 with the intellectual and political tools of 1792 were manifold. The first and major problem was that 'a dictatorial decree does not make up an army; nor can a patriotic song coming from another age be enough to win a war'.[47] Revolutionary songs did not make for a victory. The provinces did not on the whole share in this fever. Revolutionary wars might have been successful to begin with but the twenty years of war to which they had led were not fondly remembered by all. The old fear of conscription had not disappeared, while the fear of the 'reds' was as real in many rural and Bonapartist areas as the fear of the Prussians.[48] The second problem came from the unravelling of these new armies themselves. The Garibaldians were the only ones to win a flag, and most victories were inflated in importance and proved short-lived.[49] Ultimately the terms of the Frankfurt peace treaty resembled those offered in September 1870 and the five months of revolutionary war that had postponed this result seemed to have been fought in vain.[50] The armistice forced hasty elections, won by the party of peace, principally monarchist, which compromised the future of the Republic. In other words the existence of a republican regime depended ultimately on its assimilation to a war-emergency phase of the history of the First Republic. The other danger of a historiographical register was obviously that by 1870 the revolutionary myth had become diverse and included conflicting analyses.[51] As Hutton noted, the cult of revolutionary traditions took the place of a clear political programme for most of the extreme-left parties.[52] The Commune of Paris was thus divided between Blanquists,[53] who followed the Jacobin tradition,[54] partisans of Félix Pyat, who identified themselves with the Hébert ultra-terrorist faction of the Revolution, others who were specifically partisans of a revival of Chaumette's Paris Commune of 1793,[55] and even a few Babouvian socialists.[56] The shadow of Proudhon hung over the socialists of the Commune, while the Marxist socialists of the Commune hierarchy could be counted on the fingers of one hand. To push the re-enactment further some Communards revived revolutionary salutes like *ci-devant*, *citoyen* instead of *monsieur*, and even the Revolutionary calendar. The creation of the *Comité de Salut Public* on 1 May 1871 using the terminology of 1793, the destruction of Louis XVI's expiatory chapel, the symbolic destruction of the Vendôme column and the bronze column made with melted guns from Napoleonic victories were among the attempts to identify the Commune with the French Revolution.[57] There was a revolution within a revolution, the past living in the present.

This enthusiasm for the dregs of the past was not universally shared even in the Commune. Many felt that an impersonation could not compensate for the lack of a sense of direction or a clear social programme. In the same way that 1870 volunteers were not ultimately comfortable with the historical identity thrust upon them, some of the efforts to *identify* the Commune with the mythical revolutionary past sounded hollow. Identification and identity are different in the sense that the former can be contrived and erudite rather than experienced. The double defeat which concluded *l'année terrible* had touched many much more deeply than a few feverish proclamations; individual identities also related to history and introduced elements of self-doubt.

IDENTITY CRISIS

To describe an identity crisis of the past implies the use of a certain number of debatable psychological or even psycho-analytical phrases with their ready-made conclusions. That there was a deep anxiety as an outcome of the war seems undoubted and fits largely with the literature on *fin-de-siècle* France: 1792 had failed 1870, the historical identity of the French itself was open to questions and so were the origins of the defeat. One side counted the lost opportunities of the conflict and blamed them for the humiliating defeat, while the other would describe in fatalist terms the inexorable movement towards defeat from 1789, 1852, or 1866 onwards.[58] Others described in physical terms the decline of the French as an ethnic entity, a culture, a state and an army. The racial issues at stake in any biological definition of wars, corresponding to any evolutionist view of the world (be it Lamarckian or social Darwinist[59]), were summed up in the work of the pessimistic racialist theorist *par excellence*, Gobineau.

Gobineau summed up his views in *L'état de la France*: 'For a country to disintegrate like this, the disease must wreak its work from within; the wounds inflicted by the foreign assailant produce cuts, but never this purulent liquefaction of the marrow and the blood.'[60] Paradoxically in that context Gobineau reinterpreted the war in the light of his racial theories and political predictions only when the war had actually finished. It took him several months in 1870 to let loose an unusual optimism. The days of the war when Gobineau forced himself to believe in the chances of the French armies were unique in his life, and at odds with his previous and later writings.[61] This pattern of war-induced altered consciousness could be found in many other writers and this is perhaps a legitimate occasion for the use of the term 'identity crisis' when so many writers denied their former views and re-assessed their own contributions to the war effort. Deeply embedded in the experience of 1870–1, the languages of defeat contributed towards the *fin-de-siècle* mood.[62] The medical narratives about alcohol,[63] venereal disease,[64] tuberculosis[65] and even amputation[66] contributed strongly towards this metaphorical vocabulary which Susan Sontag and Elaine Showalter have described.[67] As Ruth Harris and Robert Nye have correctly pointed out, these ideas were not new, but the political and social context of the immediate aftermath of 1870 recast them as central to medical and social debates.[68] Even powerful reformers set their political agenda in a pessimistic perspective which questioned the racial and social makeup of French identity. Pasteur, for instance, published a highly élitist pamphlet, *Some Reflections on Science in France: Why France Did Not Find Superior Men at this Time of Danger*,[69] which called for sweeping social and political reforms of French education and selection. At the academy of medicine in Paris,[70] Dr Chauffard addressed his colleagues shortly after the armistice in these words:

> Gentlemen, in spite of the sadness and anxiety of this hour, the academy cannot have more legitimate purpose than to study the great banes which undermine the prosperity of our race, its physical development, its ability to expand and resist. After the discussion on tuberculosis came the debates on infantile mortality, these debates . . . [on] tuberculosis, infant mortality, alcoholism, are [addressing] the most active causes of destruction, and weakening of our people, especially the working and urban people. . . . Therefore it is not simple chance . . . that such questions arise in this academy. . . . It is our fate [*la force des choses*] that wants it, it is the consciousness of public dangers.[71]

The war had revealed French inferiority and the new 'racial' or political identity of the defeated became the sum of the causes of their historical failure. The superiority of German soldiers was emphasized by British observers and Frenchmen alike. The invaders paraded their 'broad chest', they had coarse manners and a unique ability to drink large amounts of alcohol without showing the signs of a debilitating drunkenness.[72] The French soldiers, on the other hand, let themselves down by drinking their way to a hospital bed. On the operating table French soldiers perished in high numbers: the defeat was in their flesh, a bodily part of French identity. The narrative of crisis faced that of *fatum*, of national decline. As a royalist delegate of the Red Cross confided in his diary: 'All great amputations, after a period of good hope, end with gangrene or haemorrhage. It is alas a sad consequence of the physical and moral depression of our soldiers since the beginning of this war.'[73] The merchants of gloom constantly compared the victors with the vanquished, the soldiers standing for the nations. More popularly the siege of Paris was perceived as the source of a specific form of madness fostered by abuse of alcohol, political speeches, unemployment and licentiousness. Maxime du Camp among many others, but more emphatically than most, denounced the Commune as the grotesque child of this insanity. Others saw the Commune as an aberration and as the product of the collective madness that seized over-excited brains after a long confinement and the abuse of alcohol. In order to explain the political turmoil of 1870–1 better, conservative medical writers invested it with teleological meanings and medical jargon.[74] They often presented the Commune as an orgy or the overflowing of a moral sewer. Paul Lidsky has shown that this literary avalanche of abuse and excuses reveals less than it hides, and was less about understanding than about condemning and erasing.[75] Maxime du Camp and a generation of naturalist writers from Daudet to Zola are largely responsible for historical views of the siege and the Commune as the combined climax of working-class excess and imperial corruption. They were supported in their analysis by a whole literature of medical history and collective psychology which took over the naïve physiology of revolutionary enthusiasm, going as far as calling it the '*morbus democraticus* or democratic madness'.[76]

This analysis of a French crisis built on biological class discourses which, as Louis Chevalier has argued, shaped the class-based political discourse in France along the lines of racial divides and antagonism.[77] This view of French society in effect denied the existence of one French identity as a political benchmark. In 1870 a revolutionary historical identity formulated through action and historical remembrance had failed to be replaced by a systematic programme of republican definitions of national identity. From a centralist point of view the defeat had been the sobering experience of French divisions. Regional identities kept under strict control by the political powers had also shown their potential for revival in time of war and the dangers they presented to the existence of an over-arching 'French imagined community' were clear. The critique of French flesh undermined any rosy view of spontaneous organization and volunteer force. The war tested to the full some of the revolutionary myths which had served many regimes over seventy years. The divided picture that emerged from the Franco-Prussian war became the basis of a reformist programme which attempted to tackle simultaneously all the aspects of this identity crisis. The educational reforms of the 1880s inculcated the French language to crush local idioms and cultures. The *garde nationale* did not survive 1871 and, after the ultimate rebellion of the citizen-soldiers, the units were disbanded for ever to be replaced by universal conscription. Conscription gradually became a unifying experience through which French as a national language[78] was reinforced and the teaching of republican values complemented school knowledge.[79] Some work on the flesh of the French themselves became a priority in postwar France, and physical education and sports became part of a republican renewal.[80] The revolutionary dogma also died in 1870 in the sense that even the 1889 celebrations of the centenary resembled more a commemoration of past events and a celebration of moderate republican stability rather than a renewed emphasis on revolutionary values.[81] A republican identity came to be constructed almost in spite of the Revolution, in spite of historical debates, through institutional practices such as conscription and education.[82] In some respects Eugen Weber's analysis remains seminal in all debates on French identity.[83] On the other hand recent political history, such as the theoretical work of Claude Nicolet or Odile Rudelle, considerably underestimates the physicality of a republican identity rooted and literally embodied in pedagogic and military practices.[84] Through these ordinary and daily practices a republican self, even if only the fiction of a 'good-citizen' identity, was developed after 1870,[85] precisely because 1870 had demonstrated the vacuity of passive historical identities.[86] Up to 1914 the republican state managed to create an identification, even if it was uncomfortable to or rejected by many, between Frenchness and republican identity.[87]

Notes

1 B.E. Palat, *Bibliographie générale de la guerre de 1870–1871* (Paris & Nancy, Berger-Levrault & Cie., 1896), p. v.

2 Michael Howard, *The Franco-Prussian War: The German Invasion of France, 1870–1871* (New York, Dorset Press, 1961, rep. 1990).

3 Daniel Pick, *War Machine: The Rationalisation of Slaughter in the Modern Age* (New Haven, Yale University Press, 1993), pp. 88–114.

4 Richard Tombs, '"L'année Terrible" 1870–1871', *Historical Journal*, 35 (1992), 713–24.

5 Allan Mitchell, *Victors and Vanquished: The German Influence on Army and Church in France after 1870* (Chapel Hill, University of North Carolina Press, 1984). The second volume of Mitchell's trilogy is by far the most convincing. His third volume, *The Divided Path: The German Influence on Social Reform in France after 1870* (Chapel Hill, University of North Carolina Press, 1991) and his first volume *The German Influence in France after 1870: The Formation of the French Republic* (Chapel Hill, University of North Carolina Press, 1979) describe more subtle changes and more difference than convergence between France and Germany. See Edmond P. Dreyfus-Brisac, *L'université de Bonn et l'enseignement supérieur en Allemagne* (Paris, Hachette, 1879).

6 François Furet, *La Révolution, 1770–1880* (2 vols, Paris, Hachette, 1988), vol. 2, pp. 399–419.

7 Jacques Gouault, *Comment la France est devenue républicaine* (Paris, Armand Colin, 1954).

8 See two classic examples: Henri Lefebvre, *La proclamation de la Commune* (Paris, Gallimard, 1971). Vladimir Illitch Lénine, *La Commune de Paris* (Paris, François Maspéro, 1971).

9 Karl Marx & Friedrich Engels, *On the Paris Commune* (Moscow, Progress Publishers, 1976), pp. 48–99.

10 In many ways texts about the Commune also echoed the 1848 Revolution. See F. Lidsky, *Les écrivains contre la Commune* (Paris, François Maspéro, 1982), p. 22.

11 Jacques Rougerie, *La Commune: 1871* (Paris, Presse Universitaire Française, 1988); *Procès des Communards* (Paris, Julliard, 1964). Jacques Rougerie has often been criticized for his analysis of the Commune movement. Recent work by William Serman, *La Commune de Paris (1871)* (Paris, Fayard, 1986), confirms his theory.

12 Charles Olivier Carbonnel, 'Les historiens français chroniqueurs de la guerre franco-allemande et de la Commune, naissance du nationalisme historiographique (1871–1875)', *Bulletin de la société d'histoire moderne*, 13 (1974), 37–56. A. Dupuy, *Sedan et l'enseignement de la revanche* (Paris, Institut National de Recherche et de Documentation Pédagogique, 1975); Henry Contamine, *La Revanche, 1871–1914* (Paris, Berger-Levnault, 1957); Henri Guillemin, *Nationalistes et nationaux (1870–1940)* (Paris, Gallimard, 1974), pp. 9–54.

13 *La guerre illustrée*, 20 (1/10/1870), 154.

14 Jules Michelet, *Histoire de la Révolution française* (2 vols, Paris, Robert Laffont, 1979), vol. 1, pp. 861–5.

15 The *levée en masse* in 1870 was also circumscribed and did not affect specialized workers: see Archives du département de la Seine, Vd6 955, Exemptions de service accordés aux gardes travaillant chez Godillot, dans la boulangerie et les chemins de fer.

16 Jules de Marthold, *Mémorandum du Siège de Paris* (Paris, Charovay Frères, 1884), pp. 68–9. Jacques Olivier Boudon, 'Une promotion épiscopale sous le second empire, l'abbé Darboy à l'assaut de Paris', *Revue d'histoire moderne et contemporaine*, 39 (1992), 472–81. Darboy had been a moderate republican until 1857.

17 Colonel D'Albiousse, *Le drapeau du Sacré-Coeur, campagne de France (zouaves pontificaux)* (Rennes, Goupy, 1873); Abbot J.S. Allard, *Les zouaves pontificaux, ou journal de Mgr Daniel, aumônier des zouaves* (Paris, Hugny, 1880); Henri d'Arsac, *Les mercenaires ou les zouaves pontificaux en France* (Reims, Imprimerie Coopérative, 1872). The Zouaves were French soldiers who had volunteered to defend the Papal state. They represented the most ultramontaine Catholic tendencies.

18 Jules Claretie, *Paris assiégé, tableaux et souvenirs, septembre 1870 – janvier 1871* (Paris, Alphonse Lemerre, 1871), pp. 190–3. On Catholics in Brittany see Caroline Ford, *Creating the Nation in Provincial France: Religion and Political Identity* (Princeton University Press, 1993).

19 See Robert Middleton, *Garibaldi, ses opérations à l'armée des Vosges* (Paris, Garnier Frères, 1872), pp. 249–77. Louis Philippe de Ségur, *Les marchés de la guerre à Lyon et à l'armée de Garibaldi* (Paris, Henri Plon, 1873). Those two texts attacked Garibaldian troops for their lack of discipline and for the unscrupulous requisitions they made. This denunciation of Garibaldi does not undermine the originality of a foreign volunteer movement in a war like this one, nor their relative effectiveness at defending Dijon and then Lyon. In fact the Garibaldians won the only German flag to fall into French hands for the whole duration of the war. See Riciotti Garibaldi, *Souvenirs de la campagne de France 1870–71* (Nice, La Semaine Niçoise, 1899), pp. 118–19; P.A. Dormoy, *Les trois batailles de Dijon, 30 octobre, 26 novembre, 21 janvier* (Paris, Librairie Militaire Dubois, 1894), pp. 370–3. The latter gives a more balanced account of the defence of the South.

20 Archives de l'Armée de Terre, Li (Gouverneur militaire de Paris, Chef du Gouvernement), 26 corps francs commissionés; Li36 Historique, garde nationale et corps francs.

21 Paul Gaulot, *L'expédition du Mexique d'après les documents et souvenirs de Ernest Louet* (Paris, Société d'Éditions Littéraires et Artistiques, 1906). N.N. Barker, *The French Experience in Mexico, 1821–1861: A History of Complete Misunderstanding* (Chapel Hill, University of North Carolina Press, 1979).

22 This topic has been hotly debated especially after the Second World War. I.P. Trainin, 'Questions of Guerrilla Warfare in the Law of War', *American Journal of International Law*, XI (1946), 534–62.

23 Geoffrey Best, 'Restraints on War by Land before 1945', in Michael Howard (ed.), *Restraints on War: Studies in the Limitation of Armed Conflict* (Oxford University Press, 1979), pp. 17–39, 33.

24 Howard, *The Franco-Prussian War*, pp. 251–2.

25 For an early example see Charles de Martens, *Causes célèbres du droit des gens* (2 vols, Leipzig, F.A. Brockhaus & Paris, Ponthieu & Cie, 1827). I am indebted to Andrew Jones for this reference. Individual rights were not discussed in an international convention until the Hague congresses of 1899 and 1907. See Donald A. Wells, *War Crimes and Laws of War* (London, University Press of America, 1984), pp. 44–5; James Brown Scott, *The Hague Conventions and Declarations of 1899 and 1907* (Oxford University Press, 1915).

26 Hector de Condé, *La Prusse au pilori de la civilisation (crimes et forfaits des prussiens en France)* (Brussels, Devillé, 1871); C.A. Daubant, *La guerre comme la font les prussiens* (Paris, Plon, 1871). Amédée Marteau, *Le droit prime la force, page d'histoire de l'Empire d'Allemagne* (Paris, Librairie Internationale, 1876); *Recueil de*

documents sur les exactions, vols et cruautés des armées prussiennes en France (Bordeaux, Férot et Fils, 1871); A. Vavasseur, *La paix honteuse ou le droit des gens selon les prussiens* (Paris, Lacroix, Verboeckhoven et Cie., 1871). German governments reacted violently through Bismarck's telegram (9 January 1871), and later in an extended denunciation of the numerous French breaches of the Geneva Convention. *Les violations de la convention de genève par les Français en 1870–1871* (Berlin, C. Duncker, 1871). *Comment les français font la guerre, recueil de faits pour servir à l'histoire des moeurs et de la civilisation au xixème siècle* (Berlin, C. Duncker, 1871), simultaneously published in German, French and English and usually attributed to the Prussian foreign office. The need for an appropriate jurisdiction, acting at government level, was felt and exposed as early as 1872, see Gustave Moynier, *Notes sur la création d'une institution judiciaire internationale, propre à prévenir et à réprimer les infractions à la Convention de Genève* (Geneva, Comité International, 1872).

27 *The Times* (London) (15/09/1870) which reported the first massacre of civilian population by the Bavarians. E. Govoy, *Le Service de Santé Militaire en 1870* (Paris, Lavauzelle, 1894), p. 21. Simultaneously the Germans published reports of the attack on a German ambulance in Bazeilles. Dr Weil, manuscript report, Archives du Service de Santé de l' Armée de Terre, box 64/30, 'in Stuttgart', p. 9. A meeting in Brussels in 1874 attempted to solve the vexed question of the status of irregular warfare. Peter Karsten, *Law, Soldiers and Combat* (Westport, Greenwood Press, 1978), pp. 22–3.

28 Laurent Llopez, 'La garde mobile de l'hérault: défendre le territoire national de Paris à l'Algérie', *Histoire et défense, les cahiers de Montpellier*, 33 (1996), 31–62.

29 Georges Carrot, 'La garde nationale, une institution de la nation' (Thèse de doctorat, histoire du droit, troisième cycle, Université de Nice 1979), p. 224. Arthur de Grandeffe, *Mobiles et volontaires de la Seine pendant la guerre et les deux sièges* (Paris, Dentu, 1871), p. 66.

30 Archives de la Seine, VD6 1331–2; élections d'officiers et sous-officiers.

31 Samuel F. Scott, *The Response of the Royal Army to the French Revolution: The Role and Development of the Line Army, 1787–93* (Oxford, Clarendon Press, 1978), pp. 169–208.

32 Commandant L. Rousset, *Histoire générale de la guerre franco-allemande, 1870–1* (7 vols, Paris, La Librairie Illustrée, c. 1894–6), vol. 6, pp. 329–30.

33 Baron von der Goltz, *Gambetta et ses armées*, pp. 2–73. The book was originally published in the *Preussische Jahrbücher* in 1874–5.

34 Richard Holmes, *The Road to Sedan: The French Army 1866–70* (London, Royal Historical Society, 1984), pp. 11–27.

35 Colmar von der Goltz, *Gambetta et ses armées* (Paris, Librairie Sandoz, 2nd edn 1877), pp. 46–7.

36 Archives du département de la Seine, VD6/1567/1, VIIème arrondissement, Assistance aux gardes nécessiteux, letter of 14 December 1870. Characteristically this petition to form a more cohesive unit was addressed to the mayor rather than to the military administration. The 1870 organization meant that civilian authorities gathered units before they came under military jurisdiction.

37 Robert Tombs, 'Prudent Rebels: The Second Arrondissement during the Paris Commune of 1871', *French History*, 5 (1991), 393–413. Also see Archives de l'Armée de Terre, Ly35, Historiques des bataillons fédérés 3 à 250, interrogatoire de police; Ly94 Corps francs de la Commune.

38 Gérard Conte, *Éléments pour une histoire de la Commune dans le XIIIe arrondissement, 5 mars – 25 mai 1871* (Paris, Éditions de la Butte aux Cailles, 1981).

39 Prosper Olivier Lissagaray, *History of the Paris Commune of 1871* (London, New Park Publications, 1976), pp. 173–4. Also see Jean Dantry & Lucien Sheler, *Le Comité Central Républicain des vingts*

arrondissements de Paris (septembre 1870 – mai 1871), d'après les papiers inédits de Constant Martin et les sources imprimées (Paris, Éditions Sociales, 1960).

40 Archives du département de la Seine, VD6 1329–31/1 Engagements volontaires dans la garde nationale & VD6 1274–6 Engagements volontaires dans les armées de terre et de mer.

41 J.P.T. Bury, *Gambetta and the National Defence: A Republican Dictatorship in France* (London, Longmans, 1936), p. 273. The theme of a 'republican dictator' is old and originally had negative connotations: H.R. Blandeau, *La dictature de Gambetta* (Paris, Amyot, 1871); Edmond Beraud, *Gambetta dictateur* (Poitiers, Oudin, 1881), p. 5. Alphonse Glais-Bizoin, *Dictature de cinq mois, mémoires pour servir à l'histoire du gouvernement de la défense nationale à Tours et à Bordeaux* (Paris, Dentu, 1873).

42 Georges d'Heylli, *Télégrammes militaires de Léon Gambetta, documents officiels* (Paris, L. Beauvais, 1871) (9/10/1870), p. 20.

43 Fernand Braudel, *The Identity of France* (2 vols, London, Collins, 1990), vol. 2.

44 Alphonse V. Roche, *Provençal Regionalism* (Evanston, Northwestern University Press, 1954), p. 62. Louis M. Greenberg, *Sisters of Liberty: Marseille, Lyon, Paris and the Reaction to a Centralized State, 1868–1871* (Cambridge, Mass., Harvard University Press, 1971), p. 48. The Lyons Commune had much to do with rebuilding municipal government after eighteen years of direct autocratic rule.

45 Joannès Guetton, *Six mois de drapeau rouge à Lyon* (Paris, P.N. Josserant, 1871).

46 See Jeanne Gaillard, *Communes de Province, Commune de Paris 1870–1871* (Paris, Flammarion, 1971).

47 Léonce de Cazenove, *Compte rendu du comité sectionnaire Lyonnais* (Lyons, Société de Secours aux blessés des armées de terre et de mer, 1871), p. 43.

48 Alan Forrest, *Conscripts and Deserters: The Army and French Society during the Revolution and Empire* (Oxford University Press, 1989).

49 Rousset, *Histoire*, vol. 6, pp. 285–369.

50 Robert I. Giesberg, *The Treaty of Frankfurt: A Study in Diplomatic History, September 1870 – September 1873* (Philadelphia, University of Pennsylvania Press, 1966), pp. 157–67.

51 For an excellent and recent summary see Pamela M. Pilbeam, *Republicanism in Nineteenth-Century France* (London, European History Series, Macmillan, 1995).

52 Charles Rihs, *La Commune de Paris, 1871, sa structure et ses doctrines* (Paris, Seuil, reprint, 1973). Rihs made perhaps more sense from the confusion of the Commune than was perceptible in 1871. It remains mostly an intellectual history of the Commune, using the most articulate texts to make sense of the whole period.

53 See the work of the biographer and specialist on Blanqui: Auguste Dommanget, *Auguste Banqui au début de la Troisième République (1871–1880), dernière prison et ultimes combats* (Paris, Moraton, 1973).

54 One of the dominant leaders of the Jacobin faction, fed on historical traditions and readings of Robespierre and Saint Just, was Charles Delescluze (1809–71). Marcel Dessol, *Un révolutionnaire jacobin; Charles Delescluze* (Paris, Marcel Rivière et Cie, 1952), pp. 333–412. Miguel Abensour, 'Saint-Just and the Problem of Heroism in the French Revolution', in Forenc Fehér (ed.), *The French Revolution and the Birth of Modernity* (Berkeley, University of California Press, 1990), pp. 133–49.

55 Paul Sainte-Claire Deville, *La Commune de l'An II, vie et mort d'une assemblée révolutionnaire* (Paris, Plon, 1946), pp. 118–45.

56 See Bernard Noël, *Dictionnaire de la Commune* (Paris, Fernand Hozon, 1971); on Baboeuf, see Victor Advielle, *Histoire de Gracchus Baboeuf et du Babouvisme* (2 vols, Paris, Éditions du CTHS, reprint, 1990).

57 François Marotin, 'Légende et Révolution avant et après la Commune', in Christian Croisille & Jean Ehrard (eds), *La légende de la Révolution* (Clermont Ferrand: Université Blaise Pascal, 1988), pp. 473–84.

58 Carbonnel, 'Les historiens français', pp. 60–7.

59 Darwinism only slowly permeated the French scientific world but French evolutionists gradually accepted Darwin as the successor of Lamarck. See Y. Conry, *L'introduction du darwinisme en France au XIXieme siècle* (Paris, J.Vrin, 1974), particularly livre II & III; E. Gautier, *Le darwinisme social* (Paris, Deveaux, 1880). Armand de Quatrefages, *Charles Darwin et ses précurseurs* (Paris, Bibliothéque Scientifique Internationale, 1870).

60 Michael Biddiss (ed.), *Gobineau: Selected Political Writings* (London, Jonathan Cape, 1970), pp. 204–5.

61 Michael D. Biddiss, *Father of Racist Ideology: The Social and Political Thought of Count Gobineau* (London, Weidenfeld and Nicolson, 1970), pp. 210–11.

62 J.P.T. Bury, *Gambetta and the Making of the Third Republic* (London, Longman, 1973), p. 25. Bury makes some interesting and useful comparisons between Renaissance Italian political thought at the time of successive waves of invasions and the French political thought of the thirty years following the war. See also Claude Digeon, *La crise allemande de la pensée française* (Paris, Presses Universitaires de France, 1959), pp. 4–8; Koenraad W. Swart, *The Sense of Decadence in Nineteenth-Century France* (The Hague, Martinus Nijhoff, 1964), pp. 124–38.

63 See T. Gallard, *Leçon de clinique médicale* (Paris, J.B. Baillière et fils, 1872), pp 7–9. Paul Brouardel, *La profession médicale au commencement du vingtième siècle* (Paris, J.B. Baillière et fils, 1903), p. 210. Jacques Léonard, *La France médicale au dix-neuvième siècle* (Paris, Archives, Gallimard/Julliard, 1978), pp. 172–210. Martha L. Hildreth, *Doctors, Bureaucrats and Public Health in France 1888–1902* (New York, Garland Publishing, 1987), pp. 36–106.

64 See B. Taithe, 'Consuming Desires: Female Prostitutes and "Customers" at the Margins of Crime and Perversion in France and Britain *c.* 1836–1885', in Meg Arnot & Cornelie Usborne (eds), *Gender and Crime in Modern Europe* (London, University College London Press, 1998).

65 Pierre Guillaume, *Du désespoir au salut: les tuberculeux aux xixème et xxème siècle* (Paris, Aubier, 1986), pp. 112–15.

66 Jill Harsin, 'Syphilis, Wives and Physicians: Medical Ethics and the Family in Late Nineteenth-Century France', *French Historical Studies*, 16 (1989), 72–95.

67 Elaine Showalter, *Sexual Anarchy: Gender and Culture at the Fin-de-Siècle* (New York, Viking, 1990); Susan Sontag, *Illness as Metaphor* (New York, Viking, 1979); William Greenslade, *Degeneration, Culture and the Novel* (Cambridge University Press, 1994), pp. 15–31.

68 Ruth Harris, *Murders and Madness: Medicine, Law and Society in the Fin-de-Siècle* (Oxford, Clarendon Press, 1989), p. 51. Robert Nye, *Masculinity and Male Codes of Honour in Modern France* (New York, Oxford University Press, 1993), pp. 72–97.

69 *La gazette médicale de Paris*, 3rd series, tome 26 (22/04/1871), 522. A. Bopierre, *Pourquoi la France n'a pas trouvé d'hommes supérieurs au moment du péril? Réponse à M. Pasteur, de l'Institut* (Paris, Masson, 1871).

70 On the Academy see George Weisz, *The Medical Mandarins: The French Academy of Medicine in the Nineteenth and Early Twentieth Centuries* (Oxford University Press, 1995).

71 *Bulletin de l'Académie Nationale de Médecine* (Paris, J.B. Baillière et fils, 1870), tome xxxvi, p. 56. William H. Schneider, *Quality and Quantity: The Quest for Biological Regeneration in Twentieth-Century France* (Cambridge University Press, 1989), pp. 20–7.

72 *The Lancet* (3/09/1871), vol. ii, pp. 349, 579. Dr A. Flamarion, *Le livret du docteur, souvenirs de campagne contre l'Allemagne et contre la Commune de Paris, 1870–1871* (Paris, Le Chevalier, 1872), p. 30.

73 Adolphe Môny, *Notes d'ambulance, août 1870 –février 1871* (Paris, Plon-Nourrit, 1907), p. 324.

74 Jean-Baptiste Vincent Laborde, *Les hommes et les actes de l'insurrection de Paris devant la psychologie morbide* (Paris, G. Baillière, 1872).

75 Paul Lidsky, *Les écrivains contre la Commune* (Paris, François Maspéro, 1982), pp. 24–76.

76 A. Brierre de Boismont, *L'union médicale* (24/06/1871); 'A Lunatic Asylum during the siege of Paris', *The Lancet* (4/03/1871), vol. I, pp. 301–2.

77 Louis Chevalier, *Classes laborieuses et classes dangereuses à Paris pendant la première moitié du dix-neuvième siècle* (Paris, Hachette, 2nd edn 1984), pp. 707–21. Barrie M. Ratcliffe, 'Classes Laborieuses et Classes Dangereuses à Paris Pendant la Première Moitié du Dix-Neuvième Siècle? The Chevalier Thesis Reexamined', *French Historical Study*, 17 (1991), 542–74.

78 Many anthropological studies emphasize the conflicting messages and identities attached to the use of French and patois. See Anne Stamm, *L'échange et l'honneur, une société rurale en haute-Corrèze* (Limoges, S.E.L.M. 1983), pp. 226–33.

79 See Katherine Auspitz, *The Radical Bourgeoisie: The Ligue de l'Enseignement and the Origins of the Third Republic, 1866–1885* (Cambridge University Press, 1982).

80 Pierre Arnaud (ed.), *Les athlètes de la république, gymnastique, sport et idéologie républicaine 1870–1914* (Toulouse, Privat, 1987).

81 This is an argument expressed in Paul Farmer, *France Reviews its Revolutionary Origins: Social Politics and Historical Opinions in the Third Republic* (New York, Octagon Books, 2nd edn, 1973 [1944]).

82 Michel Bazon, *Les conscrits* (Paris & Limoges, Berger-Levrault, 1981). Jean-Paul Aron, *Anthropologie du conscrit français* (Paris, Montin, 1972).

83 Eugen Weber, *Peasants into Frenchmen: The Modernization of Rural France* (London, Chatto and Windus, 1977), pp. 95–114, 392–402, 452–70.

84 Odile Rudelle, *La République absolute, 1870–1889* (Paris, Publications de la Sorbonne, 1982); Claude Nicolet, *L'idée républicaine en France, essai d'histoire critique* (Paris, Gallimard, 1982), pp. 273–7. Both undermine considerably the necessity to a republican state of creating an identification, even if often uncomfortable or rejected, between Frenchness and republican identity.

85 See for instance Edouard Guillon, *Le nouveau soldat du service obligatoire* (Paris, n.p., 1873). On the minutiae of the slow reform of the French army see Allan Mitchell, *Victors and Vanquished: The German Influence on Army and Church in France after 1870* (Chapel Hill, University of North Carolina Press, 1984), pp. 15–41. On schools see Mona Ozouf, *L'école, l'église et la république* (Paris, Cana/Jean Offredo, 1982). On the sectarian divide in schools which opposed the Catholic Church and the state on ideas of citizenship see Yves Déloye, *École et citoyenneté, l'individualisme républicaine de Jules Ferry à Vichy: controverses* (Paris, Presses de la fondation nationale des sciences politiques, 1994), pp. 17–35, 287–348. Déloye makes the point forcefully that the Catholic Church attempted to present an alternative model of citizenship which mirrored and reflected the then unavoidable republican identity.

86 A historical anthropology of the practices of ordinary identity in nineteenth-century France is in the making and follows the work of Michel de Certeau. See Michel de Certeau, Luce Giard & Pierre Mayol, *L'invention du quotidien* (2 vols, Paris, Gallimard, 2nd edn 1994).

87 Brian Jenkins, *Nationalism in France: Class and Nation since 1789* (London, Routledge, 1990), pp. 72–4.

Part Three

MICRO-IDENTITIES/ MACRO-WAR

The First World War takes the lion's share of the historiography of war and identity in general, and the following two sections reflect mostly the trauma of this all-engulfing and senseless war. Within mass armies and 'total war' many other forms of identity were questioned, contested or reinforced. Gordon Urquhart shows how even in a global conflict a cultural identity as limited in its original geographical locale as the Scottish Highlands could be opened to Scots abroad and 'Scotophile' Englishmen. The artefacts summoned to revive ancient or invented traditions illustrate how 'quaint' volunteering practices had become in the age of ultimate mass armies. In a sense the war revived a cultural identity which could then serve the state, the natives and those who associated themselves, romantically or genealogically, with it.

Claire Herrick on the other hand demonstrates how testing the war could become to the identity of a profession jealous of its privileges and the guarantor of its own knowledge. The Barker controversy introduced an element of doubt about the British medical profession and its ability to adapt and take account of the new physical and mental challenges of the war. The rigidity of a well-established body of experts and their ability to defuse the situation enabled the profession to survive the war relatively unscathed after a minimal number of concessions.

Matthew Seligmann shows how the war could become an overpowering test of integration for the German-Jews. Using a selection of documents from American diplomats whose profession it was to observe and report before, during and after the war, Seligmann shows how the hyphenated identity of the Jewish minority became violently contested and grew so weak as to disappear for the non-Jewish Germans. In this instance the war, and particularly the postwar experience of defeat in Germany, destroyed generations of mostly peaceful and integrated coexistence. The war experience lingered on into the aftermath of the conflict and led to renewed ethnic and political tensions.

Roisín Higgins' paper shows that modern ideological wars could be appropriated by communities at a considerable distance and, in some sense, be distorted. The loyalties of the Catholic and Protestant communities in Northern and Southern Ireland overcame non-sectarian affiliations when they responded to the Spanish Civil War. In their response they included considerations relating to their conception of democratic and legitimate communities, which inflamed further the divisions of the island.

The globalization of war, either because it was a world war, or because it was an ideological war of opposing universal political extremes, affected small communities, ethnic and sectarian forms of identity in direct and indirect ways. Peace and war cannot exist in ignorance of the other in the age of media and mass communications. Contemporary responses to war abroad shape our own societies by proxy, along the lines described by these four papers.

10

NEGOTIATIONS FOR WAR: HIGHLAND IDENTITY UNDER FIRE

G. Urquhart

'Anybody will tell you; the Scots make good soldiers. Like my brar, Billy.' [1]

In the First World War on the Western Front, the 51st (Highland) Division, though composed entirely of Territorial Battalions, created for itself a reputation unmatched by any in the Allied army. The Division, a combination of battalions from the Argyll and Sutherland Highlanders, the Gordon Highlanders, the Queen's Own Cameron Highlanders and the Seaforth Highlanders, was raised by Major General G.M. Harper. There were early doubts about the division's ability as a fighting unit which were expressed in the hijacking of the Highland Division acronym: 'Harper's Duds'. By the latter stages of the war, however, it had became one of several fighting units that prided themselves on being at the top of the *Furchtbarkeit* list as the Germans' most feared opponents.

Even more than from an ally, such respect from an enemy is flattering. Such acclaim, however, can only consolidate an already existing reputation. Military morale is dependent on the ability of the soldier to have a clear self-image and concomitant purpose. None more so, it is alleged, than the Scottish soldier, according to Captain L. Gameson who served with the Cameronians: 'With some notable exceptions . . .', he stated, 'they are a race so ready to admire themselves, that an outsider's opinion may pass them unheeded.' [2]

So what then was the origin of such confidence? What enabled the soldier of the Highland regiments to maintain this pride in the face of annihilation? The answer lies in the symbolic universe created by, and for, the Highlander, and its use as a material gateway to a particular ideology, founded upon both myth and accepted historical explanation.

SYMBOLISM AND IDENTITY

For Durkheim, social phenomena are social facts, which endure over time, external to the biological life of individuals. They are 'endowed with coercive powers by . . . which they impose themselves upon him, independent of his individual will'. [3] By virtue of this coercive power, these constrain his free will to channel desires and action. These social facts are maintained through symbols which, in the military culture, may take the forms of military codes, standing orders, rituals, gestures and so on. In such a highly cohesive and structured way of life as an army, the norm is maintained by a high density of symbolism, to preserve discipline, morale and sense of purpose. In the Scottish regiments, however, where the cluster of symbolic practices known as 'Highlandism' came into being, there is another stratum of cultural activity which has a historical basis. According to Durkheim, 'the determining cause of a social fact should be sought among the social facts preceding it, and not among the states of the individual consciences'.[4] This paper discusses the particular dynamics and restraints of that symbolic culture on each category group. This discourse of the emotions has four variants: Highlanders 'proper', that is, native soldiers from the north of Scotland; Scottish soldiers from non-Highland regiments; Highlanders from abroad, in particular Canada; and finally, English soldiers in the Highland regiments. All are considered in terms of their veneration of these symbols.

KEY SYMBOLS – KILTS, PIPES AND GAELIC

John Keegan surmised that regiments of 'irregulars' in the great standing armies of the eighteenth century had certain characteristics. Among these was the creation of spectacle in their battle formations. Central to this spectacle was the uniform or costume, the 'exotic scraps of barbaric clothing'.[5] These are now only worn for ceremonial occasions. Though they were issued briefly before being withdrawn at the start of the Second World War, the First World War was the last major conflict in which kilts were valued as standard fighting kit by the military authorities. The spectacle afforded by that battledress, as a visual badge of warriordom, is celebrated by the sobriquet, 'the ladies from Hell', bestowed by the Germans upon the Scottish troops. It is the masculinity of the fighting vigour juxtaposed with the misreading of the feminine associations of the kilt which may have served to heighten the masculine ferocity of Scottish soldiers.[6] To understand the Scottish attachment to the kilt in the First World War, it is necessary to look to the history of the garment in the context of Highland history.

After the defeat of the clans at Culloden in 1746, kilt wearing, along with bagpipe music and the Gaelic language, were banned in a wholly successful attempt to eradicate the clan system as a functional economic and social regime. Thus the precedent of their being the concrete expression of a cultural ideology had been established: by eradicating the symbols the code on which they were based was extinguished. It was only after the raising of the Highland regiments for service in the British cause later in that century that kilts and pipes were reassigned to their appropriate military context. Thus the military identity of the Highlands was reinstated through these artefacts of material culture, and with them, the mythic associations with the pre-Culloden era and the notion of the Highlander as savage outlaw.

Bagpipes have the distinction of being the only musical instrument recognized by a court of law as a weapon. After Culloden, James Reid, a piper in the Jacobite army, was tried in York for treason; his defence was that, as a piper, he had never born arms against the king. The judge, in response, argued that as bagpipes were so essential to the Highland military arsenal they must in themselves be instruments of war. Reid was duly executed.[7] Military piping was never so strong as during the First World War, but the cost in manpower was disproportionately high: over 500 pipers were killed and 600 wounded. Irrespective of the trench myth about the first man being the safest, as every soldier assumed someone else would get him, pipers were valued targets. Though the music was often inaudible in the heat of battle, as a visual symbol they were heartening and were often decorated, occasionally as the nominated representative of the unit. The ability of pipers and their tunes to motivate, rally and stir martial effort on the part of Highlanders is a truism. Though Irish, Indian and Ghurka regiments all employed pipers to similar effect, they are undoubtedly associated with Scotland. *The Times* of 21 September 1918 described a Colonel Leslie, a Russian of Scottish descent, who had never prior to the war spoken to a Highlander or heard the 'great war pipes of the North'. On hearing the piper of the Punjabi batallion playing the 'The Campbells are coming' and 'Scotland the Brave', he nearly wept.[8]

This story informs us of two cultural assumptions: first, that the pipes are capable of reaching beyond the intellect to the seat of the emotions, and secondly that they and the emotions associated with them 'belong' to the Scots, though capable of stirring any of the Allied troops to charge. As stated above, the pipers were responsible for celebrating regimental exploits by creating commemorative pipe tunes. 'The Battle of Arras', 'The Highland Brigade at Mons', 'Battle of the Somme' and 'Eyes Front' are just some that survived among many lost on the battlefields, largely untranscribed as was the tradition.[9]

After Loos, where they suffered great losses, it was decided that pipers should no longer lead charges, but they were often given privileged status as runners and carriers. Though this dictum irked, and was often disobeyed, the pipes were thereafter largely reserved for marching, recreation and ceremonial occasions.

For Highlanders from the Highlands, the prime key, the exclusive category sign, is the Gaelic language. For many soldiers, even in 1914, it was not only their first tongue, but for some, at least initially, the only one. There are reports of some Highland recruits getting as far as France in 1914, before being sent back as unusable, most commissioned officers being monoglot English speakers.[10] H.A. Munro, son of the novelist Neil Munro, tells the story of the English artillery observer catching the sergeant of the Ballachullish platoon instructing his men in Gaelic. He had neither heard of, far less heard the language before. 'You're worse than these bloody Indians!' he exclaimed, surprised at having such exotica within the uniformity of his own army.[11] The Colonial Soldiers in the next trench had at least the good grace to be truly foreign.

RECRUITING

Recruitment for the First World War in Great Britain went through two distinct phases: volunteering and conscription. War had long since been anticipated, so when it came the recruiting offices were thronged with eager and excited young men who sought to grab some glory before Christmas, when, it was alleged, the war would all be over. Propaganda of German atrocities maintained the momentum, and peer pressure, catalysed by 'Pals Regiments' from business institutions and communities, guaranteed a sufficient and steady flow of soldiers for the trenches. By the start of 1915, the British Expeditionary Force, 'the old contemptibles', had absorbed approximately one million new recruits, 'Kitchener's Army', and two million by September.[12]

In the Highlands images associated with the pre-Culloden legacy were to surface in an attempt to motivate the civilians of the region to enlist. Under the ancient clan system, feudal fealty was evoked in the ritual of the fiery cross. The manner of convoking the clan on a sudden emergency was by means of the *Crois* or *Crann-tàra*, or fiery cross. This signal consisted of two pieces of wood placed in the form of a cross. One of the ends of the horizontal piece was either burnt or burning, and a piece of linen or white cloth was suspended from the other end. Two men, each with a cross in his hand, were dispatched by the chief in different directions. They ran shouting the slogan or war-cry of the clan and naming the place of rendezvous. The cross was delivered from hand to hand, and as each fresh bearer ran at full speed, the clan assembled with great celerity.[13] In September 1914, Locheil, hereditary chief of the Clan Cameron, was asked by Lord Kitchener, to raise a regiment of his clansmen and others.

> From the capital of the Highlands, he sent forth what one might call the fiery cross of the old days, and from there to every part of the world he asked Highlanders to come and serve in the war. . . . You take your Highlanders from all over the globe, wherever there is a Highlander, there you can take him.[14]

Military manrent, as perpetuated under the clan system, involved the tenants of the clans' lands responding to the clarion by virtue of their occupancy. The fiery cross was evoked, in this context, with reference to expatriate Highlanders and their descendants. Locheil appealed to memory, to the ancestors of those displaced by the clearances, famines and voluntary emigration, most particularly in the New World. The call was not only a plea to honour the old country in her present plight, but also a demand for ancestral loyalty due to the clan chief.

The Stuart pretenders justified their claim to the throne through the Divine Right of Kings. Pittock has it that 'Jacobites confessed no treason and asserted their own righteousness'.[15] As in the clan risings of the eighteenth century, the justice of the British cause in the First World War was emphasized, both nationally and regionally: 'the whole nation was unanimous that the war was right . . . let them come and show what Highlanders are made of.'[16]

That 1914 was the sexcentenary of the Battle of Bannockburn was not lost on Sir Robert Finlay, addressing a rally in Nairn Public Hall:

> How nobly Nairn, both town and county had done its duty. . . . Many of them had read that most interesting book published lately . . . about the Scottish Wars of Independence in which was pointed out the conspicuous part which the province of Moray played in repelling the aggression of Edward I. The province of Moray in these days was a very large one, and included Nairnshire. He rejoiced to know that the spirit that animated the province in the Scottish Wars of Independence was still alive, and that Nairnshire was still sending recruits to both the Army and Navy.[17]

As so often in warfare, the then enemy was now an ally. The same speaker, four days later in Kingussie, used a more recent campaign, but the same techniques of precedent and flattery:

> He appealed to the young men of Badenoch – a district renowned for soldiering. In the Peninsular War, Highlanders played a great part, and it is to the Highlands they again look for men like those who rallied to Wellington during that trying campaign. The present struggle is one of life or death, and the more Highlanders we have the more certain we are of winning.[18]

Thus, the historical precedent for the call to arms in the Highlands was established. It is worth quoting from a poem published in September 1914 in the *Inverness Courier*, 'The Territorial War Song':

> Our battlepipes are piping for the gathering of the men –
> They come from croft and clachan, from Island and from Glen;
> In every town from hillside brown from East and West and North,
> Is heard the heartsome music while the men come marching forth.
> The martial fires that stirred our sires are burning bright today.
> The Highlandmen and Islandmen are ready for the fray.[19]

The icons of the fiery cross and bagpipes were evoked in this locally written poem. In a syndicated poem, published in the *Inverness Courier*, which also addressed the specific characteristic of the other subgroupings in the United Kingdom, the third verse goes:

Sons of Scotland, ever foremost
When the cry of honour rings.
From the hill and silent moorland
See the sturdy clansman springs.
Skirl of pipes and beat of drummers!
Lo, Ye tally Britons all!
For the mother country calls you,
And you hear her call.[20]

The images are those of a barren countryside, redolent of James McPherson's Ossianic verses. The volunteers appear directly from the land, as if part of it. Strangely, though kilts are never mentioned, they are implicit in the imagery.

'HIGHLANDING' THE SCOTS

Of course, this powerful iconic grouping was, and is, not evocative for Highlanders alone. Their sole ownership of such a symbol set had long since lapsed. These images had assumed the status of a signified of 'Scottishism', propelled by the Romantic era and the patronage accorded by Sir Walter Scott.[21] Many from the central belt of Scotland, non-Highland regiments, like the Cameronians and, paradoxically, the Highland Light Infantry, who recruited from the Glasgow area, had adopted these trappings for their own military identities, unlike, it should be noted, the Border Regiments who have not historically been kilted. This military culture was so pervasive in Scotland that its symbols have come to represent even a civilian, non-military 'Scottishness'.[22]

J.H. Beith, who worked under the pen-name of Ian Hay, was already a writer of happy-go-lucky school stories when war broke out. Though born in Manchester, his Highland parentage ensured an affection for all things Scottish. He thus enlisted in the Argyll and Sutherland Highlanders, using his experiences as a captain there to fuel his best-selling novel, *The First 100,000*. Narrated in omniscience, though in the inclusive third person, it is the story of a platoon of clearly drawn characters, a 'gang show', in the pseudonymic Bruce and Wallace Highlanders and their adventures, through training in England up to the battle of Loos. Initially serialized in *Blackwoods Magazine*, its light-hearted optimism ensured a wide reading and mass acceptance of the representation of the Highland soldier as being fiercely patriotic, brave and obedient, with his heart in the right place. It is an extension of the 'kailyard' novel, full of couthy wit and unabashed sentiment.

Now we are out on the road again, silent and dusty. Suddenly far to the rear, a voice of singular sweetness strikes up 'The banks of Loch Lomond'. Man after man joins in until the swelling chorus runs from end to end of the long

column. Half the battalion hail from the Loch Lomond district, and of the rest
there is hardly a man there who has not indulged during some Trades holiday
or other in 'a pleesure trup' upon its historic, but inexpensive waters.

On we swing full throated. An English battalion halted at a crossroads to let
us go by gazes curiously upon us. Tiperary they know, Harry Lauder they have
heard of; but this song of ours has no meaning for them. *It is ours.* The feet of
Bobby Little hardly touch the ground. His head is in the air. One day he feels
instinctively he will hear that song amid sterner surroundings. When that day
comes, the song, please God, for all its sorrowful wordings, will reflect no
sorrow from the hearts of those who sing it – only courage, and the joy of
battle, and the knowledge of victory. . . . A shrill whistle sounds far ahead. . . .
Loch Lomond dies away with uncanny suddenness.[23]

Arguably Loch Lomond, the locale rather than the song, is an icon of a general
'Scottishness'; it has greater importance for Glaswegians than for anybody north
of the Highland Line. Hay, however, uses the song as a totem of unity for
countryman and town dweller, and commensurately in Scotland's case, agrarian
North and industrial South. (The catchment area of the Argyll and Sutherland
Highlanders, more so than any other Scottish regiment, contained those two
extremes.) The intensely specific topography is sentimentally stated, the song's
lyrics equating the loss of romantic love with the cessation of connection to the
land.

HIGHLANDERS ABROAD

As alluded to in Locheil's 'fiery cross' address quoted above, not all 'Highlanders'
lived in, or were even born in, the Highlands of Scotland. Two groupings are of
interest here: expatriates and adoptees. Locheil's speech was evoked by Colonel
A.B. Grant, in a meeting of clan societies in the Kenilworth Hotel in Glasgow:
'The Chairman said how the fiery cross had gone abroad and he was sure that
men of the proper stamp would come forward.'[24] Locheil had received a cable
from Canada:

to which so many of their Highlanders had gone, offering the service of 500
men of the Cameron Highlanders of Canada. . . . He also knew that a large
number of Highlanders wished to come over from Toronto. He knew that he
would get Highlanders for the Battalion not only from Toronto and Winnipeg,
but from the whole Dominion of Canada.[25]

Canada had its own regional versions of Highland regiments for some time, most
of which would see action in France. The uniforms of the Cameron Highlanders
of Canada were identical to those of the Camerons of Inverness. Many were

descendants of Highlanders, and many were themselves Highland- or Scottish-born. William Peden, a Scottish emigrant to Canada, surveyed the linkages with Scotland which the war had revitalized:

> The make-up of the unit [8th Battalion, 90th Winnipeg Rifles] was composed mostly of men of Old Country extraction, many of whom . . . had seen service with the British Army in India and South Africa. . . . The others, like myself, had no previous military experience, but they had one thing in common, all were young and apart from the patriotic motive and the spirit of adventure, was the opportunity of visiting their home-land and of seeing again the parents and relatives they had left behind, when emigrating to Canada.[26]

Ian McKay, of the 4th Cameron Highlanders, had tea with the colonel of the 48th Toronto Highlanders, and found other expatriate connections.

> He was Canadian born but spoke Gaelic so was greatly pleased when I addressed him in it and we had a Gaelic conversation together. Their acting Adjutant . . . was a MacKay descended from a MacKay who was in one of Wolfe's Highland regiments and settled in Canada afterwards. He was tremendously interested in the Clan. . . . Most of their officers were Macgregors or 'Macs' of some description and all very keen on claiming connections with Balquhidder, Lochaber or other Highland districts.[27]

The Canadian Highlanders are seen in the context of Scotland both by themselves and by Highlanders. Dugald MacEchern, Bard of the Gaelic Society of Inverness, elegized them thus in 1923:

> Wielding the axe of the settler
> Far in the depths of the forest,
> Digging the yellow gold
> Low in the depths of the canyon,
> Struggling on far fields of battle,
> Struggling and falling with glory.[28]

Like the Highland regiments, the Canadians are represented in the natural environment, battling against the elements: 'far' and 'low' are stressed at the starts of the lines; their Highland forbears were 'near' and 'high'. Their subsequent battle would be in 'fields', easier territory, though the soldiers, like the trees in the forest, would fall. The fourth line is an eerie adumbration of the trenches. As J.D.E. Mackie of the Argylls noted, they betrayed their hybrid personal characteristics, combining a clannish comradeship overlaid with a New World brashness: 'A Canadian Battalion was also in the camp and the Scots were impressed by their friendliness although a little shocked at their familiarity.'[29] From South Africa came a battalion of infantry, the South African Scottish, to join the 9th (Scottish) Division. Scottish regiments also came from other expatriate regions closer to home, Tyneside, Liverpool and London, all of whom were kilted.

What, however, of those having no Highland roots? In the heady early days of the First World War, it comes as no surprise that enlisting decisions could rely upon something as spurious as a fashion. In the towns where the Highland regiments trained and where they marched, such as Bedford, Basingstoke and Aldershot, their aesthetic swagger, military cachet and perhaps even the rebel chic of the Highland dress brought crowds of young men in their wake. The cinema topical, or newsreel, film from Bedford in 1915 of the 4th Camerons marching through the town, shot, presumably, by a local cameraman, framed the kilts centrally, to the exclusion of the heads and faces of the Highland soldiers.[30] The sense of spectacle was played upon; the townsfolk had seen kilted soldiers before, but never in such numbers. One of the social functions of the newsreel topical was often to provide a reflected representation of local community, but as these incomers had no individual identities their personalities became subsumed to the charisma of the kilt fetish. Many English recruits to the Highland regiments were taken up to the north of Scotland for basic training in the early part of the war. Private W.G. Crask of Bradford tantalized himself when allocated his uniform. After being initially disappointed in his Balmoral bonnet when expecting a Glengarry, he 'went back to billet and tried kilt on. Looks A1. My landlady didn't recognise me in my military rigout as I look much bigger. In fact, it was only the smile which let out the fact that I was I.'[31]

We are reminded of Carroll's Cheshire cat, and it is indeed curious how Crask vanishes. The early part of his diary, in Bradford, is replete with trivia, romantic suspicion and an amount of angst. Against his father's wishes, he chose the Seaforths over a local regiment, and by the time he has settled into Fort George, near Inverness, for training, the residual aspects of his civilian life have disappeared. His days are repetitive – drill in the morning, sea swimming in the Moray Firth and band concerts in the evening – and warrant little illustrative comment from him. The inner man is absorbed in regimental activity. Mentions of the hard-won, but flighty, Mabel recede and then disappear, suggesting a new, more contented love in his life.

Eric Linklater argued that in the course of the First World War a strange thing happened to the 51st Highland Division: regimental loyalty, the staple of the soldier, became subsumed to a greater pride in the Division.[32] A divisional identity, an agglomerated identity of 'Highlandness', came to the fore. This phenomenon was at least partially attributable to the influx of non-Scots, including a lot of Irishmen, to the Highland regiments, thus effectively diluting the extremely territorial origins of the Highland regiments. The inductees were thrust into a military environment premised on what was for them an alien culture.

If, as one of its lesser effects, war offers the chance for unprecedented cross-cultural encounters, and even in this case immersion, how did these ersatz Highlanders navigate through such novelty? Even if kilts and bagpipes were 'gateway' icons, there must have been more difficult straits of 'Highlandness' to encounter. The desire for integration was strong. Wrench notes how many Englishmen, having been drawn by the 'magnetic' kilt to become, as he puts it, without further qualification, 'Highlanders', played with their identities: 'Redhead and Metcalfe were both pals in the Durhams and like the others changed their names to something more Scottish. Theirs were respectively Robertson and MacGregor. What a pity none of them could disguise their native accents.'[33] We can, however, imagine them trying. Stainton, who joined the Liverpool Scots, had invented a Scottish lineage to justify his recruiting decision. His real motivation was 'a great love for that sweet, stirring and mournful music of the pipes'.[34]

On meeting a Gordon Highlander, he was thrown into self-examination. His admission that he felt 'a rank imposter', without any 'moral right' to wear a kilt, echoed the privileged status of ethnic origin. The awareness of history and lineage overruled even national patriotism. Others, however, were less conscience-stricken. The Town Major at Izel-le-Hameau made an attempt at integration. A.E. Wrench described, with delight, the Englishman's first taste of haggis, the national dish of Scotland:[35]

> He liked it, and said he was quite proud to be a Scotsman now. 'You know' he said 'you Scots folk do eat some funny things. But I liked it. It was damn good, . . . and I asked him for more.'. . . he still spoke as if the haggis was bothering him.[36]

The allusion to becoming a Scotsman is, of course, heavily ironic, but the subtext of 'foreign muck' is plain, and the chasm widened rather than narrowed. Steve Bradbury, who joined the Seaforth Highlanders in Ripon, had similar difficulty with certain Highland rituals. He was disappointed that 'Christmas Day was not celebrated like it is amongst the English Regiments, the Scots preferring to keep New Year's Day'.[37] After the event his disappointment was compounded by disgust. There is a sense of betrayal, in his detached observation, though we are reminded, in parts, of an anthropologist's account of a primitive ritual:

> New Years Eve [1915] was one of the worst nights I ever spent. Half the fellows in my tent were drunk, several fights took place, and Scotch patriotic songs were shouted and sung until 12 struck when someone blew a call on a

bugle. This seemed to be a sign for everyone to go mad, for all raced out and commenced kicking up the most unearthly row, dancing singing and fighting until about two in the morning, when those who could get back to their tents did so and fell asleep exhausted by their exertions, the remainder lying in the sand dead drunk. I was exceptionally miserable.[38]

Bradbury, though a Yorkshireman and proud of it, identified himself as a Scot in the course of his service; he acquired a taste for Burns' poetry and transcribed into his memoirs many newspaper testimonials referring to the Highland Division at war. For example:

Never very far away
I saw any number of men in bonnets and kilts waiting to have their wounds attended to (writes Mr Hamilton Fyfe) 'You "Highlanders," he said, 'you are everywhere. You get into all the battles.'
'Aye,' said one of them with a broad grin on his smoke-blackened features, 'we're never very far away.'[39]

The understatement, though arguably a Highland commonplace, is an authentic touch which charmed both Bradbury and the original writer. The quotation marks around 'Highlanders', which may be Hamilton Fyfe's, certainly merited inclusion in Bradbury's transcription and colluded in the irony. This is of course an example of how category shift manifests itself; 'Highlander' became a surrogate for 'soldier in the Highland Division'. Lance Corporal Vickery, 7th Seaforths, the hero of the *War Illustrated* story portraying 'The Dauntless Courage of a Highland Laddie', was from Walthamstow. Awarded the DCM, he had played the harmonica to steady the nerves of his comrades at Loos in 1916.[40]

IDENTITY

Identity, in this instance, is founded strongly on tradition. Though this is the case in all regiments, for the Highland regiments of the First World War this had resonances attuned to national history and perceived national characteristics. This was continually legitimated through cultural artefacts, practices and rituals, which were in themselves signifiers of a prior military tradition and way of life. Functionally, of course, one does not transport this baggage around consciously. Identity is not something at which one has to work; rather it is something through which one works, while doing other things. The identity symbolically forged was a technique of incorporation, an accessory to the core business of fighting and a mark that separated the 'self' from 'other'.

In the terms of the uncompromising binary that was the battlefield of the Western Front, the 'other' was across 'no-man's land' in the German trenches.

The Allied/British identity was the appropriate 'self'. Yet the Highland identity was a part of that composite: 'Jock' and 'Kilty' became subsets of the alias 'Tommy'. While categories of politics, nation and economic interest were elements of British nationalism, cultural identity, the discourse described by emotions, was discrete from the mechanistic allegiance owed, and indeed gracefully given, to the Crown by Highlanders.

Many old soldiers of the Highland regiments felt themselves to have become Highlanders not by virtue of their birthplace or residence, but through their participation in Highland culture. The fostering of 'Highlandism' in the maelstrom of the Western Front accelerated the acculturation process, burning into memory the ideology of 'Highlandness'. Those that survived, whatever their opinions on the war, capitalism, religion and the myriad ideological questions thrown up by the conflict, were assured of the part that the Highland regiments played in it and the part that Highland iconography played in that performance and the maintenance of morale. Correspondingly, in winning through, they adjudged themselves to have become more Highland.

Notes

1 I. Welsh, *Trainspotting* (London, Minerva, 1993), p. 190.

2 E. Spiers, 'The Scottish Soldier at War', in H. Cecil & P. Liddle (eds), *Facing Armageddon* (London, L. Cooper, 1996), p. 328.

3 In L.A. Coser, *Masters of Sociological Thought: Ideas in Historical and Social Context* (Fort Worth, Texas, Harcourt Brace Jovanovich, 1977), p. 129.

4 Ibid.

5 J.Keegan, *A History of Warfare* (London, Hutchinson, 1993), p. 75.

6 Spiers, 'Scottish Soldier', pp. 317–18, notes how, in an attempt to maintain an illusion of continuity in an undermanned sector of the front, the Highland Division were ordered to wear trousers, as the majority of the troops were moved in preparation for the Somme offensive. It could be postulated that the reputation of the Highland Division was at least partially due to their being one of the more conspicuously recognizable of the Allied units, and thus more easy to demonize.

7 C.A. Malcolm, *The Piper in War and Peace* (London, Hardwicke, 1993), p. 31.

8 Malcolm, *Piper*, pp. 33–4.

9 It is worth noting, however, that quite often the pipers most favoured by the men were those who could play music hall, popular and 'pantomime' songs. Malcolm, *Piper*, p. 12.

10 D. Henderson, *Highland Soldier* (Edinburgh, John Donald, 1989), p. 36. It is unlikely that this would have happened later in the war.

11 Imperial War Museum [IWM], H.A. Munro, diary, p. 24.

12 A. Marwick, *The Deluge: British Society and the First World War* (London, Macmillan, 1973), pp. 15–55. For a fuller account, L. Macdonald, *1914 – The Days of Hope* (London, Penguin, 1989). For explanation of the Highland recruiting tradition and its historical context, Henderson, *Highland Soldier*, pp. 15–53.

13 F. Adam, *The Clans, Septs and Regiments of the Scottish Highlands* (Edinburgh, Johnston and Bacon, 1970), p. 119.

14 *Inverness Courier* (4/09/1914), p. 4, col. 5. It is interesting to note the rhetorical similarity to Pitt's speech to Parliament of 1766, justifying the raising of the Highland regiments, 'I sought for merit wherever it was to be found. It is my boast that I was the first minister who looked for it, and found it in the mountains of the North. I called it forth, and drew it into your service. . . .' in Henderson, *Highland Soldier*, p. 12. The allusion is as if the Highlanders were immersed in the land, even part of it, and would require some extraction.

15 M. Pittock, *The Invention of Scotland* (London, Routledge, 1991), p. 60.

16 *Inverness Courier* (4/09/1914), p. 4, col. 3.

17 Ibid., p. 5, col. 2.

18 *Inverness Courier* (8/09/1914), p. 5, col. 3.

19 D.A. MacKenzie in the *Inverness Courier* (18/09/1914), p. 3, col. 3.

20 *Inverness Courier* (1/09/1914), p. 4, col. 4.

21 H. Trevor-Roper, 'The Invention of Scotland: The Highland Tradition of Scotland', in E. Hobsbawm & T. Ranger (eds), *The Invention of Tradition* (Cambridge University Press, 1984), p. 15.

22 Unsurprisingly perhaps, a large proportion of national costumes have a military origin.

23 I. Hay, *The First 100,000* (Edinburgh, William Blackwood and Sons, 1927), pp. 11–12. By way of contrast, J.D.E. Mackie of the Argyll and Sutherland Highlanders noted how, while encamped with them in England, he heard a battalion of the Sussex Regiment marching along to their song, 'We are the men of Sussex, Sussex by the sea'. Though this warrants no evaluative comment from him, his silence seems to voice the scorn in which he holds both the paucity and the vagueness of the geographic referent. Leeds University Library, Liddle Collection, J.D.E. Mackie, notebook.

24 *Inverness Courier* (8/09/1914), p. 3, col. 2.

25 Ibid.

26 Internet, Hugh Peden's Home Page, http://www.pacific-pages.com/hpeden/hist004.htm, 13 May 1997.

27 Ian MacKay's diary, 27 March 1915. Privately owned.

28 D. MacEchern, *The Sword of the North* (Inverness, Robert Carruthers and Sons, 1923), p. 233.

29 Leeds University Library, Liddle Collection, J.D.E. Mackie, notebook.

30 Scottish Film Archive, *The 4th Cameron Highlanders at Bedford, c.* 1915, ref. 1388.

31 The Highlanders Regimental Museum, Fort George, Private W.G. Crask, diary, 22 April 1915.

32 E. Linklater, *The Highland Division* (London, HMSO, 1942), p. 7.

33 IWM, A.E. Wrench, diary, p. ii.

34 Spiers, 'Scottish Soldier', p. 323.

35 Haggis is a pudding of various offal cuts, mixed with meal, onion, suet and spices served up boiled in a sheep's stomach. Historically, it consisted of the residue when the smallholding farmers had sold on the good meat that they could not afford to keep. It is eaten on occasions when Scottish identity is celebrated: St Andrew's Day, New Year's Day and Burn's Birthday. See Robert Burns' 'To a haggis', a celebration of poverty and integrity.

36 IWM, A.E. Wrench, diary, p. 166.

37 IWM, S. Bradbury, diary, p. 9.

38 IWM, Bradbury, diary, pp. 9–10.

39 IWM, Bradbury, diary, p. 143.

40 *War Illustrated* (5/02/1916), p. 9. The story describes him as a 'braw Scot', from the Gordon Highlanders, but concedes the rather anecdotal nature of the story. The full story is revealed in documents held at the Highlanders Regimental Museum, Fort George, ref. 84–65.

11

The Broken Soldier, the Bonesetter and the Medical Profession: Manipulating Identities during the First World War

C.E.J. Herrick

A s the papers in this volume demonstrate, the crisis conditions afforded by wars have often led individuals, groups and societies to question, reconsider, or recognize all manner of identities, be they individual, collective, national, racial, or ethnic. A similar relationship can be charted with respect to professional identity, that of the medical profession in the case of this paper. It has been argued by some historians of medicine that wars, especially the mass mechanized conflicts of the twentieth century, have presented conditions favourable to changes within the structure of medicine. According to such writers the 'unique' conditions of warfare, characterized by large patient numbers, increased availability of resources and enhanced professional cooperation, furnished conditions ideal for the development of specialization within medicine,[1] and for low-status groups to manipulate their position within the hierarchy of the profession.[2] In the context of the First World War in particular the identity of the profession was redefined, reassessed and questioned by those outside its ranks.

The structure of the modern medical profession was established in the mid-nineteenth century. By setting up a medical register composed of those individuals who had passed a recognized course of education and training, the 1858 Medical Act served to define the membership of the profession of medicine. Although other forms of medical practice were not outlawed, those on the register were granted a legal monopoly over the increasingly large field of state-sponsored medical practice. With the intrusion of medical professionals into areas formerly not considered to be within the province of the profession – for example, the home and the workplace – other healers were marginalized and defined as 'other', their definition as quacks and charlatans reinforced by their lack of the 'guild hall-mark'.[3]

Inherent in this dichotomy drawn between the two groups (and exploited by the members of the profession themselves) were the assumptions that the knowledge and methods of the orthodox profession were superior to those of its unaccredited rivals, that the orthodox profession had the interests of the patient at heart, and, moreover, that the profession could cure patients' ills where outsiders could not. The medical profession came to be identified in terms of therapeutic success based upon optimism relating to the cure and the prevention of disease, an optimism predicated on the basis of science. Such claims to 'unique' skill and expertise in the field of healing could be tested by individual and societal crises, such as individual illness and epidemics. Wars, themselves characterized by epidemics of disease and wounding, similarly brought the identity of the profession under scrutiny.

The growing status of scientific medicine was reflected in the status of medicine within the military sphere, which had been precarious in the nineteenth century. Medical men in both the army and the navy were denied the rank and privileges enjoyed by their fellow combatants and came to be associated with high mortality from disease in times of war.[4] The increasing involvement of civilian doctors in military medicine, in the form of consultants and reserve personnel from the 1890s onwards, served to infuse the formerly low-status practice of military medicine with the characteristics of the orthodox civilian profession. No longer were army medical officers perceived to be the camp-followers of old, skilled in amputation and little else besides.

The creation of an 'army' of sick and wounded soldiers during the 1914–18 war posed particular problems for a profession whose reputation was built in part on claims to expertise in the treatment of such cases. With the increasing involvement of civilians in armies rendered necessary by the nature of mass warfare, the medical treatment received by the wounded came to be of increasing relevance to the military authorities, of importance to their families at home and of increasing interest to the nation more generally. That the serviceman was variously identified as a unit of military manpower, a family and community member, as well as a potential worker, ensured that his subsequent treatment by the medical profession became a matter of 'national concern'.[5] A reflection of this was the widespread coverage of the work of the medical services in the care of the sick and wounded during the First World War in newspapers and non-medical journals.

The wartime identity of medicine was infused with the characteristics of the peacetime profession and with the rhetoric of science. Yet the medical profession was also perceived as part of the war effort. Medicine, as represented by surgery and bacteriology, was portrayed as being engaged in its own private 'war'[6] against wounding and 'the minute unseen forces of disease'.[7] In this 'splendid struggle'[8] doctors were identified as 'tireless, superb and indomitable men . . . intrepid . . . in the great work of charity and healing'.[9] More so than in any other previous campaign medical men were identified as combatants.[10] In a spirit of 'courage and self-sacrifice'[11] such men had surrendered their lucrative practices, choosing instead to serve the nation at war and, according to one article, they were 'serving [their] country well'.[12] In essence then, the medical profession was defined, at least for the public, in terms of altruism, humanitarianism and sacrifice. Such a portrayal was propagandist, being openly intended to 'increase the confidence of those at home that their loved ones who may suffer from sickness and wounds will receive every attention which skill and devotion ensure'.[13]

The profession was also defined in terms of its perceived therapeutic power. According to one article in *The Times*, doctors were 'armed with the sure knowledge of the wiles of disease'.[14] The application of that knowledge in the form of 'science, Listerism and mechanical ingenuity',[15] such articles argued, had, through the saving of countless lives, served to 'rob war of its ultimate horror'.[16] This interpretation was derived, in part, from medical successes early on in the war in the conquest of disease, the foremost being the virtual eradication of tetanus through inoculation. It related also to optimistic views on the possibility of defeating epidemic disease and infection in a military context, best illustrated during the Japanese victory over the Russians in 1904–5. This two-fold victory over both Russia and the 'silent foe', disease,[17] had highlighted the possibility of reducing wastage in war; medicine was now regarded as a potential strategic weapon.[18]

Although there were criticisms of the organization of the Army Medical Service (AMS), the overwhelming impression given was that medicine was the antithesis to war. It was creative, where war was destructive. Yet this was not the only perspective. This paper examines an episode in the medical history of the First World War which profoundly and openly challenged the identity and characteristics of the profession so often accepted without question. These challenges were not internal to medicine; they took place in journals and newspapers of the day and in the rarefied atmosphere of the House of Commons. The debate in question surrounds the abilities of the orthodox medical profession – that is, those on the medical register serving in the Royal Army Medical Corps (RAMC) under either permanent or temporary commissions – to be able to treat successfully one particular class of case, that of the partially disabled, which became a subject of growing concern as the war went on. The prominence of such cases was related to their very normality before the war. According to one writer,

> These men as a rule have no other handicap than the one they bring out of the war. They are young; with the exception of those who have contracted a chronic disease, they are fundamentally healthy; they have not been demoralized by years of privation or idleness or the habit of dependence. . . . The whole world is anxious to help them to the maximum degree of recovery, physical, social and economic.[19]

According to contemporary writers, and discussed in a number of recent histories of disability during the war,[20] the fact that 'so many young and able-bodied men [had] been maimed' in the same moment focused the attention of the public on 'the "social aspects" of disease and disability', absent in the pre-war period despite the educating efforts of the voluntary organizations involved.[21]

The claims of the profession to be able to 'repair' the broken soldier, much vaunted in newspaper headlines, came increasingly into question.[22] Central to this crisis of professional identity was the claim of one man, Herbert Barker (1869–1950), a bonesetter and self-proclaimed manipulative surgeon – that is, one who uses manipulation of the joints and tissues rather than surgery to rectify disabling afflictions of limbs and joints – to be able to cure partially disabled soldiers where the orthodox profession had failed.[23] Excluded from the profession through not having followed the prescribed course of education, Barker was effectively barred from treating such cases.

This paper charts Barker's campaign to be allowed access to wounded soldiers, thereby threatening the monopoly of the orthodox profession in the field of state service. The criticisms of the profession employed by Barker and endorsed by a vocal band of supporters centred not purely on the therapeutic failings of the profession relative to those of 'other' healers. Rather, the very attitude of the profession to their patients, to other healers and to the war effort itself was highlighted as being the antithesis to all the profession claimed to be. Widespread coverage of the debate and medical matters more generally, as well as the profound direct experience of large numbers of soldiers encountering daily interaction with doctors as yet unprecedented in peacetime, led to a more general appreciation of the characteristics of professional medical men and their unqualified rivals. The paper also examines the professional reaction to this, characterized by internal manipulations of the wartime organization and internal hierarchy of the profession made partially in defence of the territory of the orthodox profession.

In essence then, this paper is not simply concerned with surgical manipulation, but concentrates on the 'manipulations' of medical identity during the First World War. On one level this was effected through the media; however, the characteristics of the profession were also selectively used by different factions of the profession and those outside to further their own ends and professional ambitions. For Barker, the profession was an ailing patient he was destined to cure, a 'world . . . out of joint . . . to [be] set . . . right'.[24]

THE BONESETTER'S CLAIMS

Early in the war it was acknowledged that the 'price of victory' at least in part would 'be a heavy toll in maimed men',[25] compounding the wastage of manpower through the rejection of sub-standard recruits. It was regarding the treatment of such cases that the value of manipulative surgery (more commonly known as bonesetting) was raised by Herbert Barker. In the years prior to the war Barker had made efforts to gain professional recognition for his unorthodox practices, but to no avail. In 1912 in *The Times* he had been the subject of a discussion on the divisions between orthodox and alternative medical practices entitled 'What is a Quack?', although the interest in his situation was short-lived.[26] By throwing up a large number of joint injuries of the kind in which he specialized, the war presented Barker with an unprecedented opportunity to demonstrate his skills. Interestingly the treatment of joints was also an area in which it had been declared prior to the war that the 'practical surgeon with common sense has nothing to learn from the bonesetter'.[27]

At the start of the war Barker approached the War Office offering his services for the treatment of recruits who had been rejected, an offer which was refused.[28] In 1916, he again approached the War Office requesting to treat a different class of case, namely those servicemen who were 'fit and healthy were it not for the crippling of a limb or a disabling stiffness in one or more joints' and yet had been discharged from the army as unfit.[29] Barker claimed to be able to cure these partially disabled soldiers whom orthodox practitioners had apparently been unable to cure. According to the rhetoric employed by Barker and his supporters these cases numbered into the thousands. This 'constant stream'[30] represented a substantial wastage of manpower, a wastage it was alleged that was both unnecessary and caused by the deficiency of orthodox medical methods.

The subsequent rejection of Barker's second offer, which had been supported by a petition signed by a number of influential figures, all of whom had knowledge or direct experience of the therapeutic benefits of Barker's methods, was the catalyst for a debate in which the abilities and motivations of the medical profession were questioned. Many of Barker's supporters were former patients – 'the failures of the medical Faculty';[31] they came from 'every grade of society – from those who stand in the shadow of the throne, from the ranks of the learned, the aristocracy, statesmen, literary men, politicians, physicians, and surgeons, soldiers and sailors of all ranks, and from that great company indicated by the phrase "the world of sport"'.[32] He was backed by the journals *Truth* and the *English Review*, and it was the testimony of his clientele in such journals which defined the wartime identity of Barker relative to that of the profession. By questioning the therapeutic value of orthodox practices Barker implicitly challenged the identity of orthodox medicine. The writings in support of his claims represented an explicit attack on the medical profession.

The championing of Barker came at a time when manpower shortages were becoming acute. By 1916 conscription had been introduced and the debate over the virtues of manipulative surgery was dominated by the rhetoric of wastage and manpower. This perceived crisis of resources was made clear in an article by W. Llewellyn Williams in the *English Review*. He wrote, 'We are combing out every

available man from the industrial ranks. Employers of labour loudly proclaim
that the policy has been carried to dangerous lengths; that the productive
capacity of the country has been imperilled. An economy in men is as imperative
as economy in material resources.'[33]

A further impetus for the support of Barker came from the profession itself
with the publication of a report on 'Combined Physical Treatment' by the
Committee of the Section of Balneology and Climatology of the Royal Society of
Medicine, a summary of which appeared in *The Times* in August 1916. Combined
physical treatment,[34] a regime employed in the treatment of cases of chronic and
minor war disability, was described as comprising 'heat, massage, electricity,
movements' as well as manipulation. The method was widely used in France, but,
the report lamented, 'up to the present time physical remedies have not been
used with the same thoroughness and precision in England'.[35] Instead they were
regarded as 'fringe' medical practices. This difference in therapeutic emphasis
between the French and the British was significant, according to the authors of
the report, because some 80 per cent of cases of minor disability treated in
French hospitals (notably at the Grand Palais in Paris) were restored to fitness
and, more importantly, returned to duty.[36] According to Williams the report was
'an indictment of the methods so far adopted by the Faculty in dealing with the
extraordinary casualties following operations at the seat of war'.[37] It was evidence
of a deficiency in the medical armoury, one which Barker alone could solve. This
focus on the failings of medicine as justification for the need for Barker's talents
left unsaid the ambiguity of the definition between fringe and orthodox medical
practice which the report also demonstrated.

The relative abilities and character of Barker and those of the orthodox
medical profession were juxtaposed in articles which promoted the value of
manipulative surgery. The alleged 'successes' of Barker implicitly challenged the
therapeutic power of orthodox medicine and consequently threatened the
hegemony of a profession identified so heavily by its utilitarian claims. As
Jeremiah MacVeagh (MP for South Down, 1902–22) claimed in the House of
Commons, 'the skill of experts in manipulative surgery . . . [had] cured thousands
of cases in which the Faculty had been powerless'.[38] Supporters of Barker
identified the medical profession as being almost solely responsible for the
wastage of manpower through minor disability. For them, the problem of
manpower depletion was exacerbated by deficiencies in the therapeutic scope of
orthodox medicine. This left 'Thousands of soldiers . . . walking about maimed,
crippled, half-men, many of whom Mr Barker could make whole'.[39] Rather than
saving the wounded through accepting Barker's 'patriotic offer' the 'Faculty', as it
was termed during the debate, had instead sacrificed the well-being of the
wounded.[40] As Williams argued, 'To permit a cripple to be wasted because he
has not been subjected to adequate treatment, which can be obtained, is a
scandal.'[41] Although it was the military authorities who had rejected the services

of Barker the implication by Barker himself was that the military, through its dependence on the profession for the continuing supply of medical men, had been 'manipulated' by a self-serving and jealous medical profession.[42] By contrast, Barker was portrayed as working in the interests 'imperative and urgent of our disabled soldiers'.[43]

In the course of the debate the prospect of years of suffering, pain and debility were contrasted with the almost miraculous relief rendered by the manipulative operations undertaken by Barker which lasted but minutes. According to George Bernard Shaw, writing in the *English Review* in 1918 under the provocative title 'What is to be Done With the Doctors?', 'Mr Barker sets whole rows of crippled soldiers on their legs . . . whilst the Royal Army Medical Corps leaves the soldier . . . to lie on his bleeding breast and stare ghastly at the skies.'[44] Barker himself wrote: 'Is it not a tragedy that people should be left lame, in pain, enduring inconvenience for years . . . when relief can be afforded, often in a few minutes by manipulative operations?'[45] Symbolic of the contrast between the expertise of Barker and the medical profession was the case of Private Townley of the West Kent Regiment, who had been examined by some ten qualified doctors before being discharged from the army as incurable. He was allegedly 'cured in five minutes by manipulative treatment',[46] and his case was brought to public prominence by Mrs Frances Parker, sister of Lord Kitchener,[47] though the case was unusual in that it involved a member of the ranks of the armed forces, rather than one of the officer class.

The 'scientific' nature of the medical profession was questioned in the course of the debate. The continued ban on Barker was described as 'a defiance of science', contrary to the rhetoric of the profession.[48] The perceived failure of the British medical profession to recognize the value of alternative approaches to treatment, in contrast to the 'open-minded' attitude of the French was taken as evidence of the British disregard for 'scientific' principles in medicine,[49] and formed part of the wider critique of the 'British Neglect of Science'.[50] In Parliament it was wondered whether the War Office was 'making use of all science and knowledge' where the treatment of the wounded was concerned.[51]

Even from within its own ranks, the 'scientific' bent of the medical profession was questioned. From November 1916 there appeared in the *Medical Press and Circular*, a journal once fiercely opposed to Barker's claims, a 'mass of correspondence' from doctors supportive of manipulative surgery.[52] According to the editor, through its failure to establish a committee to investigate the efficacy of Barker's methods 'the profession will expose themselves to the suspicion that they do not care for science or humanity because they are thinking chiefly of the profession'.[53] He even questioned whether surgeons were the 'real seekers after truth' which they claimed to be.[54] This statement was mirrored by that from Austin Harrison, editor of the *English Review* (and a non-medical man) who saw the profession as 'deliberately opposing progress'.[55]

The most extreme version of events surrounding the treatment of the wounded and the performance of the medical profession came from the pen of George Bernard Shaw. His criticism was heavily permeated by his openly anti-medical feelings, as reflected in his support for mainstream anti-medical movements like anti-vaccination and anti-vivisection. According to one contemporary, 'Mr Shaw's Heroes' included 'osteopaths, bonesetters, Kellgrenites and medical gymnasts'.[56] For Shaw, the medical profession's attitude towards Barker, and bonesetting in general, indicated that its members saw themselves to be 'universal experts in all the arts of healing', even those – like manipulative surgery – in which they had received no instruction. They defined themselves in terms of 'omniscience, omnipotence and infallibility',[57] qualities which their singular failure in the treatment of disabled soldiers had brought into question. According to Shaw, what the profession deemed to be 'scientific progressive medicine' was 'largely dictated by the hygiene of the pocket' rather than by any rational means.[58]

However, the meaning of science in this context was ambiguous, although not in the way Shaw implied. The editor of the *Medical Press and Circular* did not call for the acceptance of Barker's methods, which Barker himself defined as 'scientific manipulative methods'.[59] Rather he simply called for an investigation of these methods to be made by the profession (and significantly, not by an independent non-medical group as was argued in Parliament).[60] A committee of medical men, while examining the substance of Barker's claims, would have served to demonstrate to the public the openness and fair-minded approach of the profession. It could also serve as a platform through which the techniques of the bonesetter could be assimilated into orthodox practice.[61] The willingness expressed by some members of the profession to give concessions to Barker were in part motivated by fears that the debate was a serious threat to the reputation of the profession and its standing in the eyes of the public.[62] This was seemingly confirmed in a letter from Major Wheeler of the 3rd Oxfords which was often quoted in articles pushing for manipulative methods to be accepted.[63] Wheeler wrote:

> It is unthinkable that professional prejudice will be so great that your efforts will fail to bring about a full investigation of Mr Barker's methods. Should you fail, no words could express the absolute disgust and profound contempt of the layman for a 'learned' faculty, which, masquerading as the servants of humanity, surpass in arrogance, ignorance and cant any act of any Trades Union or Guild of the 'non-learned' classes, whose organizations have the frankness to admit their real aims.[64]

The debate over the value of manipulative surgery was dominated by the image of suffering, maimed and crippled soldiers. Their suffering, it was argued, was a direct result of 'professional jealousy and prejudice'.[65] In Parliament the profession was described as 'a professional camarilla filled with insane jealousy of unqualified men who have beaten them in one branch of their own calling'.[66] This emphasis on the conservatism and jealousy of the profession was similar to the adversarial language used in the criticism of medicine in the nineteenth century when medicine was in the process of establishing boundaries between professional men and outsiders. In 1905, Howard Marsh had warned that treating bonesetters as 'ignorant quacks' would leave the profession susceptible to such criticism.[67] For Barker, the wartime debate on manipulative surgery was simply part of 'the history of medical and surgical progress' characterized by conflict between 'new ideas' and 'ingrained conservatism'.[68] Describing the profession as 'The Faculty' also served to imply that the profession, rather than making progress, had stood firmly still. Expressive of this was the comparison of the attitude of the profession towards Barker with that of 'the church . . . in the case of Galileo'.[69]

In the course of the debate over manipulative surgery then, the professional identity of medicine was challenged. Its claims to rationality, scientific knowledge, and therapeutic power were all disputed, the 50,000 disabled soldiers discharged from service by November 1916 standing as testimony to the failure.[70] The 'Faculty' of medicine was seen to have acted in a 'spirit of trades unionism' which sat uneasily with both the changing priorities ushered in by the war and the whole concept of a disinterested scientific profession.[71] By contrast, Barker was held up to be the paragon of all that the profession claimed to be.

It was further maintained that the attitude of the profession towards Barker, and by extension towards those injured in defence of the nation, was not in keeping with the wartime spirit of self-sacrifice, national responsibility and improvisation. The failure to exploit all resources in the care of the wounded was held up as an example of 'professional prejudice' unsuited to the emergency conditions of war. This was expressed in the following statement from one of Barker's supporters:

> We are sacrificing, more or less willingly, every day, some old rule or principle of action; we are scrapping old methods and boldly taking up new methods in every department. Is the one department to escape this revolutionary change the department which has to do with the medical and surgical treatment of our brave fellows injured in our service?[72]

It was such conditions, ushered in by the crisis of war, upon which Barker focused as the means to have his methods accepted.

In the House of Commons it was suggested that the Defence of the Realm Acts (DORA) could be invoked to allow Barker to practise for the duration of the war, thereby temporarily suspending the monopoly of practice held by qualified doctors.[73] This measure was resisted by the profession, challenging as it did the

very foundations of their professional identity. The legal status of the 1858
Medical Act was even investigated by Law Officers of the Crown, who found that
there was no legal difficulty involved in allowing Barker to practise.[74] The fact
that this was ignored by the military authorities hinted at other motivations
behind the continued refusal of Barker's offers.

DEFENDING THE PROFESSION – THE MANIPULATION OF MEDICAL BOUNDARIES

The ability of the medical profession to resist the challenge posed by the claims of
Barker was dependent on a number of factors, and was maintained through a
number of different strategies. From members of the orthodox medical profession
there was little in the way of direct refutation of Barker's claims. The *British
Journal of Surgery*, founded in 1913 and concerned primarily with the reputation of
British surgery, was silent on the issue,[75] as was the *Journal of the RAMC*. In *The
Hospital* in March 1917, the stance of the supporters of Barker was ridiculed in a
letter from 'A Friend of the House of Commons' titled 'Mr Squealer the Rat-
Catcher'.[76] The letter implicitly questioned the motives behind support for
Barker:

> It is well known that the trenches are swarming with rats, and many
> professional rat-catchers have failed lamentably and disgracefully to cope with
> the plague. We are acquainted with a most skilful amateur rat-catcher, to
> whom the Pied Piper of Hamelin was but a bungling amateur. We demand
> that he shall at once be employed in the Army, and receive military status,
> with a sufficiently noble uniform, with plenty of stripes and stars and crowns,
> and an abundance of pockets to put the rats in. The trade union of
> professional rat-catchers will, of course, object. Away with them! Crucify
> them! Bang them over the head with an Act of Parliament! The rat-catcher we
> recommend is Our rat-catcher. . . . Mr Squealer the rat-catcher is a grossly ill-
> used person, and we mean to see him righted.

By August 1917, the medical profession was represented in Parliament by the
imposing figure of Sir William Watson Cheyne, consultant surgeon to the Navy,
veteran of the Second Boer War, and former President of the Royal College of
Surgeons. In his maiden speech in the House,[77] Cheyne adopted what Barker
referred to as a 'gross caricature' of manipulative surgery – which Cheyne
explicitly referred to as bonesetting – suggesting that the methods were
dangerous, and the results inconsistent and impermanent.[78] He also refused to
treat Barker as a special case superior to the general class of bonesetters, which
was contrary to Barker's intentions[79] and a testament to Barker's confused
identity as both the exception and epitome of bonesetting.[80]

Another important factor in the debate, and one largely ignored by supporters of Barker, was the organization of the AMS. The strong focus on the conservatism of medicine, and on the power of the medical 'Faculty' to manipulate the military authorities, accepted that the profession in wartime could act as an autonomous body, which, I would argue, ignored the duality of medicine as practised in the military, as well as viewing the profession as a unified whole rather than as one composed of sub-groups ordered within a hierarchy based on gender and expertise. The threat to professional identity posed by Barker was most readily countered by modifications in the organization of the AMS and by changes to the internal hierarchy of the profession aimed at the treatment of the sick and wounded, in particular, the treatment of the disabled. Such changes were not a direct reaction to the debate over manipulative surgery, but stemmed from concerns surrounding manpower levels, and extant attitudes towards the war wounded.

Before the changes in the organization of the medical profession in wartime are discussed, the immediate context of these changes should be outlined. The height of fervour surrounding the alleged skills of Barker in 1916 and 1917 coincided with intense criticism of the army medical organization from both within and without. Behind this lay a wider concern for manpower needs and wastage, a critical issue in a mass war. However, where Barker seized on the medical profession as responsible for the ensuing crisis, other critics, in particular medical men, focused on the attitude of the military towards 'broken soldiers', that is those men wounded as a result of the war.[81]

Concern for the welfare of those rendered unfit for service was inspired by the combination of issues of national economy and wastage,[82] the move to conscription, and anxiety over the issue of pensions.[83] Articles appeared in *The Times* throughout July and August 1916 praising the work of military hospitals in the treatment of these broken soldiers, noting that 'Day by day the surgeons are giving the nation new men for old'.[84] These were balanced by critical discussions of the existing attitude of the military authorities towards wounded men which John Galsworthy summarized as follows: 'Refit the man for the Army quickly and as well as you can. If he can't be refitted for the army, pension and discharge him at once.'[85] Moreover, it was argued that such an attitude ignored the needs of the soldier, particularly his moral welfare.[86]

The responsibility for the welfare of the wounded was increasingly perceived to lie with the military authorities, and any deficiency in their treatment was regarded as a result of military rather than medical incompetence. It was, according to critics of the army, their duty not only to 'make those men who can be cured fit again', but to cater for the needs of those rendered unfit through service, especially when 'The Army alone has both the staff and specialists and the necessary powers of discipline' to effect rehabilitation.[87] As one correspondent of *The Times* noted, 'the Army has broken the soldier and the

Army should mend him.'[88] Such articles implicitly recognized the dual identity of army doctors and the conflict of interest which this engendered. These conflicts and dilemmas posed by dual responsibility to the army and to the soldier were prominent in the diaries of many medical officers, and in some cases were made explicit during the war.[89]

Much of the criticism of the military authorities pertained to their use of the skills of the profession as a whole and came from members of the profession as well as from politicians. Wastage of medical manpower through failure to utilize the expertise of specialists, employing them instead in menial jobs, was a prominent criticism and source of discontent for army doctors. Such 'misfits' of expertise and employment resulted in a 'shocking wastage of . . . medical men',[90] which in turn threatened the welfare of the civilian population, by leaving them dangerously short of doctors. This wastage of medical manpower was to be investigated by a Committee, the appointment of which was announced by the Secretary of State for War in August 1917.[91]

Discharging unfit men onto 'the already depleted civilian hospitals' was a further cause for concern.[92] Medical men questioned the common military practice of 'booting men out' before treatment had been completed.[93] As an article in the *Lancet* noted, 'The economical view under which they are now being discharged can only be justified if all that is possible is done for them, so that removal from the Army does not imply the reduction of them to civilian inutility.'[94] Doctors thereby criticized the wastage of both medical and military manpower effected by military policies, and the subsequent overspill into the civilian industrial context. This identification of manpower wastage as a military problem served as a powerful lever for those groups – both medical and non-medical – interested in the fate of the disabled.

Although medical authority was subordinate to military authority (a fact symbolized by the exclusion of a medical representative, the Director-General of the AMS, from a seat on the Army Council which was the administrative machinery of the army), where doctors could offer a solution to manpower problems the autonomy of medicine was enhanced. Members of the orthodox medical profession involved in fringe practices, like massage, electrotherapy, hydrology and orthopaedics, used the opportunities presented by the changed conditions of war to stake their claim for professional recognition, to manipulate the hierarchy of the profession, as Barker attempted to do. For example, R. Fortescue Fox, member of the Committee of Balneology and Climatology of the Royal Society of Medicine called for the 'scientific study of hydrology'.[95] Exploitation of unfavourable comparisons with the performance of the French in the systematized use of baths for the treatment of stiff joints and rheumatism helped to bring about increasing provision of these resources for wounded British soldiers,[96] a change from the early years of the war where treatment of injured soldiers by means of spas and specialized baths had been a focus for smaller-scale philanthropic ventures.[97] Such changes within the orthodox profession were not mentioned by Barker or his supporters. A review of Fox's 1917 publication *Physical Remedies for Disabled Soldiers* sharply contrasted the identity of the two groups: 'The disablements of our wounded from the war are very real and very serious, and demand most skilful treatment, based upon full and properly trained knowledge. They must, at all costs, be protected from the sensational cheap-jack methods . . . of the heterodox.'[98] Skill was ultimately seen to lie with qualified members of the profession whatever their position within the hierarchy.

In order to manipulate the existing hierarchy, medical men utilized the wartime rhetoric of manpower wastage, which came to focus not just on military utility, but also on 'the civic and industrial usefulness of every possible citizen'.[99] Unlike Barker they focused not simply on conservation of manpower levels for the military, but for the wider context of the postwar industrial struggle:[100] 'the battle of civil life'.[101] They proffered solutions to medical, military and civilian manpower problems through organizational as well as therapeutic changes, which went beyond the treatment of the disabled and filtered down into the whole approach to the sick and the wounded. This wholesale approach to treatment was particularly apt in a context where it was feared that all soldiers would return from the front to some extent 'disabled' by their efforts.[102]

Modifications of the organization of the medical services were not in direct reaction to the criticisms or claims of Barker, but in part served to render these claims inert. During the war the organization of the medical service was constantly evolving, spurred on by criticism of existing practices. Horse-drawn ambulances were replaced by motor vehicles; hospital provision increased and diversified. On the Western Front in particular, the static nature of trench warfare allowed surgery to be carried out nearer the front. This had direct implications for the prevention of wound infection.

In the treatment of other ailments which were a source of considerable manpower wastage, attempts at systematized treatment were made primarily in response to problems that faced doctors serving at the front. In the midst of war doctors experienced conditions radically different from those encountered in their civilian practices and hospitals. They only saw the patient for a limited period of his illness, the evacuation process removing him from the front in a series of discrete stages through different hospitals. Complaints that such a system interrupted the continuity of treatment – and by implication its success – were raised by medical men serving in the army, both at grass-roots level and within the hierarchy of military medicine.[103] The apparent failure of medicine to treat cases was not, from the perspective of the medical men themselves, a reflection of the failure of medicine but was rather a testament to the unusual conditions of warfare under which medical treatment was carried out. One response to this was the establishment of specialist hospitals. In such institutions, supporters of specialization argued, similar cases could be concentrated, effecting economies of

material and manpower, both medical and military. This was true of heart
disorders, shellshock, and bone and joint injuries.[104] Specialist hospitals were seen
to be successful and were actively promoted in wartime.[105]

Changes in medical provision for those cases which Barker claimed to be able
to cure also occurred throughout the campaign, rendering irrelevant many of the
criticisms of the profession implicit in Barker's claims. A softening of the military
reluctance to care for men unlikely to be returned to military service was the
immediate context in which these changes occurred. In July 1916, the Physical
Clinic was opened at 126 Great Portland Street, London, providing free
treatment along the lines of the combined physical treatment used in France.[106]
Similarly, discharged soldiers were able to obtain free treatment from the Royal
Hospital, Chelsea (a military hospital), providing it was thought that their
disability could be improved.[107] Yet these were still piecemeal attempts to provide
resources and treatment for 'broken' servicemen and ex-servicemen, rather than
organized attempts to solve what was known as 'the problem of the disabled'.
The move towards specialization had an immediate impact on the treatment of
disabled servicemen through the transformation of the status of orthopaedics, a
branch of surgery dealing with the treatment of bone and joint injuries, the kind
which Barker claimed to be able to treat, a change which, as Roger Cooter has
argued, was made partly in response to the claims of Barker.[108]

The apparent success of the medical profession in the treatment of wounds and
disease more generally in part served to counter the criticisms of the profession
made by those supporting Herbert Barker. Improvements in the treatment of
infected wounds, itself a crisis which at the start of the war had threatened the
very foundations of surgical identity, led instead to high praise of medicine in
national newspapers, bolstering the scientific reputation of the profession.[109] This
was further stimulated by the research undertaken by the Medical Research
Committee (MRC), itself a showcase for medical science. Their support for
organizational and therapeutic 'innovations' was packaged in a rhetoric of
medical progress.[110] The presence of bacteriological laboratories at the front
signalled the front-line importance of science to medicine in the war.[111] The
prominence of these changes outside the profession served as a counter to the
charge that the medical profession was unscientific, and the provision of evidence
as to the strategic value of medicine to the military authorities vindicated faith in
the orthodox medical profession and in new medical élites.[112]

Medical manpower was also an issue that only recourse to orthodoxy could solve.
The publication of manuals and dissemination of information on wartime medical
problems represented a means by which new medical recruits could be educated –
an important consideration during the war when doctors serving in the army came
from such diverse medical backgrounds. It also served as a symbol of the learned or
theoretical basis of orthodox medicine, in contrast to Barker's methods which were
shrouded in secrecy and associated with spectacular, almost magical cures.

CONCLUSION

For the military the emerging wartime medical organization founded on specialization and teamwork (and itself inherently critical of the profession) served to offer a solution to manpower and recruitment problems, and to present an alternative means of dealing with the practice of discharging men from service without looking to their long-term needs. Such changes were not made through the initiative of the profession alone; rather they received support from charitable organizations, like the Red Cross Society, and state sanction in the form of the maintenance of their monopoly.[113] The unity of medicine and charity in the rehabilitation of wounded soldiers served to signify the commitment of the profession to the wounded – contrary to the rhetoric of those supporting Barker – and, more importantly, the commitment of medicine to the war effort. That Barker's offer was rejected in August 1917 on the basis that 'If you admit bonesetters where are you to stop?'[114] – albeit with the proviso that individual servicemen could consult Barker 'on [their] own responsibility'[115] – the monopoly held by the profession was reinforced. This further cemented the symbiosis of the profession and the state inherent in the 1858 Medical Act.

The notions of teamwork and cooperation, which became widespread in medicine during the war, fitted in with the wider aims and ideology of the military authorities, unlike the individualism of Barker. Promoting as it did a regime of individual discipline and self-help, such professional medicine served to redistribute some of the responsibility for restoration of fitness onto the soldier, while demonstrating the commitment of the military authorities to the plight of those wounded in war. Part of the duties of the army medical officer lay in the maintenance of military discipline, in particular in the detection of malingering – another drain on manpower levels – which was solely the province of the orthodox profession.[116] Similarly, the regulation of pensions made use of the structures of orthodox medicine; this inherent link between the state and the profession was untouched by Barker's individualist and isolationist stance. Orthodox medicine offered hope of affecting savings in military and civilian manpower, while diverting criticism away from the military authorities. It was aimed at revealing the potentialities of both wounded men – through a combination of treatment and training – and medicine. Whether it served the needs and aims of the patient is another matter.

The ultimate failure of Barker to be accepted into the realm of orthodox medicine during the war lay in his conception of the identity of the profession relative to his own. He failed to recognize the duality of medicine within the military and the emergence of an organization aimed specifically at the solution of wartime medical problems which threatened the reputation of both the medical and the military authorities, and instead relied on a standard critique of professional identity ignoring its wartime metamorphosis. This 'new' medical

organization embodied hope of a new age of medicine based on a new hierarchy
and new distribution of resources, and on a conception of the potential, both
military and industrial, of the wounded soldier. What orthodox medicine came to
offer through this conception of the soldier was the possibility of savings of
military, civilian and medical manpower, beyond the scope of 'one man out of the
fraternity of unqualified practitioners'.[117]

Barker's claims, as well as a number of other therapeutic crises ultimately
served the making of wartime professional identity. Through such crises medicine
was forced to reassert its scientific credentials, adapt and adopt the rhetoric of
management which was so suited to the needs of the army, thereby exploiting the
already solid links forged with the state. By opening up the profession to public
scrutiny war not only presented the opportunity for internal manipulation of
professional boundaries and professional identity, but made the restatement and
manipulation of medical identity necessary.

My thanks to Deborah Brunton, Richard Hankins, and in particular Roger Cooter for their
comments on an earlier draft of this paper. I would also like to thank the editors for their insightful
comments. I am grateful to John Pickstone and the staff of the Wellcome Unit for the History of
Medicine, where this research was carried out.

Notes

1 Rosemary Stevens, *Medical Practice in Modern England: The Impact of Specialization and State Medicine*
(New Haven, Yale University Press, 1966).

2 G. Gritzer & A. Arluke, *The Making of Rehabilitation: A Political Economy of Medical Specialization,
1890–1986* (Berkeley, University of California Press, 1985), p. 9.

3 H.R., 'Modern Doctoring', *Nation and Athenaeum* (23/02/1918), 656.

4 N.D. Lankford, 'The Victorian Medical Profession and Military Practice: Army Doctors and
National Origins', *Bulletin of the History of Medicine*, 54 (1980), 511–28.

5 'Cure of Crippling Wounds', *The Times* (10/08/1916), p. 3, col. a.

6 According to 'The Sign of the Geneva Cross. The Work of the RAMC', in T.P. O'Connor (ed.),
T.P.'s Journal of Great Deeds of the Great War (2 vols, London, T.P.'s Journal Publishing Co. Ltd, 1915),
vol. 2, the work of the medical profession was a 'war for lives', p. 73.

7 'Science and the Health of Armies', *The Times History of the War*, 6 (1916), 78.

8 'Wounded and the Open-Air Hospital', *Country Life* (3/04/1915), 430.

9 'The Sign of the Geneva Cross', in O'Connor (ed.), *T.P.'s Journal*, vol. 2, p. 73.

10 'Mobilized Medicine', *The Field* (9/12/1916), 893.

11 'Surgery in War', *The Times* (6/03/1916), p. 5, col. d.

12 T.C. Wignall, 'The Day of the Doctor. Heroisms of Heart and Hand', in O'Connor (ed.), *T.P.'s
Journal*, vol. 2, p. 244.

13 D.P. Winnifrith, 'A Field Ambulance. Le Cateau, St. Quentin, the Marne, and the Aisne', in
O'Connor (ed.), *T.P.'s Journal*, vol. 2, p. 313.

14 Kenneth Goadby, 'Bacteriology and the Wounded Soldier', *Country Life* (16/01/1915), 157.

15 Lord Northcliffe, *At the War* (London, Hodder & Stoughton, 1916), p. 37.

16 'Mending the Broken Soldier', *The Times* (12/08/1916), p. 4, col. d.

17 L.L. Seaman, *The Real Triumph of Japan: The Conquest of the Silent Foe* (New York, D. Appleton & Company, 1906).

18 Mark Harrison, 'The Medicalization of War – The Militarization of Medicine', *Social History of Medicine*, 9 (1996), 267–76.

19 Edward T. Devine, *Disabled Soldiers and Sailors Pensions and Training* (New York, Oxford University Press, 1919), p. 17. This was part of a series of preliminary economic studies of the war undertaken by the Carnegie Endowment for International Peace. Although published in 1919 it was written before the end of the war was in sight.

20 Seth Koven, 'Remembering and Dismemberment: Crippled Children, Wounded Soldiers and the Great War in Great Britain', *American Historical Review*, 99 (1994), 1167–202; Joanna Bourke, *Dismembering the Male: Men's Bodies, Britain and the Great War* (London, Reaktion Books, 1996).

21 Devine, *Disabled Soldiers and Sailors*, pp. 3, 14.

22 'Mending the Broken Soldiers', *The Times* (12/08/1916), p. 9, col. d.

23 For details of Barker's career see Sir Herbert Barker, *Leaves From My Life* (London, Hutchinson, 1927).

24 '"Manipulative Surgery" and Manpower', *British Medical Journal* (3/03/1917), 303.

25 'A Land of Healing', *The Times* (21/07/1916), p. 11, col. e; 'The Care of Disabled Soldiers', *British Medical Journal* (7/08/1915), 227–8.

26 'What is a Quack?', *The Times* (7/11/1912), p. 7, col. e.

27 Edmund Owen, 'Joints', *Encyclopedia Britannica*, 15 (1910–11), 11th edn, p. 488.

28 Roger Cooter, *Surgery and Society in Peace and War* (London, Macmillan, 1993), p. 119.

29 R.F. Fox, *Physical Remedies for Disabled Soldiers* (London, Baillière, Tindall & Cox, 1917), p. 4.

30 W. Llewellyn Williams, 'Mr H.A. Barker's Offer. Military Needs and Medical Methods', *English Review*, 23 (1916), 334.

31 Williams, 'Barker's Offer', p. 334.

32 Williams, 'Barker's Offer', p. 334.

33 Williams, 'Barker's Offer', p. 330.

34 R.F. Fox & J.C. McClure, 'A Combined Physical Treatment for Wounded and Disabled Soldiers', *Lancet* (5/02/1916), 311; Williams, 'Barker's Offer', p. 332.

35 The success of the French in the treatment of such cases were praised in other articles: 'Mankind in the Re-Making', *The Times* (20/06/1916), p. 11, col. f; 'Mending the Disabled Soldier. What France is Doing', *The Times* (14/11/1916), p. 5, col. d. For a perspective on the French response to disability, see Roxanne Panchasi, 'Reconstructions: Prosthetics and the Rehabilitation of the Male Body in World War I France', *Differences*, 7 (1995), 109–40. My thanks to Roger Cooter for bringing this article to my attention.

36 'Cure of Crippling Wounds', *The Times* (10/08/1916), p. 3, col. a.

37 Williams, 'Barker's Offer', p. 330.

38 'Unqualified Medical Practitioners', *Parliamentary Debates. House of Commons* (hereafter *Parliamentary Debates*), 90 (1917), col. 430.

39 Austin Harrison, 'The War Office and Mr H.A. Barker', *English Review*, 27 (1918), 147.

40 Williams, 'Barker's Offer', p. 336.

41 Williams, 'Barker's Offer', pp. 330–1.

42 H.A. Barker, 'Manipulative Surgery: A Reply to Sir Watson Cheyne', *Nineteenth Century and After*, 82 (1917), 755.

43 Barker, 'Manipulative Surgery', p. 770.

44 George Bernard Shaw, 'What is to be Done With the Doctors?', *English Review*, 26 (1918), 18.

45 Barker, 'Manipulative Surgery', p. 767.

46 'Manipulative Surgery', *Parliamentary Debates*, 90 (1917), col. 1136. Statement by MacVeagh.

47 Mrs Frances E.J. Parker, *The Globe* (8/08/1916).

48 Harrison, 'The War Office', p. 146.

49 'Manipulative Surgery', *Medical Press and Circular* (14/02/1917), 134.

50 'British Neglect of Science', *Country Life* (12/02 /1916), 194.

51 *Parliamentary Debates*, 90 (1917), col. 1134.

52 'The Faculty and Mr H.A. Barker', *Review of Reviews*, 55 (1917), 49.

53 Harrison, 'The War Office', pp. 147–8.

54 W. Llewellyn Williams, 'Mr H.A. Barker and the Medical Faculty: The Turn of the Tide', *English Review*, 24 (1917), 116.

55 Harrison, 'The War Office', p. 145.

56 H.R., 'Modern Doctoring', *Nation and Athenaeum* (23/02/1918), p. 656. Shaw had long been a critic of the profession. During the war he was critical of compulsory inoculation against typhoid. See George Bernard Shaw, 'Sanitation Versus Inoculation', *New Statesman* (10/07/1915) reprinted in *The Works of George Bernard Shaw* (33 vols, London, Constable & Co. Ltd., 1931), vol. 22, pp. 130–4.

57 G.B. Shaw, 'What is to be Done With the Doctors?', *English Review*, 25 (1917), 488.

58 Shaw, 'What is to be Done', p. 493.

59 Barker, 'Manipulative Surgery', p. 755.

60 'Manipulative Surgery', *Parliamentary Debates*, 90 (1917), cols 1134–5.

61 Roger Cooter, 'Bones of Contention? Orthodox Medicine and the Mystery of the Bonesetter's Craft', in W.F. Bynum & R. Porter (eds), *Medical Fringe and Medical Orthodoxy* (London, Croom Helm, 1987), pp. 158–73.

62 This was best expressed by Frank Collie, MD, who, in a letter to *Medical and Press Circular*, maintained that the public were coming to 'question the single-mindedness of a profession hitherto beyond reproach', reprinted in Williams, 'The Turn of the Tide', p. 122.

63 Wheeler was one of five officers of the 3rd Oxfords who had been treated by Barker, either before or during the war. According to Wheeler they were known as the 'Barker Battalion': Williams, 'Barker's Offer', p. 335.

64 Quoted in Barker, 'Manipulative Surgery', p. 762.

65 Williams, 'Barker's Offer', p. 333.

66 Quotation from Jeremiah MacVeagh, in the *Evening Standard* (17/02/1917), reproduced in '"Manipulative Surgery" and Manpower', *British Medical Journal* (3/03/1917), 303–4.

67 Howard Marsh, 'Bonesetters and Their Work', *St Bartholomew's Hospital Journal*, 12 (1905), 115.

68 Barker, 'Manipulative Surgery', p. 756.

69 Harrison, 'The War Office', p. 145.

70 'The Problem of the Disabled Soldier', *Lancet* (18/11/1916), 867–8.

71 'Manipulative Surgery', *Parliamentary Debates*, 90 (1917), col. 1135.

72 Williams, 'Barker's Offer', p. 342.

73 'Unqualified Medical Practitioners', *Parliamentary Debates*, 90 (1917), col. 430. Statement by Mr Pringle.

74 'Manipulative Surgery', *The Times* (10/07/1917), p. 10, col. b.

75 R.J. Godlee, 'Introductory', *British Journal of Surgery*, 1 (1913–14).

76 'Mr Squealer the Rat-Catcher, by A Friend of the House of Commons', *The Hospital* (17/03/1917), 480.

77 *Parliamentary Debates*, 97 (1917), cols 1073–80. Speech by Cheyne.

78 Barker, 'Manipulative Surgery', p. 760.

79 Barker, 'Manipulative Surgery', p. 760.

80 For Cheyne's perception of Barker's identity see *Parliamentary Debates*, 97 (1917), col. 1080.

81 'The Broken Soldier', *The Times* (14/09/1916), p. 7, col. c.

82 'Broken Soldiers', *The Times* (15/09/1916), p. 3, col. b.

83 'The Broken Soldier', *The Times* (14/09/1916), p. 7, col. c.

84 'Mending the Broken Soldier', *The Times* (15/09/1916), p. 4, col. d.

85 John Galsworthy, 'Re-made or Marred? A Great National Duty', *The Times* (14/10/1916), p. 9, col. d. On Galsworthy's writings on the plight of the disabled see Koven, 'Remembering and Dismemberment'.

86 'The Care of Disabled Soldiers', *British Medical Journal* (7/08/1915), 227.

87 'The Broken Soldier', *The Times* (14/09/1916), p. 7, col. c.

88 Sophia Jevons, 'Broken Soldiers', *The Times* (16/09/1916), p. 9, col. c/d.

89 Imperial War Museum, Diary of J.H. Dible (23/08/1914), p. 11; Diary of Captain L. Gameson, p. 82.

90 *Parliamentary Debates*, 97 (1917), col. 1085. Statement by Sir Garrod Thomas.

91 *Parliamentary Debates*, 97 (1917), col. 1095.

92 'The Committee of Reference of the English Royal Colleges and the Problem of the Disabled Soldier', *Lancet* (9/12/1916), 983.

93 Imperial War Museum. Diary of J.H. Dible (9/08/1915), p. 120.

94 'The Problem of the Disabled Soldier', *Lancet* (18/11/1916), 867.

95 'The Scientific Study of Hydrology', *Lancet* (17/02/1917), 271.

96 Frank Radcliffe, 'Hydrotherapy as an Agent in the Treatment of Convalescents', *British Medical Journal* (7/10/1916), 554.

97 During the war some 50,000–75,000 cases received free treatment at British spa resorts like Droitwich, Stafford and Buxton. See David Cantor, 'The Contradictions of Specialization: Rheumatism and the Decline of the Spa in Inter-war Britain', *Medical History*, Supplement No. 10 (1990), 130; 'Droitwich Baths for the Wounded', *The Times* (5/10/1914), p. 9, col. e; 'A Droitwich Home', *The Times* (7/10/1914), p. 5, col. d; 'Wounded Officers at Bath', *The Times* (6/03/1915), p. 6, col. a.

98 'Reviews', *The Practitioner*, 99 (1917), 194.

99 Galsworthy, 'Re-Made or Marred?'

100 'A Land of Healing', *The Times* (21/07/1916), p. 11, col. e.

101 'The Problem of the Disabled Soldier', *Lancet* (18/11/1916), 868.

102 Devine, *Disabled Soldiers and Sailors*, p. 4.

103 Sir A.E. Wright, 'Address on Wound Infections', *British Medical Journal* (1/05/1915), 763.

104 G. Elliott Smith & T.H. Pear, *Shellshock and its Lessons* (Manchester University Press, 1917), p. 14.

105 G.H. Makins, 'Introductory', *British Journal of Surgery*, 6 (1918–19), 1–11.

106 'Physical Clinic for Wounded and Disabled Soldiers', *British Medical Journal* (8/07/1916), 58.

107 'Medical Treatment of Discharged Wounded Soldiers', *British Medical Journal* (29/07/1916), 148.

108 Cooter, *Surgery and Society in Peace and War*.

109 'Surgical Dressings Obsolete', *The Times* (10/07/1916), p. 3, col. c; 'Antiseptics Old and New', *Illustrated London News* (23/06/1917), 744.

110 See war issues of *Report of the Medical Research Committee* (London, HMSO).

111 W.P. Herringham, 'Bacteriology at the Front', *British Medical Journal* (23/06/1917), 832.

112 H.R., 'Modern Doctoring', *Nation and Athenaeum* (23/02/1918), 656.

113 'The Care of Disabled Soldiers', *British Medical Journal* (7/08/1915), 227. For details of these voluntary contributions see Koven, 'Remembering and Dismemberment'.

114 *Parliamentary Debates*, 97 (1917), col. 1074. Statement by Cheyne.

115 Barker, 'Manipulative Surgery', p. 756.

116 Sir John Collie, *Malingering and Feigned Sickness* (London, Edward Arnold, 1913). Collie's article on 'Malingering' in *The Medical Annual* (1914) included a section on stiff and painful joints, pp. 355–7.

117 *Parliamentary Debates*, 97 (1917), col. 1074. Statement by Cheyne.

12

THE FIRST WORLD WAR AND THE UNDERMINING OF THE GERMAN-JEWISH IDENTITY AS SEEN THROUGH AMERICAN DIPLOMATIC DOCUMENTS

M.S. Seligmann

It is often assumed that war in modern times, owing to the heightened sense of patriotism that it generates among its participants, invariably acts as a spur for the promotion and strengthening of forms of national awareness. This assumption is particularly prevalent with respect to twentieth-century 'total wars',[1] which are generally held to have impacted positively upon the development of national consciousness in two key ways.[2] First of all, the phenomenon of total war, by bringing about the collapse of several poly-ethnic empires that had previously demonstrated an ability to survive more limited forms of warfare, has been credited with enabling many nationalist movements to attain the goal of their own nation-states. The breakup of the Habsburg and Ottoman Empires and the creation of a patchwork of ardently nationalistic successor states, in which cultural identity and polity were supposedly more congruent, illustrates this clearly.[3] Secondly, total war has often been seen as an engine for the forging of national unity. Total war, because it requires a united national effort and engenders shared suffering and mutual endeavour, is attributed with the ability to facilitate the deferring of social and class differences and thus aid in the forging of a sense of solidarity. The popular perception (some would say myth) of the experience of Britain during the Second World War illustrates this paradigm in action. The Second World War, it is said, created a unity of purpose in the British people, promoted common goals and ideals among them and helped establish a consensus over the future direction of national policy. Although many of the elements in this representation of the war have recently been contested such that their validity has been called into question, it remains evident that the Second World War as a shared historical memory has provided a focal point for British national pride for several generations; its commemoration as a national golden age facilitates and maintains a common sense of national achievement.[4] In this way, therefore, total war, both in relation to, and irrespective of, its actual consequences, can be held to have bound the nation together like never before, creating in the process a new and heightened sense of national consciousness.

While total war can thus clearly be a factor that acts to advance and embolden forms of national identity, both by creating the opportunity for new nation-states to come into being and by forging national solidarity in existing ones, it must not be assumed that this is inevitably the outcome of such conflicts. Total war can also be a factor that undermines prior assumptions of national identity. This is particularly true in respect to peoples or populations that define themselves by means of a plurality of national associations. Such hyphenated identity groups,[5] so-called to highlight the compound nature of their self-perception, are rarely beneficiaries of total war. On the contrary, as several examples demonstrate, they are often among its early victims. Thus, it can be seen that in America, a society with several hyphenated groups, total war has helped to destroy some of these identities. The First World War, for instance, as has been persuasively argued, largely eradicated German-American culture and the German-American identity by making this particular compound designation unacceptable to the rest of the population.[6] Such destructive tendencies with regard to hyphenated identity were not, however, confined solely to America. The First World War similarly put pressure on certain hyphenated groups in Europe, in particular German-Jews.[7]

For Germans of all descriptions, the First World War was a traumatic experience. This was no less true for German-Jews than it was for Germans of other backgrounds. However, for German-Jews the First World War had a distinct consequence: it led to their being singled out from among the general population, a process that reversed many years of assimilation and integration. The idea that the First World War helped undermine the German-Jewish identity, such that a German-Jew ceased to be considered German and became once again just a Jew, is not a new one.[8] It is, however, an argument that is worth re-evaluating for two reasons.

First of all, there is the new historiographical context provided by the publication of Daniel Jonah Goldhagen's book, *Hitler's Willing Executioners*.[9] This highly controversial examination into the long-term origins of the Holocaust asserts the continuity in German history of genocidal anti-semitism. In advancing this thesis, Goldhagen attempts both to discount the idea that German attitudes towards Jews were ever subject to a process of change and to marginalize the contribution of factors other than extreme anti-semitism in determining the nature of the relationship between Germans and German-Jews. The First World War, for instance, plays almost no part in his analysis. In one short paragraph, its significance as a potential instigator of change is abruptly dismissed.[10] In the current debate on German-Jewish history, a debate which this book has done much to reinvigorate,[11] it would be well to reintroduce the hypothesis that war, as well as anti-semitism, could have played a part in forging German homogeneity and thereby redefining the place in German society of hyphenated identity groups, such as German-Jews.

The second reason for re-evaluating this hypothesis concerns the availability of untapped sources, the use of which will allow new evidence to be brought to bear on this question. The papers of American diplomats in Europe, which contain interesting commentaries on the changing perception of Germans with regard to the country's Jewish community, are such a source. Intrinsically interesting, because diplomats are professional external observers, these papers, a mixture of both official documents and private letters, are also valuable because of the nature of American society and the implications of this for the assumptions and outlook of its overseas representatives. American diplomats, although largely drawn from an élite stratum of American life, came from a country that was self-consciously pluralistic, ethnically diverse, and containing many hyphenated communities. An inherent awareness of the implications of multiple allegiance, if not a sympathy for it, was consequently something that American diplomats would have possessed as part of their cultural matrix. Their comments, therefore, have the potential to be of particular interest in respect to developments in Germany. Should they suggest, contrary to Goldhagen, that the First World War was not marginal but did, indeed, play a role in influencing the place of German-Jews in German society, this would be one further reason for reinstating the role of the war into considerations of this question.

The approach that this paper will adopt in order to bring American diplomatic perceptions to bear on the issue of whether or not the First World War adversely affected the position of German-Jews will be to present for comparison analyses of the place of German-Jews in German society as seen by American diplomats at three key moments: one before, one during and one after the conflict. First to be presented will be the position as it was reported in 1913. This was the last full year of peace that Europe was to enjoy before the so-called 'guns of August' transformed the continent's political and military landscape. As such it can legitimately serve as a snapshot and exemplar of the circumstances that existed just prior to the outbreak of war. It can also act as the benchmark against which German attitudes subsequent to the start of the conflict can be evaluated for indications of change. The second period of consideration is the midpoint of the war, autumn 1916. As both the chronological heart of the conflict as well as its nadir in terms of carnage and suffering, this was a moment by which any repercussions of the prolonged fighting – be they social, economic, cultural or political – might reasonably be expected to have emerged. Consequently, if the war were to affect the place of Jews in German society, then evidence of new and distinctive behaviour towards Jews should be apparent at this juncture, a fact that ought then to be reflected in the diplomatic reporting. The last of the selected time frames, 1921, comes from the period after the conflict and the signing of the Treaty of Versailles. This was an era of unparalleled psychological and material dislocation in German national life. Bounded at one extreme by the reality and consequent psychosis of unexpected defeat, it was also marked by revolution,

political upheaval and economic collapse. Most of this was already evident by
1921, a year during which the unwelcome consequences of the First World War
were immediately and starkly apparent to the German people. If the war and its
outcome were to have any impact on attitudes towards Jews, then this was a year
in which it should be evident and for which the diplomatic reporting might be
expected to be revealing.

Taken together, this montage from the diplomatic records purports to be
neither a comprehensive examination of American diplomatic coverage nor an
exhaustive evaluation of the place of German-Jews in German society. Yet
comparison of these three externally formed pictures of German-Jewish life at
these selected moments will allow certain preliminary conclusions. In particular,
the proposition will be tested that American diplomatic papers can be used to
illustrate the First World War's disruptive impact on the basic German
perception of German-Jews. Goldhagen's belief that the war was not a factor for
change in this respect will thus, in a Popperian manner,[12] be re-evaluated through
these sources.

The year 1913 belonged to a period for which it is widely accepted by historians
that Germany was an unequal and stratified society. Indeed, there is a large body
of literature that details the many divisions and inequalities that existed in
Germany along class, regional and confessional lines, among others.[13] That a
society such as this should also have been discriminatory when it came to those of
Jewish backgrounds is, therefore, hardly surprising. In Germany prejudice against
Jews was widespread, a circumstance that was noted by American diplomats, who
recorded the situation in some detail. Their opinions present a very particular
picture of the scope, force and features of anti-semitism in pre-war (Wilhelmine)
Germany.

At its most basic level, German anti-semitism acted to circumvent the legal
equality of status accorded to German-Jews by subjecting them to a variety of
disagreeable social slights and disadvantages. Such petty prejudices could be
manifested in a number of ways. A good example of their form and social impact
was recorded by Joseph Grew, then First Secretary of the American Embassy in
Berlin. His diary, a typed record of his more interesting activities and encounters
compiled both for the benefit of his family in Boston and also with a view to
posterity,[14] includes an account of a visit to the estate of the aristocratic Böcklin
family at Rust, where he noted the following incident:

> Baroness Böcklin, with her niece, Frl. Ida von Fries and her nephew, von
> Fries, arrived for tea, and afterwards we were regaled by a book which
> Böcklin possessed, a sort of Jews' Almanack de Gotha, showing all the noble
> families in Europe, Princes, Counts, Barons, etc., who were of Jewish origin,
> and containing humorous accounts of each family, among them being the

Henkel von Donnersmarks, the von Schoens, the di Paulis, Wolkensteins, etc. and of course the Friedländer Fulds and the Schwabachs. I know a good many of them who would not care to own to their origin and who must have had many heart-burnings to find themselves brought to light in this book.[15]

The reason that such minor acts of 'outing' could cause such alarm among its victims was that acknowledged Jewish antecedents could lead to more than just minor social inconveniences. Jews in Imperial Germany, notwithstanding their theoretical emancipation and legal equality, lived under a variety of civil and political disabilities that informally acted as limitations on their aspirations. The Kaiser, his government and his court, for instance, were rarely disposed to admit Jews to important positions.[16] This was well known by American diplomats. As Joseph Grew observed in a letter to his mother, this circumstance was even extended to include possible appointments to replace the then American Ambassador, John Leishman:

> The papers are talking about a certain German-born Jew named Morgenthau for his successor; I don't know whether there is anything in this, but I feel sure that the Emperor would never accept him, for though there are many estimable Jews, there are some countries to which they simply cannot be sent as ambassadors and Germany is one of them.[17]

Yet, in spite of such examples of social and political disadvantage, it was also the case that German high society did not debar those who could make a contribution to it. As a result, side-by-side with the private ridicule and career limitation detailed above, there existed a pragmatism that ensured that money, social sophistication and a willingness to entertain on a grand scale provided an entry into the highest social circles for many rich German-Jewish citizens. This, too, is well illustrated by a 1913 entry from Grew's diary:

> [Attended] dinner at the Geheimrat Goldbergers. He is President of the Berlin Chamber of Commerce, [and] one of the wealthiest Jews in Berlin . . . they have a splendid house opposite our Embassy on the Rauchstrasse and entertain magnificently. It was a large dinner of some sixty people, comprising several of the State Ministers and many interesting people. Alice sat next to the Police President, Herr von Jagow. . . .[18]

Taken together, these various extracts from the Grew Papers illustrate the nature of anti-Jewish prejudices in pre-war Germany, where antipathy and pragmatism calmly coexisted. Jews, while denied equal access to many types of opportunity, were still able to integrate themselves successfully into society, even at the highest level. No expectation is evident from the sources that any alteration in this situation, either for better or for worse, was expected by American diplomats. This, however, was to change with the advent of war.

The picture of Germany in autumn 1916 that emerges from the American diplomatic documents is, not surprisingly, dominated by the progress and effects of the war. At this stage, these were unusually pronounced. Germany was facing the combined onslaught of the Brusilov offensive, the struggle for Verdun and the battle of the Somme. This conjunction of events made autumn 1916 a particularly intense period of conflict. To compound this there were also difficulties at home, where the collapse of domestic production and the onset of the 'turnip winter' were producing major hardship. To combat the ever-increasing needs on both the military and home fronts, Germany was turning ever more consciously into a true nation-at-arms, mobilizing people and resources in an ever more comprehensive manner. In the view of American diplomats, this situation had two implications for German-Jews. At one level, it was beneficial to their position. The conflict that erupted in 1914, by defying expectations and turning into a protracted war of attrition, provided Germany's Jews with a considerable opportunity. As the war lengthened, long-standing barriers to Jewish advancement in the service of the state and, in particular, entry into the officer corps of the armed forces, became untenable.[19] As Grew, by then the American chargé d'affaires, noted, this led to a '*neu Orientierung* [new orientation]' in German politics that resulted in '[the] removal of certain disabilities from certain groups or classes, such that . . . a Jew cannot become an officer; (during the present war hundreds of Jews . . . have already become officers).'[20] Clearly, in this respect, the war was having a levelling effect, opening up opportunities that had previously been denied and providing many Jews with the chance to demonstrate that their patriotism was on a par with Germany's non-Jewish population. Indeed, this became a requirement. As Grew subsequently noted, 'there has been a great increase in the number of men called to the ranks who were previously passed as unfit or excused from service for one reason or another. A great number of Jews are being reexamined and forced into service.'[21] Although undesirable to many of those affected by this process, the fact that German-Jews were being incorporated into the nation-at-arms was a progressive measure and a mark of further integration. Unfortunately, this was not the only alteration in the position of German-Jews that resulted from the war. Other, less benign changes also took place and were recorded by American diplomats.

If, prior to the outbreak of hostilities in 1914, nothing was written in the American sources to indicate that Germany's petty prejudices, unpleasant though they might be, had the potential to take on genuinely harmful forms, this changed following German belligerence. During the war letters from the American Embassy in Berlin noted an alarming trend toward more sinister types of anti-semitic behaviour. This was particularly evident in 1916. By this stage the hardships caused by the intense fighting and growing domestic distress were beginning to create a desire for scapegoats. As a result, the same circumstances that were providing German-Jews with increased opportunities for participation in the life of the nation were also, paradoxically, beginning to isolate them from the rest of the emergent nation-at-arms. Ambassador James Gerard reported in August 1916 in letters to both the Secretary of State and to the President's closest confidant, Colonel House:

> The Jews are almost on the edge of being 'pogrommed'. There is great prejudice against them, especially in naval and military circles, because they have been industrious and have made money. Officers openly talk of repudiating the war loan which they say would only mean a loss for the Jews.[22]

Gerard's analysis of growing anti-semitism and the prospect of violence towards German-Jews is significant as it illustrates the dichotomous manner in which the war acted to redefine the boundaries of the German nation. While at one level, the conflict had a positive and integrative effect and expanded the possibilities for Jewish inclusion in German society, conversely and paradoxically it simultaneously worked in a negative and exclusionary manner by facilitating an image of German-Jews as an undesirable presense and an enemy within. During the war these incompatible developments existed side-by-side. The question of which trend was to predominate in the postwar period now needs to be addressed.

The events of 1921 lend support to the idea that the First World War and its outcome played a major part in transforming German anti-semitism into a much more virulent and dangerous prejudice, for, following Germany's defeat, anti-semitic activity became more pronounced. The activities and propaganda leaflets of the German National Protection League, the emergence of the stab-in-the-back myth and the growing violence against Jews have convinced some historians that this period saw the most extreme popular anti-semitism in German history.[23] American diplomatic sources support some of these conclusions. In the new conditions in Germany the possibility of traditional expressions of prejudice against Jews being replaced by more violent responses became the subject of evaluation by American diplomats. This is highlighted by an interesting exchange from early 1921. Writing to his friend, Ellis Loring Dresel, the American Commissioner in Berlin, Joseph Grew, now Minister to Denmark, reported,

> we have just had an interesting conversation with Mr Caro, who is the Russian expert at the French Legation here, based on a flying trip which he recently made to Berlin, during which he spent three days in that city. . . . There is . . . he says, an extraordinary antipathy against the Jews in Germany, and that a vigorous anti-Jewish propaganda is being carried on. He stated that he

brought back with him a large bundle of hand bills, posters, etc, issued by the anti-Jewish propagandists, with such inscriptions as 'Down with the Jews', 'Kill the Jews' etc, upon them. . . . He expects drastic pogroms in Germany in the near future.[24]

In reply, Dresel expressed the following: 'The feeling against the Jews, as you say, is very strong, but unless Germany really falls into a state of anarchy, I certainly do not expect pogroms.'[25]

The significance of this exchange is that it lends weight to two ideas: first of all, that the First World War strengthened German anti-semitism, a prejudice that was already prevalent at all levels; and secondly, that without a further impetus to radicalization, it is unlikely that Germany would have regressed to Russian-style anti-Jewish violence. As we know, such an impetus was later provided, with consequences that bore out, indeed exceeded, the prediction made by the American commentators.

This evidence regarding the views of American diplomats is notable for two reasons. First of all, it extends our knowledge of the reporting coverage of America's overseas representatives. The existing literature on Joseph Grew and James Gerard, although in many ways extensive (something that could not be said of the material on Ellis Loring Dresel), neglects their concerns about German anti-semitism.[26] These extracts can serve as a first step toward remedying this situation. Secondly, this evidence suggests that the First World War played a role in the development of the preconditions necessary for the Holocaust. In the view of American diplomats, the experience of total war and the shock of defeat made more radical and extreme the anti-semitism that already lurked beneath the surface of German society. Their correspondence thus casts a shadow on Goldhagen's thesis of an unchanging 'eliminationist antisemitic culture' that was largely unaffected by the First World War and serves to validate further the idea that the Holocaust was the product of an incremental process of radicalization, albeit one with more increments than current research would lead one to believe. It also tends to support the idea, put forward by Peter Pulzer, that 'if there was a golden age for the Jews of modern Germany, it came to an end in 1914'.[27]

Notes

1 The concept of total war is a hotly debated historical issue. Indeed, the very existence of the phenomenon, let alone its impact on nations and societies, has inspired controversy and dispute. A useful guide to some of the points at issue can be found in Ian F. W. Beckett, 'Total war', in C. Emsley, A. Marwick & W. Simpson (eds), *War, Peace and Social Change in the Twentieth Century* (Milton Keynes, Open University Press, 1989). A more recent examination into the distinction between limited and total war can be found in Brian Bond, *The Pursuit of Victory: From Napoleon to Saddam Hussein* (Oxford University Press, 1996).

2 Anthony D. Smith, *National Identity* (London, Penguin, 1991), p. 27.

3 John A. Hall, *Coercion and Consent: Studies on the Modern State* (Cambridge, Polity Press, 1994), p. 137.

4 For the notion of 'narrating the nation' through 'invented traditions', see Stuart Hall, 'The Question of Cultural Identity', in Stuart Hall, David Held & Tony McGrew (eds), *Modernity and its Futures* (Cambridge, Polity Press, 1992), pp. 292–5.

5 The term 'hyphenated identity' is generally deemed to refer to a person or group for whom the construction of nationality derives from the pairing, not necessarily through choice, of state citizenship with an additional cultural or ethnic designation based upon racial or ancestral origins. While the concept of hyphenated identity is capable of a positive interpretation based upon the advantages of a symbiotic twin heritage, it is more often used as a pejorative notion that stresses divided loyalties and inner ambivalences. In the recent literature, the term 'hyphenated identity' is often replaced by the word 'hybridity'. See, for example, Hall, 'The Question of Cultural Identity', p. 310.

6 Erik Kirschbaum, *The Eradication of German Culture in the United States, 1917–1918* (Stuttgart, Verlag Hans-Dieter Heinz, 1986).

7 For a discussion of how the First World War impacted on other minority groups see Panikis Panayi (ed.), *Minorities in Wartime: National and Racial Groupings in Europe, North America and Australia during the two World Wars* (Oxford, Berg, 1993).

8 C. Paul Vincent, *The Politics of Hunger: The Allied Blockade of Germany 1915–1919* (Athens, Ohio, Ohio University Press, 1985), p. 16; recently restated in Anthony Kauders, *German Politics and the Jews: Düsseldorf and Nuremberg 1910–1933* (Oxford University Press, 1996), pp. 62, 133.

9 Daniel Jonah Goldhagen, *Hitler's Willing Executioners: Ordinary Germans and the Holocaust* (New York, Alfred A Knopf, 1996).

10 Goldhagen, *Hitler's Willing Executioners*, pp. 81–2.

11 For a good (polemical) guide to the points under discussion, see Hans-Ulrich Wehler, 'The Goldhagen Controversy: Agonizing Problems, Scholarly Failure and the Political Dimension', *German History*, 15 (1997), 80–91.

12 Central to Popperian thinking is the notion that universal theories, such as Goldhagen's, can be falsified through the demonstration of exceptions. See Karl Popper, *The Logic of Scientific Discovery* (London, Hutchinson, 1959).

13 A good summary is to be found in Volker Berghahn, *Imperial Germany 1871–1914: Economy, Society, Culture and Politics* (Oxford, Berghahn Books, 1994).

14 A discussion of the nature and purpose of Grew's diary and papers can be found in Joseph C. Grew, *Turbulent Era: A Diplomatic Record of Forty Years, 1904–1945*, ed. Walter Johnson (2 vols, Boston, Houghton Mifflin, 1952), vol. 1, pp. xxii–xxiv.

15 Grew Diary, 11 December 1913. Joseph Clark Grew Papers, MS Am 1687. By permission of the Houghton Library, Harvard University (hereafter Grew Papers). The disadvantages of having a family name associated with Judaism have been described in Dietz Bering, *The Stigma of Names: Anti-Semitism in German Daily Life, 1812–1933* (Ann Arbor, University of Michigan Press, 1992).

16 John C.G. Röhl, 'Kaiser Wilhelm II and German Anti-Semitism', in *The Kaiser and his Court: Wilhelm II and the Government of Germany* (Cambridge University Press, 1995).

17 Joseph Clark Grew to Annie Crawford Clark Grew, 2 March 1913. Grew Papers, MS Am 1687.

18 Grew Diary, 8 January 1913. Grew Papers, MS Am 1687.

19 Details of these barriers can be found in Werner T. Angress, 'Prussia's Army and the Jewish Reserve Officer Controversy before World War I', in James J. Sheehan (ed.), *Imperial Germany* (New York and London, New Viewpoints, 1976).

20 Joseph Clark Grew to the Secretary of State, 17 October 1916. Quoted in *Papers Relating to the Foreign Relations of the United States: 1916 Supplement* (Washington D.C., Government Printing Office, 1929), p. 62.

21 Joseph Clark Grew to the Secretary of State, 7 November 1916. Quoted in Arthur S. Link *et al* (eds), *The Papers of Woodrow Wilson* (68 vols, Princeton University Press, 1966-1988), vol. 40, p. 146.

22 James Watson Gerard to Edward M. House, 8 August 1916. Edward M. House Papers. Manuscripts and Archives, Yale University Library. That mid-1916 was a significant moment in the history of German anti-semitism has been suggested by a number of historians. See, for example, Werner T. Angress, 'The German Army's "Judenzählung" of 1916: Genesis – Consequences – Significance', *Year Book of the Leo Baeck Institute*, 23 (1978), 117–37; George L. Mosse, *Towards the Final Solution: A History of European Racism* (London, J.M. Dent & Sons, 1978), p. 172.

23 Golo Mann, 'Deutsche und Juden: ein unlösbares Problem', Speech given to the World Jewish Congress in Brussels, 4 August 1966. Quoted in Herbert A. Strauss (ed.), *Hostages of Modernization: Studies on Modern Antisemitism* (2 vols, Berlin and New York, W. De Gruyter, 1993), vol. 1, p. 45.

24 Joseph Clark Grew to Ellis Loring Dresel, 25 January 1921. Ellis Loring Dresel Papers, bMS Am 1549 (160). By permission of the Houghton Library, Harvard University (hereafter Dresel Papers).

25 Ellis Loring Dresel to Joseph Clark Grew, 4 February 1921. Dresel Papers, bMS Am 1549 (160).

26 The main works on Grew are Grew, *Turbulent Era* and Waldo H. Heinrichs Jr, *American Ambassador Joseph C. Grew and the Development of the United States Diplomatic Tradition* (Boston, Little, Brown, 1966). The life of Gerard is considered in his autobiography, *My First Eighty-Three Years in America* (Garden City N.Y., Doubleday, 1951) and in several dissertations, including Theodore R. Bathold, 'Assignment to Berlin: The Embassy of James W. Gerard, 1913–1917' (unpublished Ph.D. thesis, Temple University, 1981) and James Lawrence Troisi, 'Ambassador Gerard and American-German Relations 1913–1917' (unpublished Ph.D. thesis, Syracuse University, 1978). In none of these works is emphasis placed on how American diplomats perceived German anti-semitism.

27 Peter Pulzer, *Jews and the German State: The Political History of a Minority 1848–1933* (Oxford University Press, 1992), p. 207.

13

FIGHTING FOR A REPUBLIC? THE RESPONSE OF THE IRISH PRESS TO THE SPANISH CIVIL WAR

R. Higgins

In 1937, the Catholic and Nationalist academic Michael Tierney argued the case for Irish neutrality in foreign affairs and advocated 'sacred egoism'. He wrote of the

> many kinds of thrill [to] be got out of participation in the disputes that agitate the great world outside [Ireland's] shores. It adds to our sense of our own importance, and the fury of the foreign combatants helps to warm our blood. Perhaps it is even healthy for us to forget our own disputes in the larger issues that press upon us from every side.[1]

It was certainly true that participation in foreign disputes gave the impression that Ireland was less than parochial in outlook. The country's response to the civil war in Spain linked supporters of the elected government to international struggles for workers or democracy. Champions of the Nationalist cause presented their case in the form of a worldwide battle for the rights of Christianity and, more specifically, the Roman Catholic Church. However, as in other countries, Ireland's response to the conflict in Spain grew out of its own problems rather than providing a healthy escape.

The Spanish conflict appeared to raise questions intrinsic to the development of the embryonic states of Northern and Southern Ireland. Historians have examined the impact of Spain's civil war on the depletion of the extreme Left and Right in Ireland and on the significance of the Free State's neutral stance. Yet the Spanish Civil War is often overlooked in more general histories of Ireland during this period, largely because it does not seem to have disrupted the narrative flow of the island's past. Despite widespread support for the Spanish Nationalists in Catholic Ireland the political order of the Free State remained securely democratic.[2] Both North and South reached intellectual and political stagnation in the 1930s, which made it difficult to see the Spanish ripple.

This essay is not concerned with the impact of the Spanish Civil War on the Irish nation. Rather it examines the way in which the conflict was depicted. It looks at the confusion of loyalties in Ireland and more significantly the way in which the war is discussed and refracted through Ireland's own experience. The question of depiction

therefore works on two levels. The first is concerned with the coverage of the
European conflict in the Irish press, while the second addresses the way in which the
North and South depict themselves, the image they project to their domestic and
foreign audiences. The manner in which the 'brooding trouble over the world [had]
come to a head violently in Spain'[3] allowed each country in drawing up its response
to make a statement not so much on Communism and Fascism as on the issues of
democracy, legitimacy, political violence and religious tolerance.

The Southern Irish Provisional government had been set up in defiance of
British sovereignty and gained recognition in the resolution of a War of
Independence fought between 1919 and 1921. In the two years that followed,
Ireland had fought its own civil war over the meaning of the Republic. By 1936,
although Ireland had achieved a relative peace, the Free State's constitutional
position remained unclarified, the unresolved issues being partition and the
relationship with the British Crown. De Valera had also spent his four years as
leader of the government attempting to appease a suspicious Catholic hierarchy.
As a consequence, when the Constitution appeared in 1937, it laid the twin
ideologies of Catholicism and Republicanism as the basis of Eire.

At the end of 1936, General Eoin O'Duffy gathered together a group of Irish
Volunteers to go and fight for Franco. With much less public celebration, a small
Irish Unit of the International Brigade was also formed and dispatched to Spain.
Official government policy was one of neutrality; however, as in other European
countries, this concealed the complexity of the country's response. The dilemma
for the new Free State was encapsulated in the form of its two Brigades: one
ultra-Catholic, the other left-wing and Republican.

The Northern Irish State too came of violent origins. Having thwarted the
democratic will of Ireland by threat of war, Ulster Unionists had obtained a
separate state in 1920 made up of six counties in the north-east. By the 1930s the
power of the Unionist majority in the North appeared unassailable, and the
democratic legitimacy of the state was questioned, not least by Liberals in Britain.
The international economic depression of the interwar period greatly undermined
Northern Irish industry and the consequent drain on British subsidies led to a
degree of insecurity in the Stormont government. The whole-nation nationalism of
Fianna Fail in the Free State and the Catholic population in the six counties, along
with accusations of sectarianism in Northern Irish institutions, meant that several
questions hovered over the viability of the Northern state.

For the majority of newspapers in the South of Ireland the Spanish Civil War
was clearly a conflict between the Cross and the Hammer and Sickle. To the fore in
presenting the Nationalist case was the *Irish Independent* which concurred with
Franco's declaration that this was not only a civil war 'where Spanish destinies
[were] at stake, but a war in defence of Christian civilisation'.[4] The *Independent*
described the Spanish government as the 'Red Forces' or 'Red Criminals', made up
of Anarchists and Communist rabble. It carried banner headlines such as 'Murder

and Pillage in Spain, Authentic Details of the Red Orgy, Many Shocking Crimes' followed by its own orgy of tales of the sacking of churches and beheading of nuns.[5]

The *Independent* had been edited by Frank Geary from 1936, and he had instigated a very Catholic approach for the paper. Geary sent the reporter Gertie Gaffney to cover the fight for Christianity. Gaffney (who also opened a fund to provide comforts for the Francoist Volunteers) was rewarded for her partisan reporting with a mention in O'Duffy's memoir, *Crusade in Spain*, with the observation that her 'articles were eagerly read in Spain and brought comfort to many an anxious parent at home'.[6] Even more significantly O'Duffy included in his acknowledgements all those who contributed articles to the *Irish Independent*, 'from which I got much valuable data',[7] thereby suggesting that the reports in the *Independent* had directly contributed to the shared memory of the conflict.

The *Irish Press*, which De Valera had helped to found in 1931, was a loyal vehicle for his government. It accepted the official line of neutrality, although it was accused of being 'more Catholic than the Vatican'. The other major newspaper in the Free State was the *Irish Times*. In 1936 it was described in the Catholic periodical, *Studies*, as being from the start and consistently remaining 'the organ of Protestant interest in Ireland'.[8] During the war in Spain the *Irish Times* urged a policy of neutrality on European powers and asserted that the struggle in Spain was 'between the Fascist and the democratic, not the Conservative and the Communist points of view'.[9] As a result of its failure to support the Nationalist side in Spain the *Times* felt the full weight of Catholic Ireland and lost readership and many advertisements from Catholic schools.[10] Other, less established organs met a more severe fate. The main voice on the side of the elected government in Spain came in the form of the *Irish Democrat*, which saw the Spanish conflict as an extension of its own struggle for Republican democracy; it folded in 1937. *Ireland Today*, a left-wing intellectual journal, survived only from 1936 to 1938 and its demise resulted largely from its support for the Republican cause in Spain.[11]

Coverage of the war in the pro-Franco press was predictable in that it presented the conflict in terms of good versus evil:

> on the one hand . . . there was the great leader, General Franco, at the head of the Nationalist movement, composed of all that is great and noble in Spanish national life, fighting for a Christian civilisation; and on the other hand the forces of anti-Christ and destructive communism, which aims at destroying every vestige of religion in Spain and wiping out the name of God Himself.[12]

An acceptance of this type of simplistic argument allowed the pro-Franco press to side-step the issue of Fascism. The rhetoric (which mimicked that of the clergy in Ireland) cried out for support for Catholic Spain, setting its face against questions of democratic legitimacy or religious pluralism.

In the years before the Constitution of the Free State was drawn up O'Duffy had consistently pressed De Valera as Irish president on the question, 'what is the nature of this Republic?' In its stance on the Spanish Civil War the Free State government was in effect replying that the nature of the Republic was independent and democratic. The response of the majority of the press and the country to the conflict, however, was a reminder that the Irish Republic was also Catholic by its own design. Indeed the Irish Free State was far from pluralist. In 1925 the Cosgrave government had prohibited divorce, and three years later state censorship of literature was instituted. The Constitution managed to marry and enshrine these various elements and 'embodied the language of popular sovereignty, with strong theocratic implications'.[13]

Ireland Today offered one of the few forums for pluralism. It attempted to diffuse the hysteria surrounding any discussion of the war, and in 1937 John Fitzgerald warned, 'Let the people of this country realise, as the world realises, that Spain has just the ill-fortune to be the cockpit in a very normal and sordid, though singularly ruthless and tragical, war.'[14] More importantly, *Ireland Today* also confronted the problematic issues which were lost in the debate elsewhere. In December 1937 the journalist and novelist Garrett O'Driscoll wrote a piece which challenged the polarization of issues in Spain and the fact that the 'Catholic who does not favour Fascism is subtly given to understand that she or he must therefore, favour Communism', thus transmitting a 'skilfully-injected feeling of unease, which is altogether unnecessary and even a bit ridiculous'.[15] He also noted the way in which 'the cause of the Fascist [was] untruthfully and stubbornly put forward by innuendo as the cause of the Catholic . . .' despite the fact that, of the Fascist countries Japan and Germany, the former was hardly fighting for Christ and Germany had labelled the Catholic Church 'Public Enemy Number Two'.[16] In the previous issue Fitzgerald had attacked the supression of a proper debate in Ireland and argued that 'the claimed loyalty of the Irish people to the side of the Nationalists [*sic*] Spain would be very different, were the case as capable of free presentation here as in other countries'.[17] He asserted that religion had no place in the Spanish tragedy because it (religion) was 'immaterial, of the spirit, whereas the Spanish war [was] now on a strictly material basis'.[18]

It was, however, more convenient for the Irish press to reduce the complexity of the issues which the Spanish war raised. Southern Ireland was itself still negotiating the relationships between Church, citizen and nation. Although the country's official stance was in line with Britain, France and the United States, questions of democracy and legitimacy had been problematic throughout the island in its recent past. Owen Sheehy Skeffington, the foreign correspondent for *Ireland Today*, argued that 'the true democrat . . . must defend the people's right to choose a form of government which he personally thinks disastrous. Upon the people's right to make mistakes, and to learn thereby, depends the whole stability of democratic forms of government'.[19] This statement had particular resonance in Ireland. De Valera had ignored the democratic will of the people in rejecting the Treaty in 1921 and with his followers had forced a civil war. W.B. Yeats recorded in his diary in 1933, 'De Valera has described himself to somebody as an autocrat expressing the feeling of the masses. If we must have an autocrat let him express what Swift called "the bent

& current" of a people not a momentary majority.'[20] Furthermore, in 1932 the election to power of Fianna Fail (a party which had borne arms against the Cumman a Gael government and was closely associated with the IRA) provoked the fear of further conflict if the government party refused to relinquish power.

Much of the coverage of the war, therefore, self-consciously drew parallels between the Spanish war and the history of Ireland. Ambrose Martin argued in *Ireland Today* that the war was the result of the implosion of an ongoing battle between the 'privileged classes and the always oppressed Spanish people – not against what they call the rabble, but against those not of their caste – against the Spanish nation'.[21] This spoke a language which was easily understood in Ireland. Irish nationalism was necessarily other-defined, institutionalizing the dichotomies of Saxon and Celt which had been born of the colonial relationship and the definition of identities. Nevertheless, as the genesis of the new state demonstrated, there were competing definitions of the nation and of nationalism. De Valera's Ireland privileged the notion of a Gaelic, Catholic Ireland in a romanticized notion of the nation, a rejection of what were perceived to be the values of the Anglo-Irish and the English.

Martin's article was included in a symposium on Spain in the September 1936 edition of *Ireland Today*. A contribution from Mairin Mitchell asserted that the background of the war in Spain was poverty and starvation and the resistance of the land owners to reform. Visiting rural Spain, Mitchell was 'reminded of Irish social problems', adding, 'It might not be an over-statement to say that "Up Republic" in Ireland, means at bottom what "el reparto" or "divide the land" does in Spain.'[22] Mitchell drew clear parallels between the agrarian problems in Spain and those of Ireland's past, suggesting that even in a journal which attempted to be European in outlook, the population of Ireland was educated about the struggle through reference to its own experience. The empathy which resulted left little room for neutrality.

The process of telling the tale of a foreign war by drawing on personal experience was also true of the Northern Irish newspapers. In the North of Ireland foreign policy was determined by the government in Westminster; however, the Spanish issue also raised important questions regarding this embryonic entity. Unsurprisingly, there was support for the Spanish Republicans among organizations of the Left while the Catholic minority largely championed the cause of the Francoists. The Northern Catholic newspaper, the *Irish News*, mirrored the *Independent* in the South. The focus of its coverage was Catholic persecution – a very emotive issue for Catholics in the North of Ireland – rather than the question of Fascism. However, anti-Communist rhetoric peppered all reports and the struggle which was depicted was between diametric opposites. Commenting on the Fascist marches in London in October 1936, it discussed the triumph of Communist counter-demonstrations saying, 'East London was forgotten in their cry for arms for a Spanish democracy. . . . Unhappy workers are being forced to take pride in the thought that they are crushing the tyranny of Fascism. They do not know that they are becoming part of the tyranny of Communism.'[23]

The *Irish News* was also guilty of a failure to address the central issue of the illegitimacy of the insurgents' claim to power. Although itself a critic of the basis on which the state in which it operated was formed, it effectively overruled the democratic claims of the Spanish Republican government. In October 1936 it explained to its readers that the 'real origins of the trouble' lay in the virtual abdication of the government's responsibility to rule; the consequent outrages had the result that 'a movement which began as a military revolt grew into a great national movement, supported by all the sane elements in the country, who saw that the salvation of Spain was the issue at stake'.[24]

The politics of the *Irish News* during the Spanish Civil War were an expression of its vision of itself as the Catholic voice in the North. Sectarian riots in 1935 in Northern Ireland indicated the depth of religious division, and the *Irish News* offered a platform for the grievances of the Catholic minority with limited vision and a distinct lack of sophistication. In 1938 it recorded that a Belfast priest had paid tribute to the *Irish News* as 'catholic to the core': 'it will not tell us of divorce . . . it will tell the peoples of the horrors of Spain. . . . It will tell Lord Craigavon what we think of him, and it will tell the truth.'[25] The priest had inadvertently summarized the Catholic position of the *Irish News*: socially and politically conservative, nationalist and refusing to challenge its own rhetoric.

More interesting in some respects was the position of the Protestant papers in the North. Historians largely ignore the coverage given to the war in these newspapers because it was apparently neutral. Certainly the *Newsletter* and the *Northern Whig* received most of their reports from Reuters and the Press Association and they urged a policy of neutrality on the Westminster government. However, they faced the dilemma of conservative Protestant newspapers (the *Newsletter* referred to the Labour party in Britain as the Socialist party) which had little sympathy with either side in the Spanish struggle and recognized that whichever side won, 'the cause of government by the people for the people will have lost. . . .'[26]

Editorials in both the *Newsletter* and the *Northern Whig* used the Spanish war to discuss domestic politics and particularly the way in which Northern Ireland was perceived in Britain and in the Free State. Therefore, they very often juxtaposed discussion of democracy and religious tolerance in Spain with a defence of these aspects of the Northern Irish system. The *Newsletter* did carry reports of the persecution of priests and nuns in its news section but in August 1936 it commented that the massacre of religious was open to serious doubt:

Ulster people are not without experience of the lengths to which a campaign of falsehood can be carried, and reports of massacres of priests and nuns in Spain may rest on no more a substantial basis than allegations that the Roman Catholics in Ulster are being 'persecuted and exterminated'.[27]

The *Newsletter* continually returned to the point that the Roman Catholic Church depicted any erosion of its authority as a form of persecution.

In February 1937 Anglican and Free Church clergy paid a visit to Spain and concluded that 'if the leaders of the Roman Church in Spain could frankly and sincerely adopt a policy which separated the practice of religion from improper political activities, toleration would be assured'. An editorial on this issue in the *Newsletter* gathered pace to become a scathing attack on the hypocrisy of British liberalism and the *News Chronicle* in particular. The latter had accused Catholic Spain of acting as a zealous and powerful propagandist for the insurgents' cause in a way that could not go unchecked by any government. The *Newsletter* responded:

> The Ulster Government is confronted with an armed conspiracy which aims at its overthrow, and for daring to take measures for the protection of the Province Ministers are being accused of being a dictatorship, established in the interests of one creed. Again the Roman Catholic Church in Ulster, as in Spain labours to destroy a popularly elected Government. It complains of 'bigotry, injustice and persecution' because it is not placed in a privileged position, and at all times it ranges itself with the opponents of the Ulster government and State. In doing so it has the support of the Liberals and Socialist movements in Great Britain, in the eyes of whose members it is a glorious thing to see Spanish democracy protecting itself against clerical interference, but a most discreditable thing for an Ulster democracy to struggle against attempts to place it under the dictatorship of the Roman Catholic Hierarchy.[28]

In the process of defending the Northern Irish State, the Spanish Civil War could also be used as a means of drawing attention to the hypocrisy of the Free State's attitude. In November 1936 a heated debate preceded De Valera's rejection of the opposition's motion that the Dail should recognize Franco's government in Spain. De Valera used the fact that the Vatican had made no such step in support of his own inaction. The *Northern Whig* noted that the Free State government in considering its attitude looked first to the Vatican for a lead and suggested that the Protestants in the North would look on this voluntary subservience as a fact of great significance:

> Northern Catholics have made great play with the phrase 'A Protestant parliament for a Protestant people'. If this is a term of reproach, as they have sought to make it, what is to be said of a Roman Catholic Parliament in Dublin taking its cue not from the will of the Irish people but from Vatican City?[29]

Therefore the Northern Protestant newspapers attempted to create arguments which would underline the legitimate nature of their state by using the war in Spain to illustrate their commitment to liberal democratic values and also to attack their many detractors.

The Spanish Civil War focused international attention on the competing ideologies of the 1930s. In response, Ireland revealed itself as mired in its own religious debates. In the Catholic press the Spanish Republicans were depicted as Communist and anti-Christian. As within the Free State, debate over the true meaning of Republicanism was substituted by the idea of nation which consolidated the position of the Catholic Church and strove to maintain its democratic structure through illiberal means. This reaction left little room for self-reflection. The Unionist press was also incapable of moving beyond its own boundaries. It created potentially interesting debates on the legitimacy of the Spanish Nationalists' claims and the position of the Church but these were constantly used as a way of justifying the much-criticized state of Northern Ireland. The Spanish Civil War touched many people in Ireland in a significant way; thousands went to fight and more gave financial assistance. The war was, however, depicted as an extension of Ireland's own problems and this is certainly how it was understood.

Notes

1 M. Tierney, 'Ireland in the European Chaos', *Ireland Today*, 2, No. 4 (1937), 9.

2 T. Brown, *Ireland: A Social and Cultural History, 1922–1985* (London, Fontana,1985) p. 166.

3 'Editorial', *Ireland Today*, 1, No. 4 (1936), 1.

4 *Irish Independent* (5/10/1936).

5 *Irish Independent* (2/10/1936).

6 E. O'Duffy, *Crusade in Spain* (Clonskeagh, Brown and Nolan, 1938), p. 115.

7 O'Duffy, *Crusade*, p. vi.

8 S.J. Brown, 'The Dublin Newspaper Press: A Bird's Eye View, 1659–1916', *Studies*, 25 (1936), p. 118.

9 *Irish Times* (22/08/1936).

10 H. Oram, *The Newspaper Book: A History of Newspapers in Ireland, 1649–1983* (Dublin, M.O. Books, 1983), p. 187.

11 T. Brown, *Ireland*, p. 170.

12 O'Duffy, *Crusade*, p. 40.

13 R.F. Foster, *Modern Ireland, 1600–1972* (Harmondsworth, Penguin, 1989), p. 544.

14 J. Fitzgerald, 'Spain – Prospect and Retrospect', *Ireland Today*, 2, No. 11 (1937), 15.

15 G. O'Driscoll, 'Is Fascism Our Fate?', *Ireland Today*, 2, No. 12 (1937), 43.

16 O'Driscoll, 'Is Fascism Our Fate?', p. 44.

17 Fitzgerald, 'Spain', p. 10.

18 Fitzgerald, 'Spain', p. 15.

19 O. Sheehy Skeffington, 'A Foreign Commentary', *Ireland Today*, 1, No. 4 (1936), 7.

20 Quoted in D.T. Torchiana, *W.B. Yeats and Georgian Ireland* (Evanston, Ill., Northwest University Press, 1966), p. 161.

21 A. Martin, 'Origin of the Spanish Civil War', *Ireland Today*, 1, No. 4 (1936), 11.

22 M. Mitchell, 'The Struggle in Spain', *Ireland Today*, 1, No. 4 (1936), 14.

23 *Irish News* (5/10/1936).

24 *Irish News* (13/10/1936).

25 *Irish News* (8/04/1936).

26 *Newsletter* (19/10/1936).

27 *Newsletter* (19/08/1936).

28 *Newsletter* (17/02/1937).

29 *Northern Whig* (28/11/1936).

Part Four

WARS:
NARRATIVES OF
THE SELF

The final section of this book is about individuals and the fallacious notion of an aftermath. Niall Barr's paper discusses the uneasy representation of the veteran experience in British society and politics. It particularly emphasizes that the alleged comradeship and brotherhood of the trenches narrative did not resist the test of a class society like Britain in its chosen political vacuum. The British Legion did not become the equal of the German veteran organizations of the *Stahlhelm* and *Reichsbanner*, because it refused to allow the expression of social and political divisions.

David Taylor's paper discusses middlebrow trench literature which did not participate in the more refined aesthetics of war so popular among contemporary literary critics. The work of Patrick Macgill belongs to the 'grub-street' literary production and tapped the major sources of war's literary tropes. It reveals, however, how individual identity and sense of the self and masculinity were altered beyond recognition through war. Macgill did not return to a former life; his previous existence had never possessed the coherence and stability often attributed to pre-war life. His self, like that of many others, may not have acquired any literary value through the experience of war. Even if he borrowed his language, metaphors and images, he nevertheless managed to express something in spite of a multi-layered censorship. Many were not so lucky. Harig senior, described by his son in the novel *Ordnung ist das ganze Leben*, lost the ability to communicate anything of his war or even postwar self. There is no aftermath, and the war retains an immediacy and a terrifying freshness which can still never be translated into words or sounds. Kirstin Howard analyses a type of 'father literature' where a peace-loving generation came to terms with the deeds and crimes of their elders. Ludwig Harig's piece is unusual in its desperate empathy with a father lost in silence in spite of his son's effort. The process of mediation of this extreme case was through war when only Harig senior's comrades could translate his feelings into language.

When veterans die of old age in silence, their individual identities disappear without trace, and yet this collective shock remains inscribed in our collective consciousness and is celebrated through increasingly empty acts of remembrance. The novelist, the historian remembering his father or grandfather, or the historian of veteranship all participate in a desperate struggle to retrieve memory from death, identity from the ashes.

14

THE BRITISH LEGION AFTER THE
GREAT WAR: ITS IDENTITY AND
CHARACTER

N. Barr

In 1938 Alfred Duff Cooper propounded a popularly accepted view of the British Legion: 'Our British Legion is simply a collection of middle aged and elderly men who have been at some time in one of the Services and who meet together occasionally with the laudable purpose of wearing their medals and drinking beer. They differ in hardly any respect from a collection of Conservative working men's clubs. They have no uniform . . . and they have no organisation or officers.'[1] This view of the Legion is entirely inaccurate. The British ex-service movement was, and is, much more than a collection of social clubs and drinking dens. Just as importantly, the identity of British ex-servicemen went far beyond being a group of elderly men. All of the members of the British Legion were distinguished from the rest of society by virtue of their service in the armed forces. While the term 'veteran' implies an individual who has seen combat, and in Germany the concept of the '*Frontkampfer*', or front-line fighter, made this distinction clear and exclusive, the British idea of 'ex-service' is a wider, inclusive, term which embraces all those who have served in uniform in one of the three services. This article will trace the development of the identity of the British veteran during and after the First World War, demonstrating the importance of this new feature in British life and the manner in which the various elements and identities combined to form the British ex-service movement.

Prior to the First World War the position of the discharged veteran was precarious indeed. As a result of society's prevailing attitude of suspicion and hostility towards the army and the traditional pattern of recruitment which took men from the lowest classes in society there was little official help for the discharged soldier beyond the occasional campaign pension. Without any state provision, the old soldier could only look for help to a number of important charities, among them the Soldiers' and Sailors' Families Association, the Soldiers' and Sailors' Help Society and Lloyd's Patriotic Fund.[2] These charities were organized and run by wealthy citizens in the time-honoured traditions of benevolent paternalism, and ex-servicemen themselves took little part in them. These voluntary efforts were patchy and unreliable and the low social status of veterans, lack of public concern and paucity of funds generally left ex-servicemen to their own devices or to the Poor Law.[3] Veterans before the First World War were associated with poverty and disability as marginalized members of society.

On the outbreak of war in 1914, the voluntary efforts of the main charities were placed under immense strain almost as soon as the first wounded soldiers returned home in September 1914. Although the Prince's Fund and myriad smaller charities raised considerable sums for ex-servicemen during 1914 and 1915, and a statutory committee of the Royal Patriotic Fund incorporated and expanded much of the work of the charities from November 1915,[4] the voluntary system of provision could not cope with the unprecedented numbers of discharged and disabled men who returned to Britain during 1915 and 1916.

The lack of assistance on discharge, combined with meagre pensions, compared very badly with the grand gestures and promises made from recruiting platforms when these veterans had volunteered in 1914 and 1915.[5] The growth of veterans' associations owes a great deal to the sense of grievance felt by thousands of discharged soldiers during the war. The veterans of the First World War were very different from the 'old type of ex-soldier'. Men from every background and class in society had joined the army during the war and they were used to organizing collectively to overcome their problems and gain redress for their grievances. Unlike pre-war old soldiers who returned to civilian life in small numbers, and were quickly diluted within the civilian population, there were enough First World War veterans to organize informal local groups to discuss their grievances about discharge, pensions and employment prospects.[6] More importantly, these veterans believed that they had fought to save their country and refused to be marginalized when they returned to an ungrateful nation. During the summer and autumn of 1916, informal and disparate groups of ex-servicemen coalesced into a national organization.[7] Early in 1917, a conference held in Blackburn established the National Association of Discharged Sailors and Soldiers, which had links with the Independent Labour Party and trades union. Its main aims were a demand for employment training, better pensions and greater government consideration for the problems of discharged men.[8]

In January 1917, the National Federation of Discharged and Demobilised Sailors and Soldiers was formed out of a number of London groups incensed at the Review of Exceptions Act.[9] This Act was an attempt to comb out yet more manpower for the army by reviewing the one million men who had previously been passed unfit for service. The Act also made it possible for discharged, disabled men to be reviewed to determine whether they were still fit to fight.[10] Not surprisingly, the provisions of this Act provoked a storm of protest from veterans across the country and the newly formed Federation's cry of 'Every man once before any man twice' gained a great deal of sympathy and popularity.[11] Although senior military officers were invited to its first demonstration and meeting at Trafalgar Square, none attended,[12] and it was two radical Liberal MPs, James Hogge and William Pringle, who assumed leadership of the organization.[13] The Federation owed a great deal of its early success to the zeal and inspiration of Hogge who, although not an ex-serviceman, became its Honorary President. With a politician as leader, the Federation was connected intimately with radical Liberal politics,[14] and, from its inception, Hogge and the Federation were well aware of the usefulness of political pressure and persuasion. The Federation's main aim was for statutory war pensions based on right, rather than the grace and favour of the existing Royal Warrant. The Federation strongly believed that ex-servicemen should not be left to the vagaries of charity but should be provided with statutory assistance from the government and should have a say in that provision;[15] it demanded representation on government committees dealing with ex-service questions of employment and pensions. The barring of officers, other than those who had risen from the ranks, from membership was also indicative of the Federation's rejection of the traditional treatment of ex-servicemen.

Both the Association and Federation and many other smaller, local associations had come into existence without any central control or prompting from the establishment. The Comrades of the Great War, on the other hand, was formed in direct response to the success of the Federation's campaign over the Review of Exceptions Act. The stridency of the Federation in its call for 'Justice Not Charity' alarmed many members of the establishment who confused its demand for justice with subversion and revolution.[16] The Comrades were established after Colonel Sir Norton Griffiths wrote a letter to *The Times* in 1917 at the prompting of Lord Derby, arguing for a new, conservative ex-service association which would form a 'buttress against bolshevism'; Colonel Wilfrid Ashley, a Conservative MP, had been working along similar lines.[17] From the outset, the Comrades were linked with the Conservative Party and gained a great deal of financial support from many wealthy benefactors. Although the Comrades claimed to be a democratic organization, its first executive committee was filled almost entirely by MPs and officers[18] and, unlike the other ex-service organizations, the Comrades had no objection to traditional forms of charitable activity. After the formation of a more egalitarian council in 1918, the Comrades began to make notable progress, even converting some Federation branches to the Comrades *en masse*. Hogge portrayed the Comrades as an attempt to 'gas' ex-servicemen, with officers and members of the establishment offering beer and buns in Comrades clubs as a means of silencing protest.[19]

Given the characters of the three ex-service groups, and their different responses to the needs of ex-servicemen, there were numerous points of friction between them. Their differing political affiliations created a sense of rivalry, with the Comrades and Federation particularly suspicious of each other's motives. However, although there were serious differences between the organizations, the friction and conflict between them can be exaggerated. In general, the various organizations simply got on with the pressing task of ex-service welfare.

Indeed, the similarities between the various groups were perhaps more important than the differences. All the organizations were 'intensely loyal to the Crown',[20] although the Federation and Association combined that with a great distrust of government and the authorities. All were based on fellow-feeling, or comradeship, and all were concerned with alleviating ex-service distress to some degree or another. Apart from the National Union of Ex-Service Men which was formed in 1919, none of the groups was Bolshevist or rejected the basic framework of parliamentary government or existing structures of society.[21]

Although unity was not achieved until 1921, attempts were made as early as 1918 to bring the organizations together. A meeting was held under the chairmanship of General Sir Horace Smith-Dorrien on 30 July 1918 between thirty members of the various executives, and in 1919 a plan for an Empire Services League was discussed under the auspices of General Sir Ian Hamilton and the War Office. Even in 1918 James Howell, President of the National Association, hit upon the main elements of identity which would later exist within the Legion. He asked:

Will the new amalgamated body partake of the nature of a Trade Union? Prima facie, the question seems absurd but how is it going to be new otherwise without banging into the Scylla of a Charitable institution or the Charybidis of a Party-Political League of Khaki and Blue – and Petticoats. . . . It certainly will have to be run on democratic lines . . . and . . . the success of the new organisation will depend upon the quality of its basis or foundation, i.e. Camaraderie. We know this: what more do we want? Something in common! Must that something in common stop at the alleviation of an Ex-service Man's Distress? . . . Must it hold itself responsible for finding only employment for the class to which we belong? . . . Is it going to give a beanfeast to the veterans?[22]

Indeed it was this search for new identities and functions which later formed the character of the British Legion. When the Legion formally came into existence on 1 July 1921, as an amalgamation of the three previous bodies, it incorporated elements and ideas from all three of them. It stood for the accepted order of the British establishment and society but still reserved the right to use political pressure to gain concessions from government. Ex-servicemen could now join a unified voluntary movement with the characteristics of both a charitable institution and a trade union, which was based upon the idea of comradeship. Instead of being marginalized in British society, the British Legion represented a new identity for veterans, one based upon comradeship, pride in past service and most importantly the belief that they formed a group of men who had saved the country during the Great War.

The Legion has been described as a movement with four distinct elements: 'a benevolent society, an Old Boys Association, a quasi-religious cult and a [political] pressure group of considerable vigour'.[23] The Legion's main ideal of comradeship was sustained through social activities at branches and clubs, but Legion members also devoted a great deal of time and effort to practical schemes which assisted unemployed and disabled ex-servicemen. The Poppy Day Appeal raised the funds for these schemes and the rituals of Remembrance were taken very seriously by Legion members. The Legion also attempted to put pressure on government to improve pensions legislation and develop large-scale employment projects. A more unusual and less well-known facet of the Legion's activities was its cultivation of contacts with foreign ex-servicemen which gave the Legion a high national profile in the late 1930s. It was this very diversity which made the Legion an important organization, allowing it to harness the energies of thousands of ex-servicemen who had served in the First World War.

In 1922 Haig exhorted members of the Legion, 'Not to be content until we can count our actual financial membership not by hundreds of thousands but by millions if we are to accomplish the great task in front of us'.[24] Haig's vision was of a huge ex-service movement which, by its very size, would be able to demand large concessions from the government and assist old comrades in distress with large benevolent funds.

The British Legion grew steadily from 1922, when there were 116,433 members, until 1938, when there were 409,011. The continued growth of the Legion, until a second war intervened, proved that it was a live movement. The Legion not only replaced members who 'faded away' or lapsed in their membership, but continued to attract new members. While membership may have decreased in 1926 after the General Strike, the only period of stagnation on a national scale occurred in 1930 and 1932 with the onset of the Depression.[25]

As a voluntary movement, the Legion could never achieve the same numbers as a compulsory institution like the Armed Forces but even compared with continental ex-service groups, the British Legion was a small organization. Antoine Prost has estimated that French associations 'represented between 2,700,000 and 3,100,000 organized veterans, or almost one out of every two survivors'.[26] In Germany, both the *Stahlhelm* and *Reichsbanner* boasted membership figures in excess of a million.[27] In contrast, the Legion never amounted to more than 10 per cent of the 5 million strong ex-service community. The reasons for low membership are bound up in external factors but also with the nature of the organization itself.

In 1922 Corporal Claude Brown gave a comprehensive answer to the question 'Why am I a member of the Legion?':

Because, in the first place, I desire to perpetuate that wonderful spirit of comradeship forged in the service and especially on the battlefield, where ALL men were real chums and gave real service, friendship, shared joys and sorrows, work and play, and even their rations. I realised before hostilities ceased that Peace no less than War would want winning. I want to help all I can those chums who suffered so much with me. I want to help my fallen comrades widows and their orphans in their sad plight. . . . I want to help all those partially and totally disabled chums who nobody seems to want and whose present position appears so hopeless. All this and more can be done through the British Legion if all ex-service men will join. What baffles me is why any decent thinking comrade stands outside leaving the others to fight the cause.[28]

Brown was expounding a profoundly collective ethic of comradeship which lay at the heart of the British Legion. Comradeship meant the mutual trust, respect and friendship which grew up between men in their shared experience of army life and danger in the trenches. The value and importance of this 'brotherhood of the trenches' was a commonly accepted belief among British ex-servicemen, regardless of whether they were Legion members or not. However, Legion members identified themselves as a band of comrades who were working to help less fortunate ex-servicemen and care for the widows and orphans of the Fallen. Legion members were greatly concerned by the issues of housing, training, pensions and employment because many of them were working men who had faced these problems themselves.

There was also a strong commitment to the disabled ex-serviceman perhaps because of the large numbers of disabled veterans contained in the membership. Disabled veterans probably had a better realization of the problems that could confront ex-servicemen than many able-bodied veterans. One delegate at the 1923 Conference remarked that 'they had got to admit that 75 per cent of the members of the Legion were disabled men'.[29] This followed the same pattern found in French organizations. Antoine Prost has estimated that in the French movement 'almost all recipients of a war-pension belonged to a club, although six non-pensioned veterans out of ten remained outside the movement'.[30] The problems of disability formed an important part of Legion identity, which helps to explain the great emphasis placed on pensions work.

Although the practical efforts of relief work, pensions appeals and committee meetings were crucial aspects of the Legion, social functions and entertainment were also important. Many people joined the Legion branch to make new friends or meet old ones, but most importantly, people would only join and remain a member if they felt comfortable with the other members. The emphasis placed on sporting and social events was an echo of the sporting events encouraged by the army, but they were also a reflection of the interests of the members. As with any voluntary organization, social events were very important in maintaining interest in the more important and serious tasks which were accomplished.

Legion members also displayed pride in the achievements of the British army during the First World War – and in what the Legion accomplished for veterans afterwards. The emphasis on military symbols and trappings suggests that the British Legion was attractive to men who had found some meaning and purpose in soldiering. There was a great desire within the Legion to maintain martial pride, to remember old campaigns and battles and to retain the military trappings of parades, rallies and reviews. It is safe to assume that men who had hated the army would have few fond recollections to recount and no wish to march again on parade.

The importance of military symbols to Legion members was underlined by the long controversy concerning medals within the letters page of the *Legion Journal*.[31] There were many ex-servicemen who, although they volunteered, were never sent abroad. Those who fought in India or Ireland were not issued with any medals as this too was considered 'Home Service'. Many members believed that it was 'a great shame that the men who in 1914–15 voluntarily gave up all to serve their country were not rewarded with at least a volunteer's medal'.[32] Members felt deeply about medals or their lack of them and this could cause embarrassment on parade. An ex-regular officer who had volunteered in 1914, but had not served overseas, complained that he was asked

> why I did not wear my medals by men who, to my knowledge, were called up, as conscripts, right at the end of the war, and who, having been sent to France and never been in the firing line, wore medals. Since then I have ceased to attend all parades and rallies where it was directed that medals and decorations should or must be worn. I am quite certain that there are many men who will not join the Legion owing to this medal business.

The possession of medals formed a visible and physical distinction between members who had seen service – or active service – overseas and those who had not. Medals could open up the division between exclusive 'veterans' and the inclusive 'ex-servicemen', a division which rested uneasily within the Legion's all-embracing ethos.

In fact, many divisions existed between Legion members. Although Legion membership was open to all ex-servicemen, the Legion was filled predominantly by First World War veterans. Most members drew their sense of identity from their service in that war, even to the exclusion of other ex-servicemen. Funds were available for all ex-servicemen, but Poppy Day money was reserved exclusively for First World War veterans. Many Legion branches did not open their doors to postwar ex-servicemen and even pre-war ex-servicemen were sometimes made unwelcome. As one member put it, 'I myself belonged to a branch who resolutely refused to allow post-war men to join keeping it a close preserve for those who served in the Great War'.[33] We can thus characterize

Legion membership as a small but active number of ex-servicemen with a belief in collective action and pride in the achievements and sacrifices of the First World War.

Members of the Legion often described themselves as the 'cream of the ex-service community'[34] – a view which contrasted with the need to build a mass voluntary movement and implied that members set an example to other veterans. In 1925 Haig claimed that 'I believe, indeed I know, that the influence of the British Legion has worked powerfully in the past, not only for the fair and just claims of ex-servicemen and their dependents but for the general good of the country. Its influence has been a steadying influence in times when dire distress and bitter sense of grievance have well nigh broken the hearts of disillusioned men.'[35] The Legion was proud to claim that it formed a body of men of all ranks who stood for the good of the country. This represented a very different identity for veterans from the marginalized pre-war veteran, or the strident new identity formed during the First World War. However, within the Legion itself, it was believed that the ex-officer gave strong and stable leadership. The Legion had a highly developed hierarchy of leadership which had great influence on the character and development of the British ex-service movement. Legion leadership was not based on democratic and egalitarian lines but instead reflected traditional divisions of rank and class.

Haig believed that it was essential that the officer should play a major role in the Legion. Haig saw the ex-officer as the 'real leader' of the ex-service movement who would look after the welfare of ex-servicemen and guide them away from the 'pernicious doctrines' of socialism towards harmonious class relations. The type of officer Haig had in mind was the traditional officer and gentleman: the ex-regular, financially independent and socially confident, public-school educated man who had the time, money and energy to work for the Legion. These men were assumed to know that their duty was to help and encourage less able, less fortunate ex-servicemen.

In reality, there was a low level of officer participation in the movement which conflicted with these assumptions. L.H. Duniam-Jones expressed a common sentiment in 1926: 'The ex-officer class especially takes very little interest in the Legion, and speaking as one of them, I do feel that they are not fulfilling their moral obligation to the rank and file, to leave them to fight their battles alone.'[36] While bemoaning the lack of officers, Duniam-Jones was still supporting the assumption that officers should lead in the ex-service movement. It might be expected, given the low participation rate of ex-officers, that the Legion was dominated by ordinary ex-servicemen both in membership and leadership. However, in spite of the real and perceived lack of ex-officers in the movement, there was a concentration of ex-officers in the leadership of the British Legion. The majority of ex-officers did not involve themselves in the Legion, but those who did had a disproportionate effect and influence. Of the five National

Chairmen of the Legion 1921–1939, only the first, Thomas Lister, was not an officer.[37] In common with many of the officers involved in the Legion, the National Chairmen of the Legion were long-serving ex-regulars to whom the army and its traditions were a way of life.

The National Executive Council also contained a high proportion of ex-officers. The twenty-six representatives (once Ireland had been incorporated) were elected by the Area Conferences and then approved by the National Conference. Over the period 1923 to 1939 nearly half the representatives held the rank of captain or above and, on average, each member served for over five years, although some served for as many as sixteen years.[38] The concentration of officers in positions of responsibility continued at every level of the Legion. In the South-Eastern Area over the period 1929–32, the Area President, the Chairman, the Vice-Chairman, the Organizing Secretary and the Employment Secretary (both paid posts) were all held by officers of the rank of captain or above. In the Area Council ten out of the eighteen representatives held the rank of captain or above, while every vice-president for the four counties was a high-ranking officer.[39] This officer-heavy representation continued at every level, and in many rural branches the presence of officers was integral to the operation of the branch. At Sunbury-on-Thames the branch was not established until a retired regular officer moved to the village and called a meeting of local ex-servicemen.[40] It is clear that officer participation in the Legion leadership was much higher than the simple proportion of officers to men might have warranted.

The influence of officers had a number of important and far-reaching consequences for the movement. Many ex-officers brought the same method of leadership and command to the Legion they had utilized during the war. The hierarchy of Legion leaders was very similar to the rank structure of the armed forces and the position held by a retired officer in the Legion often depended on his military rank. Just as the Legion's hierarchy was not determined by the approval of the membership, so the egalitarian approach of democracy enshrined in the Legion charter was often overlooked by leaders more used to having orders instantly obeyed than having to compromise and persuade men to accept their position.

Colonel Crosfield, while Vice-Chairman, developed a dislike for Arthur Francks, the Metropolitan Area Chairman. He wrote to Haig in 1923 lamenting

the great detriment that Francks is to the Metropolitan Area. . . . I think Lister does appreciate the harm that Francks is doing to the movement but he does not see how he can oppose the delegates if they persist in electing Francks as Chairman. The trouble is that Francks is a terrifically hard worker. He goes round to the branches night after night, tells them what the Legion is doing and what he is doing, and the majority of the branches are, I fear, disposed to vote for him.[41]

Crosfield did not understand that such problems were part and parcel of a democratic organization. Francks had served in the ranks during the war and Crosfield clearly did not agree with Francks' values or methods. He may have been a great detriment to the Legion in London in Crosfield's view, but the branches for which Francks worked obviously did not think so. Crosfield's response was 'to get the right man elected' in Francks' stead, an aim which he achieved in 1925 by secretly canvassing support for General Bethune in direct contravention of Legion rules.[42]

The ex-officer leadership had a major influence on the character and actions of the Legion and on occasion there were serious differences in thought, action and approach between the leadership and membership of the Legion. However, although members might argue over how best to accomplish the aims of the movement, there was a very strong consensus on the main elements of Legion policy. For the majority of Legion members practical work, comradeship and entertainment in their local branch were of greater importance than any faults in the movement.

On Legion parades, members wore lounge suits with their medals but the reviewing general wore full uniform. Many Legion members were proud to be reviewed by retired officers with whom they had served and paid great attention to the details of uniform and medals. Legion members, with their fondness for military symbolism, often believed that duty and loyalty were more important than democracy. The popularity of the national officers within the Legion proved that the members were fully prepared to support strong leadership, even at the expense of proper participation in the movement. Although the members who proudly marched on Legion parades did not question the ideals of the movement they represented, the thousands of ex-servicemen outside the organization clearly did.

The methods and attitudes displayed by the ex-officer leadership did not appeal to all ex-servicemen. Many areas, particularly the large urban areas like London and Birmingham which held substantial numbers of ex-servicemen, maintained an anti-officer outlook. As late as 1929 H.E. Cheeseman, the Organizing Secretary of the Metropolitan Area, could write that the Chairman, General Bethune, had 'broken down the barrier which existed in many parts of London between ex-officers and other ranks'.[43] The effect of the anti-officer outlook was demonstrated by the membership of the Metropolitan Area Council. In 1929 the President and Chairman were both officers, as were the two paid posts of Administrative Agent and Assistant Organizing Secretary, but fifteen out of the sixteen Council representatives were rank-and-file members – a revealing contrast with the South-Eastern Area.[44] There was a definite feeling among many ordinary ex-servicemen that they should organize their own movement without the interference of the officers who had led them during the war. This undoubtedly lowered the membership of the Legion as ex-servicemen with these feelings did not wish to join an organization which had such an officer-dominated leadership.

One of the main preoccupations of Legion leaders was to construct a movement which would offer 'unwavering opposition to the Bolshies'.[45] While Haig and other Legion leaders propounded an anti-socialist theme in speeches to British Legion audiences, these did not match the beliefs of many ordinary ex-servicemen who developed a deep suspicion of Legion motives. The Legion was characterized by the *Daily Herald* as 'Haig's White Guard'[46] (an analogy to the White Russian armies which had fought against the Bolsheviks in the Russian Civil War) which would give assistance to the authorities in any civil disturbance. At the 1924 Annual Conference, the East Anglia Area moved a resolution that this 'Conference views with alarm the increasing tendency of the general public to dub the Legion as an organization with a motive for keeping ex-servicemen together with a view to their use in cases of national emergency'.[47] The delegate explained that when the Legion in East Anglia had invited a union to take part in the Remembrance Day Service, the union secretary had refused, saying, 'You are nothing more or less than Haig's White Guards.'[48] The delegate was clearly disturbed that union officials might believe there was a conflict between Legion membership and trade union affiliations. Members of the Legion were able to reconcile these different identities; other ex-servicemen were not.

There were other, more practical reasons for low Legion membership. In 1926 H.E. Cheeseman explained that 'A difficulty which every branch encounters is getting the majority of the ex-servicemen of a district sufficiently interested in the Legion to become members. It is not so much antipathy towards the Organization, as sheer apathy'.[49] Some ex-servicemen may have disliked their time in the forces and did not wish to spend their free time involved in an organization like the Legion. However, apathy and involvement in other interests do not necessarily suggest a rejection of Legion ideals and beliefs, simply that many ex-servicemen had other concerns. For many ordinary ex-servicemen, the preoccupations of work and family probably filled most of what little spare time was available.

One underlying problem which certainly affected Legion membership was the trade depression and resulting unemployment in many communities in England and Wales. The decline of Britain's main staple heavy industries of steel, mining and shipbuilding during the interwar years meant that the industrial towns of the north of England and Wales were badly affected by unemployment.[50] When we examine Legion membership figures together with the only available figures for ex-service unemployment in 1936, we find a direct correlation between low Legion membership and high unemployment in different regions.[51] In the south of the country, there were 181,387 financial members of the Legion and only 93,863 unemployed ex-servicemen. Thus, for every unemployed ex-serviceman there were two members of the Legion. In the north there were 74,363 Legion members but 177,975 unemployed ex-servicemen; for every Legion member

there were two unemployed ex-servicemen. Yet northern industrial towns like
Darlington and Newcastle were areas with large numbers of potential recruits for
the Legion. During the war the main sources of manpower had come from
London, Scotland and the industrial and mining districts of Britain; the rural
areas of the country had supplied a lower percentage of men to the army.[52] Thus,
large-scale unemployment did have a major effect on the membership and
success of the British Legion.

Unemployment could and did lower the membership of the Legion – not
because unemployed ex-servicemen were prevented from joining the Legion but
because the economic impact on the whole locality could be severe. Legion
branches depended on their local ex-service community and the general public
for support, volunteers, members and funds. In the comparatively prosperous
areas of the south, branches could recruit members who had the spare money to
pay affiliation fees and to take part in social and fundraising events, thus making
the Legion a popular and attractive organization. A branch with a strong
financial position could also utilize its large branch funds for local assistance of
hardship cases and thus present an active social and welfare organization to the
local ex-service community.

In an area with high unemployment, a branch could be starved of funds and
unable to fulfill its objectives, thus making it an unattractive proposition for most
ex-servicemen. Many of the branches in depressed areas simply did not have the
funds to build branch premises or to organize local relief funds, and the members
and the public did not have the money to spend on fundraising events or in a
clubhouse. A Wales Area delegate explained at the 1928 Conference that 'Last
year in the Rhonda Valley they collected £414, the whole amount in coppers';[53]
many people had given money, but the total amount collected remained small.
Thus, branches in depressed areas were often reduced to being centres for relief
without the many and varied activities which other more prosperous Legion
branches could pursue. Again this was unlikely to make the local Legion branch
attractive to prospective members or popular with existing ones – it was more
difficult to see the relief given out as a comradely gesture of goodwill when it was
all the branch could offer. Unemployment and poverty blighted many areas of
Britain during the interwar years and low Legion membership was only one
symptom of its overall impact.

The underlying factors of unemployment and the difficulties of organization in
urban areas could only be compounded by unfavourable perceptions of the
British Legion. Much of the explanation for low Legion membership must lie
with the predominance of ex-officers in the leadership and the anti-socialist
outlook they sponsored, both of which alienated many ex-servicemen. At no time
did Legion leaders recognize that their views or beliefs might be unattractive. At
Northampton in 1922 Earl Haig saw the membership problem in a simplistic
manner:

Private Jones will say to himself, there is Major Smith who was my boss in the army, he will want to be my boss in the Legion. Major Smith on his side will say to himself, Private Jones saw quite enough of me in the trenches, and won't want to see me hanging about his club. And so these good and true men drift apart for the rest of their lives through want . . . of realising that ours is a brotherhood where rank is naught and service everything, and that no ex-officer can get elected to a position of responsibility in the Legion unless he is prepared to give service and enthusiastic service.[54]

Not only was Haig's description of the Legion inaccurate, but his analysis of British society was mistaken. In 1920s Britain there were still large gulfs of understanding between officers and men, who did not necessarily wish to share in each other's social activities. Furthermore, the Legion could not ever be the idealistic organization which Haig wanted. Matters of class, status and rank were just as important within the Legion as in ordinary society and, while many soldiers had experienced comradeship in the trenches, their feelings did not generally extend even to men outside their own unit, let alone to staff officers. Legion membership was conceived round the idea of a universal comradeship but distinctions of service, medals and rank continued to be erected between veterans of different wars. Haig believed that his message appealed to all ex-servicemen but, in truth, it appealed only to those who still accepted the traditional tenets of loyalty, duty and deference to social superiors. It may be said that the leaders of the Legion simply did not know how to develop a mass movement based around the ideas of full democratic participation and the voluntary principle.

For the majority of the general public, however, who remained unaware of the internal dynamics of the organization, the purpose of the British Legion lay with the symbolic Red Flanders Poppy – to collect and utilize funds for the benefit of veterans facing hardship. There was certainly a great deal of hardship among veterans of the First World War. Instead of returning to a land fit for heroes, thousands of ex-servicemen returned to poor housing, unemployment and deprivation. With the slump after 1920 it was clear that government promises would not be kept.

Many men who had gone to fight found that their position at work had been filled or removed; others found their businesses ruined or their skills and training out of date. When the process of retrenchment began in 1921, such men were often the first to be laid off. Many young men had joined the army straight from school or left apprenticeships and thus missed the chance to train and gain a skill. Consequently, there were roughly 300,000 unskilled ex-servicemen throughout the interwar period.[55] The harsh economic conditions of the interwar years soon outweighed any sentiment for the men who had fought for their country and there were always a large number of veterans in the intractable million unemployed. Thousands of ex-servicemen found that the promises freely made during wartime were simply hot air, and 'The Frothblowers Anthem',[56] often sung at Legion conferences, sponsored a jaundiced view of government, politicians and their promises.

Far from representing the voice of discontent and resentment, however, the Legion believed its role was to wean ex-servicemen away from such dangerous philosophies. Haig's 1921 appeal to ex-servicemen did not sponsor disillusionment. Instead he exhorted,

> Not for doles and depression did we fight, but for progress and prosperity. The interest of the whole is the interest of each one of us. The better world and the brighter Britain we envisaged as the outcome of the Great War have not materialised. Several million men combined and fought shoulder to shoulder to win victory – the same men must now organise and play their part in winning the peace.[57]

Haig's message was that ex-servicemen should attempt to create a brighter Britain through their own efforts. The real aim of the Legion was to draw ex-servicemen together through good works – loyalty to comrades was the key motivation, rather than any belief in social justice.

In constructing this new Britain, the Legion's main 'enemy' became the British government and politicians who consistently refused Legion demands for a more equitable pensions system, better employment training and job prospects for unemployed ex-servicemen who had left their jobs to fight. Against such an 'enemy', tactical sophistication and cunning were just as important as numbers. When the Legion presented a petition to the Conservative government in 1925 with 850,000 signatures, the largest since the Chartist petition of 1848, the Legion believed that success in their demands would be achieved.[58] In fact, time after time, Legion leaders were unable to press home their demands. The Legion never learned the proper tactics to deal with politicians and most of the leaders of the Legion can be described as political innocents who had been used to receiving orders and faithfully carrying them out, not extracting concessions from an unwilling government.

In time, the Legion took on the character of a major charity rather than a political pressure group. Given the limited nature of Legion funds, the aim was to alleviate distress, and to assist as many ex-servicemen back into jobs, whether through job creation schemes or training programmes. It was not until the first Poppy Day in November 1921, however, that the Legion gained a means of regular funding to achieve these goals. This event, which began almost by accident, soon became the Legion's main source of income. The Red Flanders Poppy was an almost universal symbol of the First World War throughout the Allied countries, mainly as a result of the impact of Captain Macrae's famous poem, and the first artificial ones were manufactured by women in the devastated areas of France and Belgium for sale in America. A Madame Guerin approached the British Legion in October 1921 and asked whether they would buy poppies from her organization for sale on 11 November. A few million were purchased and demand on Armistice Day in 1921 far outstripped supply. Many of the first poppies worn on the day were produced at Legion HQ from pink blotting paper.[59] The success of the first Poppy Day prompted the Legion to establish its own source of supply by employing badly disabled men to manufacture the poppies. By 1926, when the British Legion Poppy Factory moved to a new site at Richmond in Surrey, over 200 disabled men were employed manufacturing 25 million poppies each year.[60] In 1928 the Legion Annual Report stated that:

> it can be claimed without exaggeration that the Legion Poppy Factory is the largest employer of disabled labour in the world, and that no other concern of a similar nature can claim that every man employed, from the manager downwards, is a disabled ex-serviceman.[61]

This fact contributed greatly to the success of Poppy Day as the 'public know by now that the Poppies they buy are all manufactured by badly disabled ex-servicemen who but for this would be unemployed'.[62] By purchasing a poppy the public were not only remembering the dead, but also helping the living. The Legion explained the success of the sale of poppies on Armistice Day in terms of the debt owed to ex-servicemen through their sacrifice in the First World War. However, although the Legion gained large sums from Poppy Day, it was stressed that this was not simply a means of raising funds. Captain Willcox, the Appeals Organizer, claimed,

> Poppy Day is not a flag day. A cynic might define a flag day as a day upon which one either buys an emblem in self-defence, or one to be spent in dodging flag sellers . . . the public look for poppies on November 11th and complain if they find any difficulty in buying the emblem they want.[63]

The Red Flanders Poppy became a symbol synonymous with Armistice Day, Remembrance and their spiritual connections with sacrifice and the Fallen. These symbols were taken very seriously indeed. Each Armistice Day, the Legion placed a wreath of poppies on the Cenotaph with the inscription, 'The Legion of the Living Salutes the Legion of the Dead – We Will Not Break Faith with Ye'.[64]

By 1926, the Legion Relief Departments and United Services Fund were spending nearly £1,000,000 per year and Sir Frederick Maurice could claim that 'there is no other single organisation in the country which does benevolent work on anything like so large a scale'.[65] For over 400,000 people every year, Legion relief vouchers for food and clothing provided a welcome supplement to government provision.[66] Legion business loans, employment and training schemes for disabled ex-servicemen were of great benefit to the lives of many individuals but Legion efforts could not address the underlying problems of mass unemployment and poverty.

Sadly, Legion attitudes to unemployment and poverty could be ambivalent, with reactionary and progressive opinions coexisting in an uneasy alliance. The ideal of the Legion, and its image of a 'Brighter Britain', was for all ex-servicemen to be given work and prosperity as a reward for the sacrifices during the First World War; the reality, however, was often very different.

Tension developed between the desire to help all ex-servicemen, and the limited funds available to the Legion. Very quickly a distinction came to be made between the 'waster' or 'scoundrel' and the deserving ex-serviceman, the man who had fallen on hard times and needed some assistance through no fault of his own. In 1922 Thomas Lister argued that 'The Legion had enabled men who had demonstrated their worth to stand on their own two feet and look at life with a brighter vision'.[67] The concepts of self-help and comradely assistance rather than charity were always stressed by the Legion and the attitude that the Legion should only help deserving ex-servicemen became common. Colonel Crosfield remarked at the 1929 Conference, 'Personally, I think we do not want to help the sponger and I believe in discrimination. If you have a fellow who shows no gratitude for help and comes back time and again, turn him down every time.'[68] The most disturbing aspect of such an attitude within an organization like the Legion was that such discrimination was never part of official Legion policy but operated on an informal, almost personal basis. In some minds at least, the 'deserving ex-serviceman' had changed from being 'those less fortunate than yourselves' and 'all ex-servicemen' to either members of the Legion, or someone who knew how to display old-fashioned gratitude towards what can only be described as old-fashioned charity. The most important and expansive aim of the Legion to build a brighter Britain was not fulfilled and, even within the Legion, traditional attitudes towards ex-servicemen had not entirely been eradicated.

While many ex-servicemen could express discontent with life in Britain, however, there was one pillar in Legion belief that remained unchallenged until the end of the 1930s. The Great War had been the 'War to end all Wars'; Legion belief did not admit of futility or waste. The dead had not died in vain; they had bought freedom, peace and victory for the British Empire. The Legion also believed that, as the men who had fought the war, veterans were specially marked out to play an important role in maintaining the peace which had been so dearly bought.

One editorial in the *Legion Journal* was particularly gushing on the value of international ex-service cooperation. It portrayed a Utopian vision for peace:

And how we should, many of us, like to meet with our opposite number in the various battles and other incidents of the war to talk over the effects of a bombardment, the incidents of a raid, the results of a patrol. By means such as this might we arrive at peace. For it is not the politicians who will bring peace on earth, nor the scientists, nor the professors! It is the simple soldiers – those who went through the muck and slime and the mud: the beastliness of battle: who endured the shelling and the sniping, the toll and burden of the War. The hope of the world lies in the getting together of the men who fought, and there also, is the road to peace.[69]

Veterans who knew the horrors of war could, by displaying comradeship, bring about understanding and peace between nations without any of the problems and difficulties encountered by governments.

During the 1920s the Legion policy on international cooperation was anchored around FIDAC (Federation Inter-Alliee des Anciens Combattants), an Allied international ex-service organization. However, although the Legion was willing to meet with ex-enemy organizations, the Belgian and French veterans were not. When allied and ex-enemy organizations met, in 1927 and 1928, very little was achieved. None of the FIDAC conferences demonstrated any concrete evidence for Legion convictions of the value of international ex-service cooperation, and by the early 1930s the Legion was willing to make unilateral contact with ex-enemy organizations. One stumbling block for an independent British approach to German veterans was the perceived politicized nature of the German movement – the two major organizations, the *Stalhelm* and *Reichsbanner* held violently opposed political views. When Hitler came to power he ruthlessly suppressed both bodies, forcing veterans to join National Socialist organizations. Unfortunately, the British Legion misunderstood Hitler's actions and believed that Hitler had depoliticized German veterans. The German cult of the *Frontkampfer* and its particular significance to Hitler and his colleagues help to explain why the Legion leadership became so enthusiastic about contacts with German veterans. Hitler's use of the image of the *Frontkampfer*, or front-line soldier, was a well-established part of his rhetoric. At the same time, images of martial splendour and military efficiency were integral to the Nazi party with its mass rallies, parades and uniforms. Many of the leaders of the Nazi party had fought during the First World War: Hitler and Hess had served as infantrymen while Goering had taken over command of Baron von Richtofen's flying circus on his death. Here were the new leaders of a former enemy nation who seemed to speak the same language and display the same opinions and attitudes as themselves.

With the way seemingly open for contact, the Legion's first official visit to Germany in July 1935 lasted for a week and was packed with engagements, functions and speeches. In the course of this flying visit, the delegation met

Hitler, Hess and Goering, laid wreaths on memorials to British prisoners of war and met many of the leaders of German ex-service associations. A Foreign Office official warned before the visit that Nazi propaganda was 'deliberate and carefully thought out' and 'just as insidious and, in some ways more dangerous than any communist propaganda'.[70] And although the Legion delegation did detect, and avoid, such blatant coups as placing a wreath on the Party Memorial, the entire visit was important and valuable political propaganda for the German authorities. This was the first official visit of British ex-servicemen to Germany with the blessing of the Prince of Wales and it was easy for German leaders and newspapers to argue that the visit demonstrated the honour the New Germany had won abroad, while also proving that the German *Frontkampfer* was respected even by his former enemies.

Legion contacts with German ex-servicemen increased year by year and in 1937 alone 1,700 excursions were made all over Europe. It was during 1938 that the Legion's foreign policy reached a dramatic climax, when, at the height of the Munich crisis, a plan was developed to send a 20,000-man British Legion police force to Czechoslovakia to supervise the projected plebiscites in disputed areas. This plan, which was gladly accepted by Hitler, caused serious embarrassment to the British government.[71] The British Legion's sincere and heartfelt attempts to bring about international understanding through the 'Brotherhood of the Trenches' were cynically manipulated by the Nazi authorities of Germany for propaganda advantage. After Munich it became increasingly clear that even the British government could not deliver peace to the British people.

During the interwar years, the justifications for the traditional conception of the First World War became increasingly eroded. The high hopes for prosperity and progress had been transformed into locust years of unemployment and discontent. By the mid-1930s the threat of another war was looming over Europe. The members who proudly marched on Legion parades did not, however, question the ideals of the movement which they represented or the conventional view of the First World War. In 1927 Thomas Lister remarked, 'I think that the secret of Legion success has been the fact that we have attracted to it men who, outside of their daily occupations, are determined to place the Legion first in their thoughts, and who really and genuinely want to do service in peace, just as they did service in the war.'[72] The development of a 'Legion spirit' ensured that the Legion grew into a national organization, but too many ex-servicemen lay outside Legion ranks to characterize this 'Legion spirit' as a collective veterans' mentality born out of the experience of the First World War. The Legion identity was a unique blend of local community spirit, benevolent work and pride in the armed forces and was built by veterans from the generation of the First World War whose attitudes and concerns continued to reflect the values of the early 1920s. The basic objects, ideals and principles of the Legion were fixed in the aftermath of the First World War, and they were supported by men who had developed their consciousness during that era. The Legion's 'spirit' was an internal dynamic which was constantly rehearsed through speeches, committee meetings, parades, remembrance services and social functions. Legion members were always reminded what the Legion stood for, what its members should believe and what kind of an example they should set to other ex-servicemen. Given the constant rehearsal of Legion beliefs and ideals it is unsurprising that the Legion developed its own internal dynamic, and also that it became increasingly out of date. Legion attitudes remained firmly in place, but while they were a mixture of reactionary and progressive ideals in the early 1920s, by the late 1930s they had become archaic. The Legion had remained fixed while society's values and attitudes progressed.

By 1939 Legion members began to recognize that they were old and that their attitudes and views – but not their ideals – were out of date. At the same time they were determined that the Legion should continue. In 1939 the Poppy Day collection was made on behalf of all ex-servicemen of all wars for the first time,[73] and important decisions about the future shape of the Legion were postponed until Second World War veterans could have their say. During the war Legion work continued and managed to secure greater pensions successes than at any time during the previous twenty years.[74] The Legion could not offer a new world and could not fulfill all of its high aims and ideals but it did eventually bridge the gap between old and new and thus ensured that its central ideal of comradeship would continue.

Notes

1 Public Record Office, FO371.21783, Duff Cooper, Admiralty, to Viscount Halifax, Foreign Office (29/09/1938).

2 Graham Wootton, *The Politics of Influence: British Ex-Servicemen, Cabinet Decisions and Cultural Change 1917–57* (London, Routledge and Kegan Paul, 1963), p. 16.

3 Wootton, *Politics of Influence*, p. 13.

4 Wootton, *Politics of Influence*, p. 31.

5 Wootton, *Politics of Influence*, p. 19.

6 Graham Wootton, *The Official History of the British Legion* (London, MacDonald and Evans, 1956), p. 2.

7 Wootton, *Official History*, p. 2.

8 Wootton, *Politics of Influence*, p. 79.

9 Wootton, *Politics of Influence*, pp.59–60.

10 Wootton, *Politics of Influence*, pp. 59–60.

11 Wootton, *Politics of Influence*, pp. 59–60.

12 Liddell Hart Centre for Military Archives, King's College London [LHCMA], Hamilton Papers, IH29/37/5, Major H. Jellicorse, The Ex-Service Officers and Men and the Organisations looking after their Welfare.

13 Wootton, *Official History*, p. 2.

14 Stephen R. Ward, 'The British Veterans Ticket of 1918', *Journal of British Studies*, Vol. VIII, No. 1, (Nov. 1968).

15 Wootton, *Politics of Influence*, p. 84

16 Wootton, *Official History*, p. 3.

17 Wootton, *Official History*, p. 3.

18 Wootton, *Official History*, p. 4.

19 Wootton, *The Politics of Influence*, pp. 85–6.

20 LHCMA, IH29/12, Lister to Hamilton, 3 March 1930.

21 Wootton, *Official History*, p. 10. The NUX was excluded from the USF and refused to amalgamate with the other organizations in 1921 and, by 1922, had disappeared.

22 LHCMA, IH29/37/4, James Howell to Major Jellicorse (15/12/1918).

23 Wootton, *The Politics of Influence*, p. 65.

24 British Legion Headquarters, [BLHQ] British Legion Annual Conference 1922, Field Marshal Earl Haig, Presidential Address.

25 BLHQ, British Legion Annual Reports 1922–1939 and the Affiliation Fee Receipts found in the British Legion Annual Accounts 1922–1939.

26 Antoine Prost, *In the Wake of War: Les Anciens Combattants and French Society 1914–1939* (Oxford, Berg, 1992), p. 44.

27 James M. Diehl, *Paramilitary Politics in Weimar Germany* (Bloomington, Indiana University Press, 1977), pp. 293–5.

28 BLHQ, *British Legion Journal*, April 1922, p. 222.

29 BLHQ, BL Annual Conference 1923, Res. No. 19.

30 Prost, *In the Wake of War*, p. 45.

31 BLHQ, See Letters Page of the BL *Journal*, 1932–1936.

32 BLHQ, BL *Journal*, January 1933, p. 246.

33 BLHQ, BL *Journal*, August 1932, p. 56.

34 BLHQ, BL *Journal*, March 1937, p. 317.

35 National Library of Scotland, Edinburgh, Haig Papers, Acc. 3155. No. 235b, Usher Hall Edinburgh (11/11/1925).

36 LHCMA, IH29/2, L.H. Duniam-Jones to Ian Hamilton (9/09/1926).

37 BLHQ, BL Annual Reports 1922–39: T.F. Lister served as chairman 1921–7 and was followed by Lt-Col. G.R. Crosfield (1927–30), Col. J. Brown (1930–4), and Major F.W.C. Fetherston-Godley (1934–40).

38 BLHQ, BL Annual Reports 1922–39.

39 LHCMA, IH29/15, Annual Report of the South Eastern Area Council, 1929–1931.

40 Sunbury on Thames British Legion Branch, *Sunbury-on-Thames Branch History* (privately printed).

41 National Library of Scotland, Haig Papers, Acc.3155, H227.f., Colonel Crosfield to Earl Haig (1/02/1923).

42 Ibid.; BLHQ, BL Annual Report 1925.

43 LHCMA, IH29/18, H.E. Cheeseman to Ian Hamilton (1/03/1929).

44 LHCMA, IH29/11, Metropolitan Area Council (4/12/1929).

45 BLHQ, BL Annual Conference 1923, Earl Haig's Presidential Address.

46 Wootton, *Official History*, p. 66.

47 BLHQ, BL Annual Conference 1924, Res. No. 118.

48 BLHQ, BL Annual Conference 1924, Res. No. 118.

49 BLHQ, H.E. Cheeseman, *Area Organisation*, British Legion Summer School, 1926.

50 S.V. Ward, *The Geography of Inter-war Britain: The State and Uneven Development* (London, Routledge, 1988), pp. 1, 14.

51 Total Legion membership = 375,642; Total unemployed ex-servicemen = 410,689; BLHQ, British Legion Affiliation Fee receipts and Unemployment Figures for April 1936 found in PRO, PIN15/722.

52 John Keegan, *The Face of Battle: A Study of Agincourt, Waterloo and the Somme* (London, Barrie and Jenkins), 1988, p. 196; J.M. Winter, *The Great War and the British People* (London, Macmillan, 1983), pp. 34, 38.

53 BLHQ, BL Annual Conference 1928, Res. No. 8.

54 National Library of Scotland, Haig Papers, Acc. 3155. No. 235.c., Northampton, March 1922.

55 BLHQ, General Secretary's Circular Letters to the Branches, Leaflet, *Do You Know?* 1923.

56 Unfortunately, I have not, as yet, found a copy of the words to this song.

57 BLHQ, BL Journal, July 1921, p.7.

58 Niall Barr, 'Service Not Self: The British Legion 1921–1939' (unpublished Ph.D. thesis, University of St Andrews, 1994), chapter 5.

59 Wootton, *Official History*, pp. 39–40.

60 BLHQ, BL Annual Report 1926.

61 BLHQ, BL Annual Report 1928.

62 BLHQ, BL Annual Report 1924.

63 BLHQ, W.G. Willcox, *The Appeals Work of the Legion*, British Legion Summer School, 1926.

64 BLHQ, BL *Journal*, December 1921, p. 126.

65 BLHQ, General Sir Frederick Maurice, *The Benevolent Work of the Legion*, British Legion Summer School, 1926.

66 BLHQ, BL Annual Reports 1922–39.

67 BLHQ, BL Annual Conference 1922, T.F. Lister, Chairman's Address.

68 BLHQ, BL Annual Conference 1929, Res. No. 11.

69 BLHQ, BL *Journal*, August 1927, p. 20.

70 PRO, FO 371/18882, R. Wigram (14/06/1935).

71 Barr, 'Service Not Self', chapter 6.

72 BLHQ, BL Annual Conference 1925, T.F. Lister, Chairman's Address.

73 Wootton, *Official History*, p. 257.

74 Wootton, *Official History*, p. 262. The 1939 Pensions Warrant was actually *worse* than the 1919 and 1921 Warrants, with lower rates of compensation and many other flaws. Legion pressure did, this time, gain justice by righting such anomalies.

15

'A LITTLE MAN IN A GREAT WAR': PATRICK MACGILL AND THE LONDON IRISH RIFLES

D. Taylor

'Man . . . infinitely small, running – affrighted rabbits from the upheaval of the shells, nerve-wracked, deafened; clinging to the earth, hiding eyes, whispering "Oh God!"'
L. Housman (ed.), *War Letters of Fallen Englishmen*, 1930, p. 60.

'War is a silent teacher and he who learns becomes silent too.'
Rudolf Binding, *A Fatalist at War*, 1929.

L ate twentieth-century man has learnt to kill his fellows with greater ingenuity, greater barbarity and on a greater scale than ever before, but, notwithstanding, the First World War, that 'war to end wars', still retains its ability to shock. Images of the Western Front continue to exercise a profound influence on perceptions of war and the painful adjustments required, individually and collectively, to forge a new and meaningful identity in the knowledge of hitherto unimaginable actions. The perceptions of the generation that fought, as well as of the generations who sent young (and not so young) men to the front, were shaped by powerful beliefs in the nation and the need to defend it, if necessary, in war. Similarly deep-rooted and fiercely held beliefs about the nature of masculinity shaped the perceptions of numerous young men, largely but not exclusively from the middle and upper classes, who found themselves faced with the great test, the great game as war broke out. Being a man, for those growing up in late-Victorian and Edwardian Britain, was not something that could be reduced to a simple, all-embracing formula.[1] On the surface there was a gulf separating the 'respectable' masculinity of the middle- and upper-class public-school or grammar-school boy from the 'rough' masculinity of the working-class board-school boy. There were unifying concerns, however, not least the persistent and powerful links between sporting ability, physical prowess and military virtues. The amateur sportsman was seen as the chivalric warrior in the making. Not surprisingly there were a recurring number of key concepts, such as 'loyalty', 'courage' and 'prowess and skill in combat' which were to be found in many of the differing definitions of masculinity. A true man was loyal, if necessary to the extent of sacrificing his life, not simply to his immediate fellows in the team/regiment but also to his monarch and his country. It will never be known how many men felt that it was 'sweet and fitting' to die for their country, but the creation of pals' regiments and the wholesale enlistment of football teams suggest that wider loyalties played an important part in 1914. Similarly, a true man was courageous, showing no sign of fear in combat, willing to sacrifice himself to defend the weak and down-trodden ('poor little Belgium'), especially if there was a noble cause such as liberty at stake. Furthermore, a true man was well versed in, and prided himself on, his skills in arms. The way in which a man was able 'to look after himself' may have varied from class to class, but there was a common belief in so doing.

Expectation and experience did not coincide, however. The realities of an increasingly technological war were at odds with the rhetoric of August 1914. The subsequent traumas, as naïve patriotism and simplistic notions of 'playing the game' came into conflict with the harshness of trench warfare, have been well documented, not least in literary works ranging from the well-known poetry of Owen and Rosenberg and autobiographies of Blunden, Graves and Sassoon to the lesser-known plays and novels of Aldington, Sheriff and Bartlett and Williamson.[2] Never had so many well-educated, sensitive and articulate men recorded their experiences.[3]

The impact of such writings has been immense, but it is all too easy to assume that the views they express – themselves complex and contradictory – have a universality in which these tortured souls speak for all who fought. It is these soldier-writers who, according to Samuel Hynes, created the 'aesthetics of direct experience' and in so doing were responsible for the 'creation of a new language of truth-telling about war, in poetry, prose and the visual arts'.[4] These writers, it is argued, speak with an almost unchallengable authenticity for all who had experienced the realities of the trenches. They had been there and had lived long enough to record their experiences. By implication, other writers using an older idiom are seen to have failed, for whatever reason, to tell 'the truth'. This is a powerful interpretation but not without its problems. It is by no means obvious that these well-known writers, who were for the most part drawn from a narrow segment of society (that is the English middle or upper class) articulated the feelings of the uneducated, or poorly educated, of the working classes or of those who were not English. Nor is it clear that their 'aesthetic of direct experience' was the only 'truth'. These problems, which are particularly acute in the case of so-called 'hyphenated identity', will be examined through a consideration of the war works of a relatively unknown soldier-writer – Patrick Macgill.[5]

Patrick Macgill was an unskilled but self-educated working-class Irish Catholic who fought as a British soldier and wrote of his experiences while on active service. His background and the immediacy of his response to his war experience makes him worthy of study, but there is a further reason for my interest in the man. Enlisting at the same time in the same regiment, the London Irish Rifles, was another Catholic youth, a supremely confident, if not downright arrogant first-generation Irishman from Tottenham who happily lied about his age so that he could join the British army. This was 3025 Rifleman Sidney Cadman, my maternal grandfather. His experience of war was scarcely documented. He wrote no autobiography and his letters home have long since disappeared. His 'reminiscences', to his wife and children at least, turned the war into slapstick comedy, a Fred Karno's army of jolly pranksters swatting back German bullets with frying pans, or else it was a war of good chaps, drinking and joking, playing football in no man's land as well as behind the lines.[6] Such fun and games co-existed uneasily with the nightmares which, to his dying day, reduced him to a cowering, terrified and tearful individual. In the early autumn of 1963, however, prompted by my enquiries about Patrick Macgill, whom I had just discovered as a minor war poet, there came a glimpse of his private world, so long hidden from view. In a long conversation (more a monologue) during which I was first addressed as David, but later as Jim (the name of his first-born son who had died almost thirteen years before), he talked at length about his war in a way that he had never done either to his wife or to his three children. It was a war conceived and recalled in heroic terms; a war in which comradeship rather than Catholicism provided greater security; a war in which killing and death were both serious and casual events (kill or be killed); a war of immense sorrow for dearly loved friends, killed *en masse* as their trench suffered a direct hit; and a war of guilt for having survived. Here was an old man (as he then seemed to me), recollecting by name his long-dead comrades, addressing his dead son but heard by a youth who, coincidentally, was the same age as his grandfather had been when he enlisted. From that evening, over thirty years ago, Patrick Macgill became like an absent family friend, the man I had never met but whose war experience was more accessible than that of my grandfather. This long excursion into personal history is more than self-indulgence, raising as it does two fundamental and related questions which pertain to the problem of interpretation associated with the 'aesthetic of direct experience' noted above. The first focuses on the way in which the war was experienced and then communicated to others. The second, and more profound, centres on the nature of the 'self' and the adaptability of that 'self' in circumstances which challenged and threatened to overwhelm the values and sensibilities of the individual. Each needs to be considered briefly.

The nature of knowledge is highly problematic and raises complex epistemological questions which cannot be pursued in detail here. Suffice it to say that it is extremely difficult to speak precisely of how we come to know and what it is we actually know. Events deemed to have an objective reality (the battle of Loos in which both Riflemen Cadman and Macgill fought, for example) were experienced in a variety of ways by combatants whose perceptions of events were shaped by a variety of pressures, including prior values and beliefs, experiences before the war, as well as experiences gained earlier in the war. Furthermore, the recounting of events, rather than being an account of the past 'as it was', is essentially a fiction wherein the narrator accounts for the self-that-is at the point of writing. Thus accounts written at different chronological moments give rise to different fictionalized representations of a given set of events. In this respect, the idea that there is a truth to be found in one account (and by implication falsification and distortion in another) is profoundly misleading.

Communication of the experience of a particular event is equally problematic, not least because of the sense of disjuncture caused by the events for those who wished to record their experiences. Some became silent, trapped in what Charles Carrington called the 'mental internment camp' of his '1916 fixation';[7] others turned the war into comedy; yet others sought to find a language to express their knowledge and feelings. Now the ability of the individual to verbalize an experience, which was often as much auditory and olfactory as visual, was critical, but so too was the idiom in which the observer chose to express him- (or her-) self. Thus, what might appear to be relatively straightforward accounts are, on closer inspection, complex texts which do not necessarily admit of a simple or single interpretation. In such circumstances to talk of 'truth-telling' in a manner that implies there is only one truth, or one way of relating the truth of an event, and that all other ways are, in one respect or another, flawed and untruthful, is at best naïve and misleading, at worst arrogant and dishonest.

If the nature of knowledge is problematic and the idea of 'truth' elusive, so too is the concept of the 'self'. The issues raised here are, once again, highly complex and require an understanding of psychology and anthropology that is rarely found among historians.[8] Nonetheless, a brief examination of some of the problems is essential before we move to a consideration of our central character. Historians, along with many other lay people, tend to adopt a 'common-sense' view of the 'self' and its development. It is a view in which the 'self' is thought of as being defined from within, from the experiences of the individual. Yet there is an important sense in which the self is defined by externalities, being a member of a group, not being part of another group. The preoccupation with the 'other' and 'otherness' is an important part of self-definition. Thus, in 1914 being non-German was a central element in the British soldier's definition of himself.[9] It is also a view which, while allowing for an element of chronological development, particularly in the early years of an individual, sees the 'self' as largely fixed and unchanging. Yet the 'self' can be seen not only as being more flexible and malleable but also as a fiction, albeit of considerable importance, whereby one seeks to define and come to terms with circumstances.[10] Thus, in the case of combatants in the First World War (or any other war) we can think in terms of a necessary sequence as, at its simplest, a different 'self' is constructed before, during and after the war. The new 'self' does not replace the old, however, but, as Freud observed, overlays it.[11] The story of Rifleman Macgill clearly shows how a new 'self' was constructed which coexisted with but never replaced the old as the circumstances of war called into question the persona with which he had entered the army. Likewise the brief story of Rifleman Cadman shows how a comic 'self' was carried into the postwar world as a means of coming to terms with and protecting the individual from the traumas caused by his experience of war. Once again, we are led to the conclusion that concepts such as 'reality' and 'truth' are elusive, if not illusive.

To understand the war experience of 3008 Rifleman Patrick Macgill it is necessary to look first at his earlier life. Born in 1890 into a peasant family in Glenties, Donegal, he worked from an early age as an itinerant farm labourer in Scotland before becoming a navvy working on the construction of the huge Kinlochleven reservoir. His navvying days ended in 1910, after which he made a living as a journalist until early 1912 before eventually volunteering to fight in France. His pre-war experiences are recorded in a semi-autobiographical form, notably in *Children of the Dead End*, subtitled the autobiography of a navvy, in which the central character, Dermod Flynn is closely, but not precisely, modelled on the life of Macgill himself. *Children of the Dead End*, based on a scrapbook which he had compiled during his navvying days, became a best-seller in 1914, selling 10,000 copies in a fortnight.

In many respects, the hero of the book is 'Moleskin Joe', the outsider, despised by respectable society but embodying the virtues of the itinerant labourer-cum-vagrant, who, while literally making the modern world, was not part of it. In the overwhelmingly masculine world of the navvy, strength of body and strength of character are central virtues; likewise quickness of mind which is reflected in Joe's way with words as well as in the cunning by which he conducts much of his life. Above all, comradeship is central, necessary for survival but also giving meaning to the life of the navvy. It is evident that Macgill, or his literary counterpart Flynn, admires and indeed shares some of these qualities. In addition, Flynn has self-defining qualities of his own. Although having little time for the organized Catholic Church, and even less for petty-tyrant priests, he has a strong sense of morality and justice which results in his conversion to socialism while in Glasgow. Criticizing a society that exploits the unskilled labourer (and a church that fails to criticize this exploitation), Flynn is equally outspoken in his condemnation of the exploitation of young women, driven by poverty into prostitution.

Although Flynn is presented as being politically aware, albeit in a rather naïve and sentimental manner, there is, however, no indication of any awareness of specifically Irish issues, nor are there many explicit references to Irish identity. If anything, there is a suspicion that there is an element of deliberate stereotyping to present an English audience with a familiar and picaresque figure – the hard-talking, hard-drinking, hard-fighting Irishman – but one who from the very marginality of his existence is relatively unthreatening.[12]

Unlike *Children of the Dead End*, written some four years after his experience of navvying, Macgill's war writings are much more immediate. Large parts of the three books had been written initially while on active service and had appeared as newspaper articles before being reproduced, almost unchanged, for publication in book form. This is not to suggest that there was not an element of reflection and reconstruction in these writings but rather that this took place within the context of the war, unlike other autobiographical writings which appeared many years after the war had ended. In addition, the experiences are presented through Macgill himself rather than through a fictional intermediary. There were pressures on Macgill, however. His publisher, Herbert Jenkins, had a good eye for the market, though it is difficult to determine to what extent, if any, Macgill wrote to satisfy an audience which still viewed the war in positive, heroic terms. The situation is further complicated by the pressures brought by army authorities who sought to restrict and restrain his observations of war. Adjutant-General Sir Nevil Macready, whose hatred of reporters was exceeded only by his contempt for Irishmen, threatened to court-martial Macgill when it was announced by Herbert Jenkins that his (Macgill's) experiences of the war were about to be published. In the event, Macgill was protected by Lord Esher who, as chairman of the London County Territorial Association, wrote an introduction to *The Red Push*. Macgill escaped prosecution but the threat of court martial probably explains the discrepancy between his article 'Out There', which appeared in *Pearson's Magazine* in September 1915, and the amended version which appeared as the opening chapters of *The Red Horizon* later the same year.

One of the intriguing features of the 1914–18 war was the involvement of large numbers of Irishmen who, according to all accounts, fought as bravely and loyally as their English counterparts, despite the fact that the Home Rule issue had been a major divisive issue in pre-war politics and that 'Rebellion' broke out in Dublin during the course of the war. This simple fact raises a number of complex questions: why did they enlist? how did they reconcile being Irish with fighting for an imperial power that controlled, even oppressed, them? and what impact did the experience of war itself have on their sense of being Irishmen? In other words, did it strengthen or weaken their sense of Irishness? and did it confirm or undermine their ideas of masculinity and their identity as men?

Macgill gives no specific reason for enlisting, but there is no evidence to suggest that he, in common with many other Irishmen including Cadman, felt any great personal dilemma or any contradiction between being Irish and joining the British army. Indeed, there is no evidence that the decision was ever considered in these terms. Unlike such regiments as the Dublin Fusiliers or the Connaught Rangers, the London Irish Rifles was not overwhelmingly Irish in composition, even allowing for the inclusion of first- and second-generation Irishmen in England.[13] At one point Macgill refers, in somewhat exaggerated fashion, to 'the Colonel and I [as] the only two real Irishmen in the battalion'.[14] Nonetheless, there was a real sense of Irishness about the regiment, institutionalized in the distinctive dark-green uniforms, personified by a series of distinguished Irishmen, from Palmerston to Sir John French, associated with the regiment and symbolized in a variety of ways from the ever-present harp-shaped cap badge to the uillean pipers and the celebrations of St Patrick's Day. It was a sense of Irishness which did not sit uncomfortably with being part of the British army, notwithstanding a number of brief references to an awareness among his fellow soldiers of Ireland's fight with England.[15]

Macgill created an important personal image of Ireland and Irishness which lacked an overt political dimension. Instead, there are constant references to his early life in Donegal which, although romanticized, gave him a sense of security in an increasingly threatening world. For example, on the eve of the big attack, described in *The Red Horizon*, he dreams of Donegal, while in the poem, 'A Lament', his love of Ireland is linked to doubts about his own courage. The second stanza runs:

> I wish that I was back again
> In the glens of Donegal
> They'll call me a coward if I return
> But a hero if I fall.

Elsewhere he writes with particular warmth of fellow Irishmen in the London Irish Rifles and others he had met while in action,[16] but it was a highly personal identification upon which he drew in times of trouble.

Such attitudes did not come as a complete surprise to certain contemporary observers. As early as 1843 *The Nation* bitterly rued the fact that the British army seemed 'to anglicize the Irish soldier and make him prefer the tyrant of Ireland to Ireland's self'.[17] Somewhat later, Sinn Feiners condemned such men as having no sense of politics while Sir Roger Casement (not an impartial observer, it is true) was even more scathing, dismissing those who joined the army as 'not Irishmen but English soldiers . . . more English than the English themselves'.[18] In the light of Macgill's few references to Irish issues it is tempting to agree with the Sinn Fein criticism, but the reality may have been more complex. A more convincing explanation may be found in the socio-economic background of those men like Macgill who joined the army. Many Irishmen who enlisted before 1914, as well as those who joined the new army, were drawn from the ranks of the poor and unskilled. Joining the army was a time-honoured alternative to emigration. Furthermore, such men tended to be subordinate to the 'middle-class' patriots who dominated the Home Rule cause. In such circumstances, it is not surprising that these recruits showed little sympathy for a cause that was associated with their exploiters in Ireland. Such recruits were already marginal figures but, with no clear role for them in the envisaged nation, as MacDonagh has argued, nationalism was 'too expensive a passion'.[19]

There is a further explanation which applied to Cadman, though not necessarily to Macgill. The idea that there was a contradiction between being Irish and fighting in the British army for, among other things, the British Empire was not accepted by all Irishmen. This was clearly true of John Redmond but also of others such as Sean O'Faolain who recollected that he 'had no consciousness of my country as a separate cultural identity inside the Empire. . . . I was tremendously proud of belonging to the Empire as were at that time most Irishmen. I gloried in all its trappings'.[20] Indeed, men like Redmond strongly believed that support for the British war effort would hasten the advent of Home Rule for Ireland. As Brian Griffin notes elsewhere in this volume, attitudes towards the empire were shaped, in part at least, by considerations of domestic politics. During the First World War, when the Ulster Volunteer Force were hoping that their patriotism would be rewarded by a continuation of the link with the union, Irish Volunteers felt it necessary to be equally patriotic if Home Rule was to be gained.[21]

One final point on this issue needs to be made. Loftier sentiments of nationalism, and the like, were rarely at the forefront of the soldier's mind for the simple reason that he lived in a smaller, more immediate environment created by the army. Socialization within the regiment, within the company, created new senses of loyalty and new foci of identity. Being a soldier did not necessarily replace being an Irishman but rather overlaid it. Small group loyalties which developed in peacetime were greatly strengthened by the life-threatening experiences of war. Multiple loyalties, as well as multiple identities, were created as circumstances changed but they went hand-in-hand. However, the importance attached to a particular loyalty depended upon specific circumstances. Within the army, small group loyalties were more immediate and more important for day-to-day survival. It is not surprising, therefore, that they became more powerful than any generalized appeal to nationalism. Writing in the dedication to *Soldier Songs* in 1916, Macgill had no doubt that 'the circumstances of war strengthen the *esprit-de-corps* of a soldier . . . pride of regiment in an "old sweat" is much stronger than love of country.' Further, precisely because of the life-and-death struggle at the front, actions such as the Easter Rising could be (and were) seen, at best as an irrelevance, at worst as a betrayal of equally loyal Irishmen who were fighting in France.

Particularly in the early days following enlistment, Macgill found much that was positive in army life. During his period of training at St Albans he discovered a sense of solidarity that was more than the coming together of the outcasts of society of his navvying days. The individual was subsumed into a greater entity. Robert Graves had described drill as 'beautiful . . . a single movement of one large creature' while Macgill recalled the battalion marching at night in similar language. It was a

silent monster . . . full of unrestrained power; resolute in its onward sweep, impervious to danger, it looks a menacing engine of destruction, steady to its goal and certain of its mission.[22]

This sentiment survived the experience of France. Even in the more pessimistic *The Great Push* Macgill strikes a heroic note, describing the individual soldier as being 'submerged in his regiment [and part of] an army mighty in deed, prowess and endurance'.[23] In the early days he felt a sense of shared experience that transcended the divisions of civilian life. Describing a coffee shop in St Albans, he observes,

> all sorts and conditions of soldiers drift into the place and discuss various matters over coffee and mince pies; they are men of all classes who had been as far apart as the poles in civil life, and are now knit together in the common brotherhood of war. Caste and estate seem to have been forgotten; all are engaged in a common business, full of similar risks and rewarded by a similar wage.[24]

Such unity did not survive long in France. While the members of his particular section still 'agree very well', despite their differences in civilian life, 'the same does not hold good in the whole regiment; the public school clique and the board school clique live each in a separate world and a line of demarcation between them is sharply drawn'.[25]

More striking were his observations in a passage from his article in *Pearson's Magazine* in September 1915, 'Out There', which was not included in *The Red Horizon*. Having come by chance across an (unnamed) book on the new army, he was scathing in his dismissal of its claim that the new army was a 'democratic one where there is neither poverty or riches, and where all vices are washed away from the being of a civilian when he becomes a soldier'. To the contrary,

> the new soldier is not innocent, vices ancient as Adam are not choked by khaki; they still exist; in short, the new army is a miniature pattern of the society that created it. . . . it has its poor and wealthy, the poor feed on bully-beef and army stew from start to finish; the wealthy dine well when a local hotel is not out of bounds, and can always find an impoverished private ready to take up their extra duties and fatigues at the hourly rate of a few coppers.[26]

Class divisions were abundantly clear: '[The new army] has got its officers to whom the men are not allowed to speak except through an intermediary . . . they must be saluted, and failure to observe the latter ceremonial can get a private in for any amount of trouble.'[27] In other words, the world of the exploited navvy had been re-created across the Channel in wartime France.

Although part of the greater entity of the company, the regiment and the army, Macgill's experiences had a more important personal dimension. The 'self' that he had created prior to the war was complex. It drew heavily upon the masculine virtues of the navvy, but he was distanced from that world by the very fact of standing apart and writing about it. Similarly, he drew upon his Irish Catholic background but was similarly distanced from that world, not least because of his criticism of the Church and its representatives. He was from, but not entirely of, an unskilled working-class Irish Catholic milieu, in which class, religion and ethnicity created a distinct culture. In addition, and in part deriving from this complex pre-war self, he (in common with other recruits) brought with him a set of beliefs surrounding the army, war and the responsibility of the individual at war. Donning the uniform of the London Irish Rifles set him apart from his earlier civilian 'self' but the new man retained important facets of his previous self. Macgill openly proclaimed himself to be one of the 'fighting men . . . trained to the trade and licensed to the profession' and took fierce pride in being a rifleman, a specialist within the greater body of the army.[28] The image of the new 'self' was cast in active and heroic mould. Soldiering was seen as being both manly and romantic and this was to be put to the test in France. Macgill saw himself as part of 'a great adventure, full of thrill and excitement . . . [as] we stood on the threshold of momentous events'.[29] This was to be the true test of manhood. On the eve of embarkation he pondered, 'What will it be like but above all, how shall I conduct myself in the trenches? Maybe I shall be afraid – cowardly. But no! . . . It would be a grand thing to become conspicuous daring.'[30]

The idea of the 'romance of soldiering' persisted even in the face of the realities of war. In the concluding chapter of *The Red Horizon*, reflecting upon his life in the trenches and behind the lines, he talks of 'the young soldier . . . his heart stirred with the romance of his mission' and of 'the mystery, the enchantment and the glamour' while the book concludes with the simple observation: 'there is romance, there is joy in the life of the soldier.'[31]

There is a more specific (and predictable) emphasis on the importance of physical strength and vigour as a determinant of soldierly manliness. This is most clearly seen in his war poetry which abounds with references to 'brave lusty lads' and 'supple lads and clean' with 'eager eye and stout young heart'. It is the 'brave lusty comrades' who play the 'old, old game/With glancing bayonet and trusty gun/And wild blood bursting free!' It is they who show 'a good stiff upper lip for the old pal's sake/And the old battalion's pride'. The unfit and the injured can no longer take part (and by implication are no longer truly full men). However much they might sigh for that 'old, old game', when 'an arm is crippled, a leg is gone' then 'the game's no more for me'.[32]

To see Macgill simply in terms of an unquestioned military masculinity would be misleading, however. In both *The Red Horizon* and, more so, *The Great Push* there is a growing sense of doubt about the values by which he has defined himself. The realities of the war in France undermined the optimistic Macgill of *The Amateur Army*. The offensive warrior found little scope in an increasingly immobile, trench-bound war.[33] There was too much 'everlastin' waitin'' on an 'everlastin' road' for a man who 'longed for action, for some adventure'.[34] A soldier's life was less than inspirational: 'I have come to the conclusion that war is rather a dull game, not that blood-curdling, dashing and sabre-clashing thing that is seen in pictures.'[35]

Worse, 'everything seemed so monstrously futile, so unfinished, so useless'.[36] Macgill, by now a stretcher-bearer, increasingly found himself thinking in terms of a shared humanity at the front. As well as an absence of any overt anti-Englishness, his war writings were also characterized by a growing lack of anti-German sentiment, much to the dismay of some of his early readers, which further emphasizes his crisis of identity as the distinction between friend and foe/self and non-self collapsed. On sentry duty he asks himself, 'who are these men behind the line of sandbags that I should want to kill them, to disembowel them with a sword, blow their faces to pieces? . . . I am not angry with them.'[37]

In *The Great Push* he was even more outspoken, expressing concern for the German wounded, condemning 'brotherly mutilation' and confessing that 'of those who are England's enemies I know, even now, very little. I cannot well pass judgment on a nation through seeing distorted lumps of clothing and mangled flesh pounded into the muddy floor.'[38]

The theme of uselessness is seen most strongly in *The Great Push*. On the eve of the battle of Loos, at which he was to be wounded, Macgill noted how 'my normal self revolted at the thought of the coming dawn; the experience of life had not prepared me for one day of savage and ruthless butchery'.[39] The use of the phrase 'normal self' is telling. This was not the response of a naïve and inexperienced youth. Macgill's pre-war experiences had brought him into contact with violence and brutal death while his experiences in France had shown him the realities of large-scale slaughter, the 'distorted lumps of clothing and mangled flesh pounded into the muddy floor'.[40] Now the 'harrowing sights' of pieces of bodies brought home the insecurity and frailty of man. Among the dead, dying and sorely wounded he saw 'lives maimed and finished, and all the romance and roving that makes up the life of a soldier gone forever'.[41] Descriptions of the heroism of the London Irish under fire cannot disguise the increasingly melancholy tone. In Flanders it is 'Death . . . who is holding carnival'.[42] War has become 'an approved licence for brotherly mutilation', while 'the shapelessness of Destruction reigns' as Macgill becomes more and more aware of 'the Futility of War'.[43] There is a growing sense of estrangement. Unlike the rhetoric of war that had accompanied his enlistment and early training, the realities of war no longer offered the legitimation of his initial wartime 'self'.

Finally, the experience of war brought a heightened awareness of the isolation of the individual and a questioning of his ability to withstand the pressure of events. This sense of weakness and fear haunted Macgill. (So much so that he returned to the subject later and made it the subject of a war novel, *Fear!*, published in 1921.) As he noted towards the end of *The Great Push*, 'you've found out you've been posing a little before. Alone you're really a coward.'[44] And it was as an isolated individual, dependent upon self but questioning that very self, that the soldier, in Macgill's experience, found himself: 'We were alone and lonely, nearly every man of us. For myself I felt isolated from the whole world. . . . Who are we? Who shall give an answer to that question?'[45]

The older, more positive self-image never entirely disappeared. Macgill could still speak of his 'grand courage' towards the end of *The Great Push*, but the balance has changed. The confident young man, defined by a physical and moral masculinity, who joined the army and set off to France with scarcely a doubt, had been gradually replaced – or more accurately, coexisted with – a newer, more unsure and fearful 'self'. However, old beliefs, central to his former 'self', were not to be cast aside lightly. There remained a deep-seated and tenaciously held belief in such concepts as comradeship, courage and self-sacrifice – those grand abstractions, faith in which was supposedly destroyed by the realities of war. For Riflemen Macgill and Cadman these ideals survived but not simply because the old was too deep-rooted to be swept away in its entirety, nor because these men lacked the sensibility and style to express the new 'truth' about war. Rather, under conditions of war, it was necessary for them to reassert the beliefs and values for which they had enlisted and fought; it was necessary to call upon an identity, a 'self', cast in a more heroic mould to withstand the pressures of events and to safeguard the new, unheroic, even cowardly 'self' that was coming to the fore. There was, as it were, a dual self, an internal hyphenation of identity. Macgill makes a particularly telling observation:

> All men have some restraining influence to help them in hours of trial, some principle or some illusion. Duty, patriotism, vanity and dreams come to the help of the men in the trenches, all illusions probably, ephemeral and fleeting, but for a man as ephemeral and fleeting as his illusions are, he can lay his back against them and defy death and the terrors of the world. But let him stand naked and looking at the staring reality of the terrors that engirt him and he becomes a raving lunatic.[46]

Living through unprecedented horrors, which he sought to record at the time, Macgill was not unaware of the erosion of the values with which he defined himself when he first came to France but without which his mental survival was as much in jeopardy as his physical survival. To accept Hynes' claim that 'the soldier-poet, for whom the war had been a set of traditional images, had become a man beyond metaphor'[47] is to oversimplify the process of change that took place under the pressure of events during the First World War and, more importantly, it is to understate the tensions and traumas of change. If, as Jay Winter argues so convincingly, 'the enduring appeal of many traditional motifs [of remembrance] . . . is directly related to the universality of bereavement in the Europe of the Great War and its aftermath',[48] then for the soldier, the universality of maintaining life (psychologically more than physically) explains the continuing and underestimated persistence of traditional images and values of war. In both cases a sense of identity could be created and preserved in the face of appalling horror and loss. This reassertion of traditional values and motifs prevented, or obscured, in part at least, that sense of dislocation which could (and did) destroy the very identity of individuals beset by the appalling experiences of an increasingly technological and destructive war for which they had not been prepared. The phrases may have been platitudinous, the values illusory (and the individual may very well have known this) but they served a vital function. Rifleman Cadman was haunted by the war for over sixty years but never became a 'raving lunatic'; neither did Rifleman Macgill. If, as argued earlier, Irish nationalism was 'too expensive a passion' for men such as this, so much more so was 'the aesthetic of direct experience'.

Notes

1 Among numerous books on the subject see J. Bristow, *Empire Boys: Adventures in a Man's World* (London, HarperCollins, 1991); M. Girouard, *The Return to Camelot: Chivalry and the English Gentleman* (New Haven, Yale University Press, 1981); J.A. Mangan, *Athleticism in the Victorian and Edwardian Public School* (Cambridge University Press, 1981); J.A. Mangan & J. Walvin (eds), *Manliness and Morality: Middle-class Masculinity in Britain and America, 1800–1940* (Manchester University Press, 1987); and M. Roper & J. Tosh (eds), *Manful Assertions: Masculinities in Britain since 1800* (London, Routledge, 1991).

2 I.M. Parsons (ed.), *Men Who March Away: Poems of the First World War* (London, Chatto & Windus, 1965) and J. Silkin (ed.), *First World War Poetry* (Harmondsworth, Penguin, 1979) are two of the better anthologies. B. Gardner (ed.), *Up the Line to Death: The War Poets 1914–1918* (London, Methuen, 1976) contains much familiar material but is organized on a thematic basis. Edmund Blunden, *Undertones of War* (London, Cobden-Sanderson, 1928); Robert Graves, *Goodbye to All That* (London, Jonathan Cape, 1929); Siegfried Sassoon, *Memoirs of a Fox-Hunting Man* (London, Faber & Faber, 1928) and *Memoirs of an Infantry Officer* (London, Faber & Faber, 1930). Richard Aldington, *Death of a Hero* (London, Chatto & Windus, 1929); R.C. Sheriff & Vernon Bartlett, *Journey's End* (London, Gollancz, 1930); and H. Williamson, *The Patriot's Progress* (London, Geoffrey Bles, 1930).

3 P. Fussell, *The Great War and Modern Memory* (Oxford University Press, 1975), chapter 5, 'Oh! What a Literary War'.

4 S. Hynes, *A War Imagined: The First World War and English Culture* (London, Pimlico, 1992). The quotations are from Jay Winter's critique of this stance in *Sites of Memory, Sites of Mourning: The Great War in European Cultural History* (Cambridge University Press, 1996), p. 2.

5 The main autobiographical works are *The Amateur Army* (London, Herbert Jenkins, 1915); *The Red Horizon* (London, Herbert Jenkins, 1916); *The Great Push: An Episode of the Great War* (London, Herbert Jenkins, 1916); and *Soldier Songs* (London, Herbert Jenkins, 1916). In addition he wrote a number of articles for *Pearson's Magazine* and the *Daily Mail* many of which were reproduced largely unchanged in his three main books. He returned to the subject some years later in the novel *Fear!* (London, Herbert Jenkins, 1921).

6 The London Irish were known as 'The Footballers of Loos' following an incident in which a football was kicked across no man's land to the cry of 'On the ball, London Irish!' during the assault in September 1915. Allegedly, there was a 'joyous' shoot of 'Goal!' as it was kicked into the German trench. Michael MacDonagh, 'The London Irish', *The Irish Soldier* (1/10/1918), pp. 11–15.

7 C.E. Carrington, *Soldiers from the Wars Returning* (London, Hutchinson, 1965), p. 252, cited in E.J. Leeds, *No Man's Land: Combat and Identity in World War One* (Cambridge University Press, 1979), p. 113.

8 Leeds, *No Man's Land* is an exception.

9 R. Scott, *The Fabrication of the Late-Victorian Femme Fatale: The Kiss of Death* (London, Macmillan, 1992) provides an interesting general discussion in relation to late nineteenth-century literature.

10 See M. Freeman, *Rewriting the Self: History, Memory, Narrative* (London, Routledge, 1997).

11 Freeman, *Rewriting the Self*, p. 90.

12 For a more detailed discussion of the pre-war Macgill see O.D. Edwards, 'Patrick Macgill and the Making of a Historical Source', *The Innes Review*, 37 (1986), 73–99.

13 N. Perry, 'Nationality in the Irish Infantry Regiments in the First World War', *War and Society*, 12 (1994), 65–95. P. Callan, 'Recruiting for the British Army in Ireland during the First World War', *Irish Sword*, 66 (1987), 43–56.

14 *Amateur Army*, p. 15.

15 For example, he describes a fellow Irishman, Feelan, explicitly referring to Ireland's fight for freedom before singing 'The Rising of the Moon', *The Red Horizon*, p. 45. Nor was this the only rebel song popular in the regiment. Cadman's war experience was enlivened by heartfelt renditions of such songs as 'Bold Robert Emmett' and 'God Save Ireland'.

16 See for example, *The Red Horizon*, p. 83.

17 Cited in M. MacDonagh, 'Irish Soldiers in the British Army, 1792–1922: Suborned or Subordinate?', *Journal of Social History*, 17 (1983), 31–64, at p. 42.

18 Cited in T.P. Dooley, *Irishmen or English Soldiers?* (Liverpool University Press, 1995), p. 1.

19 MacDonagh, 'Irish Soldiers', p. 54. It is perhaps significant that although Macgill returned to Ireland after the war, he was never able to settle there and emigrated to America.

20 Sean O'Faolain, 'A portrait of the artist as an old man', *Irish University Review*, 1976, cited in Dooley, *Irishmen or English Soldiers?*, p. 36. There is a general point to be made here. Not just Irishmen but also Welshmen and Scots identified strongly with the British Empire to which they made as great, if not greater, a practical contribution as the English.

21 B. Griffin, 'Irish Identity and the Crimean War', pp. 122–33.

22 Dooley, *Irishmen or English Soldiers*, p. 72. *Good-bye to All That* (Harmondsworth, Penguin, 1979), p. 156.

23 *Great Push*, p. 134.

24 *Amateur Army*, pp. 63–4. This was a common experience noted by many volunteers in the early stage of the war.

25 *Red Horizon*, p. 91.

26 'Out There', *Pearson's Magazine* (09/1915), p. 293.

27 'Out There', *Pearson's Magazine*, pp. 293–4.

28 *Amateur Army*, p. 55. There are a number of references to the pride he took in being a rifleman. See for example pp. 58–9 and p. 71.

29 *Red Horizon*, p. 26. Rifleman Cadman had a similarly elevated view of the British army and the war he was about to enter. Cadman's views on enlistment were strikingly naïve. Such was the superiority of the British army in his view that he was confident that nothing could stand between them and a speedy victory.

30 *Red Horizon*, p. 17.

31 *Red Horizon*, pp. 300–1, 306.

32 'Everyday of War' in *Soldier Songs*, 1916.

33 For a more general consideration of the tensions created by the undermining of the 'offensive warrior' and the emergence of a new ideal of the 'defensive warrior' see Leeds, *No Man's Land*, especially chapter 3.

34 *Red Horizon*, p. 130.

35 *Red Horizon*, p. 130.

36 *Red Horizon*, p. 197.

37 *Red Horizon*, pp. 91–2.

38 *Great Push*, p. 88.

39 *Great Push*, p. 69.

40 *Great Push*, p. 88.

41 *Great Push*, p. 81.

42 'Death and the Fairies' in *Soldier Songs*.

43 *Great Push*, pp. 88, 159 and 252.

44 *Great Push*, p. 172.

45 *Red Horizon*, pp. 86–7.

46 *Great Push*, p. 162.

47 Hynes, *A War Imagined*, p. 156.

48 Winter, *Sites of Memory*, p. 5.

16

ELFIN RUSTLING, AIR AND ASHES: COMMUNICATION, IDENTITY AND WAR IN LUDWIG HARIG'S *ORDNUNG IST DAS GANZE LEBEN*[1]

K. Howard

'In der Luft bleibt deine Wurzel, in der Luft'.
Paul Celan

How much can a person bear? Must one forget if one wants to survive? Had father lost his memory? Or had he, in order to save himself, lengthened the moments of well-being into heavenly eternities, thereby shrinking the days of horror into seconds of shock? (p. 474)[2]

Questions such as these shape and deform the relationships of many German children to fathers they feel they cannot fully comprehend as a result of war. In the latter third of this century there has been a plethora of novels focusing on precisely this problem which have given rise to a literary sub-genre in Germany, known variously as father literature or father portraits. When it has received attention, Ludwig Harig's novel, *Ordnung ist das ganze Leben* (1986) has been discussed in two contexts: within the confines of Harig's own œuvre and within father literature.[3] While the first association is self-explanatory, the second is somewhat deceptive and demands further attention. Harig's novel indeed shares elements with these father portraits, written in the 1970s and early '80s by such authors as Peter Handke, Christoph Meckel, Bernward Vesper and Christa Wolf. Like them, having reached middle age, Harig is faced, not only with his father's mortality but his own; as in this case, the relationship is often marked by a breakdown in communication and the author attempts a reconciliation (p. 267).[4] Like the other fathers featured, Harig's father was profoundly influenced by a war. However, this also marks a fundamental difference, such that the association with the father portrait ultimately proves unhelpful. While the central event of the father portrait is the Second World War, both Louis Harig, the father, and Ludwig Harig, the son, identify the First World War as being pivotal. This, of course, impacts first and foremost on Louis Harig, but it also affects the father–son relationship and ultimately influences the tone of the novel.

If we look more closely at the notion of war there are, in fact, three evoked in this work: the First and Second World Wars, and the Franco-Prussian War, which still exists within living memory in the novel. War constitutes a useful point of orientation for the Harig clan. Lineage is established as much in terms of involvement in past wars as in terms of occupation or marital alliance. Several family members are introduced or characterized with reference to war (pp. 21, 189–90, 457). Through the juxtaposition of the different wars (pp. 31, 250) and the passing down of military knowledge from one generation to the next, war also provides a degree of continuity (p. 457). However, because of the importance of the First World War in this text, time constraints and the attention that has hitherto been accorded the Second World War,[5] the First World War will be the focus here.

The notion of identity is obviously central to any biographical work and in this case is embodied in the question: 'What sort of man was he?'[6] Initially, it seems that Louis Harig's love of order (alluded to in the title of the work) will facilitate the author's quest. Indeed, Harig senior lived a neat life, the outline of which can be easily traced: his last day of school was the first day of his apprenticeship (p. 70) and the last day of his apprenticeship was his first as a recruit (p. 70). Yet, while this orderliness allows the rudiments of his life to be discerned, it provides only the structure not its essence. People are, of course, much more complex. Harig senior's identity operates on at least four different levels. There are the three more accessible spheres within which he moves: the familial (which emerges as a matter of course given the bio-autobiographical nature of this work), the regional and the national.

Given the predominance of wars in this account, it is not surprising that nationalism should be so important. Expressions of national identity occur throughout the text (the most obvious being descriptions of various war memorials (e.g. pp. 73, 76, 88)). The most detailed, if superficial, concept of nationalism belongs to Harig senior. Louis Harig has the nationalistic equivalent of a pantheistic outlook. His is the nationalization of the everyday, of the trivial, in which eggs (p. 403), fonts (p. 15), hats and clothing (pp. 268–70, 381, 433–4, 439), music (p. 144), chairs and colours (pp. 63, 79, 144, 190) are particularly valued for their Germanness. Harig senior's sense of national identity is not that of the politically engaged, but that of the *Kleinbürger*, the petit-bourgeois. His response to National Socialism is simply to wait until it passes (p. 177). He seems to live in an intellectual vacuum and has no idea, for example, who Ernst Jünger was (p. 91; see also pp. 145, 206). He only consults nationalistic non-fiction (pp. 249, 250, 310, 404) and his children get an initial idea of German nationalism from his collection of cigarette cards (p. 41). (Harig junior, by contrast, is much more sophisticated and cites Bloch, Keegan, Unruh, Goethe, Verlaine, Rimbaud, Rousseau and Lenz.)

Ludwig Harig's benevolent portrayal of his father has led several critics to dismiss this work as a hagiography and its subject as an opportunistic National Socialist. However, this simplistic assessment does both author and subject an injustice. By focusing on all the wars in the text, an interesting progression can be observed. While national identity only really began to crystallize following Germany's victory in the Franco-Prussian War (1870–1), the relationship of the Harig men to this nascent nationalism evolves such that this work presents a map of the disintegration of the relationship between individual and state over three generations. Too old to have fought in the previous war and believing himself to be a spent force, National Socialism offers the author's grandfather the opportunity for rebirth and a reconstituted sense of self (p. 189). (Thus even for this, the most politically, again if naïvely, committed of the Harig clan, the rise of the Nazis has more personal than political significance.) While there is no doubting the conviction with which Louis Harig enlists in the First World War, as the century progresses he retreats from nationalism. His attitude to National Socialism is ambivalent and his passivity is captured in an analogy in which his father is portrayed as a cog in a machine (pp. 45, 63). His experiences in the First World War disillusion him to the extent that, unlike his own father, he does not rush to don a uniform but distances himself from events (p. 267). Ludwig Harig is even less involved in the events of the Second World War. He spent this period playing in a youth orchestra in a remote location, practising while Frankfurt was being bombed and noticing little difference from peacetime (p. 361; see also pp. 346, 347, 350). His own understanding of nationalism receives little consideration.

Regionalism features to a lesser extent in this work. It emerges in the pride Harig senior feels for the Saarland, in the pronunciation of the local dialect (p. 436) and the 1935 plebiscite to determine the allegiance of the Saar.

While his father's familial, national and regional pedigrees are important, Harig is most concerned with his father's identity on the personal level. At the nexus of this identity is the First World War, described variously as the place 'where his life lies buried' (p. 19), a 'far off home' (p. 256), a closed paradise and as a mother's lap from which he has yet to crawl (p. 256). Frustratingly for Harig, he cannot comprehend his father's war experiences either by virtue of birthright or after ten years' intensive research. He is therefore dependent on his father's ability to communicate. From the outset it is thus clear that Harig senior's attitude to communication will be influential. Not only does it constitute an important element of his identity but it hinders its comprehension and marks a dramatic point of distinction between father and son. Highlighting this difficulty, Harig formulates and reformulates his father's relationship to language (pp. 411, 413). He somewhat misguidedly attempts to place his father's attitude to language in a much wider cultural, intellectual and political context. He posits, for example, that his father's tortuous relationship to language grew from the age when psychology had not yet been invented (p. 47), making the externalization of feelings difficult. However, given that his father is firmly *kleinbürgerlich* and so culturally, politically and intellectually naïve (p. 50), the First World War is the more likely key. This is corroborated by Harig's later claim that his father's situation is not derived from some inner failing but from his experiences in the war (p. 153).

The issue of communication provokes a series of rhetorical questions which pepper the text, underlining the breakdown in communication between father and son (p. 257): 'Who can still remember [the war]? Who is alive who can still remember? Who of those who is still alive and can remember wants to talk about it? Why did father never talk about it so that the tales could become history and perhaps provide a moral?' (p. 88; see also pp. 24, 28–9, 30, 36, 85, 140, 200).[7] However, from the first fairly innocuous comment that Harig senior did not cry at his wife's funeral (p. 12), it becomes clear that communication is problematic for him on every level.

At one end of the spectrum is communication at its most intimate, non-verbal or formulaic. The father does not, for example, sing but even finds others singing so embarrassing he flees. His unease extends to physical contact; his son has never seen him touch another living thing (p. 446). Devoid of any sensitivity for the metaphysical or metaphorical (pp. 155, 445), he is not surprisingly also roundly incapable of prayer: 'Father couldn't pray. Perhaps he didn't pray, didn't go to confession, didn't believe in God, like he couldn't cry, couldn't sing and couldn't use big words, because it embarrassed him. If he had had to clasp his hands and recite a prayer, he would have died of shame' (p. 445).[8]

At the other end of the spectrum is communication on the public level. Like many First World War soldiers, Harig senior is extremely sceptical of ideologies:

Shame? Dignity? Honour? All big words, father knew we would be more concerned with survival, with nothing else. (p. 300)

He didn't like big words, they embarrassed him, he would rather have crawled away when he heard someone using big words, his words weren't even small, he didn't have any. (p. 155)[9]

Language scepticism already existed prior to the First World War but although one of the most potent weapons, exploited with rampant indiscrimination, language also became one of the greatest casualties of the war. Propaganda was deployed for the first time systematically and the ensuing instrumentalization and inflation of language (also endemic in Wilhelmine Germany) undermined its integrity for the common soldier:

The official language and literature of Bismarck's Germany already had in them the elements of dissolution. It is the golden age of the militant historians, of the philologists and the incomprehensible metaphysicians. . . . For to the academicism and ponderousness of German as it was written by the pillars of learning and society between 1870 and the First World War, the imperial régime added its own gifts of pomp and mystification.[10]

University, officialdom, army and court combined to drill into the German language habits no less dangerous than those they drilled into the German people: a terrible weakness for slogans and clichés (*Lebensraum*, 'the yellow peril', 'the Nordic virtues'); an automatic reverence before the long word or the loud voice; a fatal taste for saccharine pathos (*Gemütlichkeit*) beneath which to conceal any amount of rawness or deception.[11]

As a result, the intellectual lost dominion over the experiential and words became ineffectual: 'The German gain in ground of scarcely 10 kilometres had cost both sides more than half a million casualties. They lay there now and had no more words with which they could have described this keeping still, this holding out, this sticking it out' (p. 163).[12] Only decades after the war does Harig senior take desperate but naïve recourse to language. When his wife falls gravely ill, he endeavours to cure her cancer by talking:

> When mother said in the morning she didn't feel particularly well, he [father] began talking, talked and talked as if he wanted to drive the illness out by talking and through the talking itself he forgot the medication and talking about the medication and its healing properties. He only talked, I never heard him talk so much as when he was talking against mother's illness, because all at once all his inhibitions had dissipated and he understood speech as therapy. . . . (p. 447)[13]

When this fails, existentially disillusioned with the failure of language, he withdraws again (pp. 447, 448): 'At mother's wake father looked like a stone guest. . . . Father sat at the head of the table as if he didn't belong, he didn't eat, he didn't drink, he didn't say a word' (pp. 450–1).[14]

Literature and the written word, which proved therapeutic for many First World War combatants,[15] also fail to offer a solution to Harig senior. He is not only handicapped by a Faustian distrust of words (p. 116), but professes anti-literature sentiments on a number of occasions:

> Verdun was no novel for him, no he couldn't have redeemed himself in images and similes. (pp. 155–6)

> His memory was overgrown, the memories no longer spoke, he never had scenes from novels in his head. (p. 75; see also pp. 271, 299, 373, 416)[16]

It is thus impossible for him to fictionalize his war experience; the past is a sealed unit which cannot be recreated:

What is there to alter and transform, what is there to turn over, to turn around, to turn inside out, to turn upside down, so that if it is no longer a war and battlefield it could be a new paradise and a field of flowers, on which lions have become tame and lie peacefully beside the lambs? Life won't turn into a novel in these heads, even if Lieutenant Thiele writes in his diary. (p. 164)[17]

Yet despite all of these problems and reservations, Harig senior did attempt to write an account of his life, not of his own initiative but at the behest of his son. Growing anxious that even in his eighties his father will not talk about his life, Harig prompts him to write about it. Having communicated so little in the past, however, the father is afraid that once he starts writing he will never stop, that floodgates will open and he will lose control (p. 161). (His fears prove unfounded for the project only occupies him for three weeks (p. 18).) What evolves, however, is not an account of his life in general but rather an account almost exclusively of his experiences in the First World War (p. 18).

Like the works of many First World War authors, Harig senior's account had a long gestation period, longer in fact at seventy years than most. Yet the text is far from elucidating. Harig claims the Prussian attitude to communication has impacted upon his father. His account is described as spartan and thrifty (p. 25; see also p. 99), his prose seldom contains a complete sentence and thus reads more like orders (pp. 75, 83), conveying little more than tactics: 'Yet in his notebook I read nothing further about these days than a few meagre key words. "Trenches flattened", he writes, "the ground ahead under heavy artillery fire. At dawn arrived in supposed position. Only shell-holes"' (p. 79).[18] Each time Harig quotes his father's notebook he cannot hide his disappointment at its inadequacy: 'but from these three sentences, which aren't even complete sentences, there is no sign of a carefree life in the barracks, no puzzling soldierly happiness' (p. 25).[19] While it seems his memories are buried too deep (pp. 18–19), even his earlier attempts during the war itself prove equally fruitless. From the front he writes thirty-seven formulaic postcards; he communicates without communicating: 'all thirty-seven postcards have almost the same tone, they read: "Your son and brother Louis who is in the best of health sends you his best wishes from the trench." Once he added "I missed out on the cake, as the rats have grown fat on it. Aside from that everything arrived intact"' (p. 159).[20]

However, it is not simply the written accounts which prove so unsatisfactory; his oral responses are also unhelpful. Whenever asked directly about the war, Harig senior lapses into a kind of fuguing, listing, for example, bus connections (p. 145) or reciting the hierarchy of military ranks (p. 144). Standing on a fort in France for which he had fought, he finally speaks, but what he says makes little sense: 'Now he looked down and for the first time he said a long, a cohesive sentence. He said: "The horse has a horse's nature and man has the nature of a man. But man is more resilient than the horse"' (p. 158).[21] The pinnacle of his

expression is 'Oh dear' ('Oje'), a phrase he uses frequently in conjunction with
war (pp. 144, 145, 153, 156, 160, 284, 299). Only on his return to the battlefield
some fifty years after the war is his 'Oh dear' qualified to indicate his frustration
(p. 160). Again language is inadequate to the task; he can find no words to
express his experiences (p. 163).

Harig attempts to compensate for the shortfalls in his father's war narrative by
retracing his progress through France several times, but when this proves
unsatisfactory, he is forced to resort to supposition (pp. 165, 344). Indeed, his own
imagination seems more helpful than his father's eye-witness account (p. 30). The
gap is most effectively bridged by a secondary character, Lieutenant Thiele,
Harig senior's friend and superior officer in the war. He acts as a useful
counterfoil as his relationship to language is seemingly unproblematic; he not
only kept a diary in the war but also wrote poetry (both are quoted by Harig).
The differing attitudes to language are highlighted by the juxtaposition of their
two accounts of Louis' wounding. While Harig senior concentrates on tactics,
concluding enigmatically, 'Then it happened' ('Da ist es passiert' p. 162), Thiele
not only informs the reader that Louis has been wounded, but writes freely of his
feelings (pp. 162–3) with all the immediacy of the present tense and the first
person singular pronoun. (Louis's account is mediated by the past tense and the
impersonal third person pronoun.) Thiele thus provides both the son and his
readers with a greater appreciation of the father's war experiences (p. 459).

Thiele mediates successfully between father and son, reader and father, but he
also has a dramatically therapeutic effect on Louis Harig. Some decades after the
war the two resume contact through letters. This is in itself surprising but it is
when the two finally meet face to face, decades after the war, that the spectacular
nature of the transformation becomes apparent:

> Only a moment passed and then they were in each others' arms. Never in my
> life had I seen father kiss someone before, I also don't know if father kissed
> Erich Thiele, I saw how two men in their mid-eighties stood on the station
> platform, their cheeks pressed together, and hugged each other. Erich Thiele
> took his hands from my father's shoulders, stretched them out, reached them
> out to him, he was the god Mars and father was Eros. (p. 459)[22]

The two quickly lapse into domestic familiarity reminiscent of a homo-eroticism
which marks so many depictions of relationships between soldiers in the First
World War. Harig senior tenderly dries Thiele's hair and when Thiele sings,
Louis does not flee but looks on in admiration in the house he has festooned with
flowers to honour his friend. Yet, despite the encouragement from both his son
and friend, Harig senior never resolves his relationship with language and
therefore cannot communicate his war experiences satisfactorily. Although a *petit
bourgeois*, Louis Harig is aware of the same inadequacies of language articulated

by the most literate of the First World War authors. While the explicit recognition
of these limitations allows them to be transcended to an extent, for Louis Harig,
who recognizes these problems only implicitly, there is no escape. With the
ageing process, communication becomes increasingly difficult: he only hears
what he wants to hear (p. 485) which is compounded by the onset of deafness
(p. 478). Eventually he has to rely on a variety of devices, false teeth, glasses and
a hearing aid (p. 404), to facilitate his interaction with the outside world. Given
his trouble communicating, it is not surprising he should die of throat cancer, the
tumour of which gradually strangles his vocal chords so he is finally incapable of
speech (p. 487).[23] In the last stages of his illness, when he chooses not to and then
cannot wear his various aids, he is virtually incommunicado (p. 488).

Although this work professes to be fictional, *Ordnung ist das ganze Leben* is in
fact the culmination of ten years' research. As mentioned, Harig employed
several non-fictional techniques to help pin his father down. He encourages his
father to chronicle his life and visits some of the battlefields several times with
his father and others; he also draws upon his own recollections, defers to
Lieutenant Thiele and cites other authorities such as regimental histories
(p. 77), the historian, John Keegan (pp. 73, 88) and several First World War
authors (pp. 86, 152). When this still proves inadequate, Harig takes recourse to
the author in himself and makes use of literary devices to force a greater sense
of immediacy between himself and his father. Not only do the structure of the
novel and the make-up of the individual chapters bear witness to this, but so
too does the juxtaposition of elements which do not chronologically belong
together: 'We are standing on the street, my brother and I, father and his NCO
are marching and puffing out their chests . . .' (p. 31; see also pp. 33, 148).[24]
Harig also turns to metaphors, symbols, and analogies to fairy-tales and other
literature for their ability to bridge the gap between the sayable and the
unsayable (pp. 53–7, 186, 250, 253, 256, 272, 300, 322, 369, 379, 391).[25] Most
of these, however, prove more effective at emphasizing the gap so that the
father, as a First World War combatant, remains an evanescent figure, evoked
in a shadow simile: 'almost near enough to grasp, but we can't grab him,
sometimes he stretches out a hand, no, it is only a breath of air which has
blown into the room from the street' (p. 39; see also pp. 379, 391). The
frustration causes Harig to comment plaintively, 'we can't catch up with him
any more' ('wir holen ihn nicht mehr ein') (p. 74).

Not only are these literary devices incapable of re-creating the war experience,
but they are also unacceptable to the very subject they are intended to capture,
Harig senior: '"Nothing more than hair-splitting . . . all twisting words and
meanings, all rubbish." He didn't have any time for literary similes, even if his life
depended on it' (p. 271).[26] Perhaps aware of this dilemma, while the father is at
pains to construct any representation of his war experiences, the son at times
struggles not to represent his father's experiences as a construct. An article by

Benno Rech offers an interesting insight into the process of committing Harig's father to paper. Rech quotes some of the marginalia from Harig's manuscript which show him constantly struggling to reign in his literary instincts and limit the literary artifice: 'go sparingly . . . don't be too penetrative', 'one turn too many'.[27]

Harig's work thus bears witness to a much more subtle generation gap than many of those portrayed in German father literature. It is a generation gap expressed in terms of communication. Harig, who came of age during the excesses of the *Wirtschaftswunder* of the 1950s (p. 392), demonstrates emphatically through this 500-page *magnum opus* that he did not inherit the communication difficulties of his father. While Harig senior believes communication cannot help, his son is more optimistic and believes new meanings for words can be created (p. 165). While his father is fettered by a lack of imagination (p. 170), Harig creates whole worlds using words and his most active imagination (pp. 160 ff., 182). Not surprisingly it takes his father some time to come to terms with his son's decision to become a wordsmith rather than a car painter. Even in his later years, Harig senior doubts the effectiveness of words (pp. 393, 412) in all but one context, when they combine to make up rules (pp. 423, 426).[28] Yet, for all Harig's fascination with his father's relationship to language and his empathetic and analytical understanding of him, Harig cannot decide whether his father cannot or will not speak: 'it was taxing and painful, I wished I could finally see and learn, hear and learn just what father and Erich Thiele saw and heard, what they knew and didn't divulge. Couldn't they or didn't they want to?' (p. 471; see also pp. 155, 473, 474).[29] However, in taking recourse to words, the anathema of his father, Harig is doomed to certain failure in this novel, a failure he alludes to towards the start of his undertaking:

> and now that father is dead, I have to invent him for the second time. Yet the air he breathed in such a lively way bursts in lots of soap bubbles made of words and when I open my mouth and begin to recount, half a century scatters between my lips in single syllables which I must continually fit together into words which I now still don't know. 'It's all elfin rustling', father would have said, 'all illusion!' (p. 20)[30]

While the act of writing was not the father's salvation, cannot convey his war experiences and does not capture him well on paper, it proves beneficial to the son. It is in the process of writing this novel and encouraging his father to write that Harig comes to realize that language is not always the great panacea; it has failed on both the literal and metaphorical levels. Ironically, it is ultimately, the non-verbal, the empathetic (championed by so many First World War combatants) which enables the son to understand his father's experiences:

he looked at me as if he wanted to say something, but he only cleared his throat, he just couldn't translate the language of the trenches, he shook his head, yet I could understand him, just as I always understood him, even when we didn't talk with one another. (p. 455)

he came out of the doorway and stood before us, small and thin, and his mouth was twitching. He didn't say a word. I no longer know if we said anything at that point. We stood opposite each other, we knew what father wanted to say to us, and father knew that he could be silent. We didn't need to talk with each other, no, it wasn't necessary for him to say anything, and it also wasn't necessary for us to say anything, we thought we were going to be sick, we couldn't have said a word. . . . Most of all we wanted to hug him, but since we had never done it before, we didn't dare, and father stood alone between us and looked at his hand. Dear, dear father! (pp. 442–3)[31]

Their closest moments are spent in, or can be reduced to, silence: 'I walked beside him as a child through the forest, as a young boy through the town, as a young man through half of Germany, for hours, days, weeks, we talked, chatted, argued, yet when I think about it carefully we were silent with one another' (p. 18).[32] Thus, the self-professed word doctor, Harig, begins to doubt the communicative powers of language when faced with the enormity of the First World War: 'Yes, what do words cost, what does speaking mean, what is worth reporting? Everything which happened in the trenches of the Somme, in the streets of Ablaincourt was a matter of right and duty and is not worth recounting' (p. 148).[33] With the realization that their closest moments are marked by silence, the silences seem less threatening and his father's evanescent quality becomes more an aspect of his character than an absence of it:

When the cemetery gardener put the urn with the ashes from father's body in the grave, all that remained of father was light and airy and it could have scattered to the four winds if someone had taken the lid off the urn and the wind had blown inside and lifted the dust and carried it away. (p. 486)[34]

Notes

1 Meaning: 'if you have order, you've won the battle'. All references to this novel are taken from Ludwig Harig, *Ordnung ist das ganze Leben. Roman meines Vaters* (Frankfurt am Main, Fischer, 1989) and all translations from the German are my own.

2 'Wieviel kann der Mensch ertragen? Muß man vergessen, wenn man überleben will? Hatte Vater sein Gedächtnis verloren? Oder hat er, um sich zu retten, die Augenblicke des Wohlgefühls zu himmlischen Ewigkeiten gedehnt, und dabei sind ihm die Tage des Entsetzens zu Schrecksekunden geschrumpft?' (p. 474).

3 Karl Riha, 'Ach, Ludwig, wie faß' ich Dich. Porträtierversuch . . . nebst Fußnote zum Geburtstag', in Gerhard Sauder & Gerhard Schmidt-Henkel (eds), *Harig lesen* (Munich, Vienna, Hanser, 1987), p. 21.

4 The silence of Peter Härtling's father has a devastating effect on his young son. Rhetorical questions point to resentment in this case (Peter Härtling, *Nachgetragene Liebe* (Darmstadt and Neuwied, Luchterhand, 1980), pp. 9–10). Language is similarly a shaping force in Christoph Meckel's gentler biography of his father (Christoph Meckel, *Suchbild über meinen Vater* (Düsseldorf, Claasen, 1980), pp. 23, 52). His father's answers are deemed inadequate (p. 28) and he is criticized for writing bucolic poetry during the Third Reich (pp. 36–7). As with Härtling's father, the withholding of language is used as a punishment by Eberhard Meckel (p. 56).

5 The backgrounds of the critics (generally men of Harig's generation) mean that Harig senior's involvement with the Nazi regime is examined to a disproportionate degree (Walter Hinck, 'Vater hält die Welt zusammen', in *Frankfurter Allgemeine Zeitung*, No. 218, 25/9/86; Hubert Winkels, 'Im Namen des Vater: Ludwig Harigs autobiographischer Roman', *Die Zeit*, No. 41, 5/10/90, LB 8; Helmut Schödel, 'Die Veteranen vor Verdun', *Die Zeit*, No. 141, 3/10/86, Lit.-Beilage). Much to the critics' frustration, Harig senior's relationship to National Socialism is simply observed and chronicled at a respectful distance while in father literature it is judged with such vehemence that incomprehension and disgust frequently take the upper hand. Even though Harig questions his father's involvement in the First World War, he never poses questions of a moral or humanitarian nature (pp. 84, 372). This is perhaps because Harig is attempting to relate the events as he perceived them as a child; for example, he describes a party symbol on a tie as a weirdly drawn ladybird (p. 190).

6 'Was war das für ein Mensch?' (pp. 17, 23, 24). This is augmented by the more general 'What sort of men were they?' ('Was waren das für Männer?' pp. 23, 24, 87).

7 'Wer erinnert sich noch daran? Wer lebt, der sich erinnern kann? Wer will, der noch lebt und sich erinnern kann, davon erzählen? Warum hat Vater nie davon erzählt, so daß die Legende uns Geschichte und vielleicht eine Lehre sein könnte?' (p. 88). Where for some authors of the father portrait this breakdown in communication is the occasion of great resentment, for Harig it only sparks regret (p. 267).

8 'Vater konnte nicht beten. Vielleicht betete er nicht, büßte er nicht, glaubte er nicht an Gott, wie er nicht weinen, nicht singen, nicht große Worte machen konnte, weil es ihn genierte. Es war ihm peinlich. Wenn er die Hände hätte falten und ein Gebet hätte sprechen müssen, wäre er vor Scham vergangen.' This also impacts on the family as a whole: Harig describes his childhood home as a house of silence in which words had neither a lasting nor a cumulative effect. What happened the day before was simply forgotten (p. 143).

9 'Scham? Würde? Ehre? Alles große Worte, Vater wußte, wir würden es mit dem überleben zu tun haben, mit sonst nichts' (p. 300); 'Große Worte mochte er nicht, sie genierten ihn, er hätte sich am liebsten verkrochen, wenn er jemanden große Worte machen hörte, seine Worte waren noch nicht einmal klein, er hatte gar keine' (p. 155). 'Big words' are also referred to on several occasions with reference to the Second World War (p. 264).

10 George Steiner, 'The Hollow Miracle', in George Steiner, *A Reader* (London, New York, Penguin, 1984), p. 209.

11 Ibid.

12 'Der deutsche Geländegewinn von knapp zehn Kilometern hatte beide Seiten mehr als eine halbe Million Verluste gekostet. Da lagen sie nun und hatten keine Wörter mehr, mit denen sie dieses Stillhalten, dieses Aushalten, dieses Durchhalten hätten beschreiben können' (p. 163); 'Everything was concluded from experience, nothing from speculation', 'Alles war aus der Erfahrung, nichts aus der Spekulation erschlossen' (p. 393; see also pp. 405–6).

13 'Wenn Mutter am Morgen sagte, ihr sei es nicht besonders gut, fing er an zu reden, redete und redete, als wolle er mit dem Reden die Krankheit vertreiben; er redete, und über dem Reden selbst vergaß er die Medikamente und das Reden über die Medikamente und ihre Heilkraft. Er redete nur noch, nie habe ich ihn so reden hören wie gegen Mutters Krankheit; da auf einmal war alle Hemmnis von ihm gewichen, er begriff die Sprache als Therapie . . .' (p. 447).

14 'Beim Leichenimbiß für Mutter sah Vater aus wie der steinerne Gast. . . . Vater saß am Kopfende des Tisches, als gehöre er nicht dazu, er aß nicht, er trank nicht, er sagte kein Wort' (pp. 450–1).

15 Erich Maria Remarque, for example.

16 'Verdun war für ihn kein Roman, nein, er hatte sich nicht in Bilder und nicht in Vergleiche retten können' (pp. 155–6); 'Sein Gedächtnis war überwachsen, die Erinnerung sprach nicht mehr, nie gab es Romanszenen in seinem Kopf' (p. 75). This is reiterated by Harig, but on a more sophisticated level; using allusions to various First World War novels, Harig states that his father is not a fictional character and refers to works by Walter Flex (p. 474) and Fritz von Unruh among others. Harig comments that Eugen Rapp, a character in Hermann Lenz's novel *Neue Zeit*, is saved by language (p. 159). Ironically, Harig disputes the fact that his own Second World War experiences can be fictionalized; nonetheless he is driven to try: 'It is not a novel, it is not a drama, it is not a radio play. But how else should I make myself understood?', 'Das ist kein Roman, das ist kein Theaterstück, das ist kein Hörspiel. Aber wie soll ich mich sonst verständlich machen?' (p. 380).

17 'Was gibt es da zu verändern und zu verwandeln, was gibt es da umzudrehen und umzuwenden, umzukehren und umzustülpen, damit es, wenn es schon nicht mehr Krieg und Schlachtfeld ist, so aber doch neues Paradies und eine Blumenwiese sein könnte, worauf die Löwen zahm geworden sind und friedlich bei den Lämmern liegen? In diesen Köpfen wird sich das Leben nicht in einen Roman verwandeln, auch wenn Leutnant Thiele in sein Tagebuch schreibt' (p. 164).

18 'Doch in seinem Heft lese ich über diese Tage nichts weiter als ein paar kärgliche Stichwörter. "Schützengräben eingeebnet", schreibt er, "das Anmarschgelände unter starkem Artilleriebeschuß. Bei Morgengrauen in der vermutlichen Stellung angelangt. Nur Granattrichter"' (p. 79). In this it shares something with the reportage of Ludwig Renn's novel *Krieg*.

19 'aber es ist aus diesen drei Sätzen, die nicht einmal vollständige Sätze sind, kein sorgloses Kasernenleben herauszulesen, kein rätselhaftes Soldatenglück' (p. 25).

20 'alle 37 Karten haben fast den gleichen Wortlaut, es heißt: "Aus dem Schützengraben sendet Euch bei völliger Gesundheit die besten Grüße Euer Sohn und Bruder Louis." Und einmal ist hinzugefügt: "Den Kuchen habe ich vermißt, denn die Ratten haben sich damit gesund gemacht. Sonst ist alles angekommen"' (p. 159).

21 'Jetzt schaute er hinunter, und er sagte zum ersten Mal einen langen, einen zusammenhängenden Satz. Er sagte: "Das Pferd hat eine Pferdenatur, und der Mensch hat eine Menschennatur. Aber der Mensch ist widerstandsfähiger als das Pferd"' (p. 158).

22 'Es verging nur ein Augenblick, dann lagen sich die beiden Männer in den Armen. Ich hatte nie in meinem Leben zuvor Vater jemanden küssen gesehen, ich weiß auch nicht, ob Vater Erich Thiele geküßt hat, ich sah, wie zwei Männer von Mitte Achtzig, ihre Wangen aneinandergepreßt, auf dem Bahnsteig standen und sich in den Armen hielten. Erich Thiele nahm seine Hände von der Schulter meines Vaters, streckte sie aus, reichte sie ihm hin, er war der Gott Mars, und Vater war Eros' (p. 459).

23 This is not only irrevocable in death but is compounded by the embalming process when his mouth is stuffed with sawdust (p. 489).

24 'Da stehen wir auf der Straße, mein Bruder und ich, Vater und sein Unteroffizier werfen die Beine, blähen die Brüste' (p. 31).

25 'fast zum Greifen nah, aber wir fassen ihn nicht, manchmal streckt er die Hand aus, nein, es ist nur ein Lufthauch, der von der Straße in die Stube weht' (p. 39). Symbolism similarly accentuates the gap. In this symbol-laden environment, areas important to Harig senior's war experiences are rendered inaccessible by overgrown plants (pp. 34, 36, 39, 266–7) and the stopped clocks (pp. 36, 39). It is the eye of the author which notices a small oak (a symbol of Germany, later used to decorate the family home (pp. 240–2) and as the background for the family tree (pp. 319, 426)) attempting to grow on the top of the high exterior wall of a military compound. The future of this sapling is jeopardized, however, by the jagged glass embedded in the wall acting as a deterrent to unwanted sightseers.

26 '"Nichts als Haarspaltereien . . . alles Wort- und Sinnverdrehung, alles Quatsch." Er hielt nichts von literarischen Vergleichen, wenn es ums Leben ging' (p. 271). Literary devices offer Harig senior no refuge as he has not learnt the language of the novel (pp. 158–9). He is not religious and the sky is always the sky, never heaven (p. 155; see also p. 163). He also rejects the neologism *Wirtschaftswunder*, claiming it is not a miracle but something hard fought for (pp. 382–3; see also p. 445).

27 'sparsam umgehen nicht zu penetrant werden'; 'eine Drehung zu viel'. Benno Rech, '"Ist aber ein Buch imstande, . . . seiner Leser frei und gesund zu machen". Ludwig Harig und seine Leser', in Sauder & Schmidt-Henkel, pp. 64, 65.

28 Rules are for this *Kleinbürger* supreme and immutable. Nothing he can say will defeat them.

29 'es war anstrengend und schmerzhaft, ich wünschte mir, ich könnte endlich sehen und lernen, hören und lernen, was nur Vater und Erich Thiele sahen und hörten, was sie wußten und nicht preisgaben. Konnten sie es nicht, oder wollten sie es nicht?' (p. 471).

30 'und nun, da Vater tot ist, muß ich ihn zum zweitenmal erfinden. Doch die Luft, die er so lebensvoll atmete, zerplatzt mir in lauter Seifenblasen aus Wörtern, und wenn ich den Mund aufmache und zu erzählen beginne, zerstiebt ein halbes Jahrhundert zwischen meinen Lippen in einzelne Silben, die ich immer und immer wieder neu zusammensetzen muß zu Wörtern, die ich jetzt noch gar nicht kenne. "Alles Elfenrauschen", hätte Vater gesagt, "alles Blendwerk!"' (p. 20).

31 'er sah mich an, er wollte etwas sagen, aber er räusperte sich nur, er konnte wohl die Schützengrabensprache nicht übersetzen, er schüttelte den Kopf, doch ich konnte ihn verstehen, wie ich ihn immer verstanden habe, auch wenn wir nicht miteinander gesprochen haben' (p. 455); 'er trat aus der Tür und stand vor uns, klein und schmal, und es zuckte um seinen Mund. Er sagte kein Wort. Ich weiß nicht mehr, ob wir in dieser Stunde überhaupt etwas gesprochen haben, wir standen uns gegenüber, wir wußten, was Vater uns sagen wollte, und Vater wußte, daß er schweigen konnte. Wir brauchten nicht miteinander zu sprechen, nein, es war nicht nötig, daß er etwas sagte, und es

war auch nicht nötig, daß wir etwas sagten, es würgte uns im Hals, wir hätten kein Wort herausgebracht. . . . Wir hätten ihn am liebsten umarmen mögen, doch da wir es nie zuvor getan hatten, trauten wir uns nicht, und Vater stand allein zwischen uns und schaute auf seine Hand. Lieber, lieber Vater!' (pp. 442–3).

32 'Ich ging neben ihm her, als Kind durch den Wald, als kleiner Junge durchs Dorf, als junger Mann durch das halbe Deutschland, stundenlang, tagelang, wochenlang, wir haben gesprochen, auch geschwätzt, auch gestritten, doch wenn ich es genau bedenke, haben wir miteinander geschwiegen' (p. 18).

33 'Ja, was kosten Worte, was bedeutet Sprechen, was ist des Berichtens wert? Alles, was in den Gräben der Somme, in den Straßen von Ablaincourt geschehen war, war Recht und Pflicht und lohnt das Erzählen nicht' (p. 148).

34 'Als der Friedhofsgärtner die Urne mit der Asche von Vaters Leib in die Grube gestellt hatte, war von Vater nur noch übriggeblieben, was leicht und luftig war und in alle Himmelsrichtungen sich hätte verflüchtigen können, wenn jemand den Deckel der Urne geöffnet und der Wind hineingeblasen und den Staub emporgehoben und fortgetragen hätte' (p. 486).

BIBLIOGRAPHICAL ESSAY

B. Taithe and T. Thornton

The joint topics of war and identity each has an enormous bibliography which could be divided chronologically and nationally for the wars and following various academic professional boundaries for identity. We cannot attempt to deal with the bibliography of even one war in its entirety. The Franco-Prussian war alone has several thousand volumes dedicated to one or another aspect of the conflict. Many more have been written about the two World Wars. As for identity, the term has different meanings in the various 'social sciences' in which it is most used. An anthropological identity and a psychological one are often deemed to be different. Historians gloriously ignore these boundaries and ransack the armouries of the social sciences without paying too much notice to the exact intellectual consequences of such borrowings. In this context this bibliographical essay will attempt to bring together some of the great intellectual traditions which have been used as so many quarries of ideas. The books on war will also be presented thematically and without any ambition to be exhaustive in our survey.

DEFINITIONS OF IDENTITY AND WAR

In terms of philosophical investigation of the meanings of identity we have, like most historians, followed a rather *bricoleur* line, roughly taking on board concepts from sociology, anthropology or even existentialist philosophy. We have perhaps erred in the direction of vague syntheses rather than having followed a strict philosophical line.

Logicians might still find the following useful: E.J. Lowe, *Kinds of Being: A Study of Individuation, Identity and the Logic of Sortal Terms*, Aristotelian Society Series 10 (Oxford, Basil Blackwell, 1989); C.J.F. Williams, *What is Identity?* (Oxford, Clarendon Press, 1989). For a literary approach, Simon Forde, Lesley Johnson & Alan V. Murray, *Concepts of National Identity in the Middle Ages* (Leeds, Leeds Texts and Monographs, new series, 14, 1995). Central to the debate on national identity is the abundant work of Anthony D. Smith: *Theories of Nationalism* (London, Duckworth, 1971); *State and Nation in the Third World* (Brighton, Wheatsheaf Books, 1983); *Nation and Nationalism in a Global Era* (Cambridge, Polity Press, 1995); *National Identity* (Harmondsworth, Penguin Books, 1991); *The Ethnic Origins of Nations* (Oxford, Basil Blackwell, 1986); Anthony D. Smith (ed.), *Nationalist Movements* (London, Macmillan, 1976); also John Hutchinson, *Modern Nationalism* (London, Fontana Press, 1994). Compare with Raphael Samuel (ed.), *Patriotism: The Making and Unmaking of British National Identity* (3 vols, London, Routledge, 1989).

For a rather mechanistic definition of identity using solid sociological techniques, see Peter Weinreich, *Manual for Identity Exploration using Personal Constructs* (Birmingham, SSRC Research Unit on Ethnic Relations, 1981). Psychologists have contributed to a large number of books dealing with the concept of identity in its wider sense, e.g. William C. McCready, *Culture, Ethnicity and Identity* (New York, Academic Press, 1983); Theodore R. Sarbin & Karl E. Scheibe (eds), *Studies in Social Identity* (New York, Praeger, 1983); anthropologists and linguists have rightly emphasized the relationship between language and identity. This idea has since been put to use by historians of the linguistic turn or even more traditional historians who pay some close attention to the production and diffusion of texts. See John J. Gumperz, *Language and Social Identity* (Cambridge University Press, 1982); on the process of identification which may or may not lead to identity see the thorough compilation edited by George H. Pollock, *Pivotal Papers on Identification* (Madison, International Universities Press, 1993).

From a purely anthropological perspective, war fits in within a range of other activities and the word often describes low-violence but constant activities. See for instance the amusingly titled book by Martin Harris, *Cows, Pigs, Wars and Witches: The Riddles of Culture* (London, Hutchinson, 1974).

For a discussion of masculine identities, see Robert A. Nye, *Masculinity and Male Codes of Honor in Modern France* (New York, Oxford University Press, 1993); Klaus Theweleit, *Male Fantasies* (2 vols, Cambridge University Press, 1987–9).

On definitions of war: Michael Howard, *The Causes of Wars and Other Essays* (London, Temple Smith, 1983); Michael Howard (ed.), *Restraints on War: Studies in the Limitation of Armed Conflict* (Oxford University Press, 1979); Daniel Pick, *War Machine: The Rationalization of Slaughter in the Modern Age* (New Haven, Yale University Press, 1993); Brian Bond, *The Pursuit of Victory: From Napoleon to Saddam Hussein* (Oxford University Press, 1996).

WAR AND SOCIETY

The fact that the two terms can even be put side by side without being considered a tautological proposition is strange and implies that there could be a society without war, a war without society. As pointed out in the introduction this dynamic duo has the same polarities as that of good and evil, and, in real life, the same blurred boundaries. Geoffrey Best, *War and Society in Revolutionary Europe, 1770–1870* (London, Fontana, 1982); *Humanity in Warfare: the Modern History of the International Law of Armed Conflict* (London, Methuen, 1983); M.R.D. Foot (ed.), *War and Society: Historical Essays in Honour and Memory of J.R. Western* (London, Paul Elek, 1973); Arthur Marwick, *The Deluge: British Society and the First World War* (2nd edn, Basingstoke, Macmillan Education, 1991); Arthur Marwick, *Women at War, 1914–1918* (London, Fontana for the Imperial War Museum, 1977).

For recent writing on statebuilding and its connections to war in late medieval England and France respectively, see Gerald Harriss, 'Political Society and the Growth of Government in Late Medieval England', *Past and Present*, 138 (Feb. 1993), 28–57; E. Fryde, 'Royal Fiscal Systems and State Formation in France from the Thirteenth to the Sixteenth Centuries, with some English Comparisons', *Journal of Historical Sociology*, 4 (1991), 236–87. War does not always lead to growth of state institutions: 'Perhaps it is not enough to contrast states on the one hand with bellicose, anarchic and peripheral impulses which would have arisen and developed through political disturbances, on the other, and to imagine a long-term conflict between them until the victory of the states.' Free

Companies show complex relationships – some states support them. Contamine, *War in the Middle Ages*, p. 248; Michael Scriven & Peter Wagstaff (eds), *War and Society in Twentieth-Century France* (Oxford, Berg, 1991). The editors and the contributors took the usual duet of war and society to explore unevenly the different forms of wars the French have experienced. Some societies however have only existed as separate states during a war and have only found some legitimacy in the fighting: see Drew Gilpin Faust, *The Creation of Confederate Nationalism: Ideology and Identity in the Civil War South* (Baton Rouge, Louisiana State University Press, 1988); see also Maris A. Vinovskis, *Towards a Social History of the American Civil War* (Cambridge University Press, 1990). The impact of wars on societies, to use this phrase, has particularly been discussed in relation to the recent French and German past and the rise of Fascist or Nazi organizations. See Antoine Prost, 'The Impact of War on French and German Political Cultures', *Historical Journal*, 37, 1 (1994), 209–17; Samuel Hynes, *A War Imagined: The First World War and British Culture* (New York, Atheneum, 1991); Modris Eksteins, *Rites of Spring: The Great War and the Birth of the Modern Age* (Boston, Houghton Mifflin, 1989).

NATIONAL, ETHNIC AND RELIGIOUS IDENTITY IN WAR

For a populist approach to identity in war see Howard Cooper & Paul Morrison, *A Sense of Belonging: Dilemmas of British Jewish Identity* (London, Weidenfield and Nicolson & Channel 4 Television, 1991); W.E. Mosse, *Jews in the German Economy: The German-Jewish Economic élite, 1820–1935* (Oxford, Clarendon Press, 1987); Daniel Jenkins, *The British: Their Identity and their Religion* (London, SCM Press, 1975). Jenkins argued that 'the connection between national consciousness and religious heritage within the British Isles is very close' and attempted to claim for religious debate, urging the transformation of the church to accommodate 'matter of Britain'. The theme of national identity (see Anthony Smith above) is widely developed and studied in many important texts which postulate a complex national identity if not always a complex relationship with wars. See Brian Jenkins & Spyros A. Sofos, *Nation and Identity in Contemporary Europe* (London, Routledge, 1996). The ethnic challenge of the colonial empires is the theme of many interesting books, for instance Herman Lebovics, *True France: the Wars over Cultural Identity, 1900–1945* (Ithaca: Cornell University Press, 1992). On Christians at war, see Gordon C. Zahn, *War, Conscience and Dissent* (New York, Hawthorn Books, 1967).

WAR AND IDENTITY

There are considerable difficulties in assessing the effect of conflict on forming individual identities in the medieval period. So few combatants recorded their impressions of war, and for the ordinary soldiery below the levels of gentility there is virtually nothing. Some of the chivalrous authors who had experienced conflict include Jean Froissart, *The Chronicle of Froissart*, ed. W.P. Ker (London, W.E. Henley, The Tudor Translations, 1901); Jean le Bel, *Chronique de Jean le Bel*, ed. J. Viard and E. Déprez (2 vols, Paris, Société de l'Histoire de France, 1904–5) and Sir Thomas Gray, *Scalachronica: a Chronicle of England and Scotland from 1066 to 1362* (Glasgow, Maitland Club, 1836). These authors are surveyed in Antonia Gransden, *Historical Writing in England* (2 vols, London, Routledge and Kegan Paul, 1982), vol. 2, *c. 1307 to the Early Sixteenth Century*, pp. 57–60, 83–9, 93–6; J.J.N. Palmer (ed.), *Froissart: Historian*

(Woodbridge, Suffolk, Boydell, 1981). One of the first authentically individual responses to war from the point of view of the front line is the account of the siege of Harfleur in Frank Taylor & J.S. Roskell, *Gesta Henrici Quinti* (Oxford, Clarendon Press, 1975), esp. pp. 26–54; cf. J.S. Roskell & Frank Taylor, 'The Authorship and Purpose of the *Gesta Henrici Quinti*', *Bulletin of the John Rylands Library*, LIII (1970–1), 428–64; LIV (1971–2), 223–40. For the early sixteenth century, there are accounts of some of Henry VIII's campaigns in France by Ellis Gruffudd, printed in translation from the Welsh by M. Bryn Davies as 'Suffolk's Expedition to Montdidier, 1523'; 'The "Enterprises" of Paris and Boulogne (A Contemporary Narrative)'; 'Boulogne and Calais from 1545 to 1550'.

On the particular makeup of specific armies see James B. Wood, *The King's Army: Warfare, Soldiers and Society during the Wars of Religion in France, 1562–1576* (Cambridge University Press, 1996); Andrew Ayton & J.L. Price, *The Medieval Military Revolution: State, Society and Military Change in Medieval and Early Modern Europe* (London, Tauris Publishers, 1995); Malcolm Vale, *War and Chivalry: Warfare and Aristocratic Culture in England, France and Burgundy at the End of the Middle Ages* (London, Duckworth, 1981). Vale argues that growing impersonalization and mechanization of war, especially through guns and the beat of the drum, produces a strengthening interest in single combat and the duel. (p. 166) Frank Tallett, *War and Society in Early-Modern Europe, 1495–1715* (London, Routledge, 1992). Among the many works of the leading French military historian, André Corvisier, see the collection of essays *Les hommes, la guerre et la mort* (Paris, Économica, 1985).

There is little writing on the impact of war on non-combatants in the middle ages; see C.T. Allmand, 'The War and the Non-Combatant', in Kenneth Fowler (ed.), *The Hundred Years War* (London and Basingstoke, Macmillan and St Martin's Press, 1971), pp. 163–83; and his *Society at War: The Experience of England and France during the Hundred Years War* (Edinburgh, Oliver and Boyd, 1973), esp. pp. 9–10 (the former focuses mainly on destruction and pillaging). For a recent study of the First World War, see Frans Coetzee & Marilyn Shevin-Coetzee (eds), *Authority, Identity and the Social History of the Great War* (Oxford, Berghahn, 1995); Eric J. Leeds, *No Man's Land: Combat and Identity in World War I* (Cambridge University Press, 1979) is older but remains challenging.

The historiography of war commemorations is turning into a minor industry which associates an anthropological study of major urban artefacts such as monuments and, in the best of them, a social study of the acts of remembrance. See Jay Winter, *Sites of Memory, Sites of Mourning: The Great War in European Cultural History* (Cambridge University Press, 1996); John R. Gillis (ed.), *Commemorations: the Politics of National Identity* (Princeton University Press, 1994); George Mosse, *Fallen Soldiers: Reshaping the Memory of the World Wars* (Oxford University Press, 1990). See also the 'forum' organized by *French Historical Studies*, 19 (1995), 1, 1–74, between Regina Sweeney, Vanessa Schwartz, Sarah Bennett Farmer and Daniel J. Sheerman.

INDEX OF NAMES, PLACES AND THEMES

INDEX OF AUTHORS' NAMES